THE MECCAN REVELATIONS

THE MECCAN

VOLUME II

SELECTED TEXTS OF **AL-FUTÛHÂT AL-MAKKIYA** ~
PRESENTATIONS AND TRANSLATIONS FROM THE ARABIC
UNDER THE DIRECTION OF
MICHEL CHODKIEWICZ

IN COLLABORATION WITH
CYRILLE CHODKIEWICZ AND
DENIS GRIL

REVELATIONS

IBN AL 'ARABI

NEW YORK · PIR PRESS · 2004

Pir Press
227 West Broadway
New York, New York 10013

Copyright © 1988 by the Rothko Chapel (edition: Sindbad, Paris)
Copyright © 2004 by Pir Press

All rights reserved. No part of this book may be reproduced or utilized in any form or by any means, electronic or mechanical, including photocopying and recording, or otherwise, without the prior written permission from the publisher. All inquiries should be sent to Pir Press at the above address.

Printed in the United States of America

Cover design: Peter Muller

Note: This edition, the second of two volumes, incorporates all French text and translations from the original 1988 bi-lingual, French-English edition, *Les Illuminations des la Mecque*, published by Sindbad (Paris), and edited by Michel Chodkiewicz.

Copyright Information:

Preface ©2002 by James W. Morris
English to French translation of this edition ©2004, Pir Publications, Inc., translated by David Streight

"Une Introduction a la Lecture des Futuhat Makkiyya" ©1988, Michel Chodkiewicz
"La Loi et la Voie" ©1988, Cyrille Chodkiewicz
"Le Terme du Voyage" and "La Science des Lettres" ©1988, Denis Gril

ISBN: 1-879708-21-3

CONTENTS

PREFACE   *James W. Morris*   1

INTRODUCTION   *Michel Chodkiewicz*   3
   Toward Reading the Futûhât Makkiyya   3
   Notes to Introduction   46

THE LAW AND THE WAY   *Cyrille Chodkiewicz*   57

   Introduction to 'The Law and the Way'   59
   Sources of the Law ~ CHAPTER 88   62
   Satan's Ruses ~ CHAPTER 318   77
   The Secrets of Forgiveness ~ CHAPTER 344   86
   The Gnostic and the Law ~ CHAPTER 437   94
   Notes to 'The Law and the Way'   98

THE SCIENCE OF LETTERS   *Denis Gril*   105

   Introduction and Chapter Analysis   107
   The Hierarchy of Letters ~ CHAPTER 2, SECTION I, PART I   150
   The Isolated Letters ~ CHAPTER 2, SECTION I, PART II   161
   The Properties of Letters ~ CHAPTER 2, SECTION I, PART III   176
   Notes to 'The Science of Letters'   187

THE END OF THE JOURNEY   *Denis Gril*   221

    On Being Liberated from Stations ~ CHAPTER 420   223
    On Proximity ~ CHAPTER 73 AND 161   229
    Notes to 'The End of the Journey'   242

BIBLIOGRAPHY   249

INDEX OF QUR'ANIC REFERENCES   255

GENERAL INDEX ~ GLOSSARY   259

PREFACE

The translations included in this volume have a long history. The guiding intention behind this project, as it was originally conceived by Michel Chodkiewicz (the foremost French student of Ibn 'Arabî, a professor at the École des Hautes Études, and then head of the major French publishing house Éditions du Seuil), was to provide, in a bilingual edition, the first representative overview of Ibn 'Arabî's magnum opus, Meccan Revelations (al-Futûhât al-Makkiya[1]). Anyone who has ever attempted to study that immense and utterly unique work—which would require perhaps fifty volumes of this scale to translate in its entirety—will recognize the daunting challenges of selection, translation and adequate explanation actually involved. Fortunately, Mr. Chodkiewicz was quickly able to assemble an international team of scholars to begin work in late 1984, and thanks to the financial support of the Rothko Chapel (and Mme. D. De Menil), as well as the tireless editorial work of our colleague Dr. Martine Gillet, the resulting volume (of some 653 pages), entitled Les Illuminations de La Mecque, was published in Paris by Sindbad in late 1988.

The impetus that this project gave to the further study and communication of Ibn 'Arabî's works, and especially the Futûhât, went far beyond the publication itself. Professor Chodkiewicz soon published two pioneering, foundational studies of Ibn 'Arabî's works (both now available in English and discussed in the "Further Readings" section of the

Introduction to this volume); Professor Denis Gril has continued to publish important editions, translations and studies of Ibn 'Arabî's works; and Professor William Chittick and I have gone on to complete (or should soon publish) several more volumes of English translations and studies of these "Illuminations." As a result, the years since the first appearance of our translations have seen an ongoing worldwide transformation—in the Islamic world at least as much as in Western academic and spiritual circles—in the understanding and appreciation of the nature and wider significance of Ibn 'Arabî's writings.

Unfortunately, the French edition—whose size, cost and foreign publication made access difficult in the English-speaking world from the beginning—soon became entirely inaccessible due to problems at the original publishers. Usually, for the past decade, only those with ready access to university libraries and Islamic research collections have been able to refer directly to these essential translations. Thus we are all immensely grateful to Pir Publications for their far-sighted initiative in undertaking to publish the entirety of the original Sindbad edition in English-language translations.

The present volume includes translations of both the original French chapters and Professor Chodkiewicz's original long Introduction to the key themes and opening chapters of the Futûhât.

James W. Morris

TOWARD READING
THE *FUTÛHÂT MAKKIYYA*
An Introduction by Michel Chodkiewicz

Contemplate the House: for sanctified hearts, its light shines openly
They look at it through God, without a veil,
and its august and sublime secret appears.

Futûhât, I, 47

Most of what this volume includes is composed of what God revealed to me as I walked the ritual circles around His noble House, or as I sat in the sacred enclosure and contemplated it.

Futûhât, I, 10

When he reached Mecca for the first time in 598/1202 and performed the pilgrim's ritual circumambulations of the Ka'ba—the "heart of the universe" *(qalb al-wujûd)*[1]—Ibn 'Arabî was thirty-eight lunar years old. Never to return, he had left the Islamic West he had so traversed—in every direction—throughout his youth. His decision to go East appears to have been made as early as 595/1198, after which he traveled through his native Andalusia visiting and taking leave of the teachers he had known. Curiously, we know nothing from 596; he says nothing about the year anywhere in his writings, and we can only guess that it was a time of retreat. In 597/1200, he was in the Maghreb: in Salé, where he took leave of another of his teachers[2]; in Marrakesh, where he received a vision with the command to choose a certain Muhammad al-Hassâr as a traveling companion (he met al-Hassâr in Fez some time later[3]); in Bougie, where, in another vision, he celebrated the marriage of the stars in the sky to the letters of the alphabet[4]; and finally in Tunis, where he would have a nine-month stay. It was there that he had met shaykh Abd al-Azîz Mahdawî[5] on an earlier trip (590/1194). Once again, he took up residence near Mahdawî, and it was for him that he would shortly thereafter, in Mecca, begin composition of the *Futûhât* and write *Rûh al-quds*.

From Tunis, Ibn 'Arabî traveled to famine-ravaged Cairo,[6] and then to Hebron, where he visited Abraham's tomb, and Jerusalem, where he prayed in the Al-Aqsâ Mosque.[7] He finally left for Mecca, on foot *(wa mashaytu ilâ Makka)*,[8] after a stop in Medina. He reached the city in time for the Pilgrimage, which took place in late August that year. He would stay until the end of 600/1204. The long sojourn would be marked by a series of major spiritual events—*futûhât*, a word that might be translated as "conquests," "openings," or "revelations"—that he would write down in the book of the same title. But Ibn 'Arabî had long since prepared himself for collecting the "secrets of the Ka'ba." He began his journey on the Path while still an adolescent; his only guides were supernatural ones: the three prophets Jesus, Moses, and Muhammad. He met Averroes around the time of his fifteenth birthday (we shall return to this event), and by that time he had already shown himself to be so exceptionally gifted that it was the philosopher who wanted to make his acquaintance. After his early years of being a solitary traveller on the path, he began to spend time with the Andalusian teachers whose exemplary sanctity would provide the material for *Rûh al-quds*. Paradoxically, the model student was also his teachers' teacher. Charismatic gifts, visions, ecstatic raptures, and infusions of Divine Wisdom were early markers of the singular fate to which he was destined. It was in Cordoba, in 586/1190, that he—among all the prophets gathered together—received the announcement of the role he was to play, the "Seal of Muhammadan Sainthood."[9] In 597/1200, in the village of Igisil, on the road from Salé to Marrakesh, he reached the "Station of Proximity" *(maqâm al-qurba)*, the final degree in the hierarchy of the saints.[10] The doctrinal authority he commanded, of which the *Futûhât Makkiyya*—which he would begin to compose shortly after his arrival in Mecca—are the broadest expression, has already been outlined on a number of occasions: by the time he left Tunis, the man who was not yet being referred to as *al-Shaykh al-Akbar*, "the greatest of the Masters," was the author of nearly sixty works.[11] Some of these are nothing more than short treatises of a few pages, but a number of them are veritable tomes. Their abundance is astounding, and is explained by the way Ibn 'Arabî composed his writings, which we will explain shortly. For the moment, let us bear in mind what he, himself, says regarding the composition of two important titles from this same period: the *Tadbîrat ilâhiyya* were written in but four days,[12] and the *Mawâqi' al-numûm* took eleven days.[13]

After reaching Mecca in late 598, Ibn 'Arabî almost immediately began the composition of the *Futûhât*. By the end of 599, he had written what—in the 1329 edition we are using as a reference (unless otherwise noted)—corresponds to the first 84 pages of the first volume, with the exception of pages 38 to 47, which would be inserted into the book later. Given the density of the printed text, that in itself represents a considerable volume. But the work, which was being composed parallel to the composition of other books, and was interrupted by frequent trips throughout the Middle East until 620 (when Ibn 'Arabi took up residence definitively in Damascus), would not be completed until the month of *Safar* in 629 (December, 1231), as the colophon for the initial version attests.[14] The handwritten manuscript, which the Shaykh al-Akbar had bequeathed to his son Muhammad,[15] was apparently lost; the oldest copy extant of this first edition dates from 683.

In 632, Ibn 'Arabî decided to revise the text of the *Futûhât*. He began work on a second edition. All written by his own hand, he finished on Wednesday, the 24th day of the month of *Rabi' al-awwal*, 636/1238, just two years before his death. The thirty-seven volumes of the handwritten manuscript were dedicated to his disciple Sadr al-Dîn Qûnawî (ob. 724/1274), who began a pious foundation *(waqf)* with them. Preserved for generations in the library of Qûnawî's *zâwiya* in Konya, up to the early 20th century, they were ultimately transferred to Istanbul[16]—when the Turkish government decided to confiscate the *awqâf*—and served as a basis for the critical edition established by Osman Yahia, whose publication has been in process since 1972.

Three editions preceded that one. The first, published in Cairo in 1274/1857-58,[17] was completed under the aegis of Emir 'Abd al-Qâdir al-Jazâ'irî, and financed by him. The second, dated 1293/1876, also in Cairo, makes reference to the preceding edition, but the editor announced that he had corrected it from a manuscript annotated by Shaykh 'Abd al-Ghânî al-Nâbulusî (ob. 1143/1731).[18] This edition, as several peculiarities in the text show, and as is confirmed by the excipit,[19] was based on the *first* edition of the *Futûhât*. The third edition, also published in Cairo (1329/1911), was based on the *second* edition of the work.[20]

"*As God is my witness, I swear that I have not written a single letter of this book other than by the effect of divine dictation* (imlâ' ilâhî), *of a lordly projection* (ilqâ' rabbânî), *of spiritual inspiration* (nafath ruhânî) *in my innermost heart.*[21] *I say nothing, I utter no judgment that does not come out of an inspiration from the Divine Spirit in my heart.*"[22] Ibn 'Arabî did not make these statements—there are a number of others just like them—only in regard to the *Futûhât*; he claims that they apply to his work as a whole: "*Neither this book your are now holding nor my other works is composed in the same fashion as ordinary books, and I do not write them according to the method usually used by authors.*"[23] An author makes his own choices when he writes. Ibn 'Arabî was not the master of his writing: he was, as he explains after the passage we just cited, nothing more than a *"heart prostrate before the door of the Divine Presence," "indigent," "devoid of any knowledge."* He transcribes (without a rough draft, he states)[24] whatever comes to him from this Presence. He tells us that such perfect submission to inspiration occasionally leads him to violate the rules of discourse by associating things that, rationally, have nothing to do with one another; it may even lead him, under order, to address a subject about which he has no prior knowledge. For example, when he raises the subject of "legal statutes" (ahkâm al-shar'), he states: "*I did not choose this order of exposition of my own accord; if it had been determined rationally, this chapter would not be placed here*"; and he has no hesitation about comparing the non-sequiturs that are so frequent in his writings to the abrupt breaks in meaning that can be seen in the Holy Book, citing the case of Qur'ânic verses 2:236-241 in this regard, where in apparent disorder the themes of repudiation, prayer, inheritance, and then repudiation again, appear. Whether people believe in the authenticity of Ibn 'Arabî's inspiration or not, we must get used to these abrupt deviations, these unexpected returns to thoughts and scattered ideas—which we might think were by choice—and these outbursts of the unique truth of which he feels he is the bearer. This is the way he writes, and this is how he should be read: any attempt to systematize his teachings—some of his well-intentioned followers have certainly tried, and they were followed by Western scholars—has tended to impose a false order upon him, and has destroyed the inner harmony that only a patient, open-minded reading can allow one to discover.

The study of Ibn 'Arabî's writings from his youth, those from the Maghrebin period, shows clearly that all the basic ideas of his metaphysical doctrine and his initiatory teachings, all the themes of his symbolism did not appear gradually; they were present from the very beginning. When he took up his pen for the first time, he did so with the authority of a teacher. A number of short works from this period, as he himself points out on a number of occasions, were used later in just the same way, or only slightly modified in the *Futûhât*. From a certain point of view, the *Futûhât* is thus a summa that gathers together, adds details, and gives order to ideas that had been dealt with earlier, albeit in a more succinct and less systematic fashion. Its style (which is not uniform; for example, there are marked differences between the tone of volume III in the 1329 edition and that of volume IV) is generally more discursive and—despite several poems in the text, particularly at the beginnings of chapters—is less poetic than the style that is characteristic of several earlier compositions: it is significant in this regard to compare the *Kitâb al-Isrâ' (The Book of the Night Journey)*, written in 594/1198 to the account Ibn 'Arabî also gives of his spiritual "ascension" *(mirâj)* in chapter 367 of the *Futûhât*.[25] It is nevertheless evident that a new spiritual inspiration is at work here, that a brighter light is shining over a landscape he had already noted, and that it clarifies aspects of the landscape that theretofore had remained hidden. The second of the citations placed in the exergue to this study is a strong explanation of the specific relationship Ibn 'Arabî established between the composition of this book and the time he spent near the Kaʿba. The work's title, and its variations *(Al-Futûh al-Makkiyya, al-Fath al-Makkî)* underscore this relationship, the nature of which the prologue in the first chapter will explain. Even though they may be that *too*, the *Futûhât* are for their author—and he emphasizes this point in a number of passages—much more than a simple recapitulation of what he says in other works.

Materially, as we noted, the manuscript of the definitive edition appears in the form of thirty-seven volumes *(sifr,* pl. *asfâr)*, each of which is divided into seven parts *(juz,* pl. *ajzâ')*, meaning a total of two hundred fifty-nine parts. But the structure to take into consideration is the one the Shaykh al-Akbar himself describes in the table of contents *(fihris)* located at the end of the prologue.[26] If it was indeed composed in 599, as seems to be the case, it shows that the outline of the book that would not be completed until thirty years later had already been given to him by the "Meccan Revelations" that determined its contents. Though the order was inspired, it was also an intangible order, and thus would be respected from beginning to end.[27]

This *fihris* divides the *Futûhât*'s five hundred sixty chapters into six sections *(fasl,* pl. *fusûl)*,[28] each of which is preceded by a prologue *(khitba)* and an introduction *(muqaddima)*. The first section *(fasl al-ma'ârif)*, which includes seventy-three chapters (to which we will return shortly) is devoted to types of "knowledge"; they outline most of the metaphysical and cosmological data that comprise both the point of departure and the end of a spiritual itinerary whose modalities and degrees it will generally outline.[29] In one hundred sixteen chapters, the second section[30] deals with *mu'âmalât*, or "behaviors." In it, sets of chapters, arranged in pairs, study—among other things—such issues as "repentance" *(tawba)* and "abandoning repentance", "invocation" *(dhikr)* and "abandoning invocation," "sincerity" *(sidq)* and "abandoning sincerity," and "certitude" *(yaqîn)* and "abandoning certitude"; in each case, "abandoning" is paradoxically seen to represent going beyond what is abandoned, despite the initiatorily positive nature of the "stations" *(maqamât)* left behind, and whose nomenclature is traditional in the *tasawwuf*: each of them actually implies in some way a trace of duality, and thus a limitation that needs to be transcended. *Dhikr*, for example, supposes both an invoker and an Invoked. "Abandoning *dhikr*"—which should not be understood as returning to its opposite, *ghafla* (inattention), or *nisyân* (forgetting God)—nullifies the distance that separates the *madhkûr*'s *dhâhir*. Invoker and Invoked are no longer anything but one.

The reader of this second section can already see a complicated network of correlations; this will continue to be the case up to the last page of the *Futûhât*, among the different parts of the book. Chapters 146 and 147 (on "heroic generosity," *al-futuwwa*, and leaving it behind) thus echo chapter 42 in the first section. An invisible thread similarly ties chapter 66 on "the secrets of Sacred Law," which is located in the *fasl al-ma'ârif*, to chapter 88, on "the foundations of Sacred Law," but also to chapter 262, which belongs to the third section and deals with "knowledge of Sacred Law." Only tremendous familiarity with the *Futûhât* allows the reader to decipher this subtle crisscrossing of internal references—we will offer other examples—or to identify and correlate the myriad variations on a single theme, each isolated treatment of which gives a glimpse of only one aspect. The apparent arbitrariness governing this hodgepodge can be trying; the fact that it looks like a test is probably deliberate, whether we accept the inspired nature of the work or not: this would be the case for any iniatitory teaching. But if we are not resigned to being led, unrefusingly, through the most disconcerting of detours and the most unforeseen recurrences, we are doomed to drawing nothing more from the Shaykh al-Akbar's knowledge than an abstract, mutilated geometry.

The subject of the eighty chapters in the third section[31] *(fasl al-ahwâl)* is "spiritual states." Like the word *maqâm*, "station," which is its correlate, the Arabic word *hâl* (pl. *ahwâl*) belongs to the classical vocabulary of Sufism, where its introduction as a technical term is attributed to Dhû'l Nûn al-Misrî (d. 245/859); it is defined in all the great treatises of *tasawwuf* literature.[32] Ibn 'Arabî keeps, and refines, these traditional definitions that oppose the instable *(ghayru thâbit)* "bestowed" *(mawhûb)* hâl to the *maqâm*, which is both stable *(thâbit)* and "acquired" *(muktasab)*, underscoring that the fundamentally impermanent nature of any spiritual state can be masked by the succession of states that have a certain similarity.[33] Although it is a precarious grace, *hâl* is also a perilous grace; like other masters before him, but perhaps more clearly, the author of the *Futûhât* emphasizes this point: *"It is the ignorant individual who says that the saint* (al-walî) *is he who has spiritual states. God sometimes confers a* hâl *upon those He loves, and sometimes upon those He does not love. But He confers knowledge only upon those He loves."*[34] In other words, the goal of the Way is not to obtain fleeting charismatic gifts, which the authentic *walî*—far from seeking them—fears; the goal is, rather, knowledge of God. *"In the perfect individual, every time his station rises, his* hâl *falls."*[35]

The *ahwâl*, both the number (one hundred for Ansârî, a thousand for Ruzbehân Baqlî...) and terminology of which vary greatly, can be reduced to a limited series that, because they still belong to the world of duality, usually arranges them into pairs of opposites: drunkenness/sobriety, contraction/expansion, extinction/permanence. These pairs are found again in the third section of the *Futûhât* (union/separation, proximity/distance, etc.), where they are included in a typology that is as broad as it is deep. But there is also a quite long chapter[36] on the breath *(nafas)* which, among other correlations, returns to a theme first mentioned in chapter 15 and, in regard to the Divine Names, brings up ideas that will come back into view two thousand pages later, in chapter 588. Similarly, also, the meaning of *qâb qawsayn* ("the distance of two bows," a Qur'ânic expression that relates to the Prophet's ascension; cf. Q. 53:9), envisioned here in chapter 260, will be returned to, in a different fashion, in a later section.[37]

Section four, the *fasl al-manâzil,* in which there are 114 chapters,[38] like the suras in the Qur'ân to which they correspond in inverse order, is devoted to the *spiritual abodes.* In accord with etymology, the word *manzil* (pl. *manâzil*) refers to "*the place where God* descends *toward you, and where you* ascend *toward Him* ('alayhi)."[39] For each act of worship, Ibn 'Arabî states, there is a corresponding effect produced in the being of the worshiper by the state *(hâl)* that the act has engendered in him, on the one hand, and an effect *in divinis,* an effect produced by the station *(maqâm)* to which the act is attached, on the other. This is what is called a *manzil.*[40] There are pages of paramount importance in this section, like those in chapter 366 on "the ministers of the Mahdî who will appear at the end of time," or the pages in chapter 367, cited earlier, where the Shaykh al-Akbar recounts his *miʿrâj,* or the page in the long chapter 371, which is accompanied by a number of the author's schemas, and which is a masterful outline of his cosmology.

The following section is the section on the *munâzalât,*[41] a word used to express the idea of reciprocity and which is here applied to the "meeting at the half-way point" between God and man, at the precise spot where the divine "descent" and the creaturely "ascent" converge.[42] This descent, which cannot affect the absolute transcendence of the Essence, is properly speaking a theophany, and, strictly speaking, the encounter in question is thus for man an encounter with a Divine Name.[43] Two of the most characteristic chapters in this part of the *Futûhât,* among the seventy-eight that comprise this *fasl,* are the chapters (427 and 439) whose subject is the *qâb qawsayn* previously mentioned in the *fasl al-ahwâl,* as we noted. Despite appearances, there is nothing redundant about this: chapter 260 hinges around ways of getting the creature to "realize" divine proximity; chapter 427 looks at this proximity more specifically, in that it concerns the Prophet himself, and chapter 439 in that it applies to the *wârithûn,* the "heirs," that is, the saints *(awliyâ').*[44] Each of the successively considered *munâzalât* is characterized by an emblematic phrase, often either of Qurʾânic origin or borrowed from a *hadîth qudsî,* that defines its nature and status: *he who has seen Me has not seen Me; he who bows before My Majesty, I descend toward his; if you held the place among the creatures that you hold with Me, it would not be Me that they adored; it is your perplexity* (hayra; we shall return to this word) *that has led you to Me.*

The *fasl al-maqâmât,* the "section of [spiritual] stations," stretches out over nearly all of the fourth volume,[45] and entails 99 chapters, a number that is identical to the number of Divine Names on the traditional lists. We mentioned the general meaning of *maqâm* earlier. A couple of additional observations might be in order here. One remark from Ibn ʿArabî's commentary in his *Tarjumân al-ashwâq* ("The Interpreter of Desires") deserves note for what it says about the reality of the "stations": "*The* maqâmât," he says, "*have no existence except through the existence of him who holds to them* (al-muqîm)."⁴⁶ The common idea of a "ladder" of stations existing by itself and available to anyone who undertakes the task of climbing up through the degrees of the ascent toward God is thus not appropriate: the rungs of the ladder appear only at the moment that the aspirant raises his foot and begins to set it down, and the way they are distributed is in line with the predispositions of each individual being; this is why we see so many differences from one author to the next in the hierarchy and number of stations. On the other hand, "*traveling through the* maqâmât *does not consist in leaving one* maqâm *behind* [in order to reach the next one], *but rather in obtaining something that is higher than it, without leaving the station you have already been in. It consists in 'going toward,' not 'leaving behind'* (fa huwa intiqâl ilâ kadhâ lâ min kadhâ)."⁴⁷ The result is that everyone in possession of a *maqâm* eminently possesses the preceding *maqâmât* also. And finally, as is also underscored in the passage cited earlier from the commentary on the *Tarjumân*, the "perfect Muhammadan heart"—that of the *awliyâ'* who have gathered together the fullness of the prophetic heritage—is "liberated from the chains of the *maqâmât ('an al-taqyîd bi l-maqâmât)*." This idea is a leitmotif that runs through all of Ibn 'Arabî's work,⁴⁸ most frequently in reference to Q. 33:13 *(Lâ maqâma lakum)*, which is cited in the first lines of this *fasl*: at the end of the ascension, there is no longer a *maqîm* and, from that moment on, there is no longer a *maqâm*.

For each station there is a corresponding state *(hâl)* and a certain kind of knowledge *('ilm)*, or rather a set of spiritual sciences. It is possible to experience the state characteristic of a station without having reached the station and, conversely, it is possible to reach a station without experiencing its corresponding *hâl*. Only the *'ilm* is important to the true *sâlik* ("traveler"), the celestial nomad who cannot be turned away from his goal by the temptation of spiritual joys. But the *'ilm* itself should be gone beyond: in the individual who is no longer closed in by the stations, it is followed by *hayra*—perplexity, a dazzled stupefaction, an absence of knowledge that transcends all knowledge in the same way that the Divine Essence transcends all perfection.⁴⁹

A significant portion of this section of the *Futûhât* is devoted the "poles" *(aqtâb,* sing. *qutb)*, a word that, strictly speaking, refers to those *awliyâ* who assume the highest roles in the initiatic hierarchy,⁵⁰ although in a more general sense it applies to any being who holds an axial position relative to a specific station whose full possession he represents (Ibn 'Arabî offers as an example the "station of leaving all trust to God," *muqâm al-*

tawakkul, whose pole, at his time, was his master Abdallâh al-Mawrûrî),[51] or relative to a specific community; for there is no place on earth, whether it is inhabited by believers or unbelievers, "*without a saint by whose presence God preserves it.*"[52] One chapter is first reserved for the twelve *aqtâb* (in the narrow sense of the word) *around whom the universe turns*, meaning the twelve spiritual types—each of which is characterized by his particular relationship to one of the suras in the Qur'ân and to a prophet whose heir he is—to whom the diversity of the successive Poles of the Muhammadan community returns. Ninety other chapters then describe as many *aqtâb* (in the broad sense), some of whom—and such was the case for Abû Madyan—assume the role of *qutb* understood in its narrow sense, the object of this long series being to illustrate not the ascending order of the degrees of sainthood but the multiplicity of forms of spiritual realization symbolized each time by a *hijjir* (a means of invocation characteristic of the *maqâm* in question) taken from a Qur'ânic verse.[53] After a brief explanation dealing with the *Seal of Universal Sainthood*—Jesus—already mentioned a number of times both in the *Futûhât* (especially in the first *fasl* in chapter 73) and in other works (like the *Anqâ mughrib*[54]), there are three final chapters, each of which is over a hundred pages long. The first, which develops a major theme in Ibn 'Arabî's metaphysics, concerns the Divine Names, *that is, the Divine Presences* (al-hadarât al-ilâhiyya) *that the statuses of "possibilities"* (ahkâm al-mumkinât) *claim, statuses that are nothing more than forms that appear in God's Being*. The second, one of the densest in the work, is the *bâb al-asrâr* ("the chapter of secrets"), where Ibn 'Arabî claims to sum up all the preceding chapters, one after the other, in a few sentences whose pithy wording is often difficult to penetrate. The third chapter, the last in the *Futûhât*, is practical advice "of benefit to both the aspirant and the individual who has arrived *(al-wâsil),*" the apparent simplicity of which should not fool us: the position these rules of conduct hold in the *Futûhât's* structure clearly encourages the reader to recognize their importance and to decipher their relationship to the whole.

Though they are short, the *Fusûs al-hikam*, another of Ibn 'Arabî's major works, have been commented upon by a number of writers, beginning as early as the first generation of his followers.[55] Such was not the case for the *Futûhât*, whose commentaries are few and far between[56] and extremely fragmentary. Most of them relate to only a few lines, if not a few words (the first eight in the text, in particular), or to a single verse (like the one at the beginning of the prologue); Abd al-Karîm al-Jîlî, for example, devoted an entire treatise to approximately the first two pages of the *bâb al-asrâr*. Another, later example was Emir 'Abd al-Qâdir al-Jazâ'irî, whose aim it was (in his *Kitâb al-Mawâqif*, "The Book of Stopping Places"[57]) to explain the meanings of several pages from the *khutba*[58] and from chapters 6,[59] 69,[60] 73,[61] 76,[62] and 373[63]: thus, a relatively large number, although in fact his study covered only a small number of pages. Sha'rânî, in two of his works[64] offers a simplified introduction (and on delicate points, a quite careful presentation) to the main subjects touched on in the *Futûhât*; but he does limit himself to gathering quotes from Ibn 'Arabî, and annotates them only cursorily. To the best of our knowledge, none of these commentaries has been translated into a European language.[65] Given this situation, an individual's exploration of the *Futûhât Makkiyya* might be as haphazard as it is difficult. We do not claim either to make the task easier or to clear away what traps the work might contain. What we do hope to do in this introduction to *reading* the *Futûhât* (and not to the *Futûhât* themselves), is at least point out a few cardinal points whose sighting might prevent the investigator from experiencing a *hayra* that has nothing in common with the erudite ignorance of the *awliyâ'* but the name.

We have referred to the importance—both in volume and in substance—of the *fasl al-ma'ârif*. These nine hundred pages are, in a sense, a long *muqaddima*: both a preamble to the book that establishes the framework wherein later developments will be set, and a prelude to the journey, instructing the pilgrim in regard to the road to take and the goal to be reached. The keys to deciphering the entire work are to be sought in this initial section. Our attention will thus focus on this section, and especially on its early chapters. However, our purpose is not to offer a summary that puts concepts and symbols into logical order. The how is just as important as the what. Consequently, our aim here is to detect the early emergence of themes, and to observe how the threads of the warp and those in the woof interweave.

Muslim authors traditionally begin their writings with a two-part doxology *(khutba)*: praise to God *(tahmîd)* and prayer over the Prophet *(taskiya)*. The form it takes may be limited to short phrases, or may unfold in a dazzling pyrotechnic display of rhymed prose that is often richer in sound than it is in content. Such is not the case for Ibn 'Arabî, whose doxologies are, in themselves, already statements of doctrine deserving of considerable reflection. The doxology that opens the *Futûhât* is a prime example of this; it is curious that it also introduces in a quite specific fashion an important event in the author's life. It is not just by chance that, as we have pointed out, the eight first words (the interpretation of which Ibn 'Arabî does not return to until much later, in the second *fasl*)[66] have given rise to a good share of the commentaries that have been penned.[67] What looks quite clear on the surface is deceiving.

Al-hamdu li-Llâh al-ladhî awjada l-ashiyâ' 'an 'adam wa 'addamahu: for anyone familiar with Ibn 'Arabî's teaching, the phrase *al-hamdu li-Llâh* (literally, "Praise be to God") does not only mean that praise rightfully belongs to God, but that it comes only from him, that He is simultaneously both the Praiser *(al-hâmid)* and the Praised *(al-mahmûd)*: "No one praises God but God Himself" *(Lâ hâmida li-Llâh illâ huwa)*, Ibn 'Arabî declares in his commentary on the *Fâtiha*, in chapter 5 of the *Futûhât*. In chapter 350, where he deals with the *hujub* ("veils," meaning the creatures themselves, in that they hide the omnipresence of God), he describes the spiritual abode *(manzil)* in which one receives the knowledge of this "praise of God by God." Emir 'Abd al-Qadîr was inspired by the same passage in chapter 5, and saw three different categories of beings in these first two words of the *khutba*: ordinary believers who praise God "by themselves" *(bi-anfusihim)*, the elite who praise God "through God" *(bi-Llâh)*, and the elite of the elite, whose praise "belongs to God" *(li-Llâh)*, since individuals in this category of being know that it is God who, through their lips, is addressing Himself. The men of the *lâm* (the first letter in the particle *li*) are thus superior to the men of the letter *bâ* (the first letter of the particle *bi*), since *bi* implies the subsistence of the praiser, while *li* implies his extinction. *Al-ladhî awjada l-ashiyâ'* can be translated "who brought things into existence." But *shay'*, "thing," which is the singular of *ashiyâ'*, refers as much to what is in existence *(mawjûd)* as to what is nonexistent *(ma'dûm)* in Ibn 'Arabî's terminology. Which is the case here? References to scripture, which underlie all of Ibn 'Arabî's doctrinal writings, are not present in this case. On one hand, verse 19:8 asserts that "*We created you while you were nothing*" *(lam taku shay'an*; literally, "while you were not a thing"); and on the other, eight verses (2:114; 3:47; 3:59; 6:73; 16:40; 19:35; 36:82; 40:68) declare that when God wants something to be, "*He says 'Be!,' and it is.*" In his commentary on these verses,[68] Ibn 'Arabî never hesitates to point out that they imply that the "thing" was not pure nothingness, since God's words are addressed to it, and it hears. The first verse we cited, on the other hand, supposes the coming into existence of something that did not exist in any respect; and this point of view appears to be prevalent in the first phrase of the *khutba*. This interpretation is reinforced by the following words: *"'an 'adam wa ...addamahu,"* the whole thus translated as *"Praise belongs to God who brought things into existence from nothing, and annihilated nothingness,"* words of creation *ex nihilo* about which the representatives of Islamic exotericism can find nothing to say. A number of the sentences that follow, however, are compatible with this only if we take the metaphysical doctrine into consideration in its totality; only the seeds of the doctrine exist in the passage, but it will be explained much more explicitly later. The key idea here is that of *thubût* (immutability), which in Ibn 'Arabî's technical lexicon means the state of the *a'yân thâbita*, the "eternal haecceities." *Thubût* is the way these "possibilities" are present in divine knowledge. They do not "exist": they are real only for God, not for themselves *(mawjûda li-Llâh ghayru mawjûda li-anfusiha)*.[69] But they are predisposed to being "clothed" with existence. The presence of these "possibles"—of these "things"—in divine knowledge is eternal, just as knowledge itself is, since God did not "become" *Al-'Alîm*, the Knower: He is the Knower, for all eternity, both past and to come.

The concept of *thubût* nevertheless seems not to resolve all the problems that need to be reconciled in the revealed Book: verse 76:1, for example, refers to that "moment in eternity" *(hînun min al-dahr*; our translation of *dahr* keeps Ibn 'Arabî's interpretation of the word in mind: it is also one of the Divine Names)[70] when man "was not a thing present to the memory" *(lam yakun shay'an madhkûran)*—in other words: when he was not *ma'lûman*, "known."[71] Here again, Ibn 'Arabî's metaphysics solves the problem—and at the same time resolves the contradiction between this passage from the Qur'ân and all the verses affirming divine omniscience: that "moment," which has no place in any time frame, corresponds to a degree of ontology, that of the *ahadiyya*, the pure Unity of absolutely undetermined Essence. Seen from this degree's particular vantage point, "things" are nothing, and it is thus *ex nihilo* that they are brought into existence. It is at the ontologically later degree (though they do not follow one another in time)—the degree of *wâhadiyya*, or *wahdâniyya* (Oneness)—that, under the effect of the "most holy effusion" *(al-fayd al-aqdas)*, we see the appearance of both these *ad intra* determinations that the Divine Names are, and the *a'yân thâbita* that—in potentiality, and then in actuality—by virtue of the "holy effusion" *(al-fayd al-muqaddas)* are the theaters of their epiphanies. *"The existence of the world after its inexistence, for our Master (Ibn 'Arabî) and for all individuals of divine unveiling,"* wrote Emir 'Abd al-Qâdır, *"refers to the consciousness that the* a'yân thâbita *obtain from their own efforts and from their states, and the fact that they become the places of manifestation of True Being* (al-wujûd al-haqq)*: for they do not acquire being, they just function as places of theophany. He Who manifests Himself in these places of manifestation* (al-zâhir fi hâdhihi l-mazâhir) *is True Being, and he alone is named by the names of the 'possibles' and characterized by their attributes."*[72]

The idea of *thubût*, which, as commentators have remarked, runs in filigree through this passage even though it is not to be explained until later, is the only thing that hints at what is to come next[73]: *Wa awqafa wujûdahâ 'alâ tawajjuh kalimihi li natahaqqaqa bi-thâlika sirr hudûthihâ wa qidamiha min qidamihi*: "and which has offered as the fulcrum for their existence the orientation toward them of His Words, so that we might realize the secret of their aventitiousness and their eternity and that we might tell the difference between their eternity and His eternity." The "Divine Words"—which can be understood as being the modalities specific to each of the "things" from the command *(kun!, "Be")* that made them go from the state of non-manifestation to the manifested state—are more properly speaking, here too, the Divine Names, the list of which is infinite and each of which is the "base of support" *in divinis (mustanad ilâhî)*[74] for a specific thing, its ontological root, and its "raison d'être." Ibn 'Arabî sums this up in one sentence a few lines later: *"For each servant there is a corresponding Name that is his lord; it is a body, and this Name is its heart."* But things are also, reciprocally, the raison d'être for the Names, since for each name there is a corresponding thing in which, and in which alone, its epiphany can take place. "Adventitious" in the sense of their manifestation, things are also "eternal" *ad extra*, from another perspective, since they are actually identified with the Names, or the Divine Speech, *kalimât Allâh*,[75] as Ibn 'Arabî would declare on a number of occasions when he compared the universe to a "great Qur'ân" *(qur'ân kabîr)*.[76] The passage we translate here nevertheless emphasizes the necessary distinction between God's eternity and that of things: God knows that He is, and that He is eternal. Things— as *a'yân thâbita*—know neither that they eternally are, nor even that they are. Objects of God's knowledge for all eternity, they become subjects and become conscious of being only after the *kun* that brings them into existence.

The next part of this same passage *"and so that we might understand, when this realization comes to us, what He has taught us regarding the* sidq qadamihi" would require a full explanation of verse 10:2 (which the last two words refer to) for it to be intelligible. Let us bear in mind, however, that *qadam* literally means "foot," (it has the same root as the word *qidam*, eternity) but that it refers etymologically to the idea of precedence. The foot is what holds a thing up, and in this sense the "true foot" is nothing other than the *mustanad ilâhî*, the essential reality *in divinis* of everything in existence, meaning the whole set of aspects or Divine Names whose unfolding *ad extra* constitutes the universe. In the sense of precedence, it refers to the mystery of predestination: those who know the secret of what in them is adventitious, and what is eternal *(qadîm)*, know that everything that comes to them is the manifestation of what was included as a fact of predisposition *(isti'dâdât)* in their *'ayn thâbita*.[77]

Considerable time could be spent on each word of the *khutba*, although there is not room to do so here.[78] We must limit ourselves to showing how extremely dense the text is, and to pointing out that from these very first lines there are fundamental ideas present, albeit discretely so. The discretion is relative, as the following quite unambiguous words later show: *"If He addresses His servant, it is He who is both the listener and what is heard; if [the servant] does what He commands, it is He Who is both obeyer and obeyed."* This statement is immediately followed by the famous distich *(Al-rabb haqq wa l-'abd haqq...)* that made Ibn Taymiyya and several polemicists after him so indignant: what Ibn 'Arabî is doing is using the same word, *haqq*, which can be translated as "Truth," "Reality," or simply "God," to denote both the Lord and the servant. The distich continues like this: *"May it please Heaven that I know who is subject to legal obligations* (al-mukallaf)! *If you say it is the servant, the servant is without life. If you say it is the Lord, then whence does the obligation upon Him come?"* The statement is twice blasphemous in the opinion of the doctors of the Law, since it makes a pronouncement regarding the identity of both the Lord and the servant *('abd)*, at the same time that it appears to call into question the very basis of sacred law. *Hulûl* (incarnationism) and *ibâha* (antinomianism), the accusations so frequently made against the Shaykh al-Akbar, appear to find their proof in this single brief passage. And we are only half way through the first page of four large volumes of the *Futûhât...* A reference to the echo *(al-sadâ)* symbolically extends what was just said. Elsewhere in the work—but in the beginning of the *Fusûs*,[79] also—Ibn 'Arabî would use a similar symbol, that of the mirror that reflects an optical echo, in the same way that an acoustic echo returns: God sees Himself in the mirror of man and, vice-versa, man, if he dissipates the illusion of his ontological autonomy, discovers that he is nothing more than a reflection in the mirror of Divine Reality. Whence the paradox of the Law: *"I give Him thanks with the gratitude of him who realizes that it is by legal obligation* (al-taklîf) *that the Name* Al-Ma'bûd (the equivalent of *Al-Rabb*, the Sovereign, the Lord) *becomes manifest and that it is through what is included in the words "There is no power or strength but through God" that Generosity,* al-jûd) *is manifested. For if Paradise were the reward of your acts, how could one speak of Generosity?"* The Lord *(rabb, ma'bûd)* exists as such only if there is a servant *('abd)* who is subjected to His order. The Law is thus necessary. But, as the Qu'rân asserts in verse 37:96, "*God created you—both you and what you do,*" the *'abd*'s act of obedience only appears to belong to him. The reward promised to the servant is not a reward, but rather a gift.

It must nevertheless be emphasized that the ideas we have just outlined represent only one aspect of the Shaykh al-Akbar's total doctrine; his teachings are certainly much more complex. The problem of the attribution of acts, which is a classic problem in Muslim theology, will be considered from other points of view later[80]; the idea of the "Oneness of being" (*wahdat al-wujûd*, a technical term that Ibn 'Arabî actually does not use[81]) could actually not be closely studied based only on the information we have just presented without it being understood in an extremely reductionist way. The *Futûhât*'s author, as we shall see, informs the reader to beware of embracing too quickly a spiritual science that is "an ocean without a shore."

The second part of traditional doxologies in Islam is obligatorily devoted to what is commonly referred to as "prayer over the Prophet," and consists in asking God's blessing and peace *(al-salâm)* upon him, his family, and his companions. In the *Futûhât*'s khutba, this eulogy has an unusual characteristic, since it introduces Ibn 'Arabî's account of a visionary incident that took place early in his stay in Mecca. We have commented on this event elsewhere; Michel Vâlsan sees it as relating to "*the Shaykh al-Akbar's investiture in the Supreme Center,*" and his consecration in the role of "*Seal of Muhammadan Sainthood,*"[82] meaning as the integral heir to the *walâya* (sainthood) that constitutes the inner aspect of the Prophet, in whom the role of prophet *(al-nubuwwa)*, properly speaking, represents only the outer aspect. The Prophet—or rather the Muhammadan Reality *(al-haqîqa al-muhammadiyya)* of which Muhammad is the final and perfect manifestation in history—addresses Ibn 'Arabî and invites him to speak: "*Celebrate the praise of Him who has sent me, and mine. For in you there is a particle of me that can no longer bear being far from me; it governs your most inner reality.*" Strictly speaking, the word we have translated as "particle" means a hair; Ibn 'Arabî uses it at other times[83] as a symbol of his relationship to the Prophet: as eminent as his own spiritual degree may be, as universal as the role he claims as the source of all sainthood[84] might be, the Shaykh al-Akbar clearly does not consider himself to be a substitute *(na'ib)* for the Muhammadan Reality that is, invisibly, the only true Seal.

After a few panegyric verses on the *haqîqiyya muhammadiyya*, whose primordial nature (the *haqîqa* is called the "noble principle of creation," *al-asl al-karîm*) is affirmed,[85] there is a description in symbolic language of the cosmological process from the time of the Pen (the equivalent of the First Intellect, *al-'aql al-awwal*) up to man, the final point of all creation, a process whose consummation takes place with the definitive appearance, in the person of the Prophet, of Muhammadan Reality in the Time of history.

Strictly speaking, the *khutba* is followed by a poem dedicating the work to shaykh 'Abd al-Azîz Mahdawî; it is the *khutba* and this poem that comprise the prologue as a whole. In the verses, as in the prose passage that immediately follows them, we find the names of certain individuals (e.g., Abû Abdallâh al-Murâbit[86] and Abu Muhammad al-Jarrâh[87]) that are seen in other Ibn 'Arabî works, and especially Badr al-Habashi,[88] who was the Shaykh al-Akbar's companion for twenty-three years. There are several references in the poem to the exceptional initiatory status of these men, and that of Ibn 'Arabî himself (page 9, verse 11), who at that point declares that he will have no successor: this point is worth bearing in mind, since it confirms other details scattered throughout Ibn 'Arabî's corpus that lead to the conclusion that the role of Seal of Muhammadan Sainthood is not transferable. No one is obligated to accept it, but it is fitting not to attribute to Ibn 'Arabî any position other than his own in this matter.[89]

There is another poem that follows this one. It had previously appeared in the *Kitâb al-isrâ*,[90] and seems to be the first of the different accounts the author gives regarding his spiritual ascension from one heaven to another, up as far as the Divine Presence. Its first, frequently quoted, verse is a sharp affirmation: *"I am the Qur'ân and the Seven oft-repeated"* (the "Seven oft-repeated" is an expression borrowed from the Qur'ân, verse 15:87, which according to current interpretations refers to the *Fâtiha*, the sura that opens the Qur'ân; it contains seven verses). *"The Qur'ân is to the other revealed Books and Pages what man is to the universe, since it contains all the Books, and man contains the universe; they are thus brothers,"* Ibn 'Arabî explains in chapter 325 of the *Futûhât*. He is of course speaking about the Perfect Man here *(al-insân al-kâmil)*, who is not only an "abbreviation of the world," a microcosm, but who also gathers together in his nature all the divine realities *(al-haqâ'iq al-haqqiyya)* and all the realities belonging to the creatures *(al-haq'âiq al-khalqiyya)*. Similarly, in another of his writings, the *Kitâb al-isrâr*, the Shaykh al-Akbar declares: "*The universal man is the Qur'ân*" *(al-insân al-kulli huwa l-qur'ân)*.[91]

This mention of the *insân kâmil* in the *Kitâb al-isrâ'* is an important reference to the concept, which is ubiquitous in the *Futûhât*, but when put back in its initial context, it is of added interest in the way it explains the incident described in chapter one of the *Futûhât*, the chapter that informs us of the supernatural circumstances of the work's composition. In the *Kitâb al-isrâ'*, the words are actually described as coming from a mysterious being that the "traveller" *(al-sâlik)*, that is, Ibn 'Arabî himself, meets "at the Arîn spring." In traditional Islamic geography, the name Arîn refers to a mythic island or city located equidistant from the four cardinal points.[92] It is thus clearly a symbolic name for the supreme spiritual center or, in the cosmic order, for what sacred anthropology calls the "heart."[93] The individual the *sâlik* meets is called the *fatâ*, which might be translated as "young hero." *Fatâ* is the word from which *futuwwa*—which we have already seen—is derived, and it is charged with Qur'ânic references, since it appears in a number of suras in regard to the "seven sleepers" (18:10, 13), the companion of both Moses (18:60, 62) and (especially) Abraham (21:60), who just destroyed the idols that his people were worshiping. In the chapter from his famous *Risâla*[94] devoted to the *futuwwa*, Qushayrî (d. 445/1054) offered a definition of the *fatâ* that was inspired by the story of Abraham: *The* fatâ *is the one who destroyed the idol,"* and he immediately adds the following pithy comment: *"and the idol of all men is their egos."* In the *Kitâb al-isrâ'*, the *fatâ*, who appears to the pilgrim early in his journey, is described as being "*of a spiritual essence*" and endowed "*with lordly attributes.*" He explains that he was sent to prescribe "*taking off both sandals*" for those with whom he came in contact; this is another Qur'ânic reference (verse 20:12), which in *tasawwuf* and especially in Ibn 'Arabî is interpreted to be a symbol for going beyond duality.[95] "*You are the cloud that covers your own sun. Learn your essential reality!*" he tells the traveller. He adds: "*Only he who rises up as far as my station understands my words! And only I rise up as far as my station!*" And then he recites a poem that would later be used in the *Futûhât*.

"*Where do you want me to lead you?*" he then asks. "*I want to reach the city of the Prophet, in search for the radiant station of Red Sulphur*"[96] is the pilgrim's reply. One verse gives the *fatâ*'s reply:

O you who search for the path that leads to the secret,
Turn back: for the entire secret is within you.[97]

We shall soon see the enigmatic figure of the "young hero" in the *Futûhât*. But after the table of contents at the end of the prologue, there is another long introduction (*muqaddima*) that precedes this second encounter. It is composed of a preamble and three "professions of faith" (*'aqîda*, pl. *'aqâ'id*), only the first of which appeared in the first edition of the *Futûhât*. Paradoxically, the preamble opens by questioning the usefulness of these formulations of the creed since, in Ibn 'Arabî, for the person who is ready (*al-muta'ahibb*), they are a distraction from what is essential: *"When he gives himself exclusively to retreat and invocation, when he empties himself of all thought and sits indigent, devoid of everything at his Lord's door"* God then illuminates him with supernatural knowledge. It is, moreover, to knowledge (*'ilm*) that the preamble is devoted.

Ibn 'Arabî sees three degrees of this knowledge: *'ilm al-'aql*, the knowledge acquired through the working of the intellect; *'ilm al-ahwâl*, the "knowledge of states," which can be obtained through inner personal experience (*dhawq*); and *'ilm al-asrâr*, the "knowledge of secrets" that comes from the insufflation of the Holy Spirit and belongs to the prophets and saints. He strongly warns both those who reject what the *sâhib al-asrâr*—the repository of divine secrets[98]—brings, and those who confuse him with the philosopher, because their messages ultimately converge: the way of access to knowledge and the degree of certitude in the one are quite different from that of the other.[99] In regard to theology (*kalâm*), he who has prepared himself to receive theophanies has nothing to do with it, and he rejects its attempts to validate or invalidate beliefs. The proof is that the normal believer (*al-'âmma*), whose faith is sound, ignores *kalâm*. and draws his belief directly from the obvious sense of Revelation (*min zâhir al-kitâb al-'azîz*). The extremes come together and the authentic gnostic (*al-'ârif bi-Llâh*) is closer to the simple believer than he is to the theologian (*al-mutakallim*).[100]

The first *'aqîda* (pp. 36-38)—let us bear in mind that it is the only one present in the early version of the text—is precisely the only one that every Muslim should adhere to, and is only a brief expression of the fundamental articles of the traditional creed. The second (pp. 38-41), that of the "theologians," is actually only a summary in rhymed prose of one of Ghazâlî's works (*Al-iqtisâd fî l-i'tiqâd*),[101] as the author mentions. It takes the form of a dialogue "under the dome of Arîn," and thus in the center of the world, among four individuals who correspond to the four cardinal points.[102] The third (pp. 41-47), that of the "elite" *(ahl al-ikhtisâs)*, constitutes a somewhat softened wording ("between speculation and spiritual unveiling": *bayna l-nazar wa l-kashf)*, quite elliptically presaging Ibn 'Arabî's metaphysics, but set in the framework of issues related to *kalâm*, while criticizing the inconsistencies of the Ash'arite position[103] at a number of points. We must nevertheless point out one important, oft-repeated (pp. 38 and 47) statement by Ibn 'Arabî: the profession of faith of the "elite of the elite" *('aqîda khulâsat al-khâssa)* is not to be sought there, nor is it to be sought in any particular place in the work: it is *"scattered throughout the chapters of this book.*[104]*"*

The title of the first chapter, "On knowledge of the Spirit in whose nature I drew what is transcribed in this book..." announces that the issue at hand is what might be called how the *Futûhât* were born. It is a birth that is located precisely in the place whence the work draws its title, "the Revelations of Mecca," and at the precise moment of the second encounter with the *fatâ*.

> *While doing the ritual circumambulation, I said to myself:*
> *How could I walk*
> *Around that which is incapable of perceiving my secret,*
> *Around a pile of stones that does not understand my movement?*

Both the role and the very existence of the Ka'ba, the "House of God" *(Bayt Allâh)*, are paradoxical in two ways: because God *"is with you wherever you are"* (Q. 57:4) and thus *"wherever you turn, there is the Face of God"* (Q. 2:115), it is thus impossible to assign His presence to a place; and also because, according to a *hadîth qudsî* (one absent from the canonical collections, but which Ibn 'Arabî and many other Sufis before him considered authentic), *"My heaven and My earth cannot contain me, but the heart of My servant contains Me,"* and because no other temple can revoke this privilege which is exclusive to the heart of the believer. According to an expression Ibn 'Arabî uses later, even though it is an *"inert body, unfeeling and blind, deprived of intellect, deaf,"* the Ka'ba is nevertheless "the heart of existence" *(qalb al-wujûd)*. For the blinded eye of a fallen man the universe has lost its original isotropy. In choosing a place for his house and designating it as the place where His creatures' prayer should be directed, as the goal of their long march, as the axis around which the perpetual turning of pilgrims should take place, God institutes an order for man commensurate with his infirmity. But the *'ârif bi-Llâh*, who sees God in all things and recognizes the signs of His presence *"on the horizons and in his soul"* (cf. Q. 41:53), is not easily resigned to this limiting of divine infinity, nor to this preeminence of mineral over man, the "vicar of God." Even the caliph 'Umar recognized this revolt and was willing to kiss the Black Stone only in order to follow the Prophet's example. In another passage from the *Futûhât*,[105] the Shaykh al-Akbar reports a dramatic nighttime conversation between the Ka'ba and him; the Ka'ba "pulled up her skirt" and prepared to pick herself up off her foundation in order to crush him. The only way to appease her anger was to dedicate a work in praise of the Ka'ba.[106]

But in the inaugural episode we are studying, Ibn 'Arabî immediately receives a supernatural reply to his question:

Contemplate the House: for sanctified hearts, its light shines openly
They look at it through God, without a veil,
and its august and sublime secret appears.

The last word in these verses is the key to what follows: it is the "secret" of the Ka'ba that appears when the mysterious *fatâ*, the "evanescent" *(fâ'it)*—meaning both present and absent at the same time—hero again comes upon the scene: he is both "simple and complex," he is "neither dead nor alive," and he "contains all things and is contained in all things." This "spirit" describes itself a little later as being "knowledge, the known, and the knower," " wisdom, the object of wisdom, and the wise man," and as "the contemplator and the contemplated" *(al-shâhid wa l-mashhûd)*. An Epiphany of the Ka'ba, or rather of Him who resides in it and constitutes its secret, the *fatâ* is also the *insân kâmil*, the Perfect Man, the Ka'ba incarnate, which places the emphasis on its manifestation in human form. From another, complementary, point of view, it might be said that this face-to-face experience—the resonance that runs through the story prevents us from thinking of it as a metaphorical encounter—makes Ibn 'Arabî confront his own eternal reality; this interpretation is confirmed when the account is juxtaposed with the text of the *Kitâb al-isrâ'* cited earlier. In both cases, the event occurs in a central place: a zero point in time, the "Ancient House" *(al-bayt al-'atîq*, Q. 22:29) standing in the "Mother of cities" *(umm al-qurâ*, Q. 6:92), and also, according to Ibn 'Abbâs,[107] the "navel of the earth," the zero point in space. Its history predates all history, just as its location precedes all geography.

The *fatâ* speaks only in silence (he is called *al-mutakallim al-sâmit*). The conversation he has with Ibn 'Arabî is a mute dialogue. The kinds of knowledge Ibn 'Arabî receives from the young hero are not transmitted via the spoken word, because they are not exterior to the *fatâ*; they are his very being. Whence the injunction: *"Examine the details of my constitution and the ordering of my form!"*[108] The last lines of the chapter will reiterate this order in a more solemn fashion: *"I am the ripe garden and the plenitude of the harvest,"* the *fatâ* says. *"Now raise my veils and read what the inscriptions within me contain! And what you look carefully at in me, place it in your book and preach it to those you love!"* Ibn 'Arabî then tells us, *"I raised his veils and looked at what was written in him. A light within him made the hidden knowledge he contains and envelopes within his being appear to me, and the first line I read, the first secret of this line I learned, is precisely what I am now going to transcribe in this second chapter."*[109]

Everything that came earlier—the *khutba*, the *muqaddima*, the story of the meeting with the *fatâ*—was thus merely a foreword, albeit one of impressive dimensions. Once this threshold is crossed, we finally get into the work properly speaking. The first steps are difficult: devoted to the "science of letters" (*'ilm al-hurûf*), a subject to which Ibn 'Arabî frequently returns both in the *Futûhât* and elsewhere[110] (we see it again especially in chapters 5, 20, and 26 in the *fasl al-ma'ârif*, the second chapter above all requires that its reader be extremely familiar not only with the Arabic alphabet, but also with the technical vocabulary of grammarians and calligraphers. Understanding it also supposes that the reader already has a sense of what this "science of letters" is in Islam; 'Alî b. Abî Tâlib—who certainly was far from unknown to the Andalusian Sufis—is traditionally considered to have been its founder. Indeed, on certain points, Ibn 'Arabî (especially early in the chapter) limits himself to reminding the reader, as he points out, of certain information found in earlier works.

Knowing texts and terminology is not enough, however. *'Ilm al-hurûf* properly speaking, is not *"the fruit of reflection and speculation: it is a gift from God."*[111] About the letter *nûn*, Ibn 'Arabî writes: *"There are marvels which none can understand who has not girded his loins with the loincloth of submission, and has not spiritually realized that [initiatory] death after which there is no objection or displaced curiosity."*[112] In another passage, as he brings up the secret of the correlations between two groups of three letters, he indicates that he has been forbidden to reveal them in his writings but that he is allowed to show them to those who are worthy, either because of their own spiritual realization, or, lacking that, because they have shown perfect submission to the gnostic *('ârif)* and they unreservedly accept his teaching.[113] What is at issue here has nothing to do with divination techniques or the magical events that certain properties of the letters can produce.[114] One of the most famous authors of treatises on these practices, Abû l'Abbâs al-Bûnî, mentions Ibn 'Arabî—probably an older contemporary—in his chain of transmission: the connection should not fool us in regard to the difference between the two men's thoughts. For the Shaykh al-Akbar, this *sîmayâ* is not an illusion, and it is not illegitimate to use it in a variety of situations. But the masters of the Way are disdainful of its use, and he, himself, vows never to use the power of letters in such a way; the only thing that is really important is the metaphysical truths that the science of letters allows us to show. Mentioning the Andalusian Sufi Ibn Barrâjân's (d. 536/1141) prediction of the taking of Jerusalem in 583/1187—a prediction that was apparently based on astrological calculations— he shows that it could also have been made via calculations based on the numerical value of the letters in the beginning of sura *Al-Rûm*. But he immediately adds that, for Ibn Barrâjân—and for the men of God in general—such explanations constitute only a way of concealing the fact that their certainty is based on an intuitive unveiling *(kashf)*.[115]

The principles of the science of letters are common to the Semitic traditions, and common points between the Hebrew Kabbalah and *'ilm al-hurûf* are quickly spotted in Islamic literature in general, and in the *Futûhât* in particular. Such is the case, for example, for correlations between letters and the elements,[116] as found in the *Sefer Yetsira*; they appear to share a concept that was long and widespread (in Lucretius, the Latin word *elementa* referred to the letters of the alphabet). We must point out one fact, however, and that is that it was in the Spain of Ibn 'Arabî's youth that the Zohar—one of the fundamental texts of the Kabbalah—would appear around 1280. Whoever its true author—or rather editor—may have been, the Zohar is not a common pseudepigraph; it contains initiatory teachings that were not invented by Moses of Leon, and, long before he put the work into circulation, it had a number of representatives on the Iberian peninsula. One might thus wonder, as did R. W. J. Austin,[117] if Ibn 'Arabî, living in a country in which Jews and Muslims were in daily contact with one another, had direct access to this teaching while he was living in Andalusia. He reports a conversation between an *isrâ'iliyyîn* "doctor" and himself that shows that he knew that the Torah begins with the letter *beth*, like the Qur'ân does with the letter *ba'*, its equivalent in the Arabic alphabet[118]; but polemics with the *Ahl al-kitâb* had long since led other Muslims to be interested in their Holy Books, and nothing in the Shaykh al-Akbar's writings leads us to believe that his knowledge of the Hebrew tradition was greater than that of any other educated non-Jew in his day. Beyond disputes over the historical development of specific points of doctrine and the complex interplay of reciprocal influences—which would be both in vain and unresolvable via any kind of certain proof—we still cannot deny the correlation, in both time and space, of major manifestations of Islamic and Jewish esotericism, and we cannot help but think about the meaning in the framework of spirituality of the "*last third of the night*" before the coming dawn of the Eternal Day.[119]

But Ibn 'Arabî encourages us to look for the source of *'ilm al-hurûf* in a very different direction from that of Judaism. In his prophetology,[120] all the different kinds of knowledge are connected to a particular prophet whose "heirs" are those who possess that particular knowledge, either partially or entirely. As he points out in chapter 20 of the *Futûhât*, the science of letters is a Christic (*'isawî*) branch of knowledge. The emphasis the Shaykh al-Akbar places on the importance of this, and the place he gives it from the very beginning of the work—where he presents it as the key to everything that follows—is undoubtedly related to the eschatological role Jesus is to play: as the second coming approaches, the knowledge specific to him holds, more than ever, a specific privilege of revealing mysteries. But this knowledge is also explained by the special relationship between Ibn 'Arabî, the Seal of Muhammadan Sainthood, and his "*first teacher*,"[121] who will soon return at the end of time, as the Seal of Universal Sainthood.[122]

The wealth of material in this chapter—an overwhelming combination of information about the shapes written letters take, their specific places of utterance in the mouth, and their numerical values—prevents us from offering a summary of it here: "*The hand would be exhausted, the pen would grow blunt, the ink would dry.*"[123] A few guiding ideas that run through it can be pointed out, however, the first of which is the idea of universal life, which is foundational for Ibn 'Arabî's cosmology. This idea is expressed in a number of passages in Ibn 'Arabî's work. "*It is not possible to subdivide the universe into those things that are living and those that are not. For us, it is alive in its totality.*"[124] In his comments on the Divine Name *Al-Muhyî*, "The Vivifier," in chapter 558, we writes: "*It is he who gives life to all things; for there is no thing that is not alive, because there is no thing that does not praise God: now only the living—whether our perceptions tell us they are alive or dead—can praise God."*[125] There is no lack of scriptural support for this idea of praise by the totality of creatures, regardless of whether they are inert to our eyes (Ibn 'Arabî usually relies on sura 17:44 on this subject). We will nevertheless see that what is at issue here is not a subtle exegesis. In another book, his *Rûh al-quds*, Ibn 'Arabî cites the Prophet talking about Mount Uhud (*"This mountain loves us, and we love it"*),[126] adding: *"For us, even the minerals love God... they constitute a community among others,"*[127] an assertion that shows through in a number of places in the *Futûhât* (*"Early in our spiritual life, we heard the stones glorifying God and invoking His name"*)[128]; there is also the reference, noted above, to his nuptial union with the stars and the letters of the alphabet. This is thus all a question of immediate perception of the secret reality of things, and not of a concept developed by reflecting on texts. Strong in his certainty, Ibn 'Arabî thus declares—in what is not one of the most singular aspects of the teachings he outlines in chapter 2—that the letters also constitute a "community" *(umma)*, that they also have their Messengers *(rusul)* and their Law *(sharî'a)*, and that among them can be distinguished the "common" *('âmma)*, the elite, and the elite of the elite, just as in human societies.[129] When he deals with the *dâl* or the *jîm* and the predominance of such and such quality or temperament in them, what he is describing is beings, not abstract signs.

The universe is a book, a "great Qur'ân," according to a phrase cited above. Conversely, the Book is a universe. To speak of the one is to speak of the other.

There is an intermediary between these two universes—or these two Books. It is man—the *insân kâmil*, of course—who shares the nature of both. He is both "brother of the Qur'ân" and *'âlam saghîr*, "little world," or microcosm. It is to him that the divine discourse is addressed in this double form, and it is his duty to decipher it, to be simultaneously *tarjumân al-qur'ân* and *tarjumân al-'âlam*, interpreter of the Qur'ân and interpreter of the created world; he is the one that gives them meaning.[130] The universal manifestation is the unfolding of *âyât Allâh*, of "God's signs" (but also of the "verses," since the word *âyât* has both meanings). These *âyât* are made up of words," *kalimât*,[131] which, in turn, are composed of letters, *hurûf*, which are in some way the elementary particles of the Book and of creation, as they are of the revealed Book. Whence the intricateness of the two hermeneutics—that of the Qur'ân and that of the universe—that the parallel between the twenty-eight letters of the alphabet and the twenty-eight degrees *(marâtib al-wujûd)* of Ibn 'Arabî's cosmology underscores.[132] Among these letters, the *alif*, from which all the others are derived—both graphically in the distinctive way it is written, and phonetically, through the modulation of the sound the *alif* represents[133]—is of particular importance. It is the "pole of letters" and, because of this, the point of departure for another series of correlations, this time with the spiritual hierarchy that supports the universe, the *qutb*, the "imam of the right side" and the "imam of the left side," having as their respective homologues the *alif*, the *waw*, and the *yâ*.[134]

As dry as it may seem, grammatical terminology is rich in symbolism, and Ibn 'Arabî makes full use of the resources it offers. This is certainly the case in the banal distinction between consonants and vowels. The latter, as their name *(harakât)* suggests, have the role of "moving" the inert consonants; they give them life, just as insufflation of the Spirit gives life to the Adam that was fashioned from a blob of clay (Q. 15:29).[135] But the only thing affected by this vocalization is the oral or written manifestation of the consonant in question; its essential reality *(haqîqa)* is unchangeable. The relationship between, for example, the final *dâl* in the name Zayd and the short vowels that determine the role it plays in speech is consequently analogous to the relationship between our own essences—our *a'yân thâbita*—and the successive forms that manifest them *ad extra*. It is this analogy that helps us understand the meaning of one of Ibn 'Arabî's most famous and oft commented verses, the first words of which go: *"We were the sublime letters" (kunnâ hurûfan 'âliyyât)*.[136]

Chapter 3, "How God transcends what is implied by the words He uses in reference to Himself in His Book in the words of the Messenger's speech," brings up the paradox of *tashbîh*, the "similarity" between God and His creatures, as is seen in Qur'ânic verses and hadith: God "sits" upon the Throne, "becomes angry," "smiles," and "holds the hearts of His believers in His hands." Reconciling these statements with *tanzîh*, divine transcendence, was a major problem in *kalâm* from very early on. It clearly was not in theology that Ibn 'Arabî sought the solution. The only kind of (speculative) knowledge possible where God is concerned is the *via negativa (al-'ilm bi l-salb)*. The powerlessness of *'aql*, the intellect, is radical. God is known only by God: a statement that, in the Shaykh al-Akbar's metaphysical doctrine, does not lead to the agnosticism one might logically deduct.

Chapter 4, *on the cause of the beginning of the world*, is the first outline that is developed to any degree (there will be others) on the role the Divine Names play "producing their effects in this world"; they constitute the "primordial keys" *(al-mafâtih al-uwwal)*: "To every reality [in this world] there is a corresponding Name that is specific to it, and that is its Lord."[137] Each of them, eager to manifest itself in accord with the preexisting model in divine knowledge, makes use of the intercession of the seven *ummahât al-asmâ'* (the "matrical Names") that, in turn, call upon the Name Allâh, which turns toward the Essence that commands that the realities *(haqâ'iq)* these Names express be brought into existence.[138]

This early sketch of a cosmogony will come up again in chapter 6, but after another, intervening, chapter—added to chapter 2 on the science of letters—leads us from the "great book" of the universe *(al-mushaf al-kabîr)* back to the Book strictly speaking, that is, to the Qur'ân. The preceding has thus prepared us for this give-and-take between the two homologous forms of divine speech. There is, necessarily, a correlation between the *Fâtiha*, the sura that "opens" the Qur'ân (and which Ibn 'Arabî will comment on here) and what "opens" the universal manifestation. Between the Book and the universe there is man, the ultimate purpose of both the one and the other, and whose calling it is to decipher both.

One further analogy is added to the symmetry between the cosmogonic process and the process of Revelation, and that is the symmetry that can be seen between the forms of divine discourse and the phases of spiritual realization through which man effectively becomes the *tarjumân* of the *kalimât Allâh*. A long exegesis on the *basmala*, the first verse in the *Fâtiha*, and more specifically on the letter *bâ* at its beginning, once again transfigures the grammatical vocabulary. We have already noted how rich traditional terminology is in regard to the *harakât* and their roles in case endings. Here, because of their etymology, the terms used to denote the genitive, the accusative, and the nominative, are related to the three degrees mentioned in one of the Prophet's maxims: *al-islâm*, outward submission to God, *al-imân*, inner faith, and *al-ihsân*, perfection. The *mîm*, that is, the last letter of the first word in the *basmala*, is "elevated" (that is, it carries the sign of the nominative, *raf'*, literally, "elevation"), while the Name is none other than the Named, and the servant is identified with his Master *(mawlâ)*.[139] This "ascension" of the *mîm* from the world of *'ubûdiyya*, of ontological servitude or indigence, is thus the exact equivalent of the *mi'râj* and, like it, reverses the process of manifestation: this is because the *bâ* in the *basmala*, which is the instrument of creation and Revelation, has the contrary effect—from a grammatical point of view— of imposing the genitive case *(khafd)* and thus, literally, of "lowering." Realizing that the *'abd* and the *rabb* are identical is thus the privilege of "man in the nominative," he whom a vertical course—the "straight path," *sirât mustaqîm*—leads back from the *asfal sâfilîn*, from the extreme depths, to the place where he again finds the "perfect stature," (*ahsan taqwîm*, Q. 95:4,5) that was originally his.

As in chapter 2, Ibn 'Arabî's hermeneutics use all the aspects—morphological, syntactical, graphic—of the text of Revelation, which is the spoken word, but which also is writing. The two dots under the *yâ'* in the Name *Al-Rahîm* (the All Merciful) are related to the Two Feet that God, seated upon the Throne, set upon the Footstool *(al-kursî)*, which themselves symbolize commandment *(al-'amr)* and interdiction *(al-nahy)*. But these two dots also represent the place of "*the taking off of the sandals*" *(khal' al-na'layn)* which, for Moses (Q. 20:12) and for anyone else who gets close to God, stands for going beyond duality.[140]

The commentary on the *Fâtiha*, whose homologue in the cosmic order is the *insân kâmil* or *haqîqa muhammadiyya*,[141] is followed by verses from sura *al-Baqara*. "Commentary" is actually a less-than-satisfactory word for what follows. Ibn 'Arabî offers neither a *tafsîr* in the classical sense of the word, nor a *ta'wîl*, which would be an allegorical[142] exegesis, but rather, to use words that come up often his his writing, *ishârât*, meaning "allusions" to certain unnoticed—and thus occasionally quite surprising—meanings. The *'ârif bi-Llâh* contemplates the divine beauty that exists in everything and of which everything is a reflection[143]; this leads him to perceive the positive meanings in the verses whose obvious meaning—about which there is no question—is negative. These "allusions" may be scandalous to the unknowing, who do not know that each word of the Qur'ân is simultaneously pronounced for all eternity and, for each being, perpetually new *(huwa jadîd 'inda kulli tâlin abadan)*[144]: since there is an incessant renewal of creation *(tajdîd al-khalq)*, there is incessant renewal of the Divine Word *(tajdîd al-qur'ân)*. In one stunning reversal—although he never deviates from the literalness of the text, upon which, moreover, all his exegesis is based—Ibn 'Arabî discovers that God "*has concealed His friends* (or "*His saints*," *awliyâ'ihi*) *in the guise of his enemies.*" The "unbelievers" in verse 6 *(al-ladhîna kafarû)* are indeed that. But, behind this meaning, there is another that reveals the etymology of the verb *kafara* ("hide," or "cover"). From this perspective, the verse describes "*those who have hidden what secrets of union have appeared to them.*"[145] Whether the Prophet exhorts them or not, "*they do not believe,*" but it is because they know with knowledge they have received from God alone. According to verse 7, where the description of unbelievers continues, "*He has placed a seal over their hearts"*—but such that there is no room in them for anyone other than Him—"*and over their ears*"—so that they might hear no other words in the universe than His. He places "*a veil over their eyes*": but it is the veil of the resplendent Divine Glory. The punishment *('adhâb)* with which they are threatened is being returned to the creatures that tear them away (in appearance only) from contemplation of the unparalleled One. But it is this return, sacrificial and painful, that will allow them to reach the summit of holiness by joining together knowledge of the One in the many and the many in the One: in a few lines, it adumbrates the theme that will come back with both additional breadth and depth in chapter 45.

With chapters 6, "On the beginning of the spiritual world," and 7, "On the beginning of human bodies," we return to cosmogenesis. There are two complementary ideas that play a central role here: that of the primordial character of the *haqîqa muhammadiyya*, the Muhammadan Reality (like the First Intellect, or the Pen), which was the first thing brought into existence out of the "dust" *(al-habâ')*—the totally indeterminate "dark substance," here symbolic of the *materia prima*[146]—under the effect of the Divine Light[147]; and that of the final character of man, created vertical "*like the pole supporting the tent, to be the pillar of the dome of the heavens.*" When the pillar disappears, the universe collapses. "*We thus know with certainty that man is the divine aim of the universe* (huwa l-'ayn al-maqsûda li-Llâh min al-'âlam)."[148]

Chapter 8, "On the earth which was created with the remains of Adam's clay, and which we call the Earth of essential reality," outlines the doctrine of the *'alam al-khayâl*, the "*imaginal world*," to use the words of Henry Corbin, who summarized the text in one of his works.[149] Let us not be deceived by the word "imaginal": the world has its own reality, independent of the use creatures make of their imaginative faculties. A participant in Adam's nature, this "earth," like him, contains all the higher and lower realities; like him, it adjoins both heaven and earth. No larger than a "sesame seed," it is, like him, a microcosm; and yet, in it are the Throne, the Footstool, and the seven heavens, "*like a ring cast off in the desert.*" It is "*the theater for the visions of the gnostics*": if it did not exist, "*it would be impossible for there to be meetings half-way* (munâzalât) *between God and us; it would be impossible for God [as the hadith states] to 'come down from heaven into this world,' or for him to be 'seated upon the Throne'*" (Q. 7:54). More generally, if this earth did not exist, bodies and spirits would never meet.[150] It is it that the Qur'ân points to as "*the vast land of God*" *(ard Llâh al-wâsi'a*, 4: 97; 29:56; 39:10). On this subject, Ibn 'Arabî brings up the words of Awhad al-dîn Kirmânî and Dhû'l Nûn al-Misrî, as well as his own, which we see scattered throughout the *Futûhât*: he penetrated into them for the first time in Tunis[151] in 590,[152] and had never stopped worshiping God at the moment he wrote these lines in 635.

In a way, this "interworld," where the difference between physics and metaphysics does not exist, is nothing other than the *insân kâmil*, the Perfect Man envisioned in the entire expanse of his cosmic function, the "isthmus" *(barzakh)* joining what is above to what is below. So here we again meet up with the theme that determined the order of the two preceding chapters. But the description of an "earth" where the invisible becomes visible announces also the subject of chapter 9, which deals with the jinn. For Ibn 'Arabî, this word, which is based on the root *JNN*, "to hide," includes in its most general meaning everything that escapes the perception of the ordinary man, and it thus applies to both angels (who are of a luminous nature, *nûriyya*) and the jinn, strictly speaking (who are of an igneous nature, *nâriyya*),[153] which explains why in the Qur'ân Iblîs was sometimes referred to as being a jinn, and sometimes an angel.

What is at issue here, however, is the *nâriyya* jinn. That they truly exist is affirmed by the Qur'ân and the hadith. Ibn 'Arabî has no doubt about their objective reality, even if he declares elsewhere[154] that their name "denotes that which is inner in man" *('ibâra 'an bâtin al-insân)*—which is a necessary consequence of the analogy of the microcosm and the macrocosm: they belong to the subtle fringe of the human world, like the animals belong to its crude fringe. But while man, created from earth and water, is stable and essentially humble, the jinn, created sixty thousand years earlier out of air and fire, do not have a stable form: they take whatever form they want. When they show themselves to us, they are prisoners of the form in which they appear as long as our eyes are still on them. If they are killed in one of these forms, they die and their fate after death is analogous to that of man. Fire, which is predominant in their constitution and which is "the most elevated of elements" brings them to pride; and it is this pride, which was theretofore without object, that at the time of man's creation leads them to rebel and turns some of them into demons *(shayâtîn)*.[155]

With chapter 10, we enter into sacred history, the broad strokes of which will be filled in in chapters 12, 14, and 15. The key term in this outline of "the cycle of the kingdom" *(dawrat al-mulk)*, that is, on the hierarchy of the human world "from Adam to Muhammad," is that of *haqîqa muhammadiyya*, even though it has never been pronounced: this

"Muhammadan Reality" is present from one end to the other of this cycle, and shows itself successively in the person of the prophets *(anbiyâ')* and the messengers *(rusûl)* through whom the *dîn qayyîm*, the *religio perennis* is periodically both restored and confirmed. As a perfect and definitive expression of the *dîn qayyîm*, Muhammadan Law, when it finally appears, abrogates all earlier laws. But, as Ibn 'Arabî tells us, this final, totalizing status of the *sharî'a* that the Prophet bears has the effect of validating preceding legislations when the communities that remain attached pay the *jizya*, the head tax: but by this, in effect, they are included in the Muhammadan community.[156] A passage from chapter 337 leaves no doubt about the meaning that should be attached to this remark: it not only implies the regularity of the status of the *dhimmî* within the *umma*, but also their happiness in the future.[157] This inhabitual position resulted in a fair amount of criticism for the Shaykh al-Akbar, to which Nâbulusî replied in an unpublished treatise.[158]

This Muhammadan Reality is the flawless figure of the *insân kâmil*, the theomorphic Man, and Ibn 'Arabî has no hesitation about ascribing to him a series of Divine Names listed in one of the first verses of the sura called "Iron" (Q. 57:3): the First, the Last, the Apparent, the Hidden, the Omniscient.

The title of chapter 11, "On the knowledge of our higher fathers and our lower mothers," may at first lead to some confusion. It covers two complementary ideas. On one level, *in divinis*, the "fathers" are the Divine Names, and the "mothers" are the *a'yân thâbita*, the essences of those things that are possible—the essences of the "possibles." The "sons" are then these same "possibilities," as long as they are brought into existence. On another level, one that is no longer metaphysical but rather cosmological, the Pen—or the First Intellect—plays the role of father, the Guarded Tablet (or the Universal Soul) being the Mother. Their union engenders nature *(al-tabî'a)* and Dust *(al-habâ')*, which here represent the form of matter; they are "brother and sister." The brother and sister, in turn, give birth to the Universal Body *(al-jism al-kullî)*. This process continues indefinitely: everything that is not God is both active relative to all that is ontologically inferior to it, and passive relative to what is ontologically superior, and thus, also at the same time, "father" and "mother."[159] The *birr al-wâlidayn*, the "filial piety" prescribed by Revelation, in this context takes on an unexpected symbolic meaning: it is an entire chain of beings that finds itself included in the veneration and gratitude owed to "parents."

The following chapter deals with the "cycle of Muhammad": theretofore present in the universe by his spirit *(bi rûhihi)*, the hidden *(bâtin)* *Verus Propheta* now becomes apparent *(zâhir)*. This accomplishment marks a "revolution" (the proper meaning of *dawra*) in time, which comes back *(istadâra,* a word with the same root as *dawra)* to its original state, as a hadith declares.[160] This is expressed by the return of the age of the Scale *(al-mîzân),* which was that of the creation of the world[161]: a restoration of the primordial perfection, but also—since the Scale, the symbol of cosmic equilibrium reestablished, is also an instrument associated with Justice—announces the end of the centuries. The Muhammadan community is "adjoining Paradise."[162]

Chapter 13 deals with the "Bearers of the Throne," the number of which is traditionally four, but which, according to the Qur'ân (69:17) will be eight on the Day of Resurrection. The four feet of the Throne, which encompasses universal manifestation, correspond to four aspects of this manifestation: the formation of bodies, that of spirits, the subsistence *(rizq)* of both, and their final destiny. Each of these aspects has an apparent face (a *zâhir*) and a hidden face (a *bâtin*). But what is hidden will become apparent at the end of time, and the four Bearers of the Throne will thenceforth be eight, by virtue of their hidden half being unveiled. We can sum this interpretation up only via details of a tradition whose symbolic expression (the Bearers of the Throne, respectively, take the shape of a man, a lion, a bull, and an eagle) extends into Islam what was common to both the Hebrew Bible (Ezechiel's vision) and the New Testament (the Apocalypse).[163] But it is noteworthy that, in passing, it offers Ibn 'Arabî the opportunity to give us the meaning of the story of the Sâmirî, an individual who, according to the Qur'ân (20:87-96), created the Golden Calf: this calf *('ijl)* is actually a small bull, and it is because, in a vision of the Divine Throne, the Sâmirî thought he recognized the God of Moses in the resplendent figure of the angel with the bull's face that he chose to worship Him in this guise. His idolatry was not vulgar idolatry. He was astray—and he still is—because the vision is not complete. But *he did see* *(basurtu,* Q. 20: 96); and it is the strength of his visionary certainty that drags along the sons of Israel.[164]

Despite several brief mentions of themes of another nature, themes to be returned to later, the thirteen chapters just outlined constitute the essential part of a coherent whole that centers around a single purpose: describing the procession of the degrees of universal Existence—the place of the perpetually new epiphanies of the Divine Names—and highlighting the central position and mediating role of the Perfect Man. It is this notion of Perfect Man that, without being clearly explained, connects this first part of the *fasl al-maʿârif* to the forty-four chapters that follow. In general—and here again, with a number of detours toward subjects that are not always clearly related to this guiding thread—what is presently going to be discussed, synthetically, is the modalities of spiritual realization; a detailed analysis will wait until later sections of the *Futûhât*. In other words, an outline of the broad strokes of Ibn ʿArabî's metaphysical and cosmological doctrine will be followed by a preliminary overview of his initiatory teachings, the object of which is to help hatch in the disciple the *insân kâmil* that each man is, in principle, destined to become. The predominant issues in this second set of chapters will thus be prophetology and hagiology, with special emphasis on the supreme degree of sainthood, that of the *malâmiyya*. We have explored this side of Ibn ʿArabî's work elsewhere,[165] where we devoted considerable time on this part of the *Futûhât*, and we thus limit ourselves here to a the briefest of examinations of his main ideas.

Chapter 14 brings up the idea—which is eminently suspect in exoteric Islam—of "free" or "general" prophecy as the ultimate form of sainthood (*walâya*): the *awliyâʾ* to whom it belongs have no lawbringing authority of their own (since this was "sealed" by Muhammad), but they do directly hear the divine speech addressed to the Prophet (this speech should not be imagined as being located in one specific moment in history rather than another, since it is eternally present). The hierarchy of the *degrees* of *walâya* referred to here is not to be confused with that of *functions*: the spiritual degree of the Pole is common to other saints—which is the reason why they are not subject to him—and his function is his only by substitution (*niyâba*). There is but one true Pole, from the beginning of time till the end of time, and this is none other than the "Spirit of Muhammad." All the human dignitaries in the invisible hierarchy that orders and protects the world—the Pole, the Seal of Muhammadan Sainthood, the Seal of Universal Sainthood—are just his "places of apparition" (*mazâhir*), his "substitutes" (*nuwwâb*). This is where the account of the vision in Cordoba comes in, as we noted earlier,[166] and the revelation of the emblematic name of the twenty-five Poles who ruled over the communities that preceded Islam. One of them Ibn ʿArabî calls *Mudâwî l-kulûm*, "he who heals wounds." He is described in more detail in the following chapter. The sciences attributed to him—alchemy (which "heals metals" and leads them back to the state of their original perfection by transforming them into gold), medicine, astrology, the knowledge of the laws of cosmology (*'ilm al-'âlam*)—show that we are here dealing with Hermes, or rather with the first of the three Hermes that Islamic tradition distinguishes: the one identified with Enoch.[167]

A new reference to the *fatâ* should be noted: "*The spirit from whom I received what I have placed in this book taught me that Mudâwî l-Kulûm one day gathered his companions together in a village and announced to them that he was going to leave this world.*" The sermon (*khutba*) the antediluvian *qutb* then preached is important, because is allusively offers us a key to Ibn 'Arabî's eschatology: this lower world and paradise, declares Mudâwî l-Kulûm, have in common "the brick and the mason." There is thus a continuity of nature between them, and they are reciprocally interlocking. Paradise is already present, here and now—and this is why, for example, one part of the mosque of the Prophet in Medina, the *rawda*,[168] is described in a hadith as "one of the gardens of paradise"—which the ordinary man is supposed to believe without seeing. The "people of unveiling," on the other hand, are able to perceive the paradisiacal nature of the *rawda* in this life. This speech also reveals the subject of the enigmatic dialogue between the young Ibn 'Arabî and Averroes, which is reported immediately thereafter, and which Corbin has translated,[169] albeit without its context. Careful study of the conversation shows that the problem the philosopher and the boy debated is the problem of the final ends; the best guess is that the specific topic was the resurrection of the body.[170]

We then return to the hierarchy of initiatory roles, with an outline of the seven *abdâl* that look over the seven terrestrial "climates" (they also correspond to the seven planetary heavens and the seven days of the week), and then, in chapter 16, of the four *awtâd*, each of which has a position that relates to one of the cardinal points and one of the corners of the Ka'ba.[171] But for those who occupy the top of the pyramid—the Pole himself and the two imams that stand at his right and left sides—Ibn 'Arabî refers us to chapter 270 (the beginning of the *fasl al-manâzil*). The most important part of what there is to say about these three figures will begin in the early pages of chapter 73.

Chapters 17, 19, and 28 might be classed under the rubric of "epistemology." In a number of ways, what is dealt with is sciences, their objects and their manners of acquisition, both from God's point of view (how does He know things?), and from the point of view of the creatures (what can they know of God, and how?). These are classic questions for *kalâm* and the *falsafa*, whose positions Ibn 'Arabî notes. But his remarks always relate to the issue of spiritual realization, and aim at defining what is characteristic of the gnostic *(al-'ârif bi-Llâh)* and the conditions under which he acquired gnosis, the knowledge of God that neither opposes nor separates His transcendence *(tanzîh)* and His immanence *(tashbîh)*. The idea of "return toward the creatures," which will be developed at length in chapter 45, quickly shows up here. The plenitude of holiness appears to him who, once he reaches the end of his ascent toward God, of his *mi'râj*, comes back toward the world. *"If you are among those who "leave" [as opposed to those who remain in bewildered contemplation of the Divine Presence] and reach the highest degree, then He manifests Himself through His Essence in your outer form."*[172] Those individuals are *"the ear through which God hears, the hand with which He grasps, the foot with which He walks."*[173] The case brought up here is the case of the *malâmiyya*, the "People of Blame" (whom Ibn 'Arabî also identifies as *afrâd*, the "solitary ones" or the "unparalleled ones"), a description of whom is given in chapter 23, and then in chapters 30, 31, and 32 (where they are referred to as the "horsemen" or "camel riders"). This particular citation[174] gives us insight into their characteristics: *"Know, and may God assist you, that this chapter deals with those servants of God that are called the* malâmiyya, *that is, the spiritual men who possess the very highest degree of* walâya. *There is nothing above them but the degree of [lawbringing] Prophecy. Their station is the station called the "station of Proximity"* (maqâm al-qurba). *Their specific verse in the Qur'ân is "houris enclosed in tents" (Q. 55:72), a verse that, with this description of women in paradise and its houris tells us about the souls of those men of God that He has chosen for Himself, that He has preserved, that he has enclosed in the tents of divine jealousy in every corner of the universe such that no gaze can fall upon them and distract them—but no, the gaze of the creatures could not possibly distract them! (...) God has enclosed their outer forms in the tents of ordinary actions and customary devotions such that, from the point of view of apparent practices, they devote themselves only to obligatory devotions or to habitual supererogatory devotions. They do not make themselves noticeable with miracles. People do not glorify them, they do not point at them because of their piety, in the sense that people commonly understand, even though no evil can be imputed to them. They are the ones who remain hidden; they are the pious, the faithful guardians of the repository in the universe."* This hidden holiness takes place in the Law, and through it.[175]

Parallel to the hierarchy of the roles they play and their degrees, a typology of forms of *walâya* begins to be drawn out in this part of the *fasl al-ma'ârif*; it will be elaborated upon in the last chapter (chapter 73), and even more so in the following sections. In Ibn 'Arabî, this typology is fundamentally based on the idea of prophetic "heritage," each of the one hundred twenty-four thousand prophets that have successively paraded through history constituting the prototype of a specific world of spiritual realization. There are thus "Mosaic" saints, "Abrahamic saints," "Davidic saints," and so forth (as well as saints that combine several "heritages"). Chapter 20 thus deals with the "knowledge specific to Jesus" (which is *'ilm al-hurûf*, because of the correspondence between the letters and the vivifying breath, *nafkh*—a reference to Q. 3:49)[176] and chapters 36 and 37 deal with the "Christic saints." But the mystery of *walâya* can be approached in other ways: from the symbolic meaning of the ritual practices that lead to it (as in chapter 18 on nighttime vigils, *tahajjud*, or in chapter 27 on liturgical prayer, where *salât* is looked upon as an initiatory journey), or by considering the Divine Name, whose authority controls one category or another of *awliyâ'* and determines the nature of the charismatic gifts that are their privilege (the case of the "People of the Breath," *ahl al-anfâs*, looked at in chapters 34 and 35, where these individuals are connected to the Name *al-Rahmân*). Similarly, the degrees of holiness, the number of which is inexhaustible, can also be put into a simple schematic where four successive levels can be defined through their similarity to the four levels of meaning in the Qur'ân that are outlined in a contested hadith whose validity Ibn 'Arabî nevertheless judges to be established for "men of unveiling." It is this schematic—based on the idea that man's vocation is to be the interpreter of the two Books—that he holds to in chapter 25, the chapter where he relates his encounters with Khadir, Moses' immortal partner in conversation in the sura of the Cave.

The structure of the three other parts that can be discerned in the *fasl al-ma'ârif* is much less complex. Chapters 59 to 65 gather eschatological details that will be expanded upon in chapter 371, the esoteric interpretation of which is scattered throughout the *Futûhât*. Esoteric, yes, and in no way allegorical in the philosophical sense. To avoid the image the common believer might have, paradise and hell are not simple metaphors; the rivers and gardens in the former, and the tortures in the latter are real, just as the resurrection of the body is real: bodies could not be excluded from the total assumption of the being that is required by the plenitude of the life to come. But this future is such only for our blind eyes. In the eyes of the *'arif bi-Llâh*, who in this world has crossed over the threshold of initiatory death, the beyond is nowhere else than here, and divine promises are fulfilled in the eternal now.

The series of chapters from 66 to 72 is devoted to the *sharî'a*, sacred Law, that other sections of the *Futûhât* will return to, as we stated earlier. After a preliminary outline of the very concept of *sharî'a*, Islam's fundamental obligations are looked at one after the other: ritual purity, bearing witness to the Oneness of God and the mission of the Prophet, prayer, alms, fasting, and pilgrimage. The list of subjects placed under each of these headings is scarcely different from what might be seen in a work of jurisprudence (*fiqh*), of which there are many, and Ibn 'Arabî is careful to mention—among all the problems he looks at—the positions taken by the different legal schools. What is more unusual is that he justifies each of them by highlighting (and in this case, in language that looks nothing like that of the *fuqahâ*) the *mustanad ilâhî*, the support *in divinis*, the metaphysical basis of each point of view and its opposing view. There is no hint here of cunning on the part of a rhetorician ready to espouse one adverse opinion after the other. It is in the bedazzled contemplation of divine infinity that the source of his irenic understanding of the differences among the *'ulamâ'* can be seen, and in the "Mercy that embraces all things" (Q. 7:156), whose inspired and conscious agent Ibn 'Arabî is, that the force that moves him when he writes these pages is to be found: for, as he says, *"the fuqahâ' have made narrow that which Allah had made wide."*[177] The information we offered above about the *malâmiyya* gives us a sense of what his emphasis on the law means (an emphasis that conforms so poorly to the image that his Muslim critics, or some of his Western defenders, have presented of Ibn 'Arabî); it might be best summed up by saying that a little knowledge takes us away from the *sharî'a*, but a lot takes us back to it.

The last part of the first *fasl* has only one long chapter (chapter 73): it can be read as a synthesis of all the precedes it. This synthesis is further divided into two subsets. One is a classification of the categories (*tabaqât*) of "men of God," which states in other words the fundamental concepts of prophetology and Ibn 'Arabî's hagiology. The other, which is a hundred pages long in the Cairo edition, answers one hundred fifty-five of the questions asked three centuries earlier as a challenge by Hakîm Tirmidhî in his *Khatm al-awliyâ*, a work whose title brings up the mysterious term "Seal of the Saints" that Ibn 'Arabî would have to explain.[178] All the significant themes already encountered in the seventy-two preceding chapters here reappear in an often quite dense form, and in an order that is clearly different—the order imposed by the list of questions raised by Tirmidhî— but which shows even more clearly the relationship between the subjects approached in the *fasl al-ma'ârif* and the completion of the course taken in *walâya*. Ibn 'Arabî is neither a "theoretician" nor a "grammarian" of esotericism, as some have chosen to call him. All his teaching, including in its most abstract aspects, is arranged with one goal in mind: that of reestablishing man in his dignity as *imago Dei (nuskhat al-haqq)* and the role of representation *(khilâfa)* he is supposed to play. As we have briefly pointed out a number of times, there are numerous passages in this first section of the *Futûhât* that refer to what the author and the *awliyâ'* he has known have experienced in regard to one point of doctrine or another. Texts of this type will be even more numerous in the remainder of the book: not one piece of information is given that is not sooner or later related back to the experience upon which it is based and to the methods that allow it to be verified. This operative—and not strictly speculative—characteristic of the Shaykh al-Akbar's *magnum opus* is declared forcefully in the *bâb al-wasâya* with which it ends.

If a logic is to be found in this immense work whose composition is so disconcerting for anyone who delves into it, it is probably a pedagogic logic. It is both surprising and disappointing to our mental penchant for classification. But, if we allow ourselves to be taken along, it does fulfill the need of the *sâlik*, the traveler, to know certain things at certain specific points along his itinerary, to lose sight of them, and then find them again, but this time with new vision and a new point of view along the spiral road that leads him to the center. This is just one way to read the *Futûhât*. There are others: for example, they can be approached like a vast Qur'ânic commentary, which they certainly are. But once we mention reading, we are surreptitiously tempted to adopt certain 21st century prejudices wherein it seems normal to think that a book, if appropriately studied, suffices to communicate what an author wants us to know. We would be careless if we forgot that in the 13th century, and indeed up to quite recent times, the book in the Islamic world was not a support all by itself for the complete transmission of knowledge. Regardless of how "profane" it might have been according to our criteria (grammar or arithmetic, for example), this knowledge was not received except under the guarantee of the teacher, and thus in a face-to-face meeting with him or with someone who, at the end of an uninterrupted series of intermediaries, represented him. This is how those who, throughout the centuries, tried to delve into Ibn 'Arabî's work understood it. This "introduction" will not be seen as useless if it manages to persuade the reader of its lack of sufficiency.

Even though a number of expressions familiar to those interested in the Shaykh al-Akbar have appeared in this brief study of the *fasl al-ma'ârif*—"perpetual creation" *(tajdîd al-khalq)*, "imaginal world" *('âlam al-khayâl)*, "theophany" *(tajallî)*, "Muhammadan Reality" *(haqîqa muhammadiyya)*, etc.—one might be surprised not to find *wahdat al-wujûd*. The fact is that the expression does not belong to Ibn 'Arabî's commonly used list of terms.[179] Correctly interpreted, the idea of "oneness of Being" that it covers certainly is present in his teaching but, as he mentions on two different occasions in the *muqaddima*, this latter expression, in its highest—and thus most obscure—aspects is scattered throughout the chapters of his book where a broad and systematic outline of it can be found nowhere. Certain abrupt phrases—there are some in the *khutba*'s first poem—might lead to hasty conclusions: *"There is nothing in existence and nothing to originate existence but God"* (fa-lâ mawjûd wa lâ mûjid illâ Llâh)[180]; *"He is Being, and what there is in the universe is nothing other than His form"* (sûratuhu)[181]; *"the 'other than God' is devoid of being"*[182]; *"both existence and that which exists are nothing other than God Himself"* (al-mawjûd wa l-wujûd laysa illâ 'ayn al-haqq).[183] A dozen, even a hundred, such sayings could be strung out one after the other. They are not implying that this world is an illusion in all respects: in one small unpublished treatise[184] Ibn 'Arabî mentions those who, during their retreats *(khalwa)*, allow themselves to be deceived by suggestions that lead them to deny the reality of that which is "other than God" *(yaqulûn bi-nafî 'ayn al-ghayr wa l-siwâ)*. Likewise, in the account of his *mir'aj* that appears in chapter 367 of the *Futûhât*, the prophet Aaron, whom he meets in the fifth heaven, emphasizes the flaw in the knowledge of those who deny the reality of the universe. Ibn 'Arabî's *wahdat al-wujûd* (in contrast to later formulations of the concept)[185] transcends duality without denying it: *haqq* is *haqq*, and *khalq* is *khalq*. To use a kind of numerical symbolism often employed by Ibn 'Arabî,[186] the number 1000 draws all its reality from the 1, without which it is nothing. But we cannot say 1 = 1000, or 1000 = 1; we cannot deny the unity of the one or the multiplicity of the multiple. The idea of theophany is capital here: the three zeros in 1000 (the word *sifr*, which is the name for zero, means "nothing," "the void") are nonexistent in and of themselves. But when preceded by the 1, they express a series of epiphanies through which this initial 1 manifests itself to itself, each of which is unique, an instantaneous flash of a name that is not God, and that is not anything other than God. This contradiction, like the contradiction of the *tashbîh*, the affirmation of His immanence and His similarity to all things, is impossible to resolve dialectically. But it it relies on Revelation, on God's discourse with Himself about Himself. So faith must accept it "without comment" *(bi-lâ kayf).* Only true knowledge, that of the *awliyâ'* who know God through God, the knowledge whose landmarks can be found in the *Futûhât,* can grasp *tanzîh* and *tashbîh* (the oneness of Being and the multiplicity of things that are) at the same time.

What we have seen ever so briefly about Ibn 'Arabî's teachings in these pages probably has not shed light on two fundamental ideas in this teaching, however. The first is that of *rahma,* a word that, in the context of the *Futûhât,* should be translated as "love" rather than "mercy," as is usually the case. It is from *rahma* that the universe is born—it takes shape in the "breath of the *Rahmân*"—it is through *rahma* that the universe is sustained, and it is to *rahma* that it will return: whence Ibn 'Arabî's denial that punishment will be eternal; whence his quest for the positivity, the *mustanad ilâhî,* in every idea, in every belief. How could the *awliyâ',* who see the face of God in all things, not conform to this model that God proposes to man, His mirror, when He calls Himself *Rahmân* before he mentions any other attribute in the Qur'ân? *"If we look at something, it is He we are looking at. If we hear something, it is He we are hearing... In every countenance, it is He who shows His epiphany, in every sign it is Him we are seeking. Every eye looks at nothing but Him. He is the Worshiped in everything that we worship... It is to Him alone that the universe addresses its prayer, it is before Him that everything is prostrate, it is Him alone that our language glorifies. Tongues speak but of Him, hearts are enraptured with desire for Him alone."*[187]

The other axis of Ibn 'Arabî's teaching is the Law, the expression of God's strictness, which is not an attribute systematically opposed to *rahma,* but rather its paradoxical complement. The Way begins with the *sharî'a,* and ends with it. The contrast between the *sharî'a* and *haqîqa,* "essential truth," exists only for the novice who sees *haqîqa* as something either beyond or within the Law, but if he continues along his way, he discovers that *sharî'a* is *haqîqa*: the *malâmiyya,* the highest of the saints, live "enclosed within the pavilion of ordinary acts and customary devotions." They arrived at the Law through the Law. He who no longer demands either to have or to be will henceforth perform no movement that has not been prescribed for him; and this is where his perfection resides.

In closing, we must echo the voice of the *fatâ* who inhabits the heart of the universe in stating, one more time, the precept the Andalusian pilgrim received at the beginning of his "nighttime journey" where he was led "to the distance of two bows, or nearer":

O you who seek the path leading to the secret
Turn back, for it is in you that the entire secret is found.

NOTES
TO INTRODUCTION

[1] *Futûhât Makkiyya*, Cairo, 1329, I, p. 50.
[2] *Rûh al-quds*, Damascus, 1964, p. 51.
[3] *Fut.*, II, p. 436. This Muhammad al-Hassâr accompanied Ibn 'Arabî all the way to Cairo, and died there.
[4] *Kitâb al-Bâ'*, Cairo, 1954, p. 11; *Kitâb al-kutub*, Heyderabad, 1948, p. 49.
[5] *Fut.*, I, p. 9. On shaykh 'Abd al-'Azîz Mahdawî, see ibn Qunfudh, *Uns al-faqîr*, Rabat, 1965, pp. 97-99.
[6] *Rûh*, pp. 60-61.
[7] *Fut.*, I, p. 10; *Rûh*, p. 59.
[8] *Rûh*, p. 59.
[9] On this idea, which will come up again later here, we refer to our study *Seal of the Saints, Prophethood and Sainthood in the Doctrine of Ibn 'Arabî*, Cambridge, 1993; on Ibn 'Arabî's biography, about which we are able to mention only a few short episodes here, we refer the reader to Claude Chodkiewicz-Addas' thesis, *Essai de biographie du Shaykh al-Akbar, Muhyî l-dîn Ibn 'Arabî*, Université de Paris I, October 1987, published in English by the Islamic Texts Society (1993) as *Quest for the Red Sulpher: The Life of Ibn 'Arabî*. The critical edition of the *Futûhât* established by Osman Yahia (in the process of publication) has a special index in each volume with autobiographical details or references that appear in the work.
[10] *Fut.*, II, p. 260-262. Cf. also *Fut.*, II, p. 19, 24-25, 41; III, p. 103, and *Kitâb al-qurba*, Heyderabad, 1948.
[11] There is a list of the works written by Ibn 'Arabî during this period of his life in O. Yahia, *Histoire et classification de l'oeuvre d'Ibn 'Arabî*, Damascus, 1964, I, pp. 100-103.

¹² *Tadbîrat ilâhiyya*, ed. Nyberg, in *Kleinere Schriften des Ibn Al-'Arabî*, Leiden, 1919, p. 120.

¹³ *Fut.*, I, p. 334.

¹⁴ *Fut.*, Cairo, 1329, IV, p. 718 consequently makes a typographical error in giving the date 669.

¹⁵ This detail is offered by Ibn 'Arabî in the notes to the second edition. Cf. *Futûhât*, ed. 1329, IV p. 554.

¹⁶ Evkaf Mûsesi, 1736-1772. A description of the *Futûhât*'s main manuscripts identified is given by O. Yahia, *op. laud.*, I, pp. 210-235.

¹⁷ Because of not having been able to consult this edition, we use the information furnished by O. Yahia. There is one problem, however: two different sources ('Abd al-Majîd al-Khânî, *Al-hadâ'iq al-wardiyya*, Damascus, 1308, p. 288; and Jawâd al-Murâbit, *Al-tawawwuf wa l-Amir 'Abd al-Qâdir*, Damascus, 1966, p. 89) tell us that the Emir sent two of his companions to Konya to check the text he possessed against the handwritten manuscript. We have in our possession the photocopy of a letter (ms. Zâhiriyya no. 142) addressed to the Emir from Konya by one of his two emissaries, shaykh Muhammad al-Tantâwî, during the trip; it is clearly dated 19 Ramadan 1287/1870, which is incompatible with the participation of 'Abd al-Qâdir (who had been living in Damascus for only about a year) on an edition published in 1274. The latter date thus appears to be in need of correction; the true date should in any case be prior to 1293, since the edition published in 1293 presents the detail (IV, p. 718) unambiguously, like the second.

¹⁸ *Fut.*, ed. 1239, IV, p. 719.

¹⁹ *Ibid.*, p. 718.

²⁰ There is an undated photomechanical reprint that was done in Beirut circa 1970.

²¹ *Fut.*, ed. 1239, II, p. 456.

²² *Fut.*, III, p. 101.

²³ *Fut.*, I, p. 59.

²⁴ *Fut.*, ed. 1239, IV, p. 718.

²⁵ We made a study of this theme of the *mi'râj* in the works of Ibn 'Arabî in chapter 10 of *Seal of the Saints*.

²⁶ *Fut.*, I, pp. 11-30.

²⁷ The only noticeable differences between the announced plan and its completion entail the way certain chapters are titled, which vary slightly from what is noted in the table of contents.

²⁸ "Six is the most perfect of numbers" *(akmal al-l'dâd)*, Ibn 'Arabî states (*Fut.*, III, p. 142). He is actually talking about the value of the letter *wâw*, which is a symbol for the "Perfect Man" *(al-insân al-kâmil)* who unifies in his person "heaven and earth": the higher and lower realities. This role is analogous to that of the copula, which is grammatically that of the *wâw*. We might point out that O. Yahia has added numbered paragraphs and subtitles to the subdivisions in the text of the *Futûhât* as it was originally written, which makes reading easier than the

often difficult task in the compact presentation of the previous editions.

[29] This first *fasl*, which represents approximately a quarter of the work, includes the totality of the first volume of the edition of the *Futûhât* and pages 1 to 139 of the second volume.

[30] *Fut.*, II, pp. 139-382.

[31] *Fut.*, II, pp. 382-571.

[32] Cf. for example, Qushayrî, *Risâla*, Cairo, 1957, p. 32; Sarrâj, *Kitâb al-Luma'*, Cairo, 1960, pp. 65-102; Suhrawardî, *'Awârif al-Ma'ârif*, in volume V of *Ihyâ' 'ulûm al-dîn*, Cairo, n.d., pp. 225-227. Ibn 'Arabî devotes chapters 192 and 193 to the *hâl* and the *maqâm*; Michel Vâlsan translated the chapters in numbers 372-373 of *Études traditionnelles*, July-October 1962), but mentioned these ideas on a number of occasions. We are looking only at the initiatory meaning of the word *hâl* here. Ontologically, it is the counterpart to haecceity (*'ayn*) for Ibn 'Arabî, like accident is to substance. In its temporal meaning, it refers to the present moment, a dimensionless point, and yet still the only real thing between a past which is no longer and a future which is not yet here. On these differences, see Su'âd Hakîm, *Al-mu'man al-sûfî*, Beirut, 1981, s.v.

[33] *Fut.*, II, p 132.

[34] *Fut.*, II, p. 385. Cf also IV, p. 151.

[35] *Fut.*, II, p. 319.

[36] Chapter 198, II, pp. 390-478.

[37] See *Fut.*, III, p. 543 and IV, pp. 39, 51. Cf. *Seal of the Saints*, p. 87.

[38] This *fasl* stretches from page 571 in volume II to page 523 in volume III. The first chapter corresponds to sura 114, the second to sura 113, and so forth.

[39] *Fut.*, II, p. 577.

[40] *Fut.*, IV, p. 169.

[41] This *fasl* goes from vol. III, p. 523 to page 73 in vol. IV. The number of its chapters (78) is, according to a famous hadith, the same as the number of "branches of the faith" (*shu'ab al-îmân*).

[42] *Fut.*, III, p. 118.

[43] Cf. *Fut.*, III, pp. 155, 523, 543.

[44] On the idea of "heritage" (*wirâtha*) as a basis for Ibn 'Arabî's hagiology, we refer the reader to our work *Seal of the Saints*, especially chapter 5.

[45] *Fut.*, IV, pp. 74-554.

[46] *Tarjumân al-ashwâq*, Beirut, 1961, p. 13 (commentary on the first poem). A similar remark appears in the beginning of the *fasl al-maqâmat* (*Fut.*, IV, p. 76).

[47] *Fut.*, III, p. 225.

[48] See, e.g., *Fut.* III, pp. 105, 177, 216, 560; IV, p. 28; *Mawâqi' al-nujûm*, Cairo, 1965, p. 141.

[49] On *hayra*, see *Fut.* I, pp. 270, 420; II, pp. 137, 607, 661; III, p. 490; IV, pp. 43, 196-197, 245, 280.

[50] On the characteristics of the Pole's role for Ibn 'Arabi, see *Seal of the Saints*, ch. 6. Chapter 555 of the *Futûhât* (IV, p. 194) specifies the reasons why the

Shaykh al-Akbar did not allow himself to describe the Poles who will come one after the other from his time until the Day of Resurrection.

51 *Fut.*, IV, p. 76.

52 *Ibid.*

53 Ibn 'Arabî replaces the word *hijjîr* in the subtitles of certain chapters with the word *manzil* (abode).

54 Cf. *Seal of the Saints*, ch. 8.

55 A list of the main commentaries on the *Fusûs* may be found in O. Yahia, *Histoire et classification..*, I, *RG* no. 150, pp. 241-255. For the Western reader, moreover, there is a systematic study of the fundamental aspects of Ibn 'Arabî's metaphysics, such as it is explained in the *Fusûs*: we are here referring to the first part of the work by Toshihiko Izutsu, *Sufism and Taoism*, Tokyo, 1966 (2nd ed., 1983).

56 See O. Yahia, *Histoire et classification...*, *RG* no. 135, pp. 232-234.

57 We have translated a few passages of this work (Emir 'Abd al-Kader's *Écrits spirituels*, Paris, 1982), the relationship to Ibn 'Arabî's work is noted in the introduction.

58 *Kitâb al-mawâqif*, 2nd ed., Damascus, 1966-67, III, pp. 1290-1336.

59 *Ibid.*, pp. 1152-1155.

60 *Ibid.*, pp. 1017-1021.

61 *Ibid.*, II, pp. 745-759, 826-841, 861-867, 870-875.

62 *Ibid.*, III, pp. 1021-1026.

63 *Ibid.*, pp. 1195-1196.

64 *Al-yawâqît wa l-jawâhir* and *Al-Kibrît al-ahmar*, published in a single volume, Cairo, 1369 A.H.

65 Nor does there exist, we suspect, an integral translation of the *Futûhât* themselves. Certain passages have been translated by authors who have worked on Ibn 'Arabî, Asin Palacios, in particular, in his *Islam cristianizado*, Madrid, 1981 (trans. in French as *L'Islam christianisé*, Paris, 1982). We are indebted to Michel Vâlsan for a series of translations whose notes are as copious as they are rich in detail. Some of these have yet to be edited, although most were published in *Études traditionnelles*: a passage from the *khutba* (no. 311, 1953), chapter 45 (no. 307, 1953), chapters 78-79 (no. 412-413, 1969), chapter 176 (no. 386, 1964), chapters 181, 192, 193 (no. 373-373, 1962), chapters 262-263 (no, 396-397, 1966). The most recent contribution in this domain is William Chittick's work, *Ibn al-Arabî's Metaphysics of the Imagination*, State University of New York Press, 1989, which devotes considerable attention to passages from the *Futûhât*.

66 *Fut.*, II, p. 281.

67 The remarks that follow are inspired in large part by the commentary by Emir 'Abd al-Qâdir, references for which we gave in note 58 above.

68 See, e.g., *Fut.*, I, p 168; III, pp. 46, 257, 314; IV, p. 210.

69 *Fut.*, II, p. 281. It is to this state that the "Hidden Treasure" mentioned in the famous *hadîth qudsî* that Ibn 'Arabî so often comments on corresponds. Cf.

Fut., II, pp. 232, 399; III, p. 267. On the *a'yân thâbita*, see E. Meyer's article "Ein kurzer Traktat Ibn Arabîs über die A'yân al-Thâbita," *Oriens*, vol 27/28, 1981; and Izutsu, *Sufism*..., ch. XII; Chittick, *op. laud*, ch. V. Ibn 'Arabî frequently emphasizes the difference between *thubût* and *wujûd*: for him the *a'yân thâbita* as such are radically devoid of existence. But some, among whom is Jîlî, for example, have compared *thubût* to *wujûd 'ilmî*. Although not illegitimate, this terminology unfortunately offers an argument to all those—Ibn Taymiyya, among others—who claim that Ibn 'Arabî is a proponent of the idea of the eternity of the world.

[70] Cf. *Fut.*, III, pp. 201-202; IV, pp. 175, 265.

[71] *Fut.*, IV, p. 315. The exoteric interpretation of this verse sees in it an allusion to the time period (traditionally thought to last 40 years) that separates the formation of Adam's body and the spirit being blown into him.

[72] *Kitâb al-mawâqif*, III, pp. 1298-1299; among other passages, to be compared with *Fut.*, II, p. 387 and IV, p. 312.

[73] Underscoring the significance of *'an* in *'an 'adam* might be in order. The particle, which is specific to the Arabic language, although frequently interchangeable with *min*, which is a common Semitic word, does nevertheless have a quite different meaning: *min* indicates the origin, while *'an* indicates the separation. Those entities that are "possible," which were not part of existence, while still not being "nothing"—since God knew them—are "separated" from pure nothingness and brought into existence *'an 'adam* but *min wujûd*, this *wujûd* being the same *wujûd* as the *wujûd* of *Haqq*, God; this takes us back to the idea of *haqq al-makhlûq bihi kullu shay'in* ("the Reality from which all things are created." Cf. *Fut.*, II, p. 60; III, pp. 77, 150, 354, 420, 444) the symbolic expression for which is the "Breath of the All-Merciful" *(Fafas al-Rahmân)*, or the "Cloud" *(al-'amâ')*.

[74] On the *mustanad ilâhî*, cf. *Fut.*, III, p. 528; IV, p. 174.

[75] *Fut.*, I, p. 366; II, pp. 400, 402, 404; III, p. 230; IV, pp. 5, 65, 166.

[76] *Fut.*, IV, p. 167.

[77] As we shall see, the symbolism of *both* feet has a very different meaning in Ibn 'Arabî.

[78] We might nevertheless point out that in contrast to O. Yahia, who in a note in his critical edition chooses to attribute two different meanings to the same verb *zahara* in the sentence that follows the one we just examined, we are of the opinion that the repetition of the verb, in its normal meaning in Ibn 'Arabî's works ("appear," "manifest oneself") is deliberate, the first time corresponding to the manifestation of God to Himself, in Himself (i.e., *fayd al-aqdas*), and the second His manifestation in things *(al-fayd al-muqaddas)*.

[79] *Fusûs al-hikam*, ed. Afîfî, Beirout, 1946, I, pp. 48-49, 61; *Fut.*, I, p. 163; IV, p. 2.

[80] *Fut.*, I, p. 177; II, pp. 66, 204, 604, 681; III, pp. 84, 211, 217, 303; IV, p. 33-34, 129, etc.

[81] The expression *wahdat al-wujûd* is seen in Sadr al-dîn Qûnawî (d. 672/1263)

(Al-nafahât al-ilâhiyya, Tehran, 1898, p. 279; *Miftâh al-ghayb*, written in the margin of Qâshânî's *Sharh manâzil al-sâ'irîn*, Tehran, 1899, pp. 294-295); Qunâwî was Ibn 'Arabî's son-in-law and direct disciple. The expression does not take on value as a technical term until Farghânî (d. 699/1299), who uses it on a number of occasions in his commentary on Ibn al-Fârid's *Tâ'iyya kubrâ* (the title of which is *Muntahâ l-madârik* in the Arabic version, and *Mashâriq al-darârî* in the Persian version). But its use in a more general sense in defining Ibn 'Arabî's metaphysics was apparently due to Ibn Taymiyya, whose intentions appear to have been polemical. The reductionist interpretations that it might justify—and for which some representatives of Ibn 'Arabî's school are responsible when they simplify and systematize the Master's teachings for their introductions to it—explain (but do not excuse) the interpretations that identify this doctrine with "existential monism," "panentheism," or even pantheism pure and simple.

[82] We refer the reader to M. Vâlsan's translation published in *Études traditionnelles*, no. 311, 1953, pp. 300-311, and to chapter 9 of our work Seal of the Saints. On the autobiographical and biographical sources that relate to Ibn 'Arabî's role as Seal, we refer the reader to the thesis by C. Chodkiewicz cited in note 9.

[83] See, e.g., *Fut.*, I, p. 106; III, p. 514.

[84] Cf. *Fusûs*, I, p. 62: "*The Messengers themselves, as saints* (min kawnihim awliyâ'), *see what we have just spoken of only through the tabernacle* (mishkât) *of the Seal of the Saints. Just think what might be the case for saints of a lower rank!*"

[85] The reference to the "revolution of time" *(istidâra zamânuhu)* in the third verse is an implicit reference to the hadith (Bukhârî, *tafsîr*, s. 9; *bad' al-khalq* 3) in which time—with the advent of Islam—returned to its original form just as God "created the heavens and the earth," which symbolically expresses the restorative function of Islamic revelation at the end of the human cycle.

[86] On shaykh al-Murâbit, see the short notice (no. 50) Ibn 'Arabî devotes to him in *Rûh al-quds*, Damascus, 1964, pp. 83-84.

[87] On shaykh Abû Muhammad al-Jarrâh, there is a short note, also in *Rûh al-quds* (no. 52), p. 84.

[88] On Badr al-Habashî, see especially *Fut.*, I, pp. 198, 221; *Hilyat al-abdâl*, Hyderabad, 1948, p. 1; *Mawâqi' al-nujûm*, Cairo, 1907, p. 6; *Tarjumân al-ashwâq* (preface to the commentary), p. 9; R. W. J. Austin, *Sufis of Andalusia*, London, 1971, pp. 158-159 (passage from the *Durra fâkhira*). The *Kitâb al-Inbâh*, where Habashî offers Ibn 'Arabî's verbal teaching, was translated by Denis Gril in *Annales islamologiques*, vol. XV, 1979, pp. 97-164.

[89] The theory of the transmissibility of the function of the *khatm* has been held at a number of different times (cf. *Seal of the Saints*, pp. 170-174) and still is today in certain *turuq*.

[90] *Kitâb al-isrâ'*, Hyderabad, 1948, p. 4.

[91] *Kitâb al-isrâr*, Hyderabad, 1948, p. 17. The preceding quote is from *Fut.*, III, p. 94.

⁹² On *Arîn*, see *EI2*, s.v. "istiwâ." The name also appears in *Futûhât*, I, p. 38, and IV, p. 82.

⁹³ The latter meaning is all the clearer in this case, since the passage from the *Kitâb al-isrâj* to which we are referring is part of the chapter titled *"Voyage of the Heart."*

⁹⁴ Qushayrî, *Risâla*, Cairo, 1957, p. 103.

⁹⁵ *"The Taking off of the Sandals" (Khal' al-na'layn)* is also the title of a work by Ibn Qasî (d. 546/1151), which Ibn 'Arabî cites frequently, and on which he wrote a commentary that, as a matter of fact, was quite severe for its author.

⁹⁶ In Arabic alchemy, "Red Sulphur" *(al-kibrît al-ahmar)* is the elixir via which silver is transformed into gold. The same expression is sometimes used in Sufism as a symbol for spiritual realization. In a more general sense, Red Sulphur is a metaphor for what is valuable and inaccessible.

⁹⁷ *Kabrît al-isrâ'*, p. 5.

⁹⁸ The believer is in no way obligated to accept what divine inspiration tells saints, since saints do not enjoy the privilege of infallibility *('isma)* that the prophet had; but he should at least suspend his judgment *(tawaqquf)* and be careful not to reject *a priori* the statements of the *sâhib al-asrâr*.

⁹⁹ Even though the knowledge that the true philosopher possesses is quite limited—in both depth and breadth—and in all cases greatly inferior to that of the *walî* (see ch. 167 of the *Futûhât* for an illustration of this) Ibn 'Arabî in no way considers it to be pure illusion. Cf., e.g. *Fut.* II, p. 523, where he refers to the "divine Plato" *(Aflâtûn al-ilâhî)* who, in his opinion, is not only a "man of speculative thought" but he also speaks *'an al-dhawq*, meaning "from inner, personal experience."

¹⁰⁰ Ibn 'Arabî (*Fut.*, I, p. 36) does not conclude a condemnation of *kalâm* from this, where he recognizes a certain defensive utility against heresy. But, as he says, each country needs but one *mutakallim*.

¹⁰¹ There is a Spanish translation of this work by Asin Palacios (*El justo medio en la creencia*, Madrid, 1929). Ghazâlî declared that the work was a more appropriate preparation for Sufi knowledge than the other *kalâm* treatises on the same subject; cf. *Kitâb al-arba'în*, Cairo, 1344, p. 24.

¹⁰² *Arîn* is clearly nothing more here than a simple metaphor to say that what is at issue is a "middle" *'aqîda* upon which consensus can be built. We thus see the idea of *iqtisâd*, which Asin Palacios translated as "just medium."

¹⁰³ These comments presage others that are much more critical, to come later in the work. The more personal accent placed on this third *'âqîda* becomes clear especially in the reference (p. 47) to a spiritual event that occurred in Cairo in 603 (about which, cf. *Mahâdarat al-abrâr*, Cairo, 1968, II, p. 54, and complemented by *Fut.*, I, p. 410). As indicated by the author, the third *'âqîda* is an abbreviated reprise of his *Kitâb al-ma'rifa al-ûlâ*, or *Kitâb al-masâ'il*, printed in Hyderabad, 1948.

¹⁰⁴ This statement, which Ibn 'Arabî was still claiming four years before his

death (cf. in O. Yahia's critical edition, I, p. 214, the last certificate of reading dated 15 *shawwâl* 634) is one reason among others to suspect the authenticity of the *Tadhkira* edited and translated by R. Deladrière (Ibn 'Arabî, *La Profession de Foi*, Paris, 1978); on this work, see the summaries by D. Gril, *Bulletin critique des Annales islamologiques*, 1984, p9. 337-339, and James W. Morris, *J. A. O. S.*, vol. 106, no. 4, 1986, pp. 741-744.

[105] *Fut.*, I, pp. 700-701. See also *Tarjumân al-ashwâq*, . 42: "How could the rank of the House be comparable to the dignity of manâ"

[106] The work at issue is the *Tâj al-rasâ'il*, Cairo, 1328 A.H.

[107] Cited by Makhzûmî, *Al-jâmi' al-latîf fî fadl Makka*, Cairo, 1357 A.H., p.18.

[108] *Fut.*, I, p. 48.

[109] The encounter with the *fatâ* described in the first chapter of the *Futûhât* was commented on superficially and incorrectly by Fritz Meier in *The Mystery of the Ka'ba: Symbol and Reality* in *Islamic Mysticism, Eranos Yearbooks*, Bollingen Series, XXX, vol. II, pp. 149-166. Corbin made a much more perceptive study, in *L'imagination creatrice dans le soufisme d'Ibn 'Arabî*, Paris, 1958, pp. 207-211 and 278-281.

[110] On the science of letters, other than chapter 2 (I, pp. 51-92), see, e.g., *Fut.* I, p. 191; II, p. 222; III, p. 319; IV, p. 367. A number of short treatises are also devoted to the subject: *Kitâb al-alif, Kitâb al-bâ', Kitâb al-mîm wa l-waw wa l-nûn, Kitâb al-yâ', Kitâb al-jalâla*, about which see the notes in O. Yahia's Répertoire Général, in *Histoire et classification*. The *Kitâb al-asrâr al-hurûf*, mentioned in *Fut.*, I, p. 71, was written in Mecca before chapter 2, of which it might have been an early version. The *Kitâb al-mabâdî wa l-ghayât*, to which Ibn 'Arabî makes reference a number of times during this chapter, saying that it was incomplete (I, pp. 53, 57, ...), and which also went by the title *Al-fath al-fâsî*—which places at least the beginning of his composition during the Maghrebin period—is not to be confused with the poems (excerpted in the *Futûhât*) that appeared under this title borrowed from the appendix in the Damascus edition of *Rûh al-quds* in 1970.

[111] *Fut.*, I, p. 57 for the first citation, p. 65 for the second.

[112] *Ibid.*, p. 53.

[113] *Ibid.*, p. 54.

[114] On these practices, cf. Toufic Fahd, *La divination arabe*, Strassburg, 1966, 2nd ed., Paris, 1982, pp. 219-234; see also chapter IV of Edmond Doutté's *Magie et religion en Afrique de Nord*, Algiers, 1908, 2nd. ed., Paris, 1984.

[115] *Fut.*, I, p. 60. Cf. *Mawâqi' al-nujûm*, Cairo, 1325 A.H., p. 155. On Ibn 'Arabî's oath, see *Fut.*, I, p. 190.

[116] *Ibid.*, p. 56.

[117] Cf. his introduction to the English translation of the *Fusûs al-kikam, The Bezels of Wisdom*, London, 1980, p. 23.

[118] *Fut.* I, p. 83.

[119] "*We are at present in the last third of the night of the sleep of the universe.* The

theophany that gives graces, the sciences, and perfect knowledge in their most thorough forms is that of this last third of the night..." Fut., III, p. 188.

[120] See *Seal of the Saints*, ch. 5.

[121] Cf. *Fut.* I, p. 155; III, pp. 43, 341; IV, p. 77.

[122] Cf. Seal of the Saints, ch. VIII. In the *khutba* for the *Futûhât* (I, p. 3) Ibn 'Arabî emphasizes the common status that he and Jesus share *(al-istirâk baynî wa baynahu fî l-hukm)*.

[123] *Fut.*, I, p. 57.

[124] *Fut.*, III, p. 324.

[125] *Fut.*, IV, p. 289.

[126] Bukhârî, *I'tisâm*, 16.

[127] *Rûh al-quds*, pp. 98-99.

[128] *Fut.*, I, p. 382. See also I, p. 147.

[129] *Ibid.*, p. 58. Elsewhere (II, p. 448) the letters are defined as being angelic in nature.

[130] The word *tarjumân* has special importance in Ibn 'Arabî. It appears in the title to his famous collection of poems (*Tarjumân al-ashwâq*, "The Interpreter of Desires"), but we see it used in reference to his particular role, in the beginnings of both the *Fusûs al-hikam* and the *Kitâb al-Abâdila*.

[131] *Inna l-mawjûdât kalimâtu Llâh, Fût*, II, p. 390. The same idea is expressed in *Fut.* I, p. 366; II, pp. 391, 400, 402, 404, 603; III, p. 230; IV, pp. 5, 65, 166, 167, etc.

[132] On this parallel, see *Fut.* II, p. 395; On Ibn 'Arabî's cosmology, see also *'Uqlat al-mustawfiz* (in *Kleinere Schriften...*); M. Asín Palacios, *El místico murciano Abenarabi*, IV, *Su teologia y sistema del Cosmos*, Madrid, 1928; Titus Burckhardt, *Clé spirituelle de l'astrologie musulmane*, Milan, 1974; Nasr Hâmid Abû Zayd, *Falsafat al-ta'wil*, Beirut, 1983, pp. 45-149.

[133] *Fut.*, II, pp. 122-123.

[134] *Fut.*, I, p. 78; in order to have a series of the seven *abdâl*, the *nûn, tâ', kâf,* and *hâ'* must be added. From another perspective, one we pointed out earlier, the *wâw* invisibly connects the *kâf* and the *nûn* of the *kûn!* that brings things into being is a symbol for the *insân kâmil*, or the *haqîqa muhammadiyya* (*Fut.* III, p. 283). It might also be noted that adding the numerical values of the letters in the word *alif* gives 111, which is also the total of the numerical values of the letters in the word *qutb*.

[135] *Fut.*, I, p. 85.

[136] This verse is from a work that has unfortunately been lost, the *Kitâb al-manâzil al-insâniyya*. On commentaries, see O. Yahia, *Histoire et classification*, pp. 533-537. Commentators have agreed in their interpretation of "sublime letters" being the symbol for the *a'yân thâbita*.

[137] *Fut.* I, p. 99.

[138] *Ibid.*, pp. 100-101. The seven *ummahât al-asmâ* are *Al-hayy, Al-'alim* (sic), *Al-murîd, Al-qâdir, Al-qâ'il, Al-jawwâd,* and *Al-muqsit*.

[139] Cf. *ibid*, p. 103. It might also be noted that vocalization in *u*, which is the

sign of the nominative, is called by the word *damma*, which literally means "junction"; this opens the way for a complementary symbolic perspective.

[140] Ibid., p. 110.

[141] Ibid., p. 111. The idea of *mithl munazzah*, the transcendent similarity, refers to the interpretation Ibn 'Arabî gives to verse 42:11, on numerous occasions. Cf. *Fut.*, I, pp. 62, 97, 220; II, pp. 510, 516, 517, 541, 563, 603; III, pp. 109, 165, 266, 282, 340, 412, 492; IV, pp. 135, 141, 306, 311, 431.

[142] H. Corbin's insistence on using the word *ta'wil* in reference to Ibn 'Arabî is all the more questionable because Ibn 'Arabî himself tends most often to use the term in a pejorative sense.

[143] This attitude is illustrated by the Prophet's behavior when in the presence of a rotting carcass, as described in chapter 36 of the *Futûhât* (a similar event is often mentioned in Islamic texts about Jesus).

[144] *Fut.*, III, p. 93. Cf. also III, p. 108: *Lâ yanzil 'alâ qulûb ummatihi ilâ yawm al-qiyâma*.

[145] *Fut.*, I, p. 115.

[146] *Ibid.*, p. 121. Ibn 'Arabî says that he is borrowing the word *al-habâ* from 'Alî b. Abî Tâlib, who actually uses it in a quite different sense (cf. Suyûtî, *Al-durr al-manthûr*, Beirut, n.d., V, p. 66). In Ibn 'Arabî's vocabulary, *habâ* (or its philosophic equivalent *hayûlâ*) appears with two meanings, or rather two levels, which is also the case in the Ikhwân al-Safâ (cf. *Rasâ'il*, Beirut, n.d., vol IV, pp. 5-17) and refers sometimes to *prime matter (al-hayûlâ al-ûlâ)*, and sometimes to secondary matter *(al-hayûlâ al-thânîya)*. In the first of these two functions, *al-habâ* has as synonyms *al-'amâ'*, *al-khayâl al-mutlaq*, and especially *nafas al-Rahmân*.

[147] *Fut.*, I, p. 119.

[148] *Ibid.*, p. 125.

[149] *Corps céleste et terre de résurrection*, pp. 213-225. This summary is unfortunately marred by contradictions. On page 221, for example, the sentence from Ibn 'Arabî to which Corbin refers does not mean that the pilgrims "are not wearing the ritual clothing," but that the Ka'ba is "stripped of her veil" (her *kiswa*) and that her secrets are thus available for discovery by the visitors from the *ard al-haqîqa*, whose characteristic is precisely that the invisible *(al-ghayb)* thus becomes visible. This "stripping" of the Ka'ba is related to the very nature of the *Futûhât Makkiyya*, as it is described by the *khutba* and the first chapter. Ibn 'Arabî points out (I, p. 131) that he devoted a sizeable volume to this Earth; its title is mentioned in the *Anqâ mughrib* (p. 74), although it has not been found. On the *'alam al-khayâl*, see *Fut.*, II, pp. 309-313 (chapter 177).

[150] *Fut.*, III, p. 525.

[151] *Fut.*, I, p. 173.

[152] *Fut.*, III, p. 224.

[153] *Ibid.*, p. 367.

[154] *Ibid.*, p. 354.

[155] On the jinn, see T. Fahd, "Anges, démons et djinns en Islam," in *Génies*,

Anges et Démons, Paris, 1971, collection Sources Orientales, where there are a number of references, and *EI2*, s.v. "Djinn," The story of 'Amr b. Jâbir al-Jinnî that Ibn 'Arabî mentions is found in Dâmirî, *K. hayât al-hayawân al-kubrâ*, Cairo, 1867, I, p. 258. On the supposed relationship between Ibn 'Arabî and the jinn, cf. Sakhâwî, *Al-qawl al-munbî*, Berlin, 2849, spr. 790, f. 39; for examples of *fatwa*s on relations between human beings and the jinn, cf. Ibn Hajar al-Haythamî, *Al-fatâwa al-hadîthiyya*, Cairo, 1970, pp. 67-69.

156 *Fut.*, I, p. 135.

157 *Fut.*, III, p. 145.

158 Ms. Zâhiriyya 1418, ff. 53-100b.

159 It should be noted that in *Fut.* I, p. 139, Ibn 'Arabî is clearly stating that the four elements do, in fact, come from a fifth element, which is their common source, and, moreover, that it establishes (p. 138) a correlation between them and the four wives allowed by Islamic law (by referring to the case of a Yemenite king who was allowed to have five wives).

160 *Qaq istadâra l-zamân*, cf. Bukhârî, *Tafsîr*, sura 9; *badʿ al-khalq* 2, etc.

161 For Ibn 'Arabî, this restoration of the Original Time explains the injunction (Q. 9:37) against the postponing or interspersing of supplementary months that the Meccan polytheists had done in the calendar.

162 The first cycle—from Adam to Muhammad—lasted for a period of time symbolic of the number 78,000 years (*Fut.*, I, p. 146), which corresponds to six times the "Great Year" of the Persians and Greeks, or three times the period of precession of the equinoxes. The second cycle, which begins with Muhammad and is a synthetic recapitulation of the first, is marked by the contraction of time as it accelerates upon the approaching of the Hour; it is thus much shorter.

163 The first mention in Islam of these four figures symbolic of the Bearers of the Throne appears to be in Wahb b. Munabbih, who died in the early second century after the *hijra*.

164 Chapter 13 provides a number of other details on Ibn 'Arabî's cosmology that we are unable to deal with here. They are complemented both by the information in chapter 371 (which includes a section on the Throne), and by information in the *'Uqlat al-mustawfiz* (ed. Nyberg, see especially pp. 52-60) and the *Tadbîrât ilâhiyya* (ed. Nybert, see especially p. 152). We might point out that in *Fut.* III, p. 431, Ibn 'Arabî identifies himself with the Bearer of the Throne who is the one responsible for the four feet where the "Treasure of Mercy" is enclosed, adding: *"And* [God] *has made me absolutely merciful."*

165 Cf. *Seal of the Saints*, chapters 5 to 8 in particular.

166 *Ibid.*, chapters 1 and 9.

167 The two other Hermes are *Hirmîs al-babilî* (from Babylonia) and *Hirmîs al-misrî* (the Egyptian).

168 *Fut.*, III, p. 13. The *rawda* is the space in the mosque in Medina between the Prophet's tomb and his seat *(minbar)*.

169 H. Corbin, *L'imagination créatrice...*, pp. 32-36.

170 *Fut.*, I, pp. 153-154.

171 The *rajul habashî* in question in shaykh Abû 'Alî Hawarî's remarks reported by Ibn 'Arabî (*Fut.* I, p. 160) is certainly the companion of the latter, Badr al-Habashî (cf. *Fut.* I, p. 7).

172 *Fut.*, I, p. 167.

173 We are here referring to a famous *hadîth qudsî* (Bukhârî, *Riqâq*, 38) where God "becomes" the ear, the eye, the hand, and the foot of the one He loves; for Ibn 'Arabî, (*Fut.* I, p. 406) this is a clear expression of the effective realization by the *'abd* of an identity that the veil of illusion was keeping him from seeing: God has *always* been his ear, his eye..., in short, his very being. But in the case of the "perfect servant" who comes back toward the creatures, this identity is, in a way, reversed: it is the *'abd* who, this time, is the ear, the eye, the hand of God. On this hadith, cf. *Fut.* I, pp. 203, 406; II, p. 189; III, pp. 63, 67, 68, 143, 189, 298, 531; IV, pp. 20, 24, 30, 312, 321; *Fus.*, I, p. 81; *Naqsh al-fusûs*, Hyderabad, 1948, p. 4.

174 *Fut.*, I, p. 181.

175 Ibn 'Arabî's primary texts relating to the *malâmiyya* are studied in *Seal of the Saints*, ch. 7.

176 The object of this knowledge is defined as *al-tûl wa l-'ard*, the "height" and the "width," or the "exaltation" and the "breadth," terms whose cruciform symbolism is obvious, and whose introduction into Sufism goes back to the *K. al-sahhûr fî naqd al-dahhûr* (Leningrad, Firk. 4885) written by Hallâj, a "Christic" saint par excellence. Massignon interprets them relatively flatly as references to the "two dimensions of understanding" (*Passion*, III, p. 16, note 8). For Ibn 'Arabî, they refer, respectively (*Fut.*, I, p. 169; cf. also p. 176) to the "invisible world" (*'âlam al-ghayb*) and the "manifested world" (*'âlam al-shahâda*).

177 *Fut.*, I, p. 392.

178 In the critical edition of the *Khatm al-awliyâ* (Beirut, 1965) done by O. Yahia, based on two manuscripts in Istanbul, there are 157 questions.

179 See note 81.

180 *Fut.*, I, p. 551.

181 *Fut.*, III, p. 245.

182 *Fut.*, IV, p. 293.

183 *Ibid.*, p. 40.

184 *Risâlat al-khawlwa*, Bayazid 1686, f. 6b; Yahya Ef. 2415, f. 4a.

185 On this point, see our introduction to Awhad al-dîn Balyânî's *L'épître sur l'unicité absolue*, Paris, 1982, where we underscore the distinctions that should be made between this author and his master's (Ibn Sab'în) teachings, on the one hand, and Ibn 'Arabî, on the other.

186 On Ibn 'Arabî's symbolic interpretation of the way numbers progress, see, for example, *Fut.*, III, p. 494; *Kitâb al-fanâ' fî l-mushâhada*, Hyderabad, 1948, pp. 2-3 (trans. by M. Vâlsan, *Le livre de l'extinction dans la contemplation*, Paris, 1984, p. 29).

187 *Fut.*, IV, p. 449.

THE LAW AND THE WAY
Cyrille Chodkiewicz

INTRODUCTION
TO 'THE LAW AND THE WAY'

Whether Ibn 'Arabî's reputation is good or bad—whether he is seen as the "Doctor Maximus" (as is the case with Corbin), or disdained as a "grammarian of esotericism" (as he is by Massignon)—rarely does the reputation take his actual position vis-à-vis the *sharî'a*, sacred law, into account; and often it misrepresents his position. Muslim polemecists can certainly claim both precedence and perseverance in this domain: Sakhâwî's 15th century compilation, *Al-qawl al-munbî*[1] minutely documents the monotonous calumnies leveled against Ibn 'Arabî, like the crimes of *ibâha* (permissiveness) and *tahrîf* (distorting the meanings of words in the Qur'ân); and the Shaykh al-Akbar's 20th century adversaries unimaginatively rehash the same old arguments with the same out-of-context quotes that have ensured the longevity of such misunderstandings. One recent example was seen when a 1979 decision in the Egyptian parliament slapped a provisional condemnation on the publication of the critical edition of the *Futûhât*. A careful reading of the *Futûhât* is sufficient both to show—and the number of pages is additional evidence—the considerable attention the author paid to legal questions, and to verify (a topic to which we shall return) that the *sharî'a* is not, for him, the opposite of *haqîqa*, Essential Reality. We must nevertheless be fair to one of the most outspoken of the Shaykh al-Akbar's critics, the one whose prolific pen furnished the most ammunition for later writers denouncing the pernicious influence of the Andalusian master's teachings. Ibn Taymiyya (728/1328), more subtle than those who carried on his tradition, does allow that Ibn 'Arabî "speaks eloquently in a number of domains [...]. His position regarding what is prescribed and what is forbidden, and regarding everything concerning the Law in general, is in accord with the way it should be."[2] He even admits to finding some things of profit in his work.[3] Our purpose in translating Ibn 'Arabî's passages here is certainly not to convince his detractors of his orthodoxy—for such a task would be futile—but rather to show that it would be much more serious to admire him for what he is not and to turn him into a *bâtinî*, in the usual sense of the word, that is, into a man who destroys the Law in order to discover what it conceals. The countless pages Ibn 'Arabî devoted to the *sharî'a* do not constitute a concession to the constraints Islamic society might have imposed upon a 13th century author, a forfeit paid to the *fuqahâ'* (whom he did not treat lightly, by the way, as can be seen in the passages from chapter 366 translated by James Morris in the companion to the present volume). Despite appearances, they relate to the most central aspect of his teachings. Our hope is that the title we have chosen for this section of our anthology looks vaguely pleonastic. In a way, the Law and the Way are one and the same thing. Better said: the Law, which is the Way, leads back to itself. It is the point of departure, the way, and the point of return. The very word *sharî'a*, which appears only once in the Qur'ân (43:13), suggests as much. According to *Lisân al-'arab*,[4] the verb *shara'a* means "to take a drink" and, in its first meaning, the noun *sharî'a* refers to the place where animals used to drink and, by extension, to the road that leads there (the latter meaning finally becoming autonomous in the word from the same root, *shâri'*, which in Arabic refers to the legislator, the lawgiver, but also, quite simply, to "the street").

Ibn 'Arabî did not limit himself to spelling out generalities concerning the Law: he dealt with the traditional problem of usûl *(principles or sources) and* furû' *(the consequences that devolve from them). In chapters 68 through 72, he dealt at length, point by point—for over 400 pages in a text so dense that its translation would require 2500 pages in a book like the present one—with all the legal questions raised on the subject of* 'ibâdât *(ritual practices), envisioning in each case the various solutions that had been proposed and, although he did express his preference, justifying each of them. We have chosen to present texts of a more methodological nature here, even though, paradoxically—this paradox will be explained by Ibn 'Arabî himself—they do not appear in the* Futûhât *until after the detailed sections that are based on them.*

In an unpublished treatise, the "Book of auspicious visions" (Kitâb al-mubashshirât), *the Shaykh al-Akbar tells of a dream in which he saw the Prophet embrace Ibn Hazm (456/1064),*[5] *the greatest of the masters of the* madhhab zâhirî,[6] *the legal school (no longer in existence) founded in Baghdad by Dâwûd b. Khalaf (270/884).*[7] *Then, he says, "a light enveloped both of them such that it was as if they had but one body."*[8] *Ibn Hazm's importance in Ibn 'Arabî's eyes, and thus the importance of the school he so eminently represented, can be seen in other ways, also. A small treatise Ibn Hazm devoted to one of the essential points of his teaching, the* Kitâb ibtâl al-qiyâs, *("The annihilation of reasoning by analogy") was published a number of years ago; the treatise was based on a manuscript established from the copy of the* Kitâb ibtâl al-quyâs *that Ibn 'Arabî had personally transcribed.*[9] *Similarly, the Shaykh al-Akbar composed a summary (no longer extant) of the thirty volumes of Ibn Hazm's* Muhallâ,[10] *which reveals, at least, meticulous attention to the latter's thought. The similarity in juridical positions between the two is, moreover, often striking, as we shall have occasion to see. In domains other than* fiqh, *there are correlations that clearly are not coincidental. For example, both use the* hadîth qudsî *reported by Bukhârî,*[11] *and consider the word* al-Dahr, *"Time," to belong on the list of Divine Names, which is at least unusual in Islam.*[12] *It may be noted, moreover, that part of Ibn 'Arabî's youth in Andalusia was spent under the reign of the Almohad sultan Abû Yûsuf Ya'qûb al-Mansûr, with whom he had personal contact.*[13] *This same sultan is credited with an attempt, albeit unsuccessful, to establish the* madhhab zâhirî *in his land. This probably explains why Muslim authors, and later Orientalists, ended up classifying Ibn 'Arabî among the followers of the school. This was the opinion of historian al-Maqqarî (17th century),*[14] *whose work Goldziher expanded upon.*[15] *The reputation, by the way, did not begin with modern authors; the Shaykh al-Akbar himself mentioned that he was living under its shadow: "They associate me with Ibn Hazm"* (nasabûnî ilâ Ibn Hazm), *he declared in one of the poems in his* Dîwân.[16] *But he made the statement so that he could immediately follow it with a protest against the supposed affiliation, since he added: "I am not one of those who say, 'Ibn Hazm said...,'" immediately clarifying that nothing he said had a source other than the Qur'ân, the hadith, or Community consensus* (ijmâ'). *The truth is that, if Ibn 'Arabî's teachings regarding matters of* fiqh *are carefully studied—and superficial similarities are avoided—he can be associated no more with one legal school* (madhhab) *than another; to put it more clearly, he constitutes a perfectly autonomous* madhhab akbarî *all by himself; such has been the conclusion of the handful of authors who have taken an interest in this aspect of his teachings.*[17]

THE SOURCES OF THE LAW[1]
CHAPTER 88

This chapter—the complete title of which is "On knowledge of the secrets pertaining to the bases of legal prescriptions"—is a methodical outline structured along the traditional framework for presenting usûl al-fiqh; *its contents, however, are an early indication of the originality of Ibn 'Arabî's position. His concept of* ijtihâd, *"the effort of interpretation" the author will define elsewhere, but to which references to* 'ilm ladunnî *(the knowledge that Khadir receives directly from God Himself) or to the light that guides the God-fearing man refer, can be seen from the chapter's earliest lines. Ibn 'Arabî is more explicit in another* Futûhât *passage*[18]: *"We are not saying that* ijtihâd *is what the men of exoteric sciences claim it is. For us,* ijtihâd *is the effort that allows that inner disposition* (isti'dâd al-bâtin) *to be reached through which one becomes capable of receiving the particular inspiration* (hadha l-tanazzul al-khâss) *that no prophet or messenger was able to receive during his time of prophecy—since this revelation could not cast doubt over legal status firmly established by the Messenger." In other words: in response to situations that do not appear to be expressly foreseen by the Qur'ân or the Sunna, divine grace can allow meanings and applications to appear that theretofore were not perceived in the scriptures. This idea is not unlike the concept of the "descent of the Qur'ân upon the* awliyâ', " *the saints through whom God's Book remains a permanent reality*[19] *for those He has chosen. For the jurist, this is not a question of innovating. Even if he is not among those whom God has thus favored with a specific inspiration, he should know that the only two "active foundations" of the Law are* the Qur'ân and the Sunna, and that nothing is omitted from them: his efforts should aim at finding them within these two sources. Ibn 'Arabî returns to this fundamental point frequently, relying especially on verse 3 of sura 5 ("Today, I have perfected your religion for you").[20] What follows from this divine declaration is that man should try to learn everything the Law says, but only what it says, since "that upon which the Law is silent is left no more to chance than what it says. If each word of the sharî'a means something, then the absence of a word also has meaning, and man, if he is not to transgress against the word of God, is not to fill God's silences for Him. The 'gaps' in the Law are part of its plenitude."[21] The use of "passive" foundations, of derived sources—which consensus (ijmâ') and reasoning by analogy (qiyâs) are—should lead neither to additions nor to deletions.

These four usûl are juxtaposed with the quaternary structure of the Universal Manifestation: the four Divine Names through which Creation takes place, the four elements that constitute the world of Nature, the four qualities, the four temperaments, and others. This is an Ibn 'Arabî theme par excellence; we see it in his writings on the science of letters; in the relationships he outlines between the three harakât (short vowels) and the sukûn (the "stop" sign in Arabic script), on the one hand, and the higher degrees in the initiatic hierarchy on the other; and in his reflections on the symbolism of the Ka'ba[22]: the correlations thus established among cosmology, anthropology, law, and grammar may seem surprising. They are not the result of some rhetorical concern for artificial analogies; quite the contrary, they are evidence of a cohesive doctrine whose justification can be seen in other sections of the present anthology.[23]

Much of the text translated here concerns the problem of the legitimacy of qiyâs. It shows what makes Ibn 'Arabî look like the madhhab zâhirî and what separates the two. Like Ibn Hazm, Ibn 'Arabî refuses to use qiyâs: the 'ârif bi-Llâh, the gnostic (in the etymological sense of the word), benefits from a special light that precludes his need to use this dangerous instrument. A second reason for his refusal will be addressed below. But, in contrast to the Zâhirites, he vigorously condemns those who absolutely forbid its use: the Qur'ân itself, after all, prescribed the use of reasoning, of which qiyâs is just a specific form, and this was in the most fundamental domain of all: beliefs ('aqâ'id). Its use was thus—and all the more so—perfectly licit, not in matters of establishing metaphysical principles, but in establishing simple rules for practical application.

After a short paragraph where through the inspired nature of his writings the Shaykh al-Akbar justifies the apparent lack of logic in their structure—in this case, the presence of a chapter on principles (usûl) long after the chapters where he deals with their consequences (furû')—and with no fear of the parallel he draws between their composition and that of the Qur'ân, he methodically spells out a set of rules through which the contradictions among different legal pronouncements can be resolved; he then touches on the extensively argued question of abrogation (nashk).[24] Doing away with a legal measure that had been initially formulated in the Qur'ân or the hadith, or replacing one measure with another is neither the result of a whim on God's part nor of an innovation in divine knowledge (which would be tantamount to what is implied by the Shi'ite idea of badâ' so strongly criticized by Sunni theologians)[25]; it corresponds, rather, to the expiration of a possibility. In passing, we might note Ibn 'Arabî's insistence on the necessity of having words retain the meaning they had in the language of the Arabs, if the Law is to be interpreted correctly: it shows up quite characteristically in his exegetical method, where the most surprising of esoteric interpretations are consistently backed by painstaking analysis of the literalness of the text. This is also the position of the Zâhirite authors, at least theoretically, but it did not help them develop a hermeneutics capable of discovering the spiritual meanings Ibn 'Arabî manages to tease out of the verses in the Qur'ân.[26]

Regarding the use of ijmâ' as a "source for the Law"—which he considers to be consensus among the Companions of the Prophet rather than among the 'ulamâ' of later generations—Ibn 'Arabî has a position that is similar in every respect to that of Ibn Hazm, whose position itself is in line with that of the founder of his school.[27] In contrast to the mainstream doctrine, where ijmâ' is defined as "the unanimous agreement of the community, through the voice of its specialists, at a given time," this position has the apparent effect of "petrifying" the Law, of depriving it of ways to respond to situations that were unknown to the first generation of Muslims, but it actually leads to restricting ijmâ's field of application, since agreement among the Companions was clearly not seen except on a quite limited number of subjects. This position, as we shall see, is perfectly in line with the one that Ibn 'Arabî personally applied to the use of qiyâs. "I forbid myself to use *qiyâs* only because it leads to adding to the explicit prescriptions," he wrote in a passage from this same chapter 88, the translation of which follows. For him, in the absence of a formal text (nass) that determines a specific legal status, everything preserves its original status, which is its *legality: the label "forbidden," "discouraged," "obligatory," or "recommended" that ultimately gets attached to something by the Lawgiver is accidental (in the philosophical sense of the term), added to its essence. Metaphysically based on the doctrine of* wahdat al-wujûd, *this stance highlights the central axis of Ibn 'Arabî's spiritual teaching: compassion for beings, like that of the Prophet for his community, which, in turn, devolves from that of the Creator for His creation. This is not a case of laxism: in another chapter in the* Futûhât—*although in this case he is implicitly addressing the* murîd, *the individual who has chosen to fight the Greater Holy War—Ibn 'Arabî recommends keeping the most restrictive of the different legally admissible solutions for oneself but, if asked about it, reserving the least difficult solution for others.*[28] *This same concern for not "shrinking what God has expanded" leads to setting strict limits on forays into interpretation* (ijtihâd): *it should not aim at "completing" the Law—in which nothing is missing by definition, since it was established by Him Whose knowledge encompasses all things—but only at seeking an answer (or at observing the absence of a response, which is also a response, since it leads back to the principle of "original licitness") in the Qur'ân and the hadith. Nor should it apply to anything other than concrete cases that arise from time to time; anyone who has perused collections of* fatwa *and appraised the casuistic ingenuity they display in their attempts to resolve imaginary problems will quickly understand the wisdom in this rule. This point of view, which has precedents in Islam—here Ibn 'Arabî is referring to Mâlik b. Anas, although the Companion Masrûq b. al-Ajdâ' might also be mentioned—should not be considered solely as a condemnation of intellectual frivolity in the doctors of the Law. The Sufi is a "child of the moment"* (ibn al-waqt). *He does not need to anticipate the measures of Divine Wisdom, but rather to conform to what Divine Wisdom requires at any particular moment.*

Foundation of the Law
and the universal fourfold division[29]

Know that there is unanimity regarding three entities upon which legal prescriptions are based: the Book, the *sunna mutawâtira*,[30] and consensus *(ijmâ')*. The experts are not in complete agreement regarding reasoning by analogy *(qiyâs)*: some claim that it constitutes proof *(dalîl)* and is one of the foundations for legal prescriptions, while others maintain—and this is my position—that it should be avoided. God said: "Fear God and He will teach you" (Q. 2:282). He also said: "If you fear God, He will give you discernment *(furqânan)*" (Q. 8:29); "Fear God and believe in His Messenger so that He might give you two measures of His Mercy, that He might give you a light to help you walk, and pardon you" (Q. 57:28). Similarly, He said in regard to His servant Khadir: "We have given him a mercy coming from Us, and We have given him knowledge from Us" (Q. 18:65).

This is how God transmits the knowledge He in His mercy grants to His servant. Fearing God is work *('amal)* that is prescribed for us and whose status relates to one of the [scriptural] references, or all of them, regardless of how it is imposed upon us. Junayd said: "This knowledge of ours is related to the Book and the Sunna."

These are the two "active" foundations *(aslân fâ'ilân)* of the Law, while *ijmâ'* and *qiyâs* were established only by the Book and the Sunna, and are thus passive foundations.

It is from these four things that the legal prescriptions whose performance leads to happiness *(al-sa'ada)* came into being. In the same fashion, everything in existence *(al-mawjûdât)* proceeds from four Divine Realities. These are Life *(al-hayât)*, Knowledge *(al-'ilm)*, Will *(al-irâda)*, and Power *(al-qudra)*. Moreover, bodies also proceed from four realities: heat *(al-harâra)*, cold *(al-barûda)*, dryness *(al-yubûsa)* and humidity *(al-rutûba)*.

Beings that are engendered *(al-mutawalladât)* proceed from the four elements *(arkân)*: fire *(nâr)*, air *(hawâ')*, water *(mâ')*, and earth *(turâb)*. Finally each human body is produced from four humors *(akhlât)*: bile *(safrâ)*, black bile *(sawdâ')*, blood *(dam)*, and phlegm *(balgham)*. Heat and cold are active qualities, while humidity and dryness are passive qualities.

Reasoning by analogy *(al-qiyâs)*[31]

(…) There are differences of opinion regarding reasoning by analogy and its use in argumentation *(dalîl)* or as a source of fact. Indeed, from a certain point of view, it is intellectually justifiable, and in certain cases, using it seems preferable to rejecting it, while in other cases, the opposite is true. Whatever the case, *qiyâs* does not constitute a decisive argument in and of itself. The same is true for an account that comes from a single source *(khabar al-âhdât)*; there is agreement that it should be accepted, even though it does not in itself confer certain knowledge and it is one of the sources that help determine the legal prescriptions. The same should be true for *qiyâs* when it is so clear that no room can be left for doubt. Even though I am opposed to it for my own personal use, I do accept its use by others to make decisions on legal questions if their effort at interpretation *(ijtihâd)* has led to affirming its validity [as a legal source]. It matters little whether the individual is right or wrong [in his effort of interpretation]: the Lawgiver has in fact validated the *mujtahid*'s judgment (even if he is in error), and has rewarded him. But if, in his attempt to legitimize *qiyâs*, he has not supported his opinion with any proof from the Book, the *sunna*, *ijmâ'*, or all three at the same time, it is not licit for him to make a ruling based on *qiyâs*. In issues regarding legal statutes, it nevertheless does happen that an equitable man's thinking ability allows him to formulate a stronger proof through the use of clear analogy *(al-qiyâs al-jallî)* than through authentic information that happened to come from a single source *(khabar al-wâhid)*: such information, after all, is allowable only because of the good opinion we have of those who reported the information, but we do not consider it as providing certain knowledge regarding God, since the Law forbids this, and all we can say is "I think..." or "in my opinion it is true that..." On the other hand, for us, clear *qiyâs* is associated with authentic speculative thought; we have recognized the validity of speculative thought *(al-nazar al-'aqlî)*, which we are legally ordered to practice in the divine words: "Did they not consider *(yanzurû)* the Kingdom of the Heavens and the Earth (...)?" (Q. 7:185); "Were they not thinking *(yatafakkarû)* that their companion was not possessed by the jinn (...)" (Q. 7:184). There are a number of other, similar, passages in the Qur'ân! The Lawgiver thus recognizes the ability of speculative thought to establish the existence of God—that is, of the most fundamental of principles—and then to recognize the oneness in all the roles He plays as divinity *(ulûha)*. He prescribed that we know intellectually that there is no god but Allah; we then thought about what the status of this divinity should necessarily be, according to rational argument *(al-dalîl al-'aqlî)*; then, using the speculative thought we are prescribed to employ, we reflected on what might confirm the truthfulness of what the Messenger brought from Him, even though he was nothing more "than a man like us" *(basharan mithlanâ*; cf. Q. 14:10, 11; 18:110; 21:3; 23:24, 33; 26:145, 186; 36:15, 41:6). With our reasoning abilities, we reflected on His signs *(âyâtihi)* and on the proofs He manifested regarding the truthfulness *(sidq)* of the Messenger, and we established that it was true. These are fundamental principles: if a single one of them collapsed, the laws of the religion would be null and void. It is speculative thought that allows their firm establishment. Thus, Divine Law relies on it, and asks the faithful to use it: reasoning by analogy is a form of speculative thought *(wa l-qiyâs nazar ʿaqlî)*. Do you believe that God *(al-Haqq)* would authorize its use in such issues and in such fundamental principles, and forbid its use in practical matters *(masʾala farʿiyya)* about which we find no mention in the Holy Book, in the Sunna, or in *ijmâ*? It is our firm opinion that it necessarily has a legal status of divine origin, and that, when the other roads have been closed, there is no other way out than to return to this principle, that is, to speculative thought.

By basing ourselves on the Book and the Sunna we both established this and, after careful consideration, concluded that *qiyâs* is indeed—in this procedure and from the moment it is recognized as authoritative in the very principles of the religion—one of the sources of proof where legal prescriptions are concerned.

When it becomes a necessity, and when we find no decisive scriptural support, we thus seek to define the status of things that the Law does not speak of, basing our thinking on the status of things about which it does speak, as soon as we can consider it to be logical that the Lawgiver's intention is the same in the two cases, and allows them to be dealt with in the same fashion. Whoever declares blameworthy the individual who affirms the legitimacy of reasoning by analogy, or condemns the *mujtahid* who uses such reasoning—regarding either the bases of laws or derived questions—is behaving improperly in regard to the Lawgiver, since it was He who established its legitimacy. [...]

Thus,[32] even though we object to the use of reasoning by analogy for our own personal use, we do maintain that its use is licit, because God has approved it for those whose efforts at interpretation lead to the need for its use. If he looks at it fairly, the individual who disagrees would refrain from discussing the issue, since the question is not really a matter for discussion. "And God tells the truth and guides on the path!" (Q. 33:4).

The principles of legal prescriptions

In the present chapter we shall outline that which pertains to the fundamental principles of legal prescriptions for experts, as we did for the practice of religious duties *(al-ʿibâdât)*.[33] It certainly would have been more logical for this chapter to precede the chapters dealing with *ʿibâdât*, but such is not the way the task was given to us. The decision regarding the present arrangement was not a personal decision. If we were proceeding rationally, the place of this chapter in the hierarchy of Wisdom *(tartîb al-hikma)* would be quite different. It is like the verse that says: "*Perform prayers and the middle prayer attentively (wa l-salât al-wustâ)*" (Q. 2:238). This verse is placed between the verses relating to repudiation *(talâq)* of marriage *(nikâh)* and the verses dealing with testamentary measures, which precede and follow, respectively.

It may look as though the verse is not in the right place. It is, however, placed right where God destined it to be, because He knows what is appropriate for [all] things. The Wise Man *(al-hakîm)* is the man who does as he is supposed to do, when he is supposed to do it, in the way it is supposed to be done, even if ignorance keeps us from knowing why all this is fitting. It is God Himself who imposed this arrangement of subjects upon my hand. This is why I have kept my opinions and my thoughts to myself [...].

Cases of contradictory verses or hadiths[34]

When two verses or two authentic traditions contradict one another—but it is still possible to set them side by side and use them together—we should not refuse to use them. If it is not possible to use them together because one of them contains an exclusion *(istithnâ')*, we should choose the one in which the exclusion is found. If one of them contains an addition *(ziyâda)*, it should be adopted and used. When neither of these is present, and the two verses are totally contradictory, then the date *(ta'rîkh)* [of the revelation of each] should be checked, and the more recent of the two should be used. And finally, if the date is unknown or difficult to ascertain, then we should take the one that is most apt to remove hardship in the matter of religion *(raf' al-haraj fî l-dîn)* and apply it, for this point of view is confirmed by the verse: "*There is no hardship* (haraj) *weighing upon you in religion*" (Q. 22:78), and Allah's religion is easy. "*And God wishes for you what is easy, not what is difficult*" (Q. 2:185). [The Prophet also tells us:] "*What I have commanded you to do, perform it to the extent that you are able, and refrain from what I have forbidden you to do!*"[35] If the two contradictory texts are equivalent in this regard, neither should be abandoned, but you should choose to follow whichever one you wish.

When a verse and an authentic tradition that comes from a single source are contradictory, and the date is unknown, the verse should be chosen and the tradition abandoned, since the former is certain while the latter is only a presumption. If the tradition in question is one that is reported by a number of authorities *(khabar mutawâtir)*, and thus is as certain as the verse, but their chronological relationship is unknown and it is impossible to reconcile them, the rule is that either of the two may be chosen freely. However, if there is a lessening of hardship *(raf' al-haraj)* in one of the texts, that is the one that should be preferred.

Whenever two traditions or two verses contradict one another, or when a verse and an authentic tradition stand in contradiction—whether the tradition is reported by a number of authorities or by only one—but one of the two contains an added detail *(ziyâda)* in the matter of legal prescriptions, this detail should be kept in mind and followed.[36] The balance then shifts to the tradition containing this addition, rather than to the tradition that contradicts it. However, only traditions that are authentic should be considered. The individual who follows one of the juridical schools in legal matters—but who hears a weak *(da'îf)* hadith attributed to God's Messenger that contradicts the opinion of one of the imams [the founders of the legal schools] or one of the Companions—should give preference to the weak hadith and reject the opinion in question, if he is not aware of any convincing *(dalîl)* argument for it. Even if the hadith is in reality not authentic, at least it has the same degree of probability as the contrary opinion, and one should not stray from it. And most of all, one should not stray from it if it is authentic, and it is imperative that one disregard the contrary opinion of a Companion or an Imam.

If the tradition is "unattached" *(mursal,* meaning that it is reported without a chain of transmission or with an incomplete chain) or "stopped" *(mawqûf,* meaning that it goes only back to one of the Prophet's companions but not to the Prophet himself), it can only be trusted if it is known that the second reporter *(tâbi')* did not hear the tradition from anyone other than the Companion. If such is the case, even if which Companion it came from is not stated, the *hadîth mursal* may be adopted. Such a tradition actually has the same status as a hadith reported by the Prophet *(al-musnad)*. Such is the case when the reporter from the second generation says "God's Messenger said…" without mentioning the Companion from whom he is reporting the hadith, provided we know that he was someone who saw the Companions and was a member of their entourage, that he was certain in matters of faith, and that he was not one of those individuals who claimed that remarks not made by the Prophet could be attributed to the Prophet if they were for the good of the community. If he does not fulfill these conditions, the hadith he reports should not be used, even if it has a complete chain of transmission. In summary, it is not licit to reject a verse or an authentic tradition in favor of the opinion of one of the Companions or one of the Imams; he who does so commits a blatant error, and places himself outside God's religion.

When a tradition comes from individuals about whom nothing is known *(mastûrîn)*, individuals who are spoken of neither in terms of disapproval *(jarh)* nor approval *(ta'dîl)*, what they are transmitting should be accepted. But if one of them is believed to have some fault that casts doubt upon his sincerity *(sidq)*, this tradition should be discarded. However, when this defect is not related to the narration *(naql)* in question, it should be accepted unless the person in question was a wine drinker or was speaking in a state of intoxication *(sukr)*. On the other hand, if it is known that the statement was made by someone in a state of sobriety *(sahw)* and that it is characteristic of the individual in question, the tradition reported should be accepted. [...]

In all this, there is no difference between using the authentic *khabar al-wâhid* and the tradition called *mutawâtir*, except when there is a contradiction between the two, as we have pointed out. God in no way obliges us to accept what others say about His Messenger, even if we are enjoined to respect and love them.

The problem of abrogation

I do not define abrogation *(naskh)* as it is generally defined. For me, abrogation means that the period of time during which, in God's wisdom, a certain legal statute was supposed to be observed has come to an end. When this period is over, there is nothing wrong with another measure in the Qur'ân or the Sunna of the Prophet replacing it as law. If this is what is referred to as "abrogation," I am among those who affirm its existence.

Based on the preceding, the abrogation of one verse in the Qur'ân by another, or by a tradition, is completely conceivable. Actually, the purpose of the Sunna is to clarify [that which is not clear], since the Prophet was commanded to explain to people what had been revealed [in the Qur'ân] and, in so doing, to speak from what God had shown him, and not from what his own ego *(nafs)* had shown him. Whether the issue was Qur'ânic or not, everything he said was in complete accord with what had been revealed *(lâ yattabi' illâ ma yûhâ ilayhi)*. A tradition might also be abrogated by a verse from the Qur'ân, or by another tradition. When we are in the presence of an explicit legal measure *(nass)* announced in a verse or a tradition, it is not permissible to refrain from following it until such point that the existence or the absence of another contrary measure is verified: the latter arriving measure should immediately be put into practice. If we subsequently happen upon a tradition or a verse that abrogates *(nâsikh)* one that precedes it, or narrows its scope *(mukhassis)*, or does just the opposite and widens it *(mu'ammin)*, we should follow what we have learned, although we must still respect certain conditions: the chronology of the two texts should be determined, since on some occasions it is the more restrictive verse that precedes the other, and sometimes vice-versa. The principle is that the last to be revealed is the one that is authoritative.[37]

When a verse or tradition contains a word that is not common in language *(lisân)*, the principle is to accept it with its meaning in the language of the Arabs. If the Lawgiver used the word in a sense different from what it might normally have in everyday language, like, for example, the words *salât*[38] (prayer), *wudû'* (ablution), *hajj* (pilgrimage), or *zakât* (legal alms),[39] the meaning to be taken is the one the Lawgiver explained and established. If at some later point a tradition containing the word comes along, using it with its common meaning, such an interpretation for the word in question will be restricted to that particular tradition [not to be extended to other uses of the same word in contexts where the Lawgiver had given it a different meaning].

Everything the Law establishes in the form of an order *(awâmir)* should be understood as belonging to the category of obligation *(al-wujûb)*, and everything it establishes as a prohibition *(nawâhî)* should be seen as belonging to the category of the forbidden *(al-hazr)*, unless the context tends to make what is [formally] an order slip from the category of obligation into the category of "recommended" *(nadb)* or simply "licit" *(ibâha)*, or what is [formally] a prohibition from the domain of the forbidden slip into that of the simply blameworthy *(karâha)*. [Conversely,] when the order entails no context that allows it to be interpreted as being actually a recommendation or a permission, what it prescribes is absolutely obligatory, as is also the case for what concerns prohibition. [The possibility for such an interpretation is explained by the fact that] occasionally, for example, the purpose of an [apparent] command is simply to end a prohibition, and not to make something obligatory.

Consensus

"Consensus" *(ijmâ')* refers solely to the common thinking of the Companions after [the death of] God's Prophet. What takes place after their time is not a consensus upon which decisions regarding legal questions can be based.

Consensus exists when it is known that a problem was submitted to each of the Companions and that each handed down a judgment on the issue that was in line with the pronouncements of the others, to the point where each had dealt with the question, and each offered the [same] opinion on the issue. If it is reported that even one of the Companions had a different opinion on the matter, there is no consensus. Nor is there *ijmâ'* if it is reported that one kept his silence, or if it is learned that there was a disagreement on the matter. When this is the case, one should go back to the Book or to the prophetic traditions in order to make a pronouncement. This is the best, the most perfect, way to proceed in one's search for the first meaning *(ta'wîl)*.

The Original Status

It is not permissible to interpret divine will on the basis of personal opinion *(ra'y)*, by which I mean a point of view expressed in the absence of proof or reasoning from the Book, or the Sunna, or one based on *ijmâ'*.

Even if I, personally, do not use reasoning by analogy, I do not fault the individual who considers it valid if the cause *(al-'illa)* common [to the two things between which the analogy is being established] is clear and understandable, and it seems probable that it is what the Lawgiver had in mind. No, I forbid myself to use *qiyâs* only because it leads to increasing the number of explicit prescriptions. I have understood that the Lawgiver wished for this community's burden to be lightened *(al-takhfîf)*. The Prophet said: "*Leave me alone as long as I leave you alone!*"[40] and he reproached those who quizzed him for fear he might reveal some [new] prescription that the community would be incapable of respecting, like staying awake during the night during Ramadân *(qiyâm Ramadân)*, performing the pilgrimage *(al-hajj)* every year, or something of the sort. Thus, when I saw what was at issue here, I forbade *qiyâs* in matters of religion. Neither the Prophet nor God Himself commanded its use [in legal matters]. Abandoning it is thus an obligation, for me, since it is something the

Prophet condemned. The original status *(hukm al-asl)* [of things] is the absence of legal obligation *(lâ taklîf)*.⁴¹ Indeed, God created everything on earth for us, and the person who attempts to impose a limitation *(tahjîr)* upon us is obliged to provide proof—from the Book, from the Sunna, or from *ijmâ'*. So I do not practice *qiyâs*, and I recognize absolutely no authority in its use.

Imitation of the deeds and gestures *(af'âl)* of the Prophet is not an obligation *(wujûb)*—if it were, it would amount to the heaviest of burdens—except when it comes to an act that we are specifically prescribed to perform in order to obey God, in which case the act is obligatory. For example, when he said: "Pray as you see me pray, and take your rites *(manâsik)* from me,"⁴² or in matters concerning the different parts of the pilgrimage. If there were not details concerning certain specific actions, performing them would not be an obligation for us. The Prophet was a man subject to emotions, as are all men; he could feel satisfaction and anger, just like anyone else. We are only expected to imitate him in actions and deeds when he [expressly] commanded us to do so; and he was ordered not to perform any action [of this nature] in secret, so that he could be seen by others, just as, when he received the order to transmit *(tablîgh)*, it was incumbent upon him not to say what he had heard while he was alone, because no one would be there to hear it and to communicate the content of the revelation to others who had not heard.

We are not obligated to follow any religious laws previous to ours, except in those cases where our own law has confirmed them, despite the fact that they are authentically sacred laws for the communities to which they were addressed and we do not accuse them of being false. Quite the contrary, we believe in God, in his Messenger, and in what was revealed to him [but also] in the Books and the laws that were revealed before him. (cf. Q. 2:4, 136, 285; 3:84; 4:126, etc.).

Blind conformity *(al-taqlîd)* [to the opinion of another] is not permissible in matters of religion, in our opinion, regardless of whether the individual is dead or still living. In fact, it is incumbent upon the individual who questions a scholar to tell him: "I want to know what God or His Messenger prescribed on such and such an issue!" If the individual questioned replies: "Here is the divine prescription on this matter," or "here is His Messenger's," the questioner should put it into practice, because the respondent in this case is merely a reporter *(nâqil)* of God's decision for us, or of His Prophet. On the other hand, when the person questioned says "Here is my opinion *(ra'yî)*" or "This is the way I see the matter," or even

"I do not know what the procedure is for this question; however, an analogous judgment shows that the status is the same in regard to this question as for the one uttered in regard to such-and-such other question," in this case it is not licit for the person who asked the question to take the opinion into consideration. He must thus seek out Men of Memory *(ahl al-dhikr)* and question them in the manner we have described. It is the duty of every Muslim not to question individuals other than either these *ahl al-dhikr*, meaning the men of the Qur'ân—God said: "*It is, indeed, We Who revealed* dhikr (...)" (Q. 15:9)—or the men of hadith. If the questioner knows that the person he is going to ask uses *ra'y* and *qiyâs*, he should avoid the person and ask the man of hadith. If he knows that he uses *ra'y*, *qiyâs*, and hadith, then he can ask the question. But when the person asked offers his opinion, he must specify if it is based on *ra'y*, on *qiyâs*, or on hadith. If he says it is based on *ra'y* or *qiyâs*, the judgment should be rejected; on the other hand, if he bases it on a tradition *(khabar)*, it should be accepted.

No juridical sanction applies to involuntary transgressions *(al-khatâ')* or forgetfulness *(nisyân)*, except in those specific cases where the Qur'ân or the Sunna stipulate that there is one, and where such sanctions apply to cases like the prayer of the forgetful person *(salât al-nâsî)* or involuntary homicide *(qatl al-khatâ')*. Anything about which the *sharî'a* keeps silence has no legal status other than original licitness *(al-ibâha al-asliyya)*. The prescriptions of Sacred Law apply to names *(al-asmâ')* and states *(al-ahwâl)*, and not to beings as such *(al-a'yân)*. [In other words,] a legally obligatory act *(fard)* is imposed only upon the person who is capable of accepting the obligation; this applies to orders and prohibitions, and to things that should and should not be done. Consequently, this law does not apply to anyone who is incapable of performing something that God has prescribed. In truth, God has imposed *(mâ kallafa)* "*upon a soul only what it can do*" (Q. 2:233, 286; 6:152; 7:42; 23:62) "*and according to what has been given to it; God brings about ease* (yusr) *after difficulty* ('usr)" (Q. 65:7).

A moment *(waqt)*—short or long—is assigned to each act, and it is not permissible to perform it other than during the time that was assigned to it, no sooner and no later; such are the limits prescribed by God, and they should not be transgressed.

The effort of personal interpretation *(ijtihâd)*

Personal interpretation always has the same legal status, whether it pertains to interpreting fundamental principles *(al-usûl)* or to how these principles are applied *(al-furû')*.[43] The moment God gave man the right to use personal interpretation in practical matters—He did so for the benefit of the *mujtahid*, and He only states what is true—all effort in personal interpretation [in both domains: *usûl* and *furû*] was founded in law.

The *mujtahid* who does not succeed in discovering what has been prescribed by God or His Messenger in regard to a given question commits an involuntary error *(al-khatâ')* [according to a hadith] and he will consequently receive only one reward. God nevertheless makes the answer that his personal effort *(ijtihâd)* has led him to lawful. [He is consequently rewarded] even though his answer does not, in the eyes of God, conform to the Truth, since God has made the answer lawful for the *mujtahid*. Now God affirms nothing that is false *(bâtil)*. If the *mujtahid* later learns of a prescription from God or His Messenger on this issue—with information different from what he was originally thinking—and if he also learns that this prescription came chronologically later than the one upon which he based his reasoning *(dalîl)*, he must give up his earlier position, and it would be illicit to hold to it.

This is why Mâlik b. Anas was showing knowledge, faith, and great scrupulousness when questioned about a problem of a religious nature; he asked: "Is the case [about which you are enquiring] asked concretely?" If the answer was affirmative, he offered his opinion; but if the reply was that this case had not really come up [and that it was, thus, purely theoretical] he did not answer (...).[44] It is because of this that scholars have said that [in a way] any *mujtahid* gives a just reply since either his answer coincides exactly with God's decision on the issue, or at least it coincides with God's decision regarding the person who has not found the correct answer and has thus involuntarily erred. The above entails the basic principles of canon law to the extent a book of this sort allows, as a complete study is not possible here [...].

SATAN'S RUSES
CHAPTER 318

Set in the fourth of the Futûhât's six sections—the section devoted to the "spiritual abodes" (al-manâzil)—this chapter begins by returning to a previously-encountered theme: when they prefer their personal opinion or the opinion of the founder of their school to the only truly decisive proofs—the Qur'ân and the hadith—the fuqahâ' are the toys and tools of Satan. The particular climate of Andalusian conformist Mâlikism during the time of Ibn 'Arabî's youth probably explains some of the rigor of this condemnation. But we shall see that the eastern fuqahâ' were not spared to any greater extent.

In the early pages of chapter 88, the author laconically mentioned the "light" the Qur'ân promises the God-fearing. He is more explicit here, with specific details regarding the forms that divine assistance can take in illuminating the men of the Path and sending them just solutions without their needing recourse to erudite research or speculation. Ibn 'Arabî speaks from experience, and says so. Several pages in the Shaykh's work are devoted to the inspiration (ilhâm) God grants to His saints[45], but in this passage we find phenomenological details not encountered elsewhere that shed considerable light on the central role the Law plays in Ibn 'Arabî's esotericism.

As was the case in the preceding chapter, this chapter highlights the inexhaustibility of Divine Mercy by offering a subtle analysis of pardon (maghfira).

Abrogation of the Law
by the desires of the soul[46]

(...) Know, my close friend, that, regarding this issue, it was reported to us by 'Abd Allâh b. 'Abbâs that a man who had slandered him came to request that the act be rendered licit. "O Ibn 'Abbâs," he said, "I have slandered you; make it licit for me." Ibn 'Abbâs replied: "May God keep me from making licit that which He has forbidden! In truth, God has forbidden attacking the honor *(a'râd)*[47] of Muslims. I will thus not make it licit. May God forgive you, however." Note how admirable such a course of action is, and how thorough his knowledge is! In a similar line, there is an oath by which one commits to do, or not to do, something licit[48]: God has thus made fulfilling oaths *(tahillat al-aymân)* obligatory. All this is part of progressive changes of degree *(al-istidrâj)* and the divine ruse *(al-makr al-ilâhi)* from which only the individual God has preserved by calling his attention to the danger is preserved.[49] There is no Lawgiver other than God—may He be exalted! God told His Prophet: "*[We revealed the Book with Truth to you] so that you might judge among men according to what God has you see*" (Q. 4:105). He did not say: "according to what you see." Moreover, He reprimanded the Prophet when he declared [Mary the Copt] to be illicit for him because of the oath he took during the time of the dispute with 'Ayshâ and Hafsa, asking him: "*O Prophet, why do you declare illicit what God has made licit, simply to give satisfaction to your wives?*" (Q. 66:1) This is part of what his own soul showed the Prophet.

So here is an indication that the divine words "according to what God has you see" really mean "what He inspires [in the Prophet]" and not "what he sees by himself." But if, in matters pertaining to religion, we took personal opinion *(ra'y)* into account, the opinion of the Prophet would be superior to that of anyone else. If such were the case for the Prophet, however, in regard to what his soul showed him, what would happen to the person who, not being infallible *(laysa bi ma'sûm)*, has a better chance of erring than of being correct?

This also shows that the *ijtihâd* God's Messenger speaks of consists solely in seeking proof *(dalîl)* in order to determine the legal status applicable to a question that is asked. It does not consist in legislating on the question, since that is not authorized by God.

The White Road

The qadi 'Abd al-Wahhâb al-Azdî al-Iskandarî[50] told me the following in Mecca, in 599: "While sleeping, I saw one of the pious ones shortly after his death, and asked him 'What did you see?' He then told me certain things, one of which was: 'I saw books that were lowered *(mawdû'a)*, and others that were elevated *(marfû'a)*.' I asked: 'But what were these elevated books?' 'They were books of hadith,' he replied. 'And the books that were lowered?' I inquired. And his reply was: 'They were books explaining personal opinions *(al-ra'y)*, and their authors will have to answer for them.'" This is how I realized that the issue was a serious one.

Know—and may God assist you—that the *sharî'a* is the white road *(al-mahajja al-baydâ')*, the road of the blessed and the way of beatitude *(tarîq al-sa'âda)*. He who follows this road is saved, and he who abandons it is lost.

When the verse "*Such is my way, in its rectitude*" (Q. 6:153) was revealed, God's Messenger drew a line on the ground, and then made a number of marks to the left and the right of the line. Then, placing a finger on the line, he began to recite: "*Such is My way, in its rectitude! Follow it, do not follow the tracks* (al-subul) " and then he showed the marks he had made on either side of the line—"*for they will make you stray from His way*" (Q. *ibid*)—and he pointed to the straight Path.[51]

In Sale, a city on the Atlantic shore of the Maghreb, where they say the earth stops and there is no land any farther out, one of the pious ones from among the common people told me: "I saw in my sleep a white, very flat road with a uniform light shining on it. To the right and left of this road I saw ditches, paths, and ravines with brambles growing all over of them. It was not possible to walk there because of how narrow they were, because of the difficulty of the terrain, and because of how many thorns there were, in addition to how dark it was. I saw everyone taking those paths in the darkness of the night, leaving the flat white road. God's messenger was walking on this road, accompanied by a small group of others. He was looking at the people behind him. In the group, toward the back, was shaykh Abû Ishâq Ibrahîm b. Qarqûl,[52] a *muhaddîth*, and an eminent master in the domain, whose son I have met. Hearing the Prophet say: "Call to the men that they might return to the good road," Ibn Qarqûl called out, but without reply: "Come back to the good road, come back!" None responded, and none returned to the good road.

Satan's ruses

Know that when the passions dominate the soul and the wise seek honor among sovereigns, they leave the "white road" and stray toward lenient[53] interpretations *(ta'wîlât)* in order to satisfy the desires that passion inspires in kings, who end up getting satisfaction by backing their actions with legal grounds. And even if the *faqîh* (jurist) does not himself believe in the well-foundedness of his decision, he pronounces a *fatwa* in this sense.

We have seen a great number of these people—both *qâdî* and *fuqahâ'*—act in such a way.

King Al-Zâhir Ghâzi,[54] son of king Al-Nâsir Salâh al-Dîn Yûsuf b. Ayyûb related a case to me in a discussion we had on this subject. He called a slave and said: "Bring me the wallet *(haramdân)*." I asked "What is in the wallet?" He answered "Do you disapprove of the blameworthy things and injustices that take place in my city and in my kingdom? By God, I am, like you, convinced that all this is blameworthy! However, Master, there is not a single blameworthy thing that is not the result of a decision handed down by a jurist *(faqîh)* and written by his very hand, which I have in my possession, authorizing it. May God's damnation be upon them! So one jurist—and he named the jurist most famous in his land for his faith and ascetic life—handed down a *fatwa* according to which it is not prescribed for me to fast during the month of Ramadân specifically, only to fast for some month during the year; it was up to me to chose the month of the year I wanted." And then the Sultan said: "In my heart I denounced him severely, but I did not let him know, because he was So-and-So," and he named him.

Know that God gave Satan power over the imagination. When Satan observes in a *faqîh* an inclination toward some passion that God condemns, he suggests an unusual interpretation that allows him to see a bad action as good and makes the discovery of an accommodating solution much easier. It was Satan who said: "The men of the first generation [that of the Prophet's Companions] absolved themselves of their religious duties by using their personal judgment *(ra'y)*; the scholars used reasoning by analogy in the matter of legal statutes. They clarified causes *(al-'ilal)*[55] and made statutes on issues about which the Law says nothing, as they also did on things about which the Law is explicit, basing their opinions on the fact that these things have a single, same cause *(li l-'illa al-jâmi'a baynahumâ)*. But they established the cause via personal deduction."

Once Satan has paved the way for him, he works to get what his passion dictates in any way he can consider legal, and he continues to do so until he owns or has subjugated every object of his desire. He rejects the Prophet's hadith, saying: "If this hadith were authentic..."—or, when the hadith is clearly authentic: "If there were not another hadith that contradicted or abrogated this one—Imâm al-Shâfi'î would have kept this solution [but since he did not do so, there is no reason to take the authentic hadith into account]." This is the way it is if the man is a Shâfi'ite. If he is a Hanafite, he will say: "Abû Hanîfa would have kept this solution." And so on and so forth, for the disciples of the imams. They claim that the hadith and its use are a source of error, and that what is imperative is blindly following the imams' opinions and their example in the judgments they hand down.

When these judgments happen to contradict traditions of prophetic origin *(al-akhbâr al-nabawiyya)*, they follow the former and leave the *akhbâr*, the Book, and the Sunna aside. And when I tell them that Shâfi'î declared: "If it happens that a hadith is in contradiction to my words, hurl my words against the wall and choose the hadith, because my teachings *(madhhabî)* are the hadith!"; or, that Abû Hanîfa stated to his companions: "It is formally forbidden for anyone who utters a *fatwa* based on my sayings to do so without knowing what I used as proof *(dalîl)*." Now I am not reporting anything coming from Abû Hanîfa that has not come to me via Hanafite channels, and nothing about Shâfi'î that has not come to me via Shâfi'ite channels, and likewise as far as the Mâlikites and the Hanbalites are concerned; so when I manage to back the jurists up against the wall during the course of a debate, they give in without a word. This has happened with them on a number of occasions, in both the West and the East. In truth, not a single one of them really belongs to the *madhhab* with which he claims affiliation! Sacred Law has been abrogated by the passions—and this, despite the fact that the *akhbâr* reported in the authentic books (the *Sahîh* by Bukhârî and Muslim), the biographies [of the transmitters where the information is found] concerning their approval *(ta'dîl)* or their disapproval *(tajrîh)*, and the collections of *isnâd* have been preserved and protected from alterations and interpolations!

But when one ceases using these *akhbâr*, and when men are concerned about *ra'y* and submit to their predecessors' *fatwa*, even if they contradict the authentic *akhbâr*, then there is no longer any difference between the inexistence and the existence of these *akhbâr*, since they no longer have any kind of authority in their eyes. What greater abrogation can there be than this? And if you happen to disagree with one of these scholars, he will reply that such is the way it is in his school *(madhhab)*. By God, what a liar! The founder of that *madhhab* told him: "When the *khabar* contradicts my own words, adopt the hadith and throw my opinions into the latrines. In truth, my school is the hadith." If this individual were truly acting with equity, belonging to Shâfi'î's school would, for him, consist in abandoning Shâfi'î's words in favor of the hadith whenever the former contradict the latter. May God assist them all!

The epiphanies of the Sacred Law

Now that I have clarified my thoughts, learn that when a man is free of all desire, when he despises his individual nature and gives preference to his Lord, God *(al-Haqq)* replaces the form *(sûra)* of his individual nature with a form of divine guidance—truth proceeding from a Truth *(haqqan min 'indi haqqin)*—to the point where he steps forward clothed in light; and this form is the Law *(al-sharî'a)* of His Prophet, the message of His Messenger. Where his true happiness lies is thus inspired within him by His Lord.

Among [the spiritual] men [who enjoy this charism] there are some who see this image as looking like the Prophet, and others who see it in the guise of their own state. If the Law shows itself to one being in the guise of the Prophet, all he needs to do to understand it is accept what the image teaches him. In fact, the devil never appears as a prophet. This image is thus very much the true image of the prophet and his spirit, or the image of an angel *(malak)* that has taken on his form and has obtained his knowledge of the Law from God Himself.

From an image like this I have personally learned a number of things relating to legal statutes that I had not learned from either scholars or books. When I spoke of what this image communicated to me regarding legal statutes with certain scholars in my country—specialists in both hadith and the different legal schools *(madhhab)*—they informed me that what I was telling them had been reported as such by the Prophet in the *Sahîh*, and that not a letter was missing. [...]

Now, if the image appears to someone in a form other than that of the Prophet, it is undoubtedly an expression either of the person's own state *(hâl)* or of the state of the Religious Law at that particular time and place, as is the case when one sees it in a dream. The only difference lies in the fact that the man in question had the vision while awake *(yaqza)*, while most people perceive it only while asleep. This man should not accept anything that pertains to legal statutes from the image when it manifests itself in such a manner. On the other hand, if the issue does not pertain to the licit *(tahlîl)* or illicit *(tahrîm)* nature of things, there is nothing wrong with his accepting the sciences or secrets it might offer, even in matters of creed *('aqâ'id)*: for the Divine Presence accepts all creeds, with the exception of polytheism *(shirk)*.[56] Indeed, [what the polytheist associates with God] is pure nothingness *('adam mahd)* and Absolute Being does not accept nothingness. [...]

The Law and Mercy

[...] God created the will in the soul so that it might want what God wants it to do or not to do without transgressing the limits set by the Lawgiver.

The principle here is the principle we have already established. The will occasionally happens to experience an intense desire for something with no thought to the legal rules concerning performing or abstaining from the act in question, to the point that, even if the legal prescription and the action performed happen to coincide, being faithful to the Law is not the first priority. This is just a case of a fortuitous coincidence with what the Lawgiver commanded. Such an individual performs the action in question because he wishes to, not because a rule has been decreed by the Lawgiver. So God will not praise this individual unless he asked himself, prior to satisfying his desire, if it was praiseworthy in the eyes of the Law, and if he performed the action only after a *mufti*'s response was that the Lawgiver judged that in this matter there was permission *(ibâha)*, recommendation *(nadb)*, or obligation *(wujûb)*, and only then did he act. At this point, it is a legal judgment that coincides with personal desire, and the interested party will be rewarded for submitting to it, in contrast to the first case, where passion and desire coincide equally with what is praiseworthy according to the Law and in view of coming closer to God: he who acts thus is doomed to perdition.

My friend, consider your soul's desires, and see what their status is in regard to the Law. If the Law prescribes that you act on them, then act on them. If, on the other hand, it prescribes that you do nothing of the sort, then refrain. If, however, after asking yourself and observing that, from a legal perspective, you should abstain, your desire gets the better of you and you transgress, I am convinced that on this point you are in the wrong, but that you will nevertheless be rewarded for a variety of reasons: because you asked yourself about the legal status of the issue before taking action; because your belief in the Law was sufficiently strong that you wondered about its stance on the issue; because you were convinced, after knowing that the action was forbidden, that it should be rejected; because you based your stance on the fact that Allâh is Forgiving *(Ghafûr)* and All-Merciful *(Rahîm)*, that He wipes away sins and forgives offenses, and that you thus had, in this case, a good opinion of God[57]; because it was not your intention to transgress against divine interdictions; and finally, because you were convinced before the fact about what predestination *(al-qadâ')* and the divine decree *(al-qadar)* had set out for you in regard to the performance of this matter, as was the case in the story of Moses and Adam.[58] These are the many reasons why you will be rewarded, in spite of your disobedience *(ma'siyya)*, since you are guilty from only one point of view: that of committing an act that was only a desire of the soul. To these reasons is added the fact that the act afflicted you, since, as the Messenger said to God: "The believer is he whose good actions give him joy and whose bad actions afflict him!"[59]

The Veil and Forgiveness

And out of all this God has made a way for the believer to push away Satan, who embellishes in man's eyes the villainy of his acts. In truth, Satan pushes us toward turpitude *(fahshâ')* (cf. Q. 2:169, 268; 24:21) while God promises forgiveness *(maghfira)* (cf. Q. 2:268; 5:9; 24:26; 48:29), that is [in line with the etymological sense of *maghfira*] the veil *(sitr)* that He places between the rebellious believer and the infidelity *(kufr)* that comes upon him at the moment he commits an act of disobedience,[60] so that he firmly believes that the act is an act of disobedience and he does not profess the licitness of what God has forbidden. This all takes place through the blessings of this veil.

But there is another *maghfira*, such that the one about which we were just speaking is a veil behind two other veils: one is the veil that covers the believer in this world, and thanks to which he does not go beyond the limits that God instituted concerning the sin he is tempted to commit; the other is the veil that will cover him in the life hereafter and keep him from being punished for his transgression.

The first of these two other veils [in contrast to the second] works instantaneously. God said: "*And God promises you a forgiveness* (maghfira) *coming from Him, and grace* (fadl)" (Q. 2:268). The "forgiveness" or the "veil" corresponds to the command Satan gives to engage in turpitude; the "grace" corresponds to the poverty *(faqr)* Satan promises in the verse ("Satan promises you poverty [if you show generosity toward others] and pushes you to turpitude"). God places the believer under shelter in the sense that He takes his place, and rejects what Satan wants him to do. Thus, God pushes a satanic promise away from His believing servant with a divine promise. No one can resist Him and no one can be victorious over Him! Forgiveness is certain, grace is certain, and the rout of Satan is clear! It is because of this Essential Reality *(haqîqa)* that Allâh has commanded us to make Him guarantor *(wakîl)* in our affairs.

Thus the Truth *(al-Haqq)* Himself has taken responsibility for preventing any harm to the believer in these matters. Satan's goal is not sin itself. His actual goal is getting the servant accustomed to his power. He tempts him until he can order him to attribute associates to God, so that he can lead him to eternal unhappiness. This can only take place when the protective veil *(al-sitr al-i'tisâmî)* that is placed between the servant and infidelity is raised. "*And God speaks the truth and leads to the way!*" (Q. 33:4).

THE SECRETS OF FORGIVENESS
CHAPTER 344

The existence of a law concomitantly implies the existence of positive and negative sanctions. But are the two balanced? For Ibn 'Arabî, if the happiness promised to the chosen ones is eternal, such is not the case for punishment: the predominant themes in this chapter—which complements the chapter that precedes it and, like it, belongs in the section on the manâzil*—are forgiveness, intercession, and, more generally, infinite divine Mercy. But this outline also gives him the opportunity to elaborate on another aspect of his teaching (an aspect about which there is additional information in the presentation and notes that accompany James Morris's translation of chapter 367 in the companion to the present volume): there is no path superior to Revealed Law. The* sharî'a *is not a shell that needs to be cracked open in order to find* haqîqa*: "Revealed Law," he writes elsewhere, "is identical to essential reality." "It is identical on the inside to what it is on the outside."*[61] *It is the Way. It is also the end and the goal of the Way. In the absence of submission to the Law, the ascetic disciplines, the domination of the passions, and the methodical exercise of the powers of the intellect can still certainly lead to knowledge at a high level. But the highest knowledge—that of the Divine Principle in both its transcendence and its immanence, simultaneously—is unattainable.*

The density and scope of this chapter prevents us from offering anything but short excerpts from it. These excerpts will, however, be complemented by explanations of the most important of the passages that are not translated.

The Two Mercies

[...] We have already shown that there are two Mercies belonging to God: a universal mercy *(rahma 'âmma)* and a specific mercy *(rahma khâssa)*; likewise, we know that He blessed [Muhammad's] community with a specific mercy. God's Messenger said: "*In truth, my community is enveloped in Divine Mercy: no punishment will come to it in the Life Hereafter* (al-âkhira), *for its punishment will have taken place in its life on earth* (al-dunyâ) *in the form of earthquakes, mortal combat, and trials.*"[62]

[...] Just as it is reported in an authentic hadith that God's Messenger said: "*The men of fire* (ahl al-nâr) *who are doomed to live there definitively will truly be neither dead nor alive. But there will also be men [for whom, in contrast to the former, the stay in hell will only be temporary and] whom the fire will reach because of their sins.*"[63] He did not specify to which community these men belonged, nor, in this case, did he say: "Men of my community." Now, this is a universal mercy for those who are among the men of fire. In fact, the Prophet added: "*And God will strike them dead* [literally, "*will put them to death with a slaying*"], *reinforcing the meaning of the verb by adding a noun of action* (masdar)—*all of which will happen before the "putting to death of death"* (dhabh al-mawt).[64] Now if God has them die, it is so that they will not feel the flames biting at them.[65]

The Hierarchy of Intercessions

Perfect souls are souls that affirm the Oneness of God, and believe *(al-nufûs al-muwahhida al-mu'mina)*. Now affirmation of God's Oneness *(al-tawhîd)* and faith *(al-imân)* keep pain and punishment *('adhâb)* from afflicting the soul. When I speak of the senses—I am referring here to physical bodies *(al-jusûm)*—they are all obedient to God and do not feel the pains of flames *(ihrâq)* that reduce them to ashes: the dead man does not feel what is being to done to him, even if he is aware of it. God has removed punishment from those who proclaim Divine Oneness, and who believe. And even if they enter the fire, God only has this take place so that His Word is fulfilled, and so that the difference is established between those who have committed evil acts *(al-sayyi'ât)* and those who have performed good acts *(al-sâlihât)*. This is an authentic hadith that applies to men as a whole [and not to a certain defined community]. Punishment is reserved for the people of the fire properly speaking [that is, those who are condemned to remain there for eternity], and it, itself, will last until a certain point in time *(ajal musamma)*[66] set by God, meaning until the point in time when the nineteen angels of punishment *(malâ'ikat al-'adhâb)*[67] intercede for them. This happens because, when the angels as a whole intercede [with God], these nineteen do not do so. Their intercession will come last, at the moment that Mercy becomes their attribute, meaning at the moment they observe divine anger: for they always give God preference over His creatures.[68]

[In order to clarify the preceding, Ibn 'Arabî then reminds his reader of the different phases of the intervention process that will gradually extend the benefit of Divine Mercy to all beings: first, to the believers, then to those who, without believing in the revealed messages, have used their intellects to lead them to the certitude of Divine Oneness, and finally to the damned themselves.]

In effect, the angels will intercede on the Day of Resurrection. It was God who said: "*The angels, the prophets* (nabiyyûn) *and the believers* (mu'minûn) *have interceded, but the intercession of the Most Merciful of the merciful* (Arham al-râhimîn)[69] *still remains,*" who will intercede both with the Terrible Punisher *(Shadîd al-'iqâb)* (Q. 2:196, 211; 3:11; 5:2, 95; 8:13, 25, 48, 52, etc.) and with the Avenger *(al-Muntaqim*—cf. *Dhû intiqâm,* Q. 5:95; 14:48; 39:37, etc.). All this refers to the intercessional powers of the Divine Names *(shafâ'at al-asmâ' al-ilâhiyya).*

At this point whoever has become convinced of Divine Oneness by an act of reason and not by an act of faith will emerge from the fire, even if he has nothing other working in his favor other than a conviction that did not come from faith. God reserved this [power] for Himself for that very reason.[70] Men in this category have borne witness, with God and the angels, that "*there is no God but Him*" (Q. 3:18) and that by virtue of their bearing witness, God's Grace will be given to them. They are known only by God and the angels; but the angels, even if they know them, are, like both men and the jinn *(al-thaqalayn),* under divine authority: they are submissive to God and prefer Him to these men; they can thus not intercede in favor of beings who have violated divine prescriptions and refused to believe. God alone, to the exclusion of all His creatures, has them emerge from the fire in His capacity as "*most Merciful of the merciful*" (Q. 1:1; 12:64, 92; 21:83). Then the only ones left in Gehenna, in an unchanged state, will be those who are condemned to remain there for eternity. This will be the case until such time as God [after manifesting Himself in His aspect of Anger] manifests Himself in a theophany of Satisfaction *(ridâ)*, where Mercy, which is composite in the world of composition *('âlam al-tarkîb)*, [where it is never present in a pure state], will alone have authority over all things, and where even the Angels of punishment will take their turn at intercession: then the state of the People of Fire will be changed, as we have already noted. [...][71]

[The traditional list of Divine Names has an apparent symmetry: attributes of Rigor correspond to attributes of Mercy in such a way that we tend to see them as being mutually balanced. As the preceding passage just reminded us, with its numerous scriptural references to the Qur'ân and the hadith, it is Mercy that will ultimately emerge triumphant. Ibn 'Arabî is thus led to declare that it is metaphysically necessary for one of the trays on the Divine Scale to win out over the other. If such were not the case, no potential would prevail over its opposite, and Universal Existence would never have come about: "Nothing comes into existence (takwîn) without inclination (mayl) [...][72] and God gave existence to the universe only by having one possibility prevail (tarjîh) over another."[73] "If we say that," he adds, "we do so in order to refute what some individuals maintain, trying to base their opinions on a spiritual unveiling (kashf) and claiming that the divine scale excludes His Justice coming out victorious over His Grace, or His Grace coming out ahead of His Justice."[74] Such an error can only be committed by beings whose spiritual training was not guided by a teacher. This latter remark introduces a series of comments on the two paths to Knowledge—the Prophetic Way, which is based on the Law, and the Speculative Way—and their hierarchical relationship, the most striking illustration of which is found in chapter 167 in the Futûhât, where Ibn 'Arabî describes the unequal "ascension" (mi'râj) between these two kinds of men.[75]]

God has not actually instituted any other way of access to His Knowledge—which the intellect, from the point of view of its speculative function, is incapable of obtaining autonomically—than the Law He promulgated through the words of His Messengers and His Prophets. I am saying this because I was saying that another way does exist (...).[76]

[This second way—whose characteristics immediately suggest a path similar to Hayy b. Yaqzân's allegorical itinerary, as it had been described a half

century earlier by another Andalusian, Ibn Tufayl—can be reached by certain privileged souls (fâdila) *through ascetic practices and the renunciation of human passions. Ibn 'Arabî explains that these souls then realize that there is something else behind the physical body that guides it. As they observe the limbs of a cadaver, they realize that the body is no longer in possession of its previous faculties, and they wonder about their own relationship to their bodies. They then note that there are differences between death and sleep: what we see in dreams does not happen to the physical body, as the body is not changed by the images we see, be they pleasant or unpleasant. The soul is thus convinced that there is a different reality beyond the body, and that there is a connection between this reality and the forms that are seen in dreams. This way leads to a station* (maqâm) *in which the soul clothes itself in Perfect Characters* (makârim al-akhlâq). *When this soul is purified by the practice of retreats* (khalwa) *and becomes transparent, like a mirror, the images of the world can then be written upon it: it sees what it did not see before, it speaks of things that are hidden* (al-ghuyûb), *and it reaches the Supreme Pleroma* (al-malâ' al-a'lâ) *in a surprising way.]*

(...) From angelic spirits, it draws knowledge that it did not earlier possess. Nevertheless, it does not know that another way exists, a way that, when followed, allows us to draw directly on God, from Whom all things come, and between Him and it there is a specific door especially for it (...).⁷⁷ He who follows the way of the Sacred Law adopts what the Lawgiver says when He informs him that there is no analogy between God and the world, and that "*nothing is similar to Him*" (Q. 42:11), that nothing in the world—from the highest summits to the depths of the earth—resembles Him, and that despite this He mentions [in the Qur'ân] His hand, or His hands, His eye, or His eyes, that He uses expressions like "*descend*" and "*sit down*" and "*rejoice*" and "*be with His servants (...).*"⁷⁸ If the speculative way can lead to divine knowledge, only the Prophetic Way allows God to be known in both His transcendence and His immanence.

This being knows that God is the "*culmination*" (al-muntahâ, Q. 53:42). "When he begins his journey on the path of the Law, what is written on the well guarded Tablet *(al-lawh al-mahfûz)* is inscribed upon him: he then sees the degree of each of the revealed laws, he sees himself and his destiny, his lot and his ultimate goal in the world. He thus acts in accord with what he has seen, and rises up seeking the face that is appropriate for him *(al-wajh al-khâss bihi)*. It is from God Himself *(al-Haqq)* that he draws [his knowledge], through inspiration *(ilhâm)* and theophanies [...].⁷⁹ He sees existence being propagated *(sarayân al-wujûd)* in created things. He knows who truly has authority over that which is apparent, and who the Apparent One *(al-Zâhir)*—in whom statutes *(ahkâm)* and spiritual and natural differences show themselves—is. And when these two beings [the one that followed the speculative way, and the one that followed the Prophetic Way] speak, perfect spiritual men perceive the difference between them, they know where the knowledge of each comes from, and why the degree of the traveller along the speculative way *(al-sâlik bi-fikrihi)* is inferior to that of the man who subjected himself to the Law.[80]

[*The superiority of the latter is then highlighted: while the man of the speculative path keeps his head bowed, attentive to the spiritual influx* (al-imdâd al-rûhânî) *he receives from the celestial spheres, the man of the Prophetic Path also bows his head, but this is because he is subdued by the unfurling of theophanies:* "He sees naught but God in all things, he speaks naught but through Him, he looks only at Him, and is unaware of anything other than Him."[81] *The Supreme Pleroma, the angelic spirits, the spheres and the stars would like to entrust him with the knowledge of which they have been the repositories, but he is in the company of his Lord and has no regard for them. It is only when God returns him to himself that he discovers the presence, in his own essence, of this knowledge that the higher and lower worlds have transmitted to him without his either knowing or wanting it (while the way of the intellect does not allow such knowledge to be obtained except through effort that distracts man from the contemplation of God). He wonders about the origins of the spiritual degrees* (darajât) *that have been conferred upon him. God then makes Himself manifest to him through the Divine Name "He Who confers degrees"* (Râfi' al-darajât, Q. 20:15) *and this theophany shows him that He grants them to those of His servants whom He wishes, and that He Himself is one of them. This knowledge allows him to address any man as a function of the degree that the man holds relative to his own: all the while observing the conventions that relate to God—and thus adequately expressing his own belief* (i'tiqâd)—*he rejects nothing that others affirm and* "clothes himself with all forms existing in this world": *just as God never epiphanizes Himself in the same way to two different beings, the man who has reached this station* (maqâm) *does not manifest himself in the same form to two individuals. If, because of this, some accuse him of infidelity or heresy, it is because of ignorance* (jahl) *or desire* (hasad). *After a passage in which, among other things, he harshly criticizes the philosopher Al-Fârâbî, Ibn 'Arabî returns to the ideas of "degree" and "pardon."*

Know also that God, in the sense that He distinguishes Himself from His creation, is an isthmus *(barzakh)* between the degrees of paradise *(darajât)* and the degrees of hell *(darakât)*. Indeed, He has described Himself as having two hands (Cor. 5:64). Now what is between the two hands is an isthmus relative to them.

To His right are the degrees of Paradise for those who are to reside in Paradise, and to His left are the degrees of Hell for those who will reside there. For Him, high and low (Heaven and Hell) are one and the same thing, for He is with His servants wherever they may be (a reference to Q. 57:4), in the higher degrees and in the lower degrees, in the fashion that is appropriate for His Majesty.

One of these degrees is the degree of pardon *(al-maghfira)*, which is, itself, subdivided into two other degrees: one being the veil that keeps sinners from the punishment that their sin calls for, and the other, the veil of impeccability *('isma)* that saves them from the very occurrence of sin.[82] It is said, regarding the former: "And save them from the punishment of Gehenna" (Q. 40:7) and regarding the latter: "And save them from evil deeds" (Q. 40:9). The former comes from Divine Generosity... The latter is a grace and a specific privilege.[83] [...]

[The most serious kind of disobedience to which the creature is exposed is ignorance, which makes the heart perish: in the human being, the heart is the place God has reserved as an abode for Himself.[84] *"Guarding the heart, and invigorating it through spiritual sciences, together constitute one characteristic of those who have followed the Prophetic path. But the most perfect of these individuals do not stop there, since they know—in accord with one of the most famous* hadîth qudsî, *and one of the most frequently cited by Ibn 'Arabî—that God does not reside solely in the heart. He is* 'the hearing, the sight, the hand of His servant' *and guarding the heart* (murâqabat al-qalb) *is thus not sufficient. It is thus in their whole being, and more generally, in every thing, that they perceive the presence of their Lord." Ibn 'Arabî concludes by saying "The choice of which of these two categories you wish to belong to is yours!" As he does at the end of all the chapters in this section of the* Futûhât *devoted to the "spiritual mansions"* (manâzil), *the Shaykh al-Akbar concludes by listing the kinds of knowledge that are the prerogative of him who reaches the* manzil *he just described. We might point out, by way of example from this list, the "knowledge of the sequence of veils" that separate God from His creatures, sometimes in order to keep them from seeing Him, and sometimes in His Mercy, in order to keep them from being burned up by the flaming Glories of*

His Face (al-subuhât al-wajhiyya)[85]; *knowledge of the "composition"* (tarkîb) *of the Divine Word, even though it is One in its essence; knowledge of the degrees of the angels; knowledge of the abode that is specific to the just imam, and of his spiritual degree; knowledge that explains why God shows Himself in some of His Names and not in others, like the Name* Allâh *or the Name* Al-Ahad, *"the One"; knowledge of what is called "the Hour" [of Judgment]; knowledge of the constitution of the human being and of what happens to his bodily elements after his death; knowledge of predestination, and of the divine decree...]*

THE GNOSTIC AND THE LAW[1]
CHAPTER 437

This chapter, which is from the fifth section of the Futûhât, *the* fasl al-munâzalât *(the* munâzala, *let us bear in mind, is a "midpoint encounter" between God, Who descends toward His servant, and the servant, who rises up toward Him*[86]*), defines this "meeting" in its title—one of the seventy-eight treatises in this part of the work—with the words: "He who knows what part of My Law is his knows what part of Me is his; for the degree to which you are in Me is identical to the degree I occupy in you." Observance of the* sharî'a *appears here, once again, not only as being imposed upon normal believers, but as constituting, for the spiritual elite, the necessary and effective means of reaching the highest perfection. In this regard, his ultimately calling these* 'ârifûn bi-Llâh *"the Guardians of the secret, the certain Men," is quite revealing: it is, in fact, always in these, or similar, terms that Ibn 'Arabî refers to those beings who hold the highest rank in the initiatory hierarchy, the* Malâmiyya, *or the "People of Blame," those who "are the hidden ones of this world," and the only individuals for whom "theophany is perpetual."*[87]

On Alms

God said: "*Mention me and I will mention you*" (Q. 2:152). I saw a beggar ask someone for alms, saying: "By the Face of God," or "by the reverence that you have for Him, give me something." I was in the company of a pious servant named Mudawwir, who was born in Ecija.[88] The man the beggar had addressed then opened a purse with silver pieces of various sizes in it, and began to look for the smallest of the pieces he could find. The pious servant then asked me: "Do you know what he is looking for?" "You tell me," I replied. "He is trying to find his price and value in God's eyes. Every time he takes out a large piece, his whole being replies: 'I am not worth that much to God!' The man then took the smallest piece of silver he could find out of his purse and gave it to the beggar. And yet God made Jealousy *(al-ghayra)*[89] one of His attributes, and He knows that most of His servants are ready to give their most precious belongings to satisfy the desires of their souls and to reach their goals. But most of them, when they give for God, limit themselves to offering a piece of dry bread, a coin, an article of used clothing, or other things of the kind; this is the most frequent case.

But when the Day of Resurrection comes, and God has what His servant has given out of love for Him appear without anyone seeing it, and then He has what this servant has given for someone other than Him appear, He will then say: "O My servant, are these goods not the ones which I bestowed upon you? And where is what you gave to those who asked you for alms in My name? And he will point to this insignificant, valueless object. Then God will ask: "So where is that which you have given to satisfy the whims of your soul?" And he will describe most of what the man had in his possession. God will then ask: "Are you not ashamed to appear before Me with something like this? And yet you knew that you would have to appear before me, and that I would assign you a place based on what you have done!" What shame he will have then! Then God will say: "I have pardoned you because of this beggar's request, and because of the joy that what you gave him caused. I have made your almsgiving action grow, and I have made what you gave to satisfy your passions disappear. I take your alms *(sadaqa)*, and I make them grow in your favor." God will then show the alms to witnesses, and the token contribution will have become larger than Mount Uhud.[90] On the other hand, what the man had given for someone other than God will have become *"scattered dust"* (Q. 25:23). God said: *"God has erased usury* (al-ribâ) *and made alms grow"* (Q. 2:276).

The "alms" of the gnostics

For the gnostics *(al-'ârifun bi-Llâh)*, the most modest gift is large, and the largest is immense; they give to God both the most precious and the basest of what they have in them. They belong to God in their totality, and everything that is theirs belongs to Him, since the slave and what he owns belong to his master. When they give, it is by the hand of God, and they also see the hand that receives as the hand of God. Whether they give or receive, it is with the same detachment, all the while conforming with perfect rectitude to good customs and to appropriate legal norms. Thus, they occupy the same place with God that He occupies in their hearts. "*They show themselves to be generous in their offerings made for Him*" (Q. 22:32) and honor "*the sacred institutions of God*" (Q. 22:30). And God will honor them on "the day when the witnesses stand up" under their eyes (Q. 40:51), and when "*the last*" are installed according to their rank. It will be "*the day of reciprocal deception*" *(yawm al-taghâbun,* Q. 64: title, and 9). He who committed evil will say: "May heaven deign to note that I have done good!" and he who has done good will say "May heaven deign to note that I did even more!" The gnostic will say nothing, because he will have no change in his state, which will be in the future just as it was in this world, I mean from the point of view of the contemplation *(shuhûd)* of his Lord and renunciation of all possessions *(mulk)* and any authority *(tasarruf)*. No act is thus attributable to him that he might be sorry for not having done more, or for not having done better. And the faults that he commits are decreed by God, and are only performed by Him under the effect of this decree [without appropriate willingness on his part]. He pardons them by substituting *(tadbîl)* something good that is the exact equivalent of these faults, with nothing added or taken away.

The gnostic comes back to God (or "repents toward God": *tâ'ib ilâ Llâh*) with each breath and in every act that proceeds from him, and his repentance is both the repentance that is prescribed by the Law *(tawba shar'iyya)* and the repentance the Essential Realities *(tawba haqîqiyya)* require.

The repentance prescribed by the Law is sorrow for infractions committed *(al-mukhâlafât)*. Sorrow that conforms to the Essential Realities consists in giving up any power, any strength, for the power and strength of God. The gnostic continually keeps himself between these two forms of repentance as long as he is in this world, the world of legal obligation *(dâr al-taklîf)*. Even if God lets him know that it has been said: "*Do as you wish,*

I have already forgiven you,"⁹¹ that does not lead to his departing from his state of renunciation. After he receives this information *(ta'rîf)*, however, he is no longer forced to repent, since all his acts are put back into the category of the licit *(mubâh)*, the recommended *(nabd)* or the obligatory *(fard)*, and none of them will ever return to the category of the blameworthy *(makrûh)* or the forbidden *(mahzûr)*. In effect, the Law made this status cease for him in the present world. This is reported in an authentic tradition coming from God, a tradition of general application even though it applied specifically to those who fought at Badr. However, since this tradition applied to those who fought at Badr, it is worded only hypothetically, while there is no doubt about its general applicability.⁹² For the one whom God has informed that he belongs to this group *(tâ'ifa)*, that constitutes good news *(bushrâ)* coming from Him for life on this earth. God said: "*Here is good news for those who believe and fear God, for both this life and the life to come. And the Words of Allah do not change!*" (Q. 10:63-64). Such is the case for the believer *(mu'min)* who fears God. How much greater might be the case for the pure gnostic, who has never donned a lying tunic *(mâ labisa thawb zûr)* and who has never been anything but a light in a light *(nûran fî nûr)*!

He who observes the rules of propriety prescribed by the Law and gives to nature *(tabî'a)* what God has enjoined him to give—what is deserved but nothing more—is one of the gnostics, respectful of the rules of propriety *(al-'ârifîn aludabâ')*; he is one of the Guardians of the secret, and one of the Safe Men! "*And God tells the truth and leads on the path!*" (Q. 33:4).⁹³

NOTES
TO 'THE LAW AND THE WAY'

1 Sakhâwî, *Al-qawl al-munbî*, Ms. Berlin 2849, Spr. 790.

2 *Kitâb ilâ l-Shaykh Nasr al-dîn Manbijî* in *Majmû'at al-rasâ'il*, ed. R. Ridâ, Cairo, n.d., I, p. 176. This indulgence is not shared by more recent reviewers: cf. Samî' 'Atif al-Rayn, *Al-tasawwuf fî nazar al-islâm*, Beirut, 1985, p. 454-455.

3 *Ibid.*, I, p. 171.

4 Ibn Manzûr, *Lisân al-'arab*, Beirut, n.d., VIII, p. 175-176.

5 On Ibn Hazm, see the quite valuable article by R. Arnaldez (in *EI2*, n.d.), which, among other things, constitutes a concise introduction to the ideas characteristic of the *madhhab zâhiri*.

6 It is our hope that R. Strothman's article in *EI2* will be replaced in the new edition by a more substantial piece. Goldziher's work, in its original German version (*Die Zâhiriten*, Leipzig, 1884) or its English version (*The Zâhiris*, Leiden, 1967, re-ed. 1971) is still indispensable despite the gaps in the documentation available to the author.

7 On Dâwûd b. 'Alî b. Khalaf, see, s.v., J. Schacht's article in *EI2*.

8 *Kitâb al-mubashshirât*, ms. Fâtih 5322, f. 90b. The same dream is described, albeit with less detail, in *Fut.* II, p. 519, and (according to Goldziher, *op. cit.*, p. 186 of the German version, p. 170 of the English version) in the introduction to the *Kitâb al-mu'alla*, a summary composed by Ibn 'Arabi of Ibn Hazm's *Kitâb al-muhalla*.

9 Ibn Hazm, *Kitâb ibtâl al-qiyâs*, ed. Sa'îd al-Afghânî, Beirut, 1969.

10 This work from his youth is mentioned by Ibn 'Arabî in his *Fihris* (no. 4) and in his *Ijâza* (no. 5). According to M. Sa'îd al-Afghânî (Introduction to the work cited in the preceding note, p. 17) there is a manuscript of this book in Tunis.

[11] "*The son of Adam offends Me when he damns Time, for I am Time,*" Bukhârî, *tafsîr*, sura 45. Minor variations of his hadith are found in both Muslim and Ibn Hanbal.

[12] Cf. *Fut.*, IV p. 265. On Ibn Hazm's position see Qastallânî's comment, reported by Goldziher, *op. cit.*, p. 143, n. 1.

[13] Abû Yûsûf Ya'qûb, especially, suggested that Ibn 'Arabî find husbands for his sisters (cf. the passage from the *Durra fâkhira* translated by Austin, *Sufis of Andalusia*, London, 1971, pp. 75-76).

[14] Al-Maqarrî, *Nafh al-Tîb*, ed. Dozy, Leiden, 1855-1861, I, p. 567.

[15] *Op. cit.*, p. 169.

[16] Ibn 'Arabî, *Dîwân*, Bûlâq, 1271 A. H., p. 47.

[17] Michel Chodkiewicz's communication in the Report from the colloquium "Mystique, culture et société" organized at the Sorbonne in May 1983 *(Ibn 'Arabî, la lettre et la Loi)* is one of the only texts we are able to cite. We should also mention the work in Arabic by Shaykh Mahmûd Ghurâb: *Al-fiqh 'inda l-Shaykh al-Akbar*, Damascus, 1981, an annotated anthology, which unfortunately cites no references; and a paper (unpublished), also in Arabic, titled *Al-ijtihâd kamâ yarâhu Ibn 'Arabî* presented at the Faculté des Lettres in Tunis in 1985 at the time of the colloquium on *ijtihâd*, by M. M. Mensia. To our knowledge, there is only one translation of the Shaykh al-Akbar's writings on this subject, the one by Michel Vâlsan, in chapters 263 and 263 of the *Futûhât* (which deal, respectively, with the *sharî'a* and *haqîqa*), published in the review *Études traditionnelles*, July-October, 1966, pp. 206-217.

[18] *Fut.* II, p. 270.

[19] On the idea of the descent of the Qur'ân upon the *awliyâ'*, see especially *Fut.* II, p. 506; III, pp. 94, 181; IV, p. 178.

[20] See, e.g., *Fut.* III, p. 502.

[21] M. Chodkiewicz, *op. cit.*, *Actes du colloque...*, p. 30.

[22] On the recurrence of fourfold structures, cf. *Fut.* II, p. 162; III, pp. 198-199, 201, 208, 261, 305, 406, etc.

[23] See the general introduction here.

[24] On this issue, see *EI1*, art. "Al-Kor'ân," no. 3. Some classical works devoted to this subject have been edited, or reedited, recently: Hibat Allâh b. Salâma b. Nasr al-Maqqarî, *Al-nâsikh wa l-mansûkh min kitâb Allâh*, Beirut, 1984.; Ibn al-Jawzî, *Ikhbâr ahl al-rusûkh fî l-fiqh wa l-hâdith bi miqdâr al-mansûkh min al-hadîth*, followed by Jamal al-dîn al-Badhûrî's *Qabdat al-bayân fî nâsikh wa masnûkh al-qur'ân*, Beirut, 1984. Cf. also Suyûti's expose, *Al-itqân*, Cairo, 1328, A.H., II, p. 20-27, and the Qur'anic commentaries relating to verses 2:106 and 16:101.

[25] On the idea of *badâ'*, see *EI2*, s.v. Goldziher and Tritton's article.

[26] On this point, we refer the reader to D. Gril's translations of passages from chapter 2 of the *Futûhât* in the present volume.

[27] Cf. Goldziher, *op. cit*, p. 34 and index s.v., *ijmâ' al-sahâba*. On the theories

of *ijmâ'* in Islam, see Camille Mansour, *L'autorité dans la pensée musulmane*, Paris, 1975, especially ch. III.

[28] *Fut.* III, p. 501.

[29] *Fut.* II, p. 162, l. 11-21. The titles and section headings of the texts translated hereafter are inserted by the French translator.

[30] *Sunna mutawâtira* : traditions that go back to the Prophet, reported by a number of authorities.

[31] *Fut.* II, p. 162, l. 33-35; p. 163, l. 1-17.

[32] *Fut.* II, p. 163, l. 20-27.

[33] The *'ibâdât* are dealt with in chapters 68 to 72 of the *Futûhât* (I, p. 329-762).

[34] *Fut.* II, p. 163, l. 28-35; p. 164, l. 1-4, l. 15-34; p. 165, l. 1-29.

[35] Bukhârî, *i'tisâm*, 6; Muslim, *fadâ'il, 130*.

[36] Such was the case, for example, for legal prayer, for which neither the exact number nor the specific form were set in the Qur'ân. Based on verses 2: 238, 11: 114, and 17:78, for example, a case could be made for only three or—depending on the interpretation—four daily prayers being prescribed. It was the prophetic Sunna that set their number at five and instituted the ritual.

[37] The ideas expressed in this paragraph on *khusûs* and *'umûm* (to which Dâwûd b. Khalaf, the founder of the Zâhirite school, devoted a treatise) are analogous to those outlined by Ibn Hazm in his *Kitâb al-ihkâm*. On this issue, the clearly different position of Al-Ash'arî is that any *formally* general statement should nevertheless be considered as being specific unless additional data confirm that it is meant to be general.

[38] According to Ibn 'Arabî (*Fut.* I, 193) the word *salât* is derived from the word *al-musallî*, a term which, in Islamic terminology, refers to "the one who prays," but in pre-Islamic vocabulary of horse racing it referred to the horse that ran behind the fastest of the animals (cf. *Lisân al-'arab*, XIV, p. 466b).

[39] The word *wudû'* appears to have had an original meaning of an "act intending to clean that which is dirty," which is thus not greatly different from the meaning is has in juridical language—except that in becoming a technical term it thenceforth, for the Muslim, no longer implied a place of lustration, but rather a ritual act with specific forms. The original meaning of *hajj* was simply "showing up somewhere." *Zakât* refers specifically to purification.

[40] Bukhârî, *i'tisâm*, 2; Muslim, *hajj*, 411. On the meaning of this hadith, see also *Fut.* I, p. 737; II, p. 56; III, pp. 151, 230.

[41] On the idea of the original licitness of things *(ibâha asliyya)*, see *Fut.* III, 195.

[42] Muslim, *hajj*, 310 ; Abû Dâwûd, *manâsik*, 77.

[43] It should be noted that Ibn 'Arabî, who disagrees with the *fuqahâ'* majority opinion on this issue, believes that the "door of *ijtihâd*" remains open not only in the domain of *furû'* (consequences, applications), but also in that of *usûl* (fundamental principles). This would be the position for, among others, his adversary Ibn Taymiyya (c.f. H. Laoust, *Contribution à une étude de la méthodologie canonique d'Ibn Taymiyya*, Cairo, 1939) and later, for the Sufi and traditionist Suyûtî (d.

911/1505), who would claim for himself the role of *mujtahid mutlaq* (see the excellent study of his thought in E. M. Sartain, *Jalâl al-dîn al-Suyûtî*, Cambridge, 1975, I, p. 61 s.).

44 According to Sha'rânî, *Kitâb al-mizân* (a work whose juridical thinking's indebtedness to Ibn 'Arabî Michael Winter could not sufficiently underscore in his recent work *Society and Religion in Early Ottoman Egypt*, New Brunswick, 1982), Cairo, 1279 A.H., I, p. 63, an analogous remark is attributed to Masrûq b. al-Ajdâ' (d. 63/683).

45 On *ilhâm* (and on what distinguishes it from *wahî*, "Revelation", strictly speaking, which is reserved for the prophets) see *Fut.* I, pp. 285-290; II, pp. 254, 569; III, p. 39, pp. 238-239, p. 316, etc.

46 *Fut.* III, pp. 69-71.

47 This is probably a reference to the hadith (Muslim, *birr*, 32; Abû Dâwûd, *adab*, 35, etc.) announcing that "the blood, the property, and the honor *('ird)*" of a Muslim are not licit for Muslims.

48 The case envisioned here is the diametric opposite of the preceding case, where the individual speaking with Ibn 'Abbas wanted him to call a forbidden act licit; in creating, via an oath or a vow, an obligation that was not instituted by the Law, the man was giving himself the power to make laws, which should belong solely to God. Even if this were done with pious intentions, he would be claiming a sovereignty that denies his ontological indigence. This is why Ibn 'Arabî considered Abû Su'ûd b. al-Shibl's paradoxical statement (in *Fut.* I, p. 188) so important: *Sufism is nothing more than the five prayers and the expectation of death*": supererogatory acts, which are recommended for the beginner, constitute an affirmation of autonomy that would be an error for the individual who reaches the end of the Path. If he performs them, nevertheless, he does so carrying out a specific divine order, and no longer by some individual choice that is incompatible with his state of absolute servitude *('ubûdiyya)*. On the highest degree of *walâya*, see chapter 7 in M. Chodkiewicz, *Seal of the Saints*, p. 109f.

49 On the "divine ruse" *(makr ilâhî)*, see *Fut.* II, pp. 144-145, 529-531, 605. Cf. also R. Brunschvig's article "De la fallacieuse prospérité," in *Studia islamica*, LVIII, 1982, pp. 5-31.

50 He is also mentioned in *Rûh al-quds*, Damascus, 1964, pp. 68-69, and in *Kitâb al-mubashshirât*, Fâtih 5322, f. 90b.

51 Ibn Mâja, *muqaddima*, 1.

52 This traditionist (whose edition of the *Futûhât* spells the name incorrectly as Ibn Qarqûr) was born in Almeria, and died in Fez in 569 A.H. Cf. Ibn al-Abbâr, *Takmila*, ed. Bencheneb, Algiers, 1910, no. 394.

53 It is noteworthy that the word *ta'wîl* is usually used by Ibn 'Arabî in a pejorative sense, and that using it in reference to the Shaykh al-Akbar's Qur'ânic exegesis (which is frequent in the works of H. Corbin) is questionable.

54 The individual in question is Saladin's son, who was the sovereign in Alep, where he reigned from 582 until his death in 613. He is not to be confused with

king Muzarrar Bahâal-dîn Ghâzî—the son of Al-Malik al-'Adil, to whom Ibn 'Arabî gave an *ijâza* that is a valuable source of the Shaykh al-Akbar's bibliography—who was mentioned a number of times in the *Futûhât* (III, p. 406, p. 472; IV, p 539).

55 The search for "causes" that explain an explicitly formulated legal status allows the proponent of reasoning by analogy to extend this statute to all cases relevant to the same causal mechanism: such a procedure is doubly blasphemous in Ibn Hazm's opinion (as was seen in the previous chapter, Ibn 'Arabî's position was less clear cut), since it implies, on the one hand, that the divine will obeys extrinsic causes, and, on the other, that man would be capable, if such were the case, of discovering God's motivations.

56 In passing, we might note this brief reference to Ibn 'Arabi's teaching on the universality of truth (a theme that his adversaries would choose to attack under the name of *Wahdat al-adyân*), which a famous verse in the *Futûhât* summarizes when the Shaykh al-Akbar states: "*The creatures profess a number of beliefs on the subject of God/ And I profess all that they believe*" (*Fut.* III, p. 131). On this subject, see W. Chittick's translation of Chapter 470, in volume I of this work.

57 Ibn 'Arabî is here implicitly referring to the well known *hadîth qudsî* (Ibn Hanbal, II, 391; Bukhârî. *tawhîd*, 15) where God declares: *"I conform to the idea that My servant has of Me."*

58 This sentence refers to the hadith (Bukhârî, *qadar*, 11, 12) that relates a conversation during which Moses scolds Adam for having caused the fall from Paradise, and where Adam replies: *"Are you reproaching me for something God had predestined forty years before He created me?"*

59 Tirmidhî, *fitan*, 7.

60 On the paradoxical consequences of this point of view, see, for example, the interpretation of the hadith about the believer who commits adultery (Tirmidhî, *îmân*, 11; Abû Dâwûd, *sunna*, 15) in *Fut.* III, p. 243.

61 *Fut.* II, pp. 562-563.

62 *Fut.* III, p. 175, l. 10-11. The final hadith is cited by Ibn 'Arabî from Bayhaqî's *Kitâb al-adab*. However, it is also found in Ibn Hanbal, IV, 410, 418, and Abû Dâwûd, *fitan*, 7.

63 Muslim, *îmân*, 306.

64 A reference to the hadith (Bukhârî, *tafsîr*, S. 19; Muslim, *janna*, 4, etc.) where on the Day of Judgment death will be brought in the form of a ram between paradise and hell and will be ritually sacrificed *(yudhbâh)* by Yahyâ (John). Mention is also seen of this "putting death to death" and the relationship between the name Yahyâ and his role in the translation of chapter 367.

65 *Fut.* III, p. 175, l. 17-21.

66 The expression *ajal musammâ* appears frequently in the Qur'ân, sometimes in reference to the sun and the moon (13:2, 31:29, 35:13, 39:5), sometimes to the heavens and the earth (6:2, 30:8, 46:3), sometimes to debts (2:282), and sometimes to the Last Judgment (42:14), to death (6:2, 60; 11:13; 14:10; 22:5, 33; 39:42; 40:67; 71:4) or to punishment (16:61, 20:129, 29:53; 35:45).

67 The number of angels of punishment (*zabâniyya*, Q. 96:18) is given in Q. 74:30; their king is Mâlik (Q. 43:77). The existence of these angels, who experience happiness despite the fact that they live in fire, is one of the arguments Ibn 'Arabî uses to show that the eternity spent in hell does not imply that the damned will have an eternity of punishment; as was the case with Abraham and fire, hell can become "*freshness and peace*" (Q. 21:69) for them because of the similarity of their natures (*Fut.*, II, p. 172).

68 *Fut.* III, p. 175, l. 21-27.

69 This *hadîth qudsî* appears in Muslim, *îmân*, 302.

70 Such a being, who affirms divine oneness by virtue of intellectual certitude and not of an act of faith and submission to the Law, cannot benefit from the intercession of the prophets and the angels, since intercession is reserved for believers. Only God Himself can save him from punishment.

71 *Fut.* III, p. 175, l. 27-35.

72 *Fut.* III, p. 176, l. 1.

73 *Fut.* III, p. 176, l. 2.

74 *Fut.* III, p. 176, l. 8.

75 The comparison between these two kinds of ascension is the main subject of chapter 167 in the *Futûhât*. Cf. section 8 in volume I of this work *(Ibn 'Arabî's Spiritual Ascension)* and M. Chodkiewicz, *Seal of the Saints*, ch. 10.

76 *Fut.* III, p. 176, l. 10-11.

77 *Fut.* III, p. 176, l. 33-34.

78 *Fut.* III, p. 177, l. 2-4.

79 *Fut.* III, p. 177, l. 11-13.

80 *Fut.* III, p. 177, l. 14-16.

81 *Fut.* III, p. 177, l. 18-19.

82 This privilege of impeccability, which Shi'ites extend to the Imams, is reserved for the prophets in Sunni theology. Ibn 'Arabî here gives it a wider meaning since, in the following lines, he uses the word *'isma* in reference to Suhayb, one of the Companions of the Prophet.

83 *Fut.* III, p. 178, l. 31-35; p. 179, l. 1-3.

84 A reference to the *hadîth qudsî* "*My heaven and My earth cannot contain Me, but the heart of My servant contains Me.*" This hadith, which does not appear in the canonical collections, is often cited in *tasawwuf* literature with an *isnâd* that goes back to Mahb b. Munabbih. Ibn Taymiyya himself does not reject it formally, but believes it to be a *hadîth ma'thûr*, that is, a tradition that is accepted and widely known, but not transmitted according to the rules of hadith, and thus not presenting the same guarantees. Cf. *Majmû' al-fâtâwa*, Riyâd, 1382 (37 vol.), II, p. 384.

85 This expression appears in a hadith in which "*Allah has seventy—or seventy thousand—veils of light and darkness. If He took them off, the burning Glories of His face would consume the creatures that His gaze fell upon*" (Muslim, *îmân*, 233; Ibn Hanbal, IV, 401).

86 On the definition of *Munâzala,* see *Fut.* III, pp. 155, 523, 543.

87 *Fut.* I, p. 181. On the category of *malâmiyya,* cf. M. Chodkiewicz, *Seal of the Saints,* chapter 7, especially pp. 111-113.

88 The word here is *Istija,* and not *Isbija,* as the 1329 edition erroneously indicated. Istija, today Ecija, is an Andalusian village southwest of Cordoba. The same anecdote is either reported or referred to a number of times by Ibn 'Arabî (*Fut.* I, p. 589; II, p. 27; *Kitâb al-'Abâdila,* Cairo, 1969, p. 138). The text of *Fut.* II, p. 27, identifies the Shaykh's companion as *"Al-Hajj Mudawwir Yûsuf, from Istija."* In the *K. al-'Abâdila,* the event is described as taking place in Seville.

89 "God's jealousy" is mentioned in several hadiths. Cf., for example, Muslim, *tawba,* 36, 38; Ibn Hanbal, II, 520, 536, 539.

90 A reference to a hadith from Bukhârî, *riqâq,* 14.

91 An indirect reference to the final sentences of a *hadîth qudsî* (Ibn Hanbal, II, 296, 405, 492) that appears (no. 91) in Ibn'Arabî's *Mishkât al-anwâr:* "*My servant has committed a sin. He knows that he has a Lord who pardons sin and removes it. Do as you wish. I have already forgiven you!*"

92 A hadith in which wording similar to the words that conclude the hadith above is reported in regard to the Combatants at Badr (Ibn Hanbal, II, 295; Bukhârî, *tafsîr,* S. 60). But in the version Bukhârî offers, the Prophet actually uses a form that suggests a possibility rather than a certitude: "*Perhaps* (la'alla) *God looked at the Companions at Badr and said: Do as you wish, as I have already pardoned you!*"

93 *Fut.* IV, p. 49, l. 9 to p. 50, l. 3.

THE SCIENCE OF LETTERS
Denis Gril

INTRODUCTION AND CHAPTER ANALYSIS
FOR 'THE SCIENCE OF LETTERS'

The density and the technical nature of the Futûhât's *long second chapter should have sufficed to discourage us from attempting a translation of anything more than part of it. But the deeper we got into our endeavor, the more important we realized it was to underscore its place in the* Futûhât. *The science of letters* ('ilm al-hurûf) *is one of the most synthetic, and one of the most allusive modes of expression in Islamic esotericism, because it represents the difficult transition of the inexpressible into that which can be expressed. This chapter immediately follows the chapter in which the "Young Man"* (al-Fatâ), *a personification of the Spirit, reveals to the Shaykh the "specifics of his constitution." Ibn 'Arabî explains the contents of the chapter, and then the different kinds of knowledge the* Futûhât *contains.*[1] *Can God's Knowledge be heard without the Word? the Word without words? words without letters, consonants and vowels?*

Beyond the chapter's obvious complexity, a brief overview of its different parts may help to shed light on how tightly organized it is. Most of the basic questions, and a number of the chapters of the book, were introduced earlier, via letters. There is good reason to believe that at an even deeper level, this chapter is one of the keys to the work.

Proof of this begins to be seen when bits of information concerning the science of letters—scattered throughout the Futûhât *and other treatises—are juxtaposed. It was in the science of letters that the Shaykh al-Akbar put the finishing touches on work he had begun by collecting information from a variety of sources, which he and his predecessors blended into a synthesis held together, precisely, by the letters themselves.*

The complete title of chapter 2 is: "On knowledge of the hierarchical degrees of the consonants[2] and vowels in the Universe and their counterparts among the Divine Names; and on knowledge of words and of knowledge itself, of the knower, and of the object of the knowledge" *(fî ma'rifat marâtib al-hurûf wa l-harakât min al-'âlam wa mâ lahâ min al-asmâ' al husnâ wa ma'rifat al-kalimât wa ma'rifat al-'ilm wa l-'âlim wa l-ma'lûm).*

The chapter comprises three sections (fasl) *of quite different lengths:*
  I. On knowledge of letters, of their hierarchical degrees, of the vowels or minor letters,[3] *and of the Divine Names that correspond to them (I 51-84; O.Y. I 231-361, paragraph 366-689).*
  II. On knowledge of the vowels or minor letters (al-hurûf al-sighâr) *by which words are distinguished (I 84-91; O.Y. II 51-81, paragraph 1-60).*
  III. On knowledge of the science, of the expert in it, and of the object of the science (I 91-92; O.Y. II 82-89, paragraph 61-76).

Section I, part I

The meanings carried by letters encompass absolute Existence in its totality: God and the Universe, or more specifically, He who imposes the Law and those upon whom it is imposed (mukallif-mukallafûn). *It is through the letter that both what is Written is drawn out, and the Law is fulfilled.*

Far from being original or simple entities, however, letters themselves are produced by the rotation and interaction of a specific number of celestial spheres (aflâk) *among all the spheres that move concentrically within the total, ultimate Sphere* (al-falak al-aqsâ). *Along with bringing letters into existence, the rotation of the spheres combines physical qualities (heat, cold, dryness and humidity) together in pairs. The letters are thus located on the edge*[4] *of the physical world* (tabî'a), *since, these qualities or Original Elements* (al-'anâsir al-uwal) *give birth to the physical elements (fire, air, water, and earth) when they combine. Each of the spheres from which the letters emerge, moreover, goes through a cycle that has a certain number of years, and passes through a set number of "mansions"* (manâzil), *just as the rotation of the ultimate sphere determines how long the total cycle will last. The science of letters can thus not be looked at independently of the science of the heavenly bodies or of the cosmic cycles. The more detailed outline of this question is to be found in chapter 60:* "On knowledge of the elements, of the influence of the higher world over the lower world, and of the cycle *(dawra)* in which our present world is located."[5]

From the very outset, the letters are divided into four hierarchical degrees (martaba *pl.* marâtib). These correspond to four kinds of beings: the Divine Presence that established the Law (al-hadra al-ilâhiyya al-mukallifa), Man, the Jinn, and the Angels.

The four letters that apply to the jinn refer to the four directions in space, since they are kept on the same plane of existence, with no possibility of rising or falling.

The three letters of the Divine Presence represent the three fundamental realities that allow one to apprehend the Divine: Essence, Attribute, and the Bond (râbita) between the quality and the qualified. Attributes and Names are thus the expression of the relationship (nisâb) between Absolute Being and conditioned, or contingent, being. At the same time, the three letters of this degree, Alif, Zay, Lam, form the word AZaL: eternity, in the sense of negation of anything coming earlier, that is, of any form of relationship.

This fundamental point comes up again in the three letters that correspond to the human plane. They are different from the letters for the divine plane— like servitude ('ubûdiyya) is different from lordship (rubûbiyya)—but the fact that there is the same number of letters for each is a reminder that Man was created in the image, or the form, of God, or, that he is "like Him" (ka-huwa). In both cases, the two faces of theophany—transcendence and similarity (al-tanzîh wa l-tashbîh), of which the "equivocal" (mutashâbihât) verses are the Qur'ânic expression[6]—are revealed through letters, while at the same time the undifferentiated identity of the Self is affirmed. It is, thus, eternity (qidâm) and contingency (hudûth) that make the distinction between the Principle and its manifestation, "for the sphere of Knowledge is one: eternal for the Eternal, contingent for the contingent."

Through its graphic and geometric symbolism, the letter nûn, the first of the letters specific to Man, ends up correlating highly with the transcendent relationship between the divine plane and the human plane. Nûn is a circle, but only its lower half and center appear in writing; the upper part belongs to the unmanifested. Its total realization represents the perfection of Existence. But, as figure 1 (page 148) shows, nûn also encloses the secret of divine eternity in man, since it is possible to retrace the three letters of the word AZaL from it. Through his divine form, the essential entity ('ayn) of Man exists eternally in Divine Knowledge in his state of immutability (fî hâl thubûtihi). It then becomes possible to speak of "human eternity" (al-azal al-insânî) hidden within Divine

Eternity. The symbolic richness of the letter nûn *is not limited to representing the metaphysical doctrine of immutable Essences* (al-a'yân al-thâbita), *however, nor even to that of the highest degree of spiritual realization; quite the contrary, like a guide wire, it runs through the entire chapter and beyond, into the commentary on the* Basmala *and the* Fâtiha, *in chapter 5.*[7]

The Angel receives the eighteen remaining letters as his share. This number confirms his cosmological role, as well as the role he plays as an intermediary, since divine and human presences, which are ternary, each entail the three degrees of the three worlds (mulk, malakût, *and* jabarût); each degree, in turn, has three aspects: exterior, interior, and intermediate (barzakh). The sum of the letters of the two "presences" (identical to the number of days of creation), multiplied by three brings us back to eighteen. If the three worlds are multiplied by their threefold division, the result is nine spheres: the seven heavens, the "Footstool" (al-kursî) and the Throne (al-'arsh). The cosmic ennead is then reduced to a heptad, if we take into consideration that the inner face of the outer world is identical to the outer face of the intermediate world, with the same being true of the intermediate and upper world.

From still another perspective, multiplication of the divine set of three letters by the three worlds produces the nine spheres of the projection of God's knowledge toward Man (aflâk al-ilqâ'). Similarly, multiplication of the human set of letters by the three worlds produces the nine spheres of reception (aflâk al-talaqqi). There are subtle connections (raqâ'iq) that run up and down between the two planes, and the Angel is nothing other than the place where these connections meet. By their upward, downward, and horizontal movement, moreover, the angels set the universe in motion, in the cosmic dynamic of these three directions of movement; they thus play a role like the three vowels do in the world of consonants (cf. section II).

This part, devoted to the fourfold division of the letters, concludes with a return to the question of the physical qualities or "mother principles" (al-ummahât al-uwal). Why does the mixture of hot and humid, out of which Life emanates, not emanate from a specific sphere? If such were the case, the completion of the cycle of this sphere would coincide with the stopping of all life. But life does not get extinguished. When it leaves a body the man only appears to die, but in reality he returns to his origin. The knowledge relative to this question will be addressed later, in connection with the science of letters[8] or with the posthumous future of man.[9]

Since they are not capable of blending with their opposites, the four qualities can engender only four elements. This observation is followed by others, on the number four and the four first numbers—the foundations for all others (usûl al-aʿdâd); *for example, 4+3=7, 7+2=9, 9+1=10, etc.—and on six, the first perfect number* ('adad tâmm), *which is a way to introduce the second hierarchy of letters.*

How do physical qualities that are incompatible among themselves (mutanâfira) *enter into a harmonious composition* (ta'lîf) *in the forms of elements? Their effects do not mix; the drying quality of fire is not due to heat, but to dryness. This is less a secondary question than it might seem. When we ask about the mystery of the composition of the elements, we inevitably run into the mystery of manifestation. Even though it is forbidden to reveal this secret, which in any case is beyond understanding, the Shaykh nevertheless shows the way by pointing out that there are two kinds of reality: reality that the intellect can isolate, such as physical qualities, and reality that exists only in composition. What is the connection between the two orders of reality? The answer is undoubtedly to be found in the science of letters, the receptacle of Divine Science.*

How, more specifically, does correspondence between the letters and the elements take place? Since both the primal letters and "Mother Principles" come from the same set of spheres, their physical consequences thus tend to have the same properties. The permutation of the phonemes in language (iqlâb) *and the transmutation of the elements* (istihâla) *can thus be related to one another. We might also note how the lines that form the bodies of letters play a certain role in their relationship to the elements.*

The doctrine of the fifth element allows for one additional parallel between the alif— *the beginning of all the letters, even if it is not a phoneme— and the element that is at the base of all the others. This also gives the Shaykh al-Akbar the chance to declare, forcefully, that even though the knowledge that the Initiated possess occasionally coincides with that of the philosophers, and, in this case especially, that of the "naturalists"* (ashâm ʿilm al-tabâ'î'), *it is in no way dependent upon; it relies, rather, solely on intuitive unveiling* (kashf), *which follows the emptying of the heart.*

To conclude this passage, and as if to reinforce what has just been stated, the author turns this question back toward the question of the origin of the world, the cause for which is to be found in the manifestation of the Divine Names. On this point, he refers the reader to his Inshâ' al-dawâ'ir *("The production of circles"). This will be dealt with in chapter four: "On the cause of the beginning of the world and on the correspondence between the hierarchy of Divine Names and the totality of the Universe."*[10]

It is at this point that Ibn ʿArabî reveals that the distribution of letters into four degrees, discussed up to his point, reflects only the most common point of *view, that of the* 'uqalâ'*, meaning those subjugated by their own intelligence* (tahta qahr 'uqûlihim). *The superior point of view is represented by the* muhaqqiqûn, *"those who have experienced the reality of things" and who divide the letters into six degrees or levels: God* (mukallif), *Man, the Jinn, animals, plants, and minerals.*

A certain number of simple elements or elementary spheres correspond to each degree; they are represented by the number of letters that the names of the letters specific to each degree contain. The divine degree is thus binary, or dual, since the nûn, *which in this case represents it, comprises two letters,* nûn *and* wâw, *the names for which have two letters each. The perspective that governs these remarks is that of metaphysical knowledge. In the preceding division, the* nûn *characterized Man; we can know God by beginning with ourselves. The duality foreseen here is not a duality of Principle and manifestation, but the principle of manifestation contained in the unmanifested. This principle has the dual result of the manifested and the unmanifested coming out of, and then returning to, it. In the human world, this result is translated by the institution of the* Khalîfa: *the "Lieutenant," or "Representative," who reproduces the fundamental duality of knowledge in the cosmic order.*

The next part of the passage sheds light on the knowledge of the muhaqqiqûn, *which, like the words of God, is inexhaustible. This is the realization of unity in multiplicity* (tawhîd al-kathra); *it is the contemplation of essence* (mushâhada dhâtiyya); *the way it flows, it spills out over the intimate secret, the spirit, and the soul. "How can one know the teachings (madhhab) of the individual with such a source (mashrab)?" This first part finishes with a prayer: "Praise to God Who has made us one of the beings of projection and reception (ahl al-ilqâ wa l-talaqqî). We ask Him to place us among the beings of reciprocal closeness and progressive elevation (ahl al-tadânî wa l-taraqqî.)"*[11] *These words of praise proclaim the completion of the cycle of spiritual realization through the descending and ascending, subtle and angelic paths of knowledge. The invocation avers that there is no limit to increases in knowledge as one passes through the abodes or stages of the Path* (manâzil) *to the meeting places* (munâzalât) *where the worshiper encounters the Worshiped and distinguishes himself from Him.*

In their divisions (fusûl) *and their degrees* (marâtib), *the twenty-eight letters of the alphabet—the same number as the number of "mansions"* (manâzil) *in the cycle of the moon and the Last Sphere—are in reality beyond number, since they are engendered by the uninterrupted intersection of the specific spheres. The science of letters thus looks very much like both the place and lan-*

guage that are common to metaphysics, cosmogony, and cosmology, as well as to the initiatory path. It also reveals the universality of the knowledge of those who master it.

Section I, Part II

In part I, the corresponding hierarchy for letters and beings gets set up in a process of dynamic formation. In contrast, the distribution in part II appears to be already established. Letters are presented both as a separate world that reproduces all the degrees of Being and, at the same time, as a specific community whose spiritual or initiatory hierarchy is like that of the human species. Its degrees are tied to the production of the sounds of spoken language, and follow the order of the places from which the phonemes are emitted (makhârij al-hurûf), *from the innermost part of the sound-producing organs to the outermost. Like individuals who are initiated in human communities, the letters are divided into "Common"* ('âmma) *and "Elite"* (khâssa); *and among the letters, there are different degrees up to the degree of the Messengers* (rusul). *Comments on the "isolated letters," which make up most of this part, relate to this division. But another distinction is made between the letters and spiritual Men, beyond the hierarchy properly speaking, and it is one that runs throughout the* Futûhât *as a whole. This is the distinction between "letters of qualification by divine characters"* (takhalluq) *and "letters of realization of essential reality"* (taharruq), *and, parallel to this, the distinction between the "people of lights" and the "People of secrets" as they relate to western and eastern differences in the numerical values of letters. The meaning of this difference can be seen in a concept of holiness where the closer an individual gets to God, the more the divine light will be hidden in him in order to act upon the world, and the more he, like the* afrâd,[12] *will escape any dependence on the world, and even on its inner hierarchy, which is guided by the "pole."*

In order to remain in the familiar universe of Qur'ânic Revelation, the Shaykh al-Akbar chooses to deal with the isolated letters that begin the suras, letters that represent the first degree of the Elite in the myriad worlds of letters. Twenty-nine suras begin with one or more of these isolated letters, the total number of which is seventy-eight. This means that knowledge of these suras (sûra, *pl.* suwar), *the number of which corresponds to the days of the lunar month, represents the perfection of Form* (sûra, *pl.* suwar), *meaning the Universal Man. The number of letters, seventy-eight, is, based on a hadith, the same number as the number of "branches" of the Faith* (shu'ab al-îmân).

Knowledge of the secret of these letters does not constitute a secondary branch of initiatory knowledge; it resides in the very heart of spiritual realization.

The technical, divinatory, or other implications of the science of letters are only a veil thrown over a much deeper kind of knowledge based on unveiling and inspiration. At the beginning of his commentary on the letters A.L.M. that open the second sura (al-Baqara), *Ibn 'Arabî adds that he will include in it his commentary on the following verse, but that this is not at his own instigation; it is, rather, an inescapable divine command.* Composing (ta'lîf) *the* Futûhât *is thus once again associated with the preferences of the divine mystery that presides over the composition of the world's languages and beings.*

The three letters A.L.M. *symbolize the All, whose two faces of transcendence and similarity, of eternity and contingency, are simultaneously both connected, and separated, by a necessary intermediary. Universal existence is thus simultaneously shared by a quality and a triad, and these correspond to the different letters divided between Man and God in part I.*

The alif—*which cannot be written connected to the letter that follows it—is thus isolated in writing, just as is the case for transcendent, unqualified Essence. The* lâm, *the Attribute, drops down to the line of manifestation where its linear extension, just like the stretching out of its vowel, makes possible its relationship* (idâfa) *to the Act drawn downward by the* mîm *(see figure 2, page 438).*

The downward strokes of both the alif *and the* mîm *likewise represent universal manifestation, from the highest states of Being to the edge of the "Lowest Heaven," and from there, toward the physical world. In this sense,* A.L.M. *is a general symbol for the Universal Man, but he is more specifically symbolized by the* lâm, *which represents Him Who gives—and him who receives—being* (nâ'ib manâb al-mkawwin wa l-kawn). *Written by itself, the* lâm *draws an* alif *and a* nûn, *only the lower part of which seen: the transcendental principle and the world, whose intelligible part is hidden (see figure 3, page 438).*

Each letter can thus have a divine interpretation and a human interpretation. The alif *that, in itself, cannot be "moved" by a vowel symbolizes both the unknowable, immutable Essence and the unknown* khalîfa *that is the immobile mover of the world. As graphic support for the vocal stress of the* hamza ('a), *the* alif *represents both the Producer and the first product of Being* (al-mubdi' wa l-mubda' al-awwal). *In other words, from the point of view of Total Reality, there is neither outer nor inner; there is only a (manifested) all in an (unmanifested) All. This observation is essential for both knowledge and spiritual realization. And it is just as much so for understanding the synthetic and analytic role of the Book.*

The commentary on the following verse: "This book, about which there is no doubt, is a guide for those who are fearful" *(Q. 2:2) takes the passage from the science of letters to hermeneutics. We see immediately why it needed to follow* A.L.M. *and precede the interpretation of the Fâtiha,*[13] *which is itself followed by a few other verses from sura al-Baqara.* A.L.M. *designates total Reality; "that book," marked by the demonstrative of distance, is a specific reference to the beginning, and the archetype, of Revelation.*

In "that book" (dhâlika al-kitâb), *the demonstrative* dhâlika *is broken into three morphologically and semantically distinct elements.* Li *("over there") marks distance and, as in the case for the* Lâm *in* A.L.M., *corresponds to the Attribute, which is an intermediary and a first separation of the Essence* (al-farq al-awwal). Dhâ *("this"), a pronoun not yet identified* (mubham), *will be so only with the appearance of the Book. Manifested nonetheless, it is the place of the second separation* (al-farq al-thânî). *It is thus a double separation: between Essence and Attribute (Knowledge) and the Book, or, in the latter case, between the Eternal and contingency. The* alif *written between the* dhâl *and the* lâm *keeps them separated, and at the same time it reminds them that without Him, they cannot be joined back together. Actually, the "that" should connect back to the divine Attribute whose demonstrative it is by referring back to it* (ishâra) *and the Attribute should connect with the Book to replace all that had been entrusted* (amâna) *to it. This* alif, *in line with its numerical value, is the One, or the Self, that "accompanies existence and gives it its reality," according to the verse:* "And He *(huwa)* is with you wherever you are" *(Q. 57:4). As the place of union and separation, of both the veil and revelation, this* alif *is also the veil of the* tawhîd *that affirms the One and denies the multiple, to bring it back together in the end. What is left is the* ka, *the second person pronoun; it means that the speech* (khitâb) *is addressed to You, meaning to the Divine Logos* (al-kalima al-ilâhiyya), *the repository of knowledge and archetype of all intelligence.*

Al-kitâb. Al, *the definite article, corresponds to the two first letters of* A.L.M., *the one difference being that* A.L. *expresses the unitive modality of knowledge or existence* (jamʻ) *and* al *their distinctive modality* (tafsîl). *Identity and correspondence on the one hand, and difference and hierarchy on the other, are the two poles of Ibn 'Arabî's hermeneutics. More than once in this chapter, the Shaykh points out that he dealt with these questions in his commentary on the Qur'ân (which to date is yet to be discovered):* al-Jamʻ wa l-tafsîl fi asrâr al-tanzîl, *"Unitive and distinctive knowledge of the secrets of Revelation."*

There are three aspects to the Book: its "unknown" (majhûl) *aspect, its "drawn"* (mastûr) *aspect, and its "inscribed"* (marqûm) *aspect. As unknown, it is seen as "the Mother of the Book"* (umm al-kitâb), *which is unknowable because it is the attribute of Divine Knowledge that encompasses all things and cannot be encompassed. This book is reflected in the Archetype traced out by the Celestial Pens, which inscribe the destiny of the beings of the upper and lower worlds in it. "That book" thus entails an allusive reference to the "inscribed book" whose two faces are separated by the edges of the letters. The Shaykh then reminds us that the reader, himself, is the place of descent* (manzil) *and the receptacle* (mahall) *of Revelation, via a process analogous to the way knowledge becomes active knowledge for the scholar, or vision takes place for the individual who sees. As a path of knowledge and spiritual realization, the role of this method of interpretation is to ensure that the path is clear between informal, supra-intelligible Reality and its receptivity in an intelligible form. It is the twenty-eight letters and their "mansions" on the cycle of universal manifestation that are the mediators along this pathway. In creating the division between the luminous letters—the fourteen single letters that open the suras—and the dark letters—the other fourteen—they split the Universe into shadow and light, and it is important to note that darkness sometimes is symbolic of the dark, inexistent face of being, and sometimes of the unmanifested unknowable.*[14] *Just as Revelation becomes intelligible only when these luminous and dark letters mix, so also is the light of knowledge actualized in the heart by being projected upon its ignorant, shady face. The letters of the alphabet* (hurûf al-mu'jam)—*literally: "of the incomprehensible"—stand on the border of Revelation to transmit the message and draw man toward the inexhaustible knowledge of "the Mother of the Book." "And say: Lord, make be grow in knowledge!"*

"There is no doubt about that book" (lârayba fîhi). *In order to reach this knowledge, the letters gathered together in the Book must be taken apart in a special way, on the cosmological plane of the "Footstool"* (kursî). *The negation "no"* (lâ) *is, in fact, comprised of a* lâm *and an* alif. *The two letters' composition and the order in which they appear correlate to the way knowledge normally takes place, as seen in the hadith: "He who knows himself (lâm) knows his Lord (alif)." This knowledge then stimulates the "outcome" of the* lâm *and the* alif. *But since both, together, were shaped like an* alif, *their separation actually ended up in their union, since, graphically, two* alifs, *one right after the other, are written as only one (see Figure 4, page 438).*

This stage of knowledge corresponds to the Throne ('arsh). *From the perspective of the initiatory path, it might be said that one* alif *has hidden anoth-*

er; it has not been blended into it. In this degree of *reunion* (ittihâd) *and junction* (ittisâl), *there is* "fusion, but not confusion."[15] *The redescent toward distinction takes place via a further separation, this time in the opposite direction, from* lâ *to* al, *to establish once again distinction and knowledge. The pair composed of union and separation, or unitive and distinctive knowledge* (al-jam' wa l-tafsîl), *is thus reproduced on all levels of Being.*

This is why the Throne is the place of investiture of the Khalîfa *who hides the Divine Presence within him. It is the veil of manifestation, the "Cloak"* (ridâ') *that his Principle "Bearer of the Cloak"* (murtadî) *puts on. How could the outside of the cloak know the inside? At the very most, it might know the imperceptible border that both connects them and separates them. Likewise, the scholar knows only knowledge, and only knowledge knows God, but "between knowledge and the object of knowledge there are seas whose depths cannot be reached."*

To conclude and extend this commentary to the rest of the Qur'ân, the Shaykh al-Akbar compares the use of the demonstrative dhâlika *to its feminine form:* tilka, *for example: "A.L.R., those are the signs [verses] of the wise Book"* (Q. 10:1-2) *(the "signs" or "verses"* (ayât), *which is the name for things, require agreement in the feminine singular, the demonstrative* tilka *meaning "that one"). While the Book brings Revelation in a unitive way, its signs represent the distinctive way. "That is the Book" refers to the existence of union* (jam') *before separation* (farq). *Then separation appeared in the signs, in the same way that all the numbers are brought together in One."*[16] *The correspondence of* dhâlika =*Adam and* tilka =*Eve underscores better the relationship between Man, letters and the Qur'ân. "Adam is for the totality of attributes, and Eve for differences among beings, since she is the receptacle of Act and of dissemination (badhr)."*[16]

In composing this passage about the Book, Ibn 'Arabî confides that "we were gripped by a theophany in which things so enormous and so frightful appeared to us; we threw our notebook from our hands and fled toward the world, which did calm us somewhat. The following day I wanted to have the theophany back, and I was thus kept in the state. I came back to the discourse on the Letters, one by one, as I had foreseen at the beginning of this chapter."[16]

Section I, part III

This last part entails a methodical list of the qualities and properties of letters and their cosmological correlations (I 65-68). It offers at least some insight into what could have, or should have, been included in a treatise on letters, which Ibn 'Arabî mentions several times in the chapter; he informs us that the treatise was only partially completed at the time of the Futûhât's *composition. The work in question was called* Kitâb al-mabâdi' wa l-thâyât fî-mâtahwî 'alayhi hurûf al-mu'jam min al-'ajâ'ib wa l'âyât *"The Book of Beginnings and Ends on what marvels and signs the letters of the alphabet contain."*

The terminology Ibn 'Arabî uses is so specific to this work that he then provides the key to understanding it (I 78-84). The letters are listed by the point from which they are uttered, from the hamza *to the* wâw. *He nevertheless begins with the* alif, *the origin of all the other letters, even though the* alif *is not truly a letter "for whoever has breathed in some of the fragrance of the essential realities. The 'Common Man' calls it a 'letter,' but for the person who reaches essential truth (muhaqqiq), what we are dealing with is a metaphorical expression."*[16]

We shall translate only one passage from this entire, quite technical, section: the passage on the letter sâd. *Its autobiographical nature shows the place that the science of letters held in the lives of the Shaykh al-Akbar and his companions.*

In the symbolism of writing, lâm-alif *and* alif-lâm *are considered to be letters in themselves. These two combinations of the* alif *and the* lâm—*the intermediary par excellence*—*show the paths through which the* alif *brings life into the universe and makes itself known to it. This passage will also be translated in its near entirety, because it adds the perspective of spiritual realization to the commentary on the first two verses of sura* al-Baqara.

Writing an introduction to the explanations Ibn 'Arabî offers for his own terminology is no simple task. We might at least attempt to focus on a few of the more important of these explanations that lead toward fuller understanding of the chapter as a whole, and of its relationship to the rest of the Futûhât.

The letters, like Man, receive the Divine Discourse. They are thus capable of expressing all realities (haqâ'iq), *especially those realities that make up the human world. Their order thus follows a hierarchy similar to that of the Initiates, as we have already seen, and as can be seen in the remarks that follow, which introduce the section on vowels. The* alif *corresponds to the unknown* qutb *("Pole"); although unknown, his presence is spread throughout the world, and he supports the world through his spiritual energy* (himma). *As a semi-vowel of prolongation (a long* a*), the* alif *looks like an extension of sound, carried by the breath from its source to its furthest reach. Like an echo, it continues to propagate itself, even when there is no longer any consonant being uttered. On the level of writing, the* alif *is nothing more than a point, thus an intelligible reality, whose extension produces all forms. In the propagation of sound, the* alif*, like the pole, is assisted by two imams, the semi-vowels* wâw *and* yâ' *(long* u *and long* i*). These three letters, to which the* nûn *is added, make up the four "pillars"* (awtâd)*; the same letters, to which* tâ'*,* kâf*, and* hâ' *are added, are the equivalent of the seven* abdâl.*[17] These seven letters actually represent the dynamic elements of the Arabic language. The* wâw *and the* yâ' *are at the base of most morphological changes. The* alif*, the* wâw*, the* yâ'*, and their vocalic counterparts:* a, u, i, *and the* nûn *are the signs of number, of conjugation, and of case endings, and thus of syntax. These same letters and the three others are responsible for the essential portion of the way pronouns work, that is, the replacement of one noun by another. This movement of permutation* (ibdâl)*, which sets discourse in motion, is brought into being on the morphological level at the same time as it is on the syntactical level, and this can be transposed for the beings of the world. The* abdâl *(replacements, or "permutants"), like these letters, insure the maintenance and the perpetual transformation of the world through the working of permutation or transmutation. The relationship to alchemy shows through here, even though it may not be clearly expressed. On the other hand, the idea of* badal—*the replacement of one letter, one word, or one being by another—gives a sense of the continuity and the perpetual renewal of existence.*

A reading of the chapter as a whole, and specifically of the explanation of these technical terms, makes it look very much as though the science of letters covers the sciences of physics, numerology, and the revolution of the celestial spheres and temporal cycles, as well as a whole set of practices, like the one based on the relationship between the way letters are drawn out and the parts of the human body. This knowledge does not become spiritually operative, however, until it is received through the archetype of Revelation, because what correspondence there is between the letters and the Divine Presence is seen in the world of inscription ('âlam al-raqm) *only through the writing of the exemplar, the* Qur'ân *(khatt al-mushaf), and in the spoken word, only through recitation* (tilâwa)*. Even though the Divine Presence does propagate Itself through all speech, whether it is part of the Recitation or not, it is not enough[18] to know that every word pronounced until the end of time is from the Qur'ân."[19]*

As soon as the universal science of letters adapts to their Qur'ânic form, the letters of the Qur'ân and the entities they make up are seen as living realities that correspond to the world of Man.

"Thus, we have taken a look at the hierarchical organization of the station of Qur'ânic writing in ourselves *('indanâ)*; at the letters with which the suras begin and end; and at the privilege bestowed upon the unknown suras[20] according to the science of metaphysical speculation *(al-'ilm al-nazarî)*, known as "knowledge from God" *(al-'ilm al-ladunî)*. We have also taken a look[21] at the repetition of *bismi 'llâhi l-rahmâni l-rahîm*, at the letters that are found neither at the beginnings nor at the ends of the suras, nor in *bismillâhi...* and we have asked God—exalted may He be—to tell us if this privilege was granted to the letters out of pure divine solicitude *(ikhtisâs i'tinâ'i)*, as is the case for prophecy among the prophets, or because of the fact that a thing was one of the first things *(al-ashyâ' al-uwal)*; or if the letters received the privilege through their own merit *(min tarîq al-iktisâb)*. The reply was unveiled to us through inspiration *(kashf ilhâm)*, and we saw that some receive it out of solicitude, and others as a reward for what they accomplished in their first condition *(fî awwal al-wad')*. But in reality, they, we, and the entire Universe were granted the privilege out of divine solicitude."[22]

Section II
"On knowledge of the vowels
through which we distinguish words,
or 'minor letters'"

As its title suggests, this section deals less with the vowels themselves than with their roles in the formation of words, and thus with the spoken word. Given Arabic writing, where only the consonants are noted, the vowels are not part of the structure of a word, but they do allow it to be pronounced: they "bring it to life." The word vowel (haraka) *means "movement," and the absence of vocalization is called "rest"* (sukûn). *The impetus the vowel gives to the inert body of the consonant is like the breath of God that gives life to the human body molded from clay:* "When I have formed him and blown My Spirit into him" *(Q. 15:29 and 38:72). It might be noted that the consonants are also produced via the breath; but the breath stops at their points of emission, while both short and long vowels are just a modality or a "coloration" of the exhalation.*[23] *Its role as originator of existence and producer of beings, or let-*

ters, and of words is only adumbrated here; it is dealt with in a long chapter that begins with specifics regarding phonetics and the science of letters.[24] On the contrary, it is its eschatological role that is fulfilled by the breath of the Archangel Isrâfîl in the *"trumpet"* (al-nafkh fî l-sûr) *that resuscitates bodies in order to lead them back toward their origins.* "Isrâfîlian Reality" *is in itself nothing more than an emanation of* "Muhammadan Reality" *in one of its modalities: the* "Exhalation of the All-Merciful" (nafas al-Rahmân), *the beginning of the substantial extension of a being. This reference to the Universal Man is explained by the very object of this passage, which is to show the parallel between the formation of words and the formation of the world. The Prophet designated himself as the one to play this role, when he said: "I have received the totalizing words"* (jawâmi' al-kalim), *which might be translated in this quite specific context: "I have received the power to bring words (written or spoken) together." The relationship between the power of the breath to bring things into existence and its eschatological fulfillment is more specifically the fact of* "the knowledge that belongs to Jesus,"[25] *and is only one of the aspects of the universal reality of these "total Words"* (jawâmi' al-kalim).

From an ontological perspective, these words transmit three kinds of essences: independent (dhât ghaniyya), *dependent* (faqîra), *and making the connection either between one kind and the other, or between two essences of the same kind. At the level of language, this division can be seen again in the parts of speech—noun, verb, and particle— and in logic, as seen in essence, adventitiousness* (hadath), *and their reciprocal relationship.*

The written vowels correspond to the movement of the body, those that are spoken correspond to the movement of spirits. Moreover, some letters that are vocalized have a stable vowel (mutamakkin), *like the non-final or invariable final vowels, while the others are "of a changing color"* (mutalawwin), *like the letters of verbal or nominal inflection* (i'râb). *Stability* (tamkîn), *however, constitutes the original state of all the vocalized letters, just as the primordial nature* (fitra) *is in man, since all letters are connected to the archtype of their "Immutable Essences"* (a'yân thâbita). *The origin of any being is actually its immutability* (thubût) *in Divine Knowledge. The "coloration" of the* dâl *in* Zayd *can change depending on its role in case ending (*Zayd*-un, -an, or -in), but it still stays the same. The cosmic movement of the spheres colors the creaturely qualities of both beings and letters, in the same way that parents, according to the hadith, imprint the form of a specific religion upon their child's soul.*[26] *The absence of a vowel or "rest" signifies a return to original immobility; vocalization is the coloration, and thus the change necessary for the cycle of manifestation's return to its origin to be completed. The speaker, through the* *movement of his thought, provokes a series of transformations through the effect of his "breaths" (anfâs), which produce spoken words and which, through their subtlety (latâfa), reproduce the orientation and the effect of the "original Realities" (al-haqâ'iq al-uwal) on the movement of the spheres.*

The second part of this second section deals less with the formation of words than with the relationship between the word and its meaning, or what it designates. From this point of view, the lexicon splits into four principal types[27]; they are, for the meanings of words and their stylistic use, what physical qualities are for the world of elements. In doing this, Ibn 'Arabî is introducing the subject of the third chapter: "On Divine transcendence in respect to the similarity and the anthropomorphism implied by the words that God Himself and His Messenger used in regard to Him." *These somewhat suggestive expressions (the hand, the face, the laughter, or the anger of God), the* mutashâbihât, *the semblance of resemblance, bring us back to the first part of the chapter, where God's letters have a three-to-three correlation with those of Man. Man is a perfect reflection of the Divine Image, but divine realities are divine; human realities are human. The Attribute marks the line that separates absolute divinity* (ulûha) *from absolute servitude* ('ubûda)*, each in its own perfection and reality. It is thus with the triple reality of knowledge, knower, and known that is continually present throughout this long chapter that the Shaykh ends, because the science of letters proceeds from the divine attribute of Knowledge that embraces all things. The only individuals capable of receiving either this knowledge or that of "equivocal" words are those who* 'have told themselves: we shall empty our hearts of all reflective speculation, and we shall sit with God—exalted may He be—practicing *dhikr* on the carpet of respect for spiritual conventions *(adab)*, of vigilance *(murâqaba)*, of the presence of the heart *(hudûr)*, and of the disposition to receive what will come from Him, so that God Himself will take charge of teaching us through revelation and the realization of our essences, for we have heard Him say: "*Fear God and God will teach you*" (Q. 2:282)..."[28]

This is how the chapter ends: "May he who wishes to know the heart of the doctrine of Unity *(lubâb al-tawhîd)* consider the verses on *tawhîd* in the Incomparable Book, the verses where God affirms His own unity, for no one knows anyone better than he knows himself. See, thus, how God has qualified Himself, and ask Him to allow you to understand it. You will begin to be aware of the kind of divine knowledge that the intellect could never achieve via reflection... May God grant that we understand Him, *Amîn!* And may He count us among those who know and who apprehend His signs!"[29]

Ibn 'Arabî's Science of Letters

The preceding pages offer but an overview of chapter 2. Despite how specific the Shaykh al-Akbar might be when he develops some themes, others are mere outlines, and in some cases he puts off explanations until later chapters, especially if the questions at issue have already been, or are planned to be, treated in other works. A synthesis of all these details would be an endeavor as delicate as it is difficult since, as we have already seen, the science of letters covers the fundamental points of his metaphysical, physical, and initiatory doctrine. There is nothing more coherent or less systematic, moreover, than a teaching based on intuitive unveiling and contemplative vision. The quite succinct information that follows aims solely at adding slightly to this overview. Our hope is also to show how letters were ever the Shaykh al-Akbar's faithful companions in his spiritual work and spiritual realization.[30]

Taking an expression from al-Hakîm al-Tirmidhî, Ibn 'Arabî reminds us more than once that the science of letters is the science of the saints ('ilm al-awliyâ'). However, he is not unaware that some individuals acquire it via means other than sainthood, and he quite rightly worries: "It is a noble science in itself, even though it is quite rare to practice it without being affected *(illâ anna l-salâma minhu 'azîza)*. It is thus preferable not to seek it, since it is a science with which, in its entirety *('alâ l-jumla)*, God has privileged His saints. Even though some individuals do possess it in small quantities, they did not receive what they know in the same way as God's pious servants *(al-sâlihûn)*. Those individuals have such knowledge for their unhappiness, not for their felicity. May God make us 'knowers through God' *('ulamâ' bi-Llâh)*."[31] *So why such a radical condemnation of the practical applications* ('amal) *of this science, about which it is also said that it is "detestable in both reason and in Law"* (mamqût 'aqlan wa sharlan), *while the properties* (khawâss) *and operative virtue* (fi'l) *of letters devolve from the principles outlined in chapter 2, especially when information is offered about these applications at the same time? From an operative point of view, a new category of letters should be considered: letters that, originally written* (raqmiyya) *or pronounced* (lafziyya), *are conceived by the reflective faculties* (fikriyya) *or are evoked* (mustahdara) *by the imaginative faculty.* "Know that letters have properties and that there are three kinds of letters: those which are written, those which are spoken, and those which are evoked. By 'evoked', I mean those letters which man brings into being by giving them form through mental representation *(wahm)* and the strength of the imagination *(khayâl)*. It is not possible to evoke anything other than written or spoken letters, since there are no others. This evocation takes place via a process analogous to writing or speaking. The letters that are spoken are nothing other than the Names; here we are dealing with the properties of Names *(khawâss al-asmâ')*. With written letters it is not necessarily a question of names, and the practitioners of this science are not in agreement on whether any single letter is, or is not, endowed with an operative virtue. I have known some who have maintained that this was impossible. Having had occasion to discuss the issue with them, I have showed them what truth their opinion contained, and what in it was false, as well as what weaknesses there were in their arguments... (and likewise, for those who held the opposite view). I then stated to both sides: experience what you have knowledge of, keeping in mind what I have just told you. And they did so. They verified what we showed them, and were pleased with it. If I had not vowed never to provoke an effect *(athar)* via a letter, what marvels they would have seen!"[32]

Ibn 'Arabî was in close association with practitioners of this science, and the techniques he mentions are quite specific. He also points out the frequent lack of exactness in the table (jadwal) *where the letters are divided, in the order of their numerical value, according to the four physical qualities, and he wonders if the error was not deliberate, for the purpose of discouraging those who are not worthy. This knowledge is explicitly related to the "disciple of Ja'far al-Sâdiq" or the emblematic Jâbir Ibn Hayyân, whose name is mentioned in other treatises.*[33] *In the* Kitâb al-Mîm wa l-Wâw wa l-Nûn, *while connecting the tradition with Ja'far al-Sâdiq, he clearly differentiates between the Imam's teaching and the operative consequences drawn by his "disciple." He clearly recognizes Islam's assimilation of the ancient tradition when he cites the name of Pythagoras* (Fîthâghurus) *in relation to where the way of Letters and the way of numerologists* ('adadiyyûn) *come together. And yet he clearly points out the distance between them, not vis-à-vis what they know, but rather the problems posed by how what they know is applied. He places himself in the line of masters of the* tasawwuf, *like Ibn Mansarra al-Jabalî,*[34] *who, while dealing with the secret* (asrâr) *symbolism of letters, are precautiously reticent in regard to their efficient properties. Ibn 'Arabî's prudence thus has a number of justifications, including the analogy between magic* (sihr) *and the applications of the science of letters* (sîmiyâ)[35] *and, at a higher degree, between letters and the theurgy of "Jesus' knowledge"* (al-'ilm al-'îsawî). *Because he is, himself, a "Spirit emanating from Him," Jesus—the "seal of universal sainthood"—identifies himself with the divine Breath that brings beings and letters into existence, and represents the perfect conjunction between the science of letters and the knowledge possessed by the Saints."*[36]

Chapter 2 does not really deal with the relationship between kun (*the* fiat *of existence) and the power of the word articulated by letters to bring things into existence. The three letters in* kun: kâf, *the* wâw *hidden in the center, and* nûn, *give rise to certain developments, among which are the symbolism specific to the letter* Wâw, *but especially the correspondence between the* kun *and the* huwa *(the Self). The* Wâw's *disappearance in* kun *reflects the* hâ' *of the unmanifested from which the* Wâw *proceeds in the* kun *of manifestation. The process of coming into existence is thus marked simultaneously by the occultation of the transcendent, unmanifested Principle and the propagation of the Self or of Divine Ipseity* (huwiyya) *in all beings.*[37]

Chapter 198 on the other hand, the chapter on the Breath (nafas), *looks like a broad continuation of all the symbolism of the production of sounds, from the uninterrupted sound of the breathy descending letter* (al-harf al-hâwî) *to the phonological characteristics of letters and the way beings are brought into existence, to the three "tendencies" vowels have, and to the principle of the formation of words. Most of this long chapter is nevertheless devoted to the universal extension of Divine Speech and the Breath, or the Exhalation of the All-Merciful between the* hâ' *and the* Wâw, *through the inexhaustible modalities of the Qur'ânic Word and the Divine Names, of which the Universal Man is the synthetic sum.*[38]

Graphically, the ability the alif *has to stand alone* (qayyûmiyyat al-alif[39]) *is a counterpart to the idea of* harf hâwî, *albeit with other doctrinal meanings. Relative to the* alif's *absolute verticalness, all the letters show inflection, a bowing* (mayl) *to one degree or another. Whether this is due to weakness or illness, this tendency is simultaneously the cause (in the two senses of the word* 'illa) *both of differences in form and of the sound due to the two "weak letters"* (wâw, *and* yâ') *that are the* alif's *"assistants." But what remains to be explained is how this principle of self-subsistence, through which all things subsist—it is characterized by verticality—can assure that this will be the case, while the generation of beings* (takwîn) *takes place horizontally. The answer is that the* alif *exists virtually in all letters, through what might be called the "principle of rectification due to weakness"* (qayyûmiyyat al-'illa). *The straightening up of the* alif *from its extended position has already been mentioned in relation to the letter* nûn. *Here it joins the movement of the vowels as the symbol of spiritual combat.*[40] *The sigh of the lover's nostalgia,*[41] *bowing backward, only reproduces the mercy that is the cause of our existence. "If it bows, it is in order to descend from its height, through mercy toward you, in order to bring you into existence as the place of your Creator's manifestation."*[42]

Lastly, we should return to the isolated letters, knowledge of which represents the fulfillment of faith. They are the key (miftâh) *to all the Divine Names, which, themselves, lie at the base of the beginning of the world.*[43] *The* Fâtiha *with which the Book of the World begins, as a key unto itself, does not begin with isolated letters for this very reason. Although they are limited in number, these letters are the first letters of a great number of Names*[44]*; relative to these names, they are thus in a situation not unlike that of the phonemes in human language that are common to a host of languages. The science of letters might thus be defined as a metalinguistics and a metaphysics announcing the principles of the production of both language and the physical world. Ibn 'Arabî does not raise the classical question about the origin of language—whether it came into existence via divine institution or human convention—since for him all names are the Names of God, all beings are His inexhaustible words; but he does wonder about the principle that allows letters and elements to enter into a harmonious* (ta'lîf) *composition. To the extent that the answer relates to knowledge of the Supreme Name* (al-ism al-a'zam)[45] *it is a secret that cannot be divulged. But to the extent that it implies the entire process of progress along the path of initiation, it can be told, even concisely, in order to show the way:* "...Regarding the question: 'where are these (isolated) letters?' the answer is: in the obstacles presented to the breath *(fî 'awârid al-anfâs)*. What presents itself as an obstacle to the breath of the All-Merciful is what brings the entity of the letter *(yuhdithu 'ayn al-harf)* into contingent existence; it is what presents itself as an obstacle to the letters that brings names into existence. The 'placement' *(ayniyya)* of names is thus located in letters; the placement of letters is the breath; the placement of the breath is spirits; that of the spirits is hearts, and that of hearts is the 'apudity'—the 'proximity'—of Him who turns them *('indiyya muqallibuha).*"[46]

In other words, the question that keeps coming back in a variety of forms is that of the encounter between the absolute and the conditioned, between the eternal and the contingent. In chapter 2, this encounter took place in an intermediate region defined by the triple relationship entailing knowledge, the knower, and the thing known. In chapter 198 on the Breath, as he goes deeper into the meaning of the divine name al-Badî', *the Inventor (of the heavens and earth*[47]*), Ibn 'Arabî remarks that, despite what some might have maintained, it cannot be said that "knowledge is the formal representation of the thing known"* (al-'ilm tasawwur al-ma'lum), *since even though form is "invented" by God—meaning that it is created with no previous model, like the heavens and the earth—such is not the case for knowledge. Since ideas* (ma'ânî), *as immutable entities, are not created, they cannot be either invent-*

ed or formally represented. *A third term is thus needed between form and idea, and this role is played by the word, written or spoken* (kalima) *whose meaning becomes a form endowed with its own existence* (wujûd 'aynî), *such as the word* Zayd.[48]

This brings us back, finally, to the Qur'ân, "for the book is the junction of one idea with another *(damm ama'nâ ilâ ma'nâ)*, and ideas cannot be joined to ideas if they are not put down in letters and words. Once letters and words contain them, they are capable of being joined to one another, after letters are joined together in what we call writing..."[49] *This joining, which is also separation, is the symbol of our condition, of our path of worship and knowledge:* "He who professes Oneness worships God in two ways: in the way of the Essence, in that the quality of absolute divinity comes back to him, and in the way of this divinity. Blessed is he who combines these two ways, for the worshiper is composed of both letters and meaning. The letter is concerned with the letter, and meaning, with meaning. This is why we do not worship Essence devoid of its quality of divinity, and divinity is not worshiped outside a relationship to some being qualified by it. Worship can only be based on what the servant's reality is—composition—and not on what divine reality requires: Unity."[50]

But if the worshiper is composed of letters and meaning, existence is one, and the self is identical to the Self. Under the jealous veil of the letter smoulders the fire of the self's love for the Self:

Existence is a letter, you are its meaning;
And in creatures I have no hope
other than Him...[51]

The Science of Letters
before and after Ibn 'Arabî

The preceding gives a sense of the complexity and the depth of the science of letters for the Shaykh al-Akbar. As original knowledge, in the sense that its origin is in the very heart of the individual interpreter, it nevertheless still has a number of antecedents. We shall limit ourselves here to outlining their development in different forms of Islamic esotericism. We note from the outstart that most of the questions Ibn 'Arabî deals with in chapters 2 and 5 of the Futûhât *had already been raised by his predecessors. In one way or another, some authors — and some of the earliest—even managed to work out this synthesis of multiple* bits of knowledge known as 'ilm al-hurûf. *Its relationship to disciplines like grammar and phonetics*[52] *or calligraphy*[53] *is not within the scope of this cursory overview. Notes on the translation will deal briefly with these topics.*

We have seen that in relation to the relationship between letters and the physical world or even in other more specific questions,[54] Ibn 'Arabî cites Jâbir Ibn Hayân either by name, or as the "disciple of Ja'far al-Sâdiq," thus admitting the tradition that sees him as the student of the sixth Imam. The problems raised by this relationship, as well as the attribution and dating of the vast corpus of (primarily alchemical) writings attributed to Jâbir have been raised a number of times without being definitively resolved.[55] Using P. Kraus's edition and presentation of selected texts from Jâbir, we shall limit ourselves to pointing out that part of Ibn 'Arabî's teaching on letters was present in Jâbir's earlier work.

The science, or the "balance of letters," really constitutes the finishing touches in the foundation of Ibn 'Arabî's alchemy, which is his theory of balance ('ilm al-mîzân). The theory is a way to evaluate, and to measure both quantitatively and qualitatively, the properties of all the beings comprised within the total sphere of manifestation. P. Kraus offers an excellent summary of Jâbir's cosmogony and cosmology:

> "It is thus within the mass of the Sphere, identical to the luminous sphere that encompasses our world and ether, that the substance first thought to be incorporeal becomes visible, takes on a distinct shape and color, and, in short, becomes a body. This same sphere is still the locus for the four incorporeal natures which, once they are united to "substance" or to the fifth Nature, will become concrete and will become material to a certain extent. Indeed, the supreme sphere in which the world of substance and the worlds of the simple Elements or the four Natures mix together represents the intermediary between the incorporeal and the corporeal: it is the last of the incorporeal beings and, at the same time, the first of the corporeal beings "endowed with passivity." As incorporeal, it is a simple, uniform substance wherein the particular and the universal exist together. As a body, it is composite, it moves, and it is subject to time and place. It is through the attachment *(tashabbuth)* of the Soul to Substance, through the mixture *(ikhtilât)* that takes place between the two, that Substance goes from the incorporeal state to where it is corporeal, that the con-

cretization of bodies takes place, that the transition of the intelligible to the sensible takes place, and that the simple thing becomes a composite thing. Once they are mixed together and have become something unique, they successively descend into the world of the four Natures and take their shape from them. At the base of this "generation" *(kawn)* of the corporeal world is the desire (called *shahwa*, or *shawq*, or *tawaqân*) the Soul experiences, which is directed toward matter.[56]

"The principle and the origin of balances *(mawâzîn)* are thus derived from the desire the Soul experiences for the elements. Whence the fact that each being endowed with a soul has its cause in the principle of balances."[57]

Corbin took this idea and applied it to its spiritual dimension.

"Measuring the Natures of a thing, regardless of what it is, means measuring quantities that the Soul has appropriated for itself; it is measuring the desire of the Soul as it descends into matter. Conversely, it is the transmutation of the Soul that is going to condition the transmutation of bodies; it is in the Soul that they transmute, for the soul is the locus of their transfiguration."[58]

The aim of the science of balance is thus not merely "to reduce all the facts of knowledge to a system that is quantifiable and measurable, giving them the characteristics of an exact science."[59] *When everything can be measured, its place in the Universal Harmony can be assigned.*[60] *All things and all higher realities in the first place are thus determined by their own balance:* "The division in balance comes after the division in existants. There is a balance for the intellect, for the soul, for nature, for form, for the spheres, for heavenly bodies, for the four natures and the animals, for plants, and for minerals. The most perfect of all is the division of letters."[61]

The division in the sciences proposed by Jâbîr in the Kitâb al-hudûd[62] *shows the extent to which the science of letters plays a central role.*

Balance, or the science of letters, holds such an important place in this general schematic of knowledge because it provides not only a way to put into words, but also to realize, the origin of both manifestation and beings, whether this be in Pythagorean terms, via the relationship between letters and numbers; in neo-Platonic terms, via the progression and movement of the celestial bodies; or in Aristotelian and Stoic terms both at the same time, via the composition and mixing of natures and elements. To a greater extent than any other, this science allows Islam to integrate the entire ancient esoteric heritage through the twenty-eight letters of the Arabic alphabet, with them, themselves, being considered as the product of the multiplication of the four "natures" via the different levels of the seven-tiered hierarchy. As the "Book of Morphology" (Kitâb al-tasrîf), and others, explain it, the words of language are formed via principles that correlate closely with the principles that govern the physical and spiritual constitutions of the realities that these words stand for.[63] It is thus clear that this balance aims not only at determining the properties of beings (khawâss), and their many magical, medical, astrological, alchemical, and other applications, but also at rediscovering, in the simple elements of language, the key to all knowledge.

One question worth asking is whether Ibn 'Arabî had access to Jâbir's works, or had heard of them, as certain passages seem to suggest.[64] In any case, the similarity in their cosmological terminology, and the number of terms they share, is striking. Both authors give the same importance to the phonic and graphic production of letters. There is a close correlation between developments in grammar and the relationships among letters, words, and meaning. A study of the relationship between the two works—which were separated by at least three centuries—is yet to be done, not on the quite secondary level of a possible transmission via books, but in order to understand how the tasawwuf *managed to integrate elements whose true origin it alone could have known.[65] On the larger scale, the two works are not really comparable, since one belongs to the field of alchemy, and the other to the* tasawwuf; *they do nevertheless share two common characteristics, the heritage of a long tradition (Hellenistic in one case, and Islamic in the other) and "shared knowledge." Although Jâbir quite clearly proclaims that the science of letters is the path one should take to "bring together that which is scattered," Ibn 'Arabî gives his reader ample time to allow himself to be imbued by the conviction.*

The "Epistles of the Brothers of Purity" (Rasâ'il ikhwân al-safâwa khillân al-wafâ), which, like Jâbir's work, were inspired by Shi'ite esotericism, also raise both dating issues and, in regard to authorship, identification issues.[66] The work contains a number of elements that are also present in Jâbir, although occasionally more clearly accented, like the Pythagorean idea of the production and ordering of the cosmos. Numerology and music for the Ikhwân thus have an importance all their own.[67] One case in question is an early, quite succinct essay on the Letters that is integrated into the fifth epistle, which is devoted to Music.[68] *It follows the epistles dealing with arithmetic, geometry, astronomy, and geography, thus with cosmology and the number symbolic of its metaphysical and physical basis.*[69] *This original passage is developed again in epistle 31,*[70] *which quite notably concludes the* rasâ'il *that deal with the corporeal, physical world* (al-jusmâniyyât al-tabî'iyyât) *and precedes those that deal with the psychic, intelligible world* (al-nafsâniyyât al-'aqliyyât). *This essay proposes to explain "the causes of differences in languages, words and sounds, of the way letters are shaped and the forms that writing takes, and how teachings, beliefs, and religions appeared... as well as the disappearance of peoples, the appearance of others who were their descendants, century after century and community after community..." This desire to establish a correlation between the development of languages and writing systems and the destiny of humanity can be seen even more clearly—among the Ikhwân as well as in Jâbir or Ibn 'Arabî—in the fact that the science of letters is intimately linked to knowledge of the trajectories of the heavenly bodies and cycles. In their argument, the Ikhwân attempt to look like they are following the philosophical procedure of going from the sensory toward the suprasensory, or from the physical to the metaphysical, via knowledge of the "substance of the soul"* (jawhar al-nafs). *They do nevertheless warn the reader about the extremely subtle and complex nature of the science relating to the common origin of letters and the physical world.*[71] *Why—regarding the obscure relationship between prime matter* (hayûlâ) *and physical nature* (tabî'a)—*would they put him on his guard against "divulging the secret of Lordship"* (ifshâ' sirr al-rubûbiyya), *if not because the science of Letters leads to this secret?*[72] *Following the* tasawwuf *authors, they consider that this science has its origin in a providential inspiration* ('inâya) *received through the prophets, sages, and scholars.*[73]

The Ikhwân's entire doctrine is based on the Triad: the One is reflected in the Intellect, from which the Soul splits off. Through the mysterious presence of hayûlâ, *the Soul is propagated in the body of the universe and gives it life, through the plane of archetypes and the imaginal. The celestial spheres, dragged along by the Soul, begin to move, and their encounter with the celestial bodies produces sounds. Movement* (haraka) *produces sound, while silence* (sukûn) *comes from rest. On the one hand, the movement of the spheres causes the physical world to be born through the blending and compounding of "natures"; on the other, "movements and sounds are the measure of eras and epochs* (mikyâl al-duhûr wa l'azmân) *and determine the duration of the worlds that correspond to them." The celestial sounds* (al-aswât al-falakiyya) *are reproduced in a similar way, in the physical world where movement and the upper parts of bodies produce audible sounds. Just as celestial bodies are spherical, sound is propagated in the physical world in a waving, spherical form, depending on whether what is taken into consideration is the effect of the sound on a certain plane (where it extends out like the waves caused when a body falls into water), or in space, where it grows spherically* (shakl kurawî).

On the cosmic plane, the Ikhwan place such importance on sound because, among the five senses, it corresponds to the fifth celestial element or nature (tabîal al-falak), *that is, the element or nature through which the upper world joins the elemental world.*[74] *On the one hand, music, in the way it imitates the celestial sounds, aims at leading terrestrial sounds toward their superior model*[75]; *on the other, the production of terrestrial sounds* (al-aswât al-ardiyya) *is closely related to that of the three kingdoms. But they are not necessarily words* (kalâm). *Only animals utter intelligible sounds, and man is the only member of the animal kingdom who articulates the sounds of language* (aswât mantiqiyya). *Given man's central place in the universe, the points of phonemic articulation, as Ibn 'Arabî explains, express the relationship between the microcosm and the macrocosm. An entire theory of speech, more logical than grammatical, is developed by the Ikhwân, starting from the idea that letters and words are to ideas what the body is to the spirit, and between the body and the spirit, the soul both diffuses life and provides the imagination with its ideas.*

In regard to writing, it might be noted that the Ikhwân's work and Ibn 'Arabî's work converge remarkably: "know that at the base of all these letters and systems of writing there are two, and only two, lines. All the letters are formed between these two, and out of them, even including their later derivations, in the same way that all of humanity comes into existence from two beings: Adam and Eve—may peace be upon them—and just like the universe as a whole, the heavens and the earth and their inhabitants, come from two original beings *(jawaharayn)*: the first and its follower *(sâbiq-tâlî)* or the simple and the composite, that is, the Intellect and the Soul (...). These two lines are the straight line *(al-khatt al-mustaqîm)*, or the diameter of a circle, and the curved line *(al-khatt al-muqawwas)*, or the circumference. The first of the letters is the straight line: the *alif*, and the second, the *bâ'* [...]. No animal or plant escapes either this rule (the hierarchical predominance of the male over the female) or this aspect. While man's form is like the straight (vertical) line, that of the animals is more like the curved line; hierarchically, plants and animals are placed below man. In the worlds of the celestial spheres, the inhabitants of the heavens have straight aspects to them, and perfect shapes, while everything that is found in the subliminal worlds corresponds to the curved shape. Such is also the case for the numbers formed from One and Two, the first of which corresponds to the straight line and the second to the curve. They are the origin and the source of all numbers, which increase and grow out of them."[76]

Reference to a primordial language and system of writing is added to the straightness and verticality of the alif, *the One, the Intellect, and the Father of humanity. Adam, who was created based on a perfect form, speaks the* suryâniyya[77] *language. Even though no system of writing was in use in his time, it is said that Adam received nine "letters" or signs* ('alâmat) *represented by the nine numerals of Indian origin that were borrowed by the Arabs shortly before the time of the Ikhwân. They correspond to the nine spheres that encompass all beings. The other systems of writing are born out of their later ramifications, but the Indians retain the privilege of these nine signs because that is where Adam came down from Paradise. For the Ikhwân, India is thus greatly representative of Adamic primordialness, while the twenty-eight letters of the Arabic alphabet are signs of the completion, and the perfection, of the tradition, just as the lunar cycle completes the solar cycle.*[78]

The revolving of the nine spheres that these nine signs symbolize is what brings about the multiplicity of writing systems and the differences among languages. There are positive aspects to this multiplicity, in the sense that it comes from a single principle, although it also gives rise to opposition and conflict. The Ikhwân see this in the Arabic language; while variations in the reading of the Qur'ân (qirâ'ât) *mean a mercy and a richness in meaning, the existence of a number of Arabic dialects even before the time of Islam shows tendencies toward discord that appeared even in the earliest days of Islamic history. Explaining power struggles and disputes over authority via this linguistic fact does appear to be somewhat limited, but it is justified by the general cosmological knowledge that the science of Letters implies, and by the connection that has always existed in Shi'ite esotericism between the science of Letters and the Family of the Prophet that the Community was supposed to have gathered around. There are thus observable differences between the teachings of the Ikhwân and Ibn 'Arabî on the subject of Letters, but there are also numerous correlations with the second chapter in the* Futûhât.

In some respects, the contribution of Ibn Sinâ (370/980 - 428/1037) to the science of letters expands on the Ikhwân al-safâ's teaching. As a medical doctor, he was interested in the production of phonemes from both a physiological and a phonological point of view. His short work titled "The Ways of Letter Production" (asbâb hudûth al-hurûf), *following the Ikhwân's example, first looks at sound as an undulating movement of air* (tamawwuj al-hawâ') *caused by contact with or projection of a body. After describing the organs of phonemic articulation, he reviews both the phonemes found in Arabic and those that exist in Persian and the Khwâriziman (Turkish) language.*[79]

But it is especially in the Risâla nayrûziyya fî ma'ânî al-hurûf al-hijâ'iyya[80] *that Ibn Sînâ belongs to the esoteric, or hermetic, tradition we have been describing here, and he includes in it his interpretation of the isolated letters found in the Qur'ân. After a short review of the hierarchy of Being from the Producer of beings* (mubdi' al-mubda'ât) *to the corporeal, ethereal* (athîrî) *world with its spherical, or circular, or elemental form, he sets up a correspondence between the letters of the* abjad,[81] *their numerical value, and the principles of manifestation, looked at first of all by themselves, and later in their interactions:*

The Creator (Bârî')	= alif *(1) and* hâ' *(5)*
The Intellect ('aql)	= bâ' *(2) and* wâw *(6)*
The Soul (nafs)	= jîm *(3) and* zây *(7)*
Physical Nature (tabî'a)	= dâl *(4) and* hâ' *(8)*
Prime Matter (hayûlâ)	= tâ' *(9): does not enter into relationships with any other principle.*

The second principles devolve from the first:

Production of beings (ibdâ')	= yâ' *(10) = (2 x 5)*
Order (amr)	= lâm *(30) = (5 x 6)*
Creation (khalq)	= mîm *(40) = (5 x 8)*
Origin of existence via kun (takwîn)	= kâf *(20) = (5 x 4)*
amr + khalq = lâm + mîm	= 'ayn *(70)*
khalq + takwîn = mîm + kâf	= sîn *(60)*
The two letters of existence: yâ' + mîm	= nûn *(50)*
amr + khalq + takwîn = lâm + mîm + kâf	= sâd *(90)*
id. + ibdâ' = sâd + yâ'	= qâf *(100)*

If bâ', jîm, dâl, *and* zây—*which are indispensable in the order of entities—are removed from these 19 letters (the* basmala *also contains 19), what remains are the fourteen isolated letters of the Qur'ân, which Ibn Sînâ inter-*

prets based on the table above. *Thus,* Alif - Lâm - Mîm *means* 'The oath by the First, the master of Order and of Creation," Alif - Lâm - Mîm - Sâd *adds the sense of* "He who establishes All" *(munshi' al-kull),* Yâ- Sîn: "Oath by the beginning of the emanation *(al-ibdâ')* and its completion "(khalq + takwîn*);* Nûn: "Oath by the world of origination and divine order,*" or* "the reunion of All" (majmû' al-kull), *etc. Massignon, who composed a detailed study*[82] *on this short* risâla, *saw Ismâ'ili influence in the hierarchy. It is nevertheless possible that this is nothing more than one variation on a quite common theme of the Principle and the process of manifestation. He also posited that the work attempted a reconciliation between Greek philosophy and Semitic—or perhaps better said, Qur'ânic—wisdom, although this was common in the work of the* falsafa. *Ibn Sînâ nevertheless had a more specific goal here. With the somewhat systematic expression of the philosopher, he shows that the letter of Revelation contains within it the explanation of both the Origin and Manifestation.*

Some of what we know about letters comes via early Shî'ite esotericism.[83] *According to the tradition, the Ismâ'ili treatises composed around the time of the arrival of the Fâtimid dynasty occasionally associate the letters with cosmogony and the doctrine of cycles. In one of the treatises included in the* Kitâb al-kashf,[84] *the letters of the alphabet were the first of God's creations; this is not unlike the idea of* hudûd, *or "borders" between the unmanifested, on this side of the Throne* ('arsh) *and the "Footstool"* (kursî),[85] *first, and then among the different stages of manifestation.*

As always in Ismâ'ili thought, the principles of manifestation are reflected in the prophets and the imams, such that the first seven of the twenty-eight letters, the "mother-principles," represent the seven nutaqâ,[86] *and the last seven, the imams.*

These two heptads, whose number reminds us of the fourteen isolated letters of the Qur'ân, are called "the door of writing" (bâb al-raqm), *or, in cosmic terms, "The Book found with Him," and "the Mother of the Book." When they join together with the other fourteen, these letters compose the* Qur'ân.

Other treatises compare these seven primordial letters to those of the kûnî qadar.[87] *The response to their manifestation is the succession of the prophets and the imams. The last letter, the "border of the beyond," thus represents* al-Qâ'im, *who finishes the cycle and instigates resurrection. In its outer, or "political" aspect of prophecy* (siyâsât al-nubuwwa) *and interior, by the purification of souls* (tahârât al-nufûs), *this prophetic history through the science of letters thus associates the move toward the original meaning of the Qur'ân with the eschatological realization of* ta'wîl.[88]

The early exegetes were quick to make reference to the divine and spiritual realities that the isolated letters in the Qur'ân stood for.[89] Similarly, the letters of the basmala, and bâ' in particular, gave rise to numerous interpretations, some of which are outlined by Sarrâj (d. 378/988-9), the author of one of the earliest manuals of tasawwuf. One quote from Abû Sa'îd al-Kharrâz (d. 286/899) gives a sense of how inextricably linked the science of letters and spiritual realization are: "Whenever one of the letters from the Book appears to you, the letter will become a source of inspiration and understanding to the extent of your proximity and your presence in Him, although other interpretations are still possible for you. When you hear His words: "Alif - Lam - Mîm...," knowledge related to the *alif* is manifested to your understanding—knowledge different from that which is related to the *lâm*. One kind of understanding is different from another, depending on the strength of one's love, the purity of one's *dhikr*, and one's proximity."[90]

While not in complete agreement with this Qur'ânic reference, other authors also see in the letters a principle of mediation between the Creator and the creatures that later gets extended into human language. This is what Ahmad ibn 'Atâ[91] says: "When God created the letters, He made them His secret. When He created Adam, He transferred this secret into him, which He had done for none of the angels. The letters then appeared on Adam's tongue in a variety of forms and languages. God turned the letters into the forms of the languages..."[92] " Shortly before that, al-Hakîm al-Tirmidhî (d. late 3rd/9th century) had even more clearly explained the relationship between the letters and the Names taught to Adam: "All the sciences are contained within the letters of the alphabet, for the beginning of science is the divine names out of which both creation and the governance of the world emerge, within the limits of God's commandment, what He has allowed and what He has forbidden. The divine names themselves come out of the letters, and return to the letters. This hidden treasure of science is known only by the saints whose intellects receive understanding from God, and whose hearts are attached to God and enraptured by His divinity, wherever the veil is raised before the letters and attributes, that is, the attributes of Essence."[93] *As can be seen in the answer Ibn 'Arabî offered to the questions in the* Khatm al-awliyâ' *about the Supreme Name and its letters,*[94] *Tirmidhî played an important intermediary role in passing on the science of letters, even though he does not appear to have added markedly to it in his work.*

A short treatise on letters and the Qur'ân[95] by Sahl al-Tustarî (d. 283/896), one of Tirmidhî's contemporaries, highlights the close correlation between his work—one of the oldest on tasawwuf—and Ibn 'Arabî's. Sahl's famous question about "prostration of the heart" might have been placed at the end of chapter 2 of the Futûhât on purpose, even though it does not appear to pertain to letters, because of the affinity between spiritual inspiration and spiritual realization.[96]

According to Sahl, the letters were originally located in the Primal Substance (al-habâ')[97] where the beginnings of things (usûl al-ashyâ') are. Their composition gives rise to the spoken word (qawl), the expression of several categories of thought by naming things (musammayât), the names of which, in turn, break down into letters. Words play an intermediary role between the Principle and its manifestation in this cycle of composition and decomposition. The letters, in turn, make a clear distinction between the language of creatures (kalâm al-khalq) and God's speech (kalâm Allâh), while still maintaining a certain correlation between one and the other, filtered by the Primordial Substance. Even though they are influenced by conventions and are composed of elements that come and go, human words are actually carried by air, whose subtlety and plasticity correspond to al-habâ' *in the elemental order.*

Divine Speech is "composed of unchangeable entities and dazzling spiritual lights, which are His will and the objects of His knowledge detached from His mystery *(ghayb).* The force that detached them is the *kun.* This *kun* manifests the Word and encompasses the Primal Substance or the letters. They have the air to support them, and they constitute the spiritual strength that makes beings noticeable as individuals.[98] They are the beginnings of things. The specific *kun*, the form *(sûra)* or reality *(haqîqa)* proper to each thing through which it comes into existence, is itself only a piece broken off from the supreme *kun* uttered for the totality of beings.[99] Not only do all things come into existence via the *kun*— they are consequently called *mukawwanât*, that is, produced by *kun*—but it is also this "force" *(quwwa)* that gives the divine attributes their existence.[100] This force is called the "Book" *(kitâb)* of beings produced by the *kun* because *kitâb* means "that which brings together." Indeed, Allah— may His mention be exalted and His Names sanctified—has two attributes: one by which He distinguishes Himself from all things, the attribute of His Essence, as in His words: *He did not engender and was not engendered, and He has no equal"* (Q. 112: 3-4); and the other by which He acts— brings them into existence—veils Himself, and calls Himself *Allâh.*

Do you not see that all His attributes come back to *Allâh*, and *Allâh* to *Huwa*[101]? *Huwa* thus encompasses all Names and Attributes. The name that Allah has given to Himself is also the name through which He created. He is the Supreme Light, the Unraisable Veil, the Extra, Mystery, Possibility *(imkân)*, the "Mother of the Book" and the Principle *(asl)*. He contains all that has been and all that will be. He is the knowledge that God reserves for Himself in His Mystery [...]. He is where decisions are made regarding all things *(al-maqâdîr)* in an undifferentiated and nondistinct manner. In uttering the word *kun*, He detaches them from His mystery. Their separation takes place either via the spoken word *(qawl)*, or via an action *(fi'l)*. Those things that are said *(maqûlât)* are spiritual realities, and the effects of His actions *(maf'ûlât)* are bodies. Bodies have their origin in water, the first of outer substances. Spirits reside in the hidden, inner "body," the spirit[102] that surrounds water and carries the All, the place and the air where the letters unfurl.[103]

Letters thus move into the space between the world of the Spirit and the world of bodies, just as the kun did between the impenetrable Divine Mystery—according to Ibn 'Arabî, the Unknown Book—and the celestial prototype of the Book containing all the creatures.

Alif, *followed by* wâw *and* yâ', *are the noblest letters because, together with vowels and the cases that correspond to them, they are symbolic of man's three main faculties: rationality, animality, and physicality. These divide up into twenty-eight faculties, whose half belonging to the physical* (tabî'iyya) *order, and other half to the psychic* (nafsâniyya) *order correspond to the division into obscure and luminous letters (the fourteen isolated letters of the Qur'ân). This dual aspect of manifestation, subtle and thick, represented by air and water, also rules over the microcosmic and macrocosmic relationship between the human being or the universe and the Book, in terms which partially presage those that Ibn 'Arabî would use.* "Letters enter into composition in order to manifest what is not manifested in what is "written," or its secret. If the medium of letters is air, the 'writing' of the creature *(kitâb al-makhlûq)* becomes the spoken word and language; and if this medium is ink, what is written becomes corporeal and visible. In the same way that the creature's writing contains the sign of his spoken word, and his spoken word, the sign of what is not manifested and is secret in him, the body of the universe and the totality of his parts is for the Creator—may He be exalted—comparable to a book containing the sign of His spoken word *(qawl)* and his speech *(kalâm)*, which contain the sign of the Divine Mystery. Glory be to Him, for there is no god but Him, the Lord of the Noble Throne."[104]

When he deals with the isolated letters of the Qur'ân from this both metaphysical and cosmological perspective, Sahl is declaring that nine of the letters,[105] the most noble of them, correspond to the nine celestial "bodies"—the seven heavens, the Kursî and the Throne—which suggests a remarkable correspondence with the nine primordial letters of the Ikhwân al-safâ.

The passage on the Qur'ân lists a certain number of descriptive words for the Qur'ân. It is the Attribute (sifa) par excellence, and, more specifically, the Science and the ensemble of the Divine Names to which the hundred degrees of Paradise correspond. The totality of the aspects of the Qur'ân can be known only through the isolated letters. Like the fourteen phases in the growth of the moon, they lead the moon, or the soul, to the perfection of the sun, or of the intellect, in a synthetic and unitive way in "Alif - Lâm - Mîm. There is the Book; there is no doubt in regard to It," and in an analytical and distinctive way in "Alif - Lâm - Râ'. Such are the signs of the Book."

This letter of Sahl's thus contains the seeds of the essential part of chapter 2 in the Futûhât.

Al-Hallaj, who was a disciple of Sahl's, is considered by Ibn 'Arabî to be one of the primary representatives of the science of letters.[106] Their cosmogonic role nevertheless appears to be less well developed in his writings than in those of his teacher, except perhaps in regard to the Kun.[107] A few sentences from the Akhbâr do however clearly show that for Hallaj the letters in their Qur'ânic form represented the path of knowledge par excellence: "The knowledge of all things resides in the Qur'ân, and the knowledge of the Qur'ân resides in the letters that are placed at the beginnings of the suras. The knowledge of letters resides in Lâm - alif; that of Lâm - alif in the Alif, that of the Alif in the Dot, that of the dot in the original knowledge (al-ma'rifa al-asliyya); that of original knowledge in eternity (azal), that of eternity in the eternal Will (mashî'a); that of the eternal Will in the mystery of Huwa. There is nothing like Him, and no one knows this but Him."[108]

"The Qur'ân is the language of all knowledge; the language of the Qur'ân is the letters as they enter into composition. They come from the axial line (khatt al-istiwâ') of which 'the trunk is stable and the branches are in the sky.' And it is around it that the knowledge of unity gravitates."[109]

The lâm - alif mentioned above is itself compared to this axial way, or to knowledge of the Self: "Whoever seeks the knowledge of Unity outside the lâm -alif opens himself to wallowing in impiety, and whoever seeks to know the huwa of ipseity (huwiyya) in some way other than in the axial way is wallowing through a baneful perplexity from which there is no respite."[110]

The Kitâb al-Tawâsîn, *whose title was inspired by the isolated letters* Tâ-Sîn, *and* Tâ' - Sîn - Mîm, *entails a certain number of references to the science of letters like the passage on the letters in the name* Muhammad[111] *or on the symbolism of "the distance of two bows." The symbolism of* mîm, *compared to the string that holds the two bows tight in relation to the mediating role of the Prophet, is not unlike the most metaphysical meaning of the letter* nûn.[112] *The role of* lâm - alif *in the knowledge of unity is illustrated by a sketch in Rûzbehân Baqlî's Persian version where four equidistant* lâm - alif*s surround four concentric circles.*[113] *Ibn 'Arabi's highlighting of the four* lâm - alif*s in the* shahâda *are probably of the same inspiration.*[114]

Thanks to the discovery and publication of the Kitâb khawâss al-hurûf wa haqâ'iqihâ wa usûlihâ (The Book on the properties of letters, on their essential realities and their principles),[115] *Ibn Masarra al-Jabalî (269-319/883-931), one of the earliest representatives of Andalusian* tasawwuf, *looks very much like the founder of a path that would lead to Ibn 'Arabî.*[116] *He brought what were probably the earliest texts on* tasawwuf *back from his journey to the East. Sahl al-Tustarî's work on letters, from which his own work borrowed heavily* [117] *was almost certainly among them. Ibn Masarra nevertheless took his own approach. While Sahl, still close to the controversy about the created or uncreated Qur'ân, took as his point of departure the difference between divine and human speech, Ibn Masarra pointed out two aspects of the Book: it is a synthetic unit in respect to its Essence, but from the creatures' point of view, three bodies of knowledge*[118] *can be seen: the science of Lordship, the science of Prophecy, and the science of Trial* (mihna). *The third of these bodies of knowledge includes everything through which God tries Humanity: the Sacred Laws and our ultimate destiny (or "the Promise and the Threat"). This knowledge includes as many degrees of perfection as God has names, according to the words of the Prophet: "God has 99 names. He who says them all will enter Paradise."*[119] *Ibn Masarra emphasizes the total, distinctive nature of this "naming"* (ihsâ'), *which associates the science of the Qur'ân with that of the divine names. Reading the Qur'ân and making spiritual progress are brought together in a hadith that Ibn 'Arabî, likewise, often cited: "On the Day of Resurrection, he who recites the Qur'ân will be told: 'recite and rise up* (iqra' wa 'rqa), *you will be placed at the last level (reached by your recitation)!'"*

A few words about the basmala *and the* Fâtiha, *and a summary of the entire Qur'ân, are followed by general observations regarding the isolated letters; borrowings from Sahl are clearly visible here. Ibn Masarra emphasizes the relationship between the phases of the moon, knowledge of cycles (which belongs to the "science of trial") and the total future of Man. The interpretation of each group of isolated letters has an inspiration of its own, which can only be partly seen in Ibn 'Arabî. On the other hand, the early part of the* Risâlat al-I'tibâr, *published after the essay on letters, makes a strong case, like Sahl and 'Ibn Arabi at the beginning of the commentary on the* Fâtiha *(chapter 5 in the* Futûhât*), for the Universe being a book whose letters are Divine Speech.*[120]

Between Ibn Masarra and Ibn 'Arabî, al-Andalus was probably never without a master in the science of letters.[121] *Ibn Qasî (d. 546/1151) made occasional references to the science in his* Khal' al-na'layn.[122] *Ibn 'Arabî cited some of these in his commentary on the book in order to explain, and occasionally even to criticize them.*[123] *Among other references, the symbolism of* nûn *comes up a number of times, sometimes in terms that presage Ibn 'Arabî's later themes, like the "alif of the* nûn*," "the inner face, and the life of the Holy Spirit."*[124]

Al-Niffarî was a peculiar individual in the tasawwuf[125] *who accorded a special place to letters*[126] *in his work. Most often he refers to them in the singular—the letter—like a general reality, with no apparent relationship to the Word, Revelation, or the Book. His silence in this regard can be explained by the meaning Niffarî gives to the letter. In it—in accord with the etymology of the word* harf—*he sees a veil that separates "him who stops and stands still"* (wâqif) *from Divine Reality and, by extension, identifies the letter with everything*[127] *it limits, that is, with everything that is other than God. Niffarî is nevertheless unaware of the role the letter plays in the reception of knowledge and the process of knowing. After the veil is lifted, he also discovers the modalities of spiritual realization in each of the degrees of Being. The text that the following passage is taken from is titled: "standing in the stance that is appropriate for letters"* (mawqif adab al-hurûf) *because* adab *is the respect for place that its state and its degree in the hierarchy of Being confer upon each being.*

'The doors of the human Heart give way into the entire Letter; the doors of the sciences of the jinn open into the intermediate world of the Letter *(wasat al-harf)*. Angels enter through the upper world of the Letter *(a'là l-harf)*. The letter asked: 'What are the intermediate world of the Letter, its upper world, and the whole Letter'? God Almighty replied: 'The upper world of the Letter is My Name; the intermediate world is My Entreaties *('azîmatî)*, and the whole letter, My Languages and My Ways of Speaking *(lughâtî wa alsinatî)*. The angel replies to the Name, for it is his door, the jinn to the entreaties, since they are his door, and man to the entire Letter, since the same is true..."[128]

Despite Niffarî's insistence that the letter remain a veil in this text, where the word harf *is somewhat naggingly repeated—no one can escape the letter—he does ultimately say:* "He said to me: My knowledge is beyond the Letter. He to whom I have given the plenitude of presence, knowledge, and contemplation, has himself become the Letter through the spiritual meaning of his being *(bi-ma'nawiyyati-hi)*, while still remaining the companion of the Letter through the psychic nature of his being *(bi-nafsâhiyyati-hi)*, and that is the prison of believers."[129]

In both aspects, Niffarî's experience can be seen completely in Ibn 'Arabî's experience, both in the vision of the world of letters and in the union of the Letter and Meaning, which alone can resolve the contrast between what is created and what is uncreated.[130]

Other authors endeavored to discover the spiritual meaning of the Arabic language through the grammatical terminology that developed during the first two centuries after the hijra *in Kufa and Basra, in regard to phonetics and spelling, morphology and syntax. This latter branch of grammar was of particular interest to al-Qushayrî (376-465/986-1027) in his* Nahw al-qulûb al-saghîr,[131] *in which he delves into the meanings of the names for the three cases from an initiatory perspective ("elevation," "establishment," " and "lowering"), marked by the three vowels of declination* (i'râb) *or the semi-consonants that correspond to them* (wâw, alif, yâ'). *This symbolism runs through all the literature of the* tawawwuf, *probably from even before the time of Sahl al-Tustarî, as well as through Ibn 'Arabî and other, more recent, authors.*[132]

The space allotted for this introduction does not allow us to go at great length into the development of the science of letters after Ibn 'Arabî. It is however important that we follow a couple of the directions it took, because they give us a sense of how the Shaykh al-Akbar played such a central role, both here and elsewhere.

Shams al-dîn al-Bûnî, who authored a number of treatises on the esoteric sciences, is generally considered to be a contemporary of Ibn 'Arabî.[133] But a careful look at his best known work, the *Shams al-ma'ârif al-Kubrâ*, shows that in its present state, it could not have been composed before the end of the 7th/13th century.[134] Although this summa of esoteric knowledge appears to be more practical than contemplative, it is not devoid of a strict spiritual aspect. The author reminds us on more than one occasion that the origin and goal of *esoteric knowledge in no way resides in the outer order, although this does not exclude the practical applications of such knowledge that have made the book so popular, even up to the present day. We must limit ourselves here to a short analysis, given the extent to which "dispersion of knowledge" was practiced. In the book, we find the tradition of both Qur'ânic commentary and the* tasawwuf *regarding the isolated letters, and all the cosmological information customarily connected to the sciences of letters; we see, especially, Jâbir's "science of balances" and alchemy, the "conjunctions"* (wafq, *pl.* awfâq)[135] *or "magic squares" and their myriad applications, the use of the* zâ'irja,[136] *and the reference to* jafr *for knowledge of future events. The fact that the chains of transmission reported are both Eastern and Western*[137] *is evidence that a number of traditions come together in the work. Al-Bunî was undoubtedly acting deliberately when he published what others either had kept under greater cover or had limited to oral transmission. In divulging certain practical, or "magical," aspects of these sciences, he was throwing a veil over the deepest meaning of the heritage, while at the same time bequeathing it to those still capable of understanding it.*[138] *In deploring, on at least two occasions, that the men of the 8th and 9th centuries after the hijra would find themselves in a position where they needed to deny they knew these sciences and to pretend that they had been lost, he was announcing both the weakening and the permanence, of the body of knowledge.*[139] *Since that time, the* tasawwuf *has never been without teachers who could explain its highest meanings.*[140]

The chapter Ibn Khaldûn devotes to the science of letters is to a certain extent a confirmation of both al-Bûnî's prediction and the growing importance of Al-Bunî's book. Absent in the version as it was conceived in the Maghreb,[141] *this chapter was inserted between the science of magic and talismans*[142] *and the science of alchemy, long after the passage devoted to* tasawwuf. *Although he does recognize that the "men of the Divine Names" do not consider the science to be a means of exercising power* (tasarruf), *he deals with it especially from the point of view of* sîmiyâ', *simultaneously citing Ibn 'Arabî and al-Bûnî.*[143] *It is strange to observe Ibn Khaldûn completely disassociating the science of letters from* jafr, *which he ties to the chapter on the expectation of the Mahdî,*[144] *while al-Bûnî does the opposite, and integrates the two.*[145]

But it was especially 'Abd al-Razzâq al-Qâshânî (d. 730/1329) who introduced it into the commentary on isolated letters, thus to a certain extent expanding on Ibn 'Arabî's work and restoring a quite old[146] *exegetical tradition in a new form: "Alif - Lam - Mim* is the promised book; in other words: the form of the Universal All (represented by the initial monogram) is what was being referred to in the idea of the *Kitâb al-jafr wa l-jâmi'a,* the

'Book of Parchment and the summa encompassing all things,' the book that was 'promised' to be with the *Mahdî* at the end of time, and will be read, such as it is in reality, by the *Mahdî* alone. The *Jafr*, the Parchment, is the Tablet of the Eternal Decree *(lawh al-qadâ')* which is the intellect of the Universal All and the *Jâmi'a*—the Summa—is the Table of Assigned Destiny *(lawh al-qadar)*, which is the Soul of the Universal All."[147]

The science of letters has also been the subject of a few presentations in the West, not from the point of view of university research,[148] but in the very spirit of the science, and in reference to the Shaykh al-Akbar's work.

In an article written shortly after his arrival in Cairo, René Guénon offered an overview of the science of letters[149] where he began with the idea of the primordial language, using the expression lugha suryâniyya *used by the Ikhwân al-Safa, as we have seen, as well as by other authors.[150] What he then says about the constitution of sacred languages when he cites chapter 2 of the* Futûhât *is not found in exactly that form in the book, but it does correspond to chapter 5 of the* Fâtiha, *and perhaps also to chapter 198, on the* nafas. *It actually appears as though this information might have been passed to Guénon orally. It is interesting that for secondary applications of the science of letters or* sîmiyâ', *he refers to Ibn Khaldûn—that is, to what Ibn Khaldûn had himself received after his arrival in Egypt, albeit without the same spiritual opening. Without reading Ibn 'Arabî, from what it would appear, Guénon nevertheless understood the importance of the science of letters in understanding the Shaykh al-Akbar, and this through its other initiatory sobriquet:* al-Kibrît al-ahmar, *"Red Sulphur." Here is how he concluded his article:*

> And only he who has reached the degree of Red Sulphur—a possibly unexpected name, in some opinions, in a comparison of the "science of letters" with alchemy—can be active in all worlds. Deep down, these two sciences are actually one and the same. What they express, in quite different ways, is nothing other than the very process of initiation, which is a strict reproduction of the cosmogonic process, the total realization of a being's possibilities taking place necessarily, passing through the same phases as those of Universal Existence.[151]

"The mysteries of the letter Nûn,*" an article published a few years later, shows how close Guénon was to Ibn 'Arabî in his interpretation of symbolism,*

especially in regard to the upper and lower parts of the nûn.[152] *In other articles, Guénon shows how appropriate the language of the science of letters in Islam is for discussing metaphysical and cosmological teachings.*[153]

The late Michel Vâlsan authored two articles on this subject, based on correspondence with Guénon that dealt, in part, with the symbolism of letters[154]*: "Un symbol idéographique de l'homme universel," and "Triangle de l'Androgyne et le monosyllabe ôm."*[155] *Guénon described a triangle with an* alif *at the top and a* dâl *and a* mîm *at the base—the three letters in the name Adam. Inside was an upside down triangle with a* hâ' *and a* wâw *at the base and an* alif *at the apex, thus giving the name Hawâ' (Eve). On the right side of the larger triangle,* Ahad *("one") can be read;* Awm *("Om") can be read on the left side; and* Dâma *and* Dâ'im *("Permanent") at the base. Based on this figure and information related to the science of letters inspired by the teachings of Ibn 'Arabî, Vâlsan drew conclusions that were of tremendous importance for the doctrine of the multiple states of being and the Universal Man. He interprets this symbolism as a—*

> "seal of the two sacred sciences of numbers and letters. In reality, these sciences are the two main branches of the more general science of Names (applicable in both the divine order and in the order of worship) that Allah taught to Adam as a privilege (*Q. 2:31*, cf. *Gen. 2:19-20*) and the fact that this *alif* is in our graph first of all the initial for the very name of Adam is a perfect illustration of the truth that these two sciences are two complementary attributes of the Universal Man..."[156]

The reference to the primordial tradition, in the person of Adam, and the Hindu Tradition, suggested by the presence of the monosyllable Awm, *through the Abrahamic tradition, explains the meeting of India and Islam, either at the beginning or at the end of the cycle. As for the Ikhwân al-safâ, the comparison of two alphabets gives tremendous meaning to this meeting, especially in the juxtaposition of the two words* Aum *and* Amîn *(the last letter of which is a* nûn*).*

The science of letters thus constitutes the key to all knowledge from the origin, the hearing of the primordial sound, to its reabsorption at the end of the cycle. We must emphasize the importance here of this study, not only because it is greatly inspired by the teachings of the Shaykh al-Akbar regarding letters, but also because it underscores its most universal dimension.[157]

What we see here is that the science of letters has two different aspects in Islam: one, cosmological and Hellenic in origin, is present especially in Jâbir and the Ikhwân al-safâ, and the other—metaphysical, spiritual, and eschatological, and inspired by the Qur'ân—is represented by both esoteric Shi'ism and tasawwuf. Neither excludes the other, however, and the two currents are interwoven, their solidarity insured by the Qur'ân, where Revelation and creation are linked when the word that brings about existence is pronounced: kun! Moreover, all the authors mentioned here are in agreement that only contemplation and unveiling allow access to the actual science of letters and all their meanings. That being said, not all strike the same balance between the different orders of knowledge that the two main currents carry within them. Of the masters of tasawwuf, it appears as though Sahl al-Tustarî and Ibn Masarra are the individuals who best presage the synthesis Ibn 'Arabî achieved. In their succinctness, their treatises devoted to the science touch on nearly all the aspects of the teaching that would later show up and be more fully developed in the Futûhât and other Ibn 'Arabî works. It is clearly not coincidental that the expression uses the language of Letters, since Letters are both a key that opens the heart to penetration by the Book and the wax that keeps sealed beneath it those revelations whose time has not yet come. On the one hand, "Those which open the suras" (fawâtih al-suwar) have nourished an uninterrupted tradition one representative of which Ibn 'Arabî naturally became; his hermeneutics entails ascending through the Qur'ânic degrees of paradise. On the other, the work of the "seal" corresponds to the trip back down, a parallel to the Word, to the "men of secrets" sent to insure the inner ordering of the universe and to guide men toward the final, total meaning of "that book." For such men, the science of letters encompasses all the orders of knowledge, metaphysical and cosmic, initiatory and cyclic. There is no doubt that Ibn 'Arabî played a considerable role in bringing together all these aspects—a multiplicity of reflections with regard to manifestation—of a single principle. From the point of view of the history of ideas, we might even see an analogy between this synthesis and the synthesis philosophers were seeking between the ancient and prophetic heritages in earlier centuries. But Ibn 'Arabî's work takes place on a different plane, a strictly initiatory plane where the Intellect, as he reminds us in the commentary on the Fâtiha, remains the faithful "vizier" of the Spirit.

Few have committed themselves, or at least few have said so, to the path of establishing an identity between letter and meaning in a being's very heart. Niffari "got stuck," while Ibn 'Arabî drew from it the spiritual energy that gave his Qur'ânic commentary, Al-Jâm' wa l-tafsîl, its interpretive power of both synthesis and analysis.[158] So closely connected are Word and manifestation that *each word composed of letters, an emanation of the "Breath of the All-Merciful," is of Qur'ânic origin.* The letters thus become the hermeneutic principle not only of the Qur'ân but of all reality, and this central fact probably constitutes the Shaykh al-Akbar's most specific, and the most profound, contribution to the science of Letters. The *"Book of Eternity"* (Kitâb al-azal)[159] *is a remarkable illustration of this hermeneutic, since the word* azal *is not found in the Qur'ân.* After dealing with the theological difficulties raised by the idea of "eternity," he wipes them all away by going into an explanation of the three letters in the word AZaL, according to *"the language of secrets,"* meaning the science of Letters, in terms similar to those in the passage on the "Eternal Man" at the beginning of chapter 2 in the Futûhât: "Know that the secret of eternity, its spirit and the basis of its existence, is nothing other than me..."[160]

If Ibn 'Arabî states that *"existence is a letter, and you are its meaning,"* it is because *"you,"* the servant, should be identified with the letter and the meaning of the Qur'ân. The book itself came from the "Unknown Book" that is as all-encompassing and as impenetrable as divine knowledge.[161] Like the Universal Man, the Book faces both toward the manifested, on one side, and the unmanifested, on the other. In the isthmus that separates these two faces of reality, the letters allow for the passage from one to the other, sometimes to wipe away the difference between them and sometimes to create it, but always to help the servant of the one and multiple Reality.

Figure 1
Symbolism of nûn and the secret of its eternity

a.) The letter nûn:

b.) The upper and lower nûn:

   upper   unmanifested

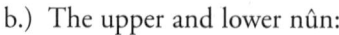

   lower   manifested

c.) Alif on its side, or the diameter touching the two ends of the nûn:

   head of the alif   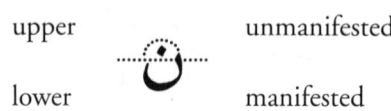   focal point (markaz)

d.) As it stands back up, the alif forms a lâm:

e.) Nûn breaks down into zây:

f.) Thus, the three letters in the word azal (eternity) are formed:

alif + zây + lâm = ازل

Figure 2
Alif - Lâm - Mîm

Line of the manifestation of the beginning of existence...... 3
Line of formal manifestation...

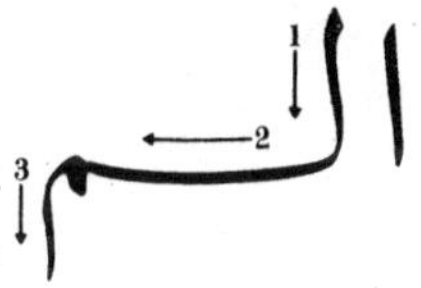

The dynamics of writing and manifestation:
1. Descent of Essence toward Attribute.
2. Extension of Attribute toward Act.
3. Descent of Act toward manifestation.

Figure 3
The Letter Lâm

ل ....alif
..(.).. ....nûn

Figure 4
Lâm - Alif and its decomposition

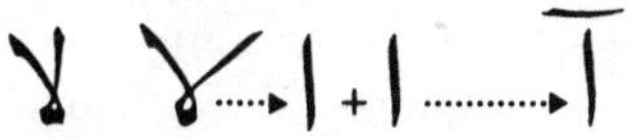

ل   ل....ا+ا........آ
1   2   3: alif and madda

Figure 5

The letters sâd and dâd and their circular shapes

nûn..... ص   ض
         sâd   dâd

THE HIERARCHY OF LETTERS
CHAPTER 2, SECTION I, PART 1[162]

Know—and may God be of assistance to us—that absolute, nonconditioned Existence includes Him who imposes the Law *(al-mukallif)* or True Being *(al-Haqq)* and those upon whom the Law is imposed *(al-mukallafûn)* or the universe *(al-'âlam)*. Just as the letters all encompass reality, it is our goal to begin from these letters and to differentiate among them in a specifically precise, verified fashion that, when they become aware of it, is in no way different for men who have been blessed with unveiling. The fashion to which we refer begins with the simple *(basâ'it)* elements of which the letters are composed, called *hurûf al-mu'jam*[163] when they are each called by name, since their meaning remains incomprehensible to the individual seeking to penetrate them via reflection. When the simple elements were revealed to us, we found that the letters divide up into four different degrees *(martaba*, pl. *marâtib)*:

- The letters whose degree entails seven celestial spheres: *alif, zây,* and *lâm*;

- The letters whose degree entails eight spheres: *nûn, sâd,* and *dâd*;

- The letters whose degree entails nine spheres: *'ayn, ghayn, sîn,* and *shîn*;

- The letters whose degree entails ten spheres: the remaining eighteen letters of the alphabet. Each of these letters is composed of ten celestial spheres, just as the preceding letters are composed of nine, eight, or seven spheres—no more, and no less.

In total, there are 261[164] celestial spheres—the simple elements, just discussed, from which the letters are brought into existence. The septenary degree, the *zây* and the *lâm*, excluding *alif*, is characterized *(tab')* by heat and dryness. The nature of the *alif* can be heat, humidity, dryness, or frigidity; it is hot with what is hot, humid with what is humid, cold with what is cold, and dry with what is dry, depending on the worlds that it stands next to.[165] The letters of the octenary degree are hot and dry. In the nonary, *'ayn* and *ghayn* have cold, dry natures, while *sîn* and *shîn* are hot and dry. Those of the decenary degree are hot and dry, except for *hâ'* and *khâ'*, which are cold and dry, and *hâ'* and *hamza*, which are cold and humid.[166] In all, there are 203 spheres whose movements produce heat. 241 produce dryness, sixty-five produce cold, and another twenty-seven[167] produce humidity, which includes their reciprocal combinations and interpenetrations *(tawâluj-tadâkhul)*, as stated above. Thus, from the movement of seven spheres on the 203 spheres, the first four elements *('anâsir)* are brought into existence, among which is *alif*, in particular. From the movement of the 196 other spheres, heat and dryness—and nothing more—are brought into existence. From these spheres come the letters *bâ', jîm, dâl, wâw, zây, tâ', yâ', kâf, lâm, mîm, nûn, sâd, fâ', dâd, qâf, râ', sîn, tâ', thâ', dhâl, zâ',* and *shîn*.[168] The movement of eighty-eight spheres produces coldness and dryness, in particular, and from these spheres come *'ayn, hâ', ghayn,* and *khâ'*. Twenty spheres bring cold and humidity into existence through their movement, and from them come *hâ'* and *hamza*. *Lâm-alif* results from the mixture of the 196 spheres if it is pronounced *lâ (lâm + alif* prolonged) or from the mixture of 196 and twenty spheres, if it is pronounced *la'a (lâm + hamza)*.[169]

There is no specific sphere in the universe that brings heat and humidity into existence. When the nature of air (which comes from them) is looked at, we see the divine wisdom that keeps it from coming from one sphere in particular.[170] Nor is there a sphere that is solely responsible for bringing one of the primary elements into existence. *Hâ'* and *hamza* are thus swept up in the rotation of the fourth sphere, which runs through the cycle of the final sphere *(al-falak al-aqsâ)* over the period of 9000 years. *Hâ', khâ', 'ayn,* and *ghayn* are moved by the rotation of the second sphere, which runs through the cycle of the final sphere in 11,000 years, and all the other letters are dragged along by the first sphere, whose course lasts

12,000 years. This final sphere entails a certain number of "mansions" *(manâzil)* for each of the spheres it encompasses; some are found on the surface, and the others in its concave part, while others still are between the two. If it would not overly extend this chapter, we would have described the "mansions" and the realities that each sphere contains. But we plan to return to this point sufficiently in chapter 60, if God's inspiration wills it, when we address the issue of the elements and the power of the upper world on the lower world; there, we will say which of the cycles of the final sphere has the world in which we presently are living located in it, and which spiritual *(rûhâniyya)* entity looks over us. Let us thus be patient until we reach that point, or until that point reaches us—God willing.[171]

The septenary degree, with its letters *zây, alif* and *lâm,* corresponds to the divine presence that imposes the Law. The octenary degree, with its letters *nûn, sâd,* and *dâd,* represents in the world of Letters that which is specific to Man. The nonary degree and its letters, *'ayn, ghayn, sîn,* and *shîn,* is specific to the jinn. The tenth degree, which is hierarchically the second and contains the rest of the letters, is specific to the Angels. The division of these four categories of beings, according to these four hierarchical degrees, is based on essential truths that are difficult to grasp; explaining them would need a volume all its own. We began a discussion of this issue in the *Book of Beginnings and Ends regarding the marvels and signs that the letters of the alphabet contain.* This work is not yet completed, but is in our hands as we write; only a few isolated sections have been fully composed.[172] I will nevertheless offer a brief overview. The jinn of Fire *(al-jinn al-nârî)* have four letters specific to them because of realities that constitute them which led them to say, as God has told us: "*Then I will come to them from before them and from behind them, and from their right-hand side and from their left-hand side*" (Q. 7:17).[173] When their four realities were thus exhausted, they did not have a fifth to help them seek a higher degree. Beware of believing that this would be possible for them, because height and its opposite would thus belong to them and could complete the six directions in space. The reality of things *(al-haqîqa)* in no way allows this, as we established in the *Book of Principles and Ends.* In it, we have shown the reason both why *'ayn, ghayn, sîn,* and *shîn* are specific to them and the correspondence between these letters and them, since their existence comes from the same spheres as these letters.

The Divine Presence has three of these letters specific to it, because of their own similarly constitutive realities: essence, attribute (or quality), and the bond *(râbita)* between the two. This bond is also the receptivity *(qabûl)* by which quality is attached to the qualifier, and to whoever is qualified by it. Science is thus connected both to him who is knowledgeable in the science, and to the thing known; will, to the individual who, with his will, wants, and to the object that is wanted. Moreover, there is an equal number of these letters.[174] What marvels there are in the constitutive realities of beings for those who become aware of them, for God asserts His transcendence in what the Other does not know, and which the breasts of those who do not know about Him cannot contain. We have also spoken of the correspondence between these letters and the Divine Presence in the above-mentioned book.[175]

The Human Presence, like the Divine Presence, has three of these letters specific to it. However, even though these two presences do coincide in number, the letters in this case are *nûn*, *sâd*, and *dâd*. The Human Presence is thus different from the Divine Presence in the material makeup of its letters. Indeed, servitude cannot be associated with lordship, because of realities by virtue of which lordship is god *(ilâh)*; by the same token, by virtue of his own realities, the servant is destined to worship God *(ma'lûh)*. Being made in the image of God,[176] man, like God *(ka-huwa)*, is endowed with three letters. If man and God shared the same constitutive realities, there would be only one unique being, God or servant, and that could not be. Essential realities thus need to be distinct from one another, even if they can be attributed to one and the same being.[177] This is why God distinguishes Himself from man in His eternity *(qidam)*, just as men distinguish themselves from Him in their reaching the point of being adventitious beings *(hudûth)*. It cannot be said that God distinguishes Himself from man by His knowledge, since the sphere of knowledge is one; it is eternal with the eternal, contingent with the contingent. The two presences have in common that they are grasped by the intellect because of three essential realities: essence, quality, and the bond between the quality and that which is qualified. The servant is subjected to three states: one state exclusively with himself (this is the moment that his sleeping heart no longer perceives anything else), one state with Allâh, and then one state with the world. The creator is different from us in this, since he has only two states, one for himself, and the other for his creatures. Since there is no being above Him, God has no quality that connects Him to it. But this is a whole sea unto itself; if we were to dive into it things would be heard that the ear could not bear. In the *Book of Principles and Ends* we mentioned the correspondence among *nûn*, *sâd*, and *dâd*, which belong to man, and *alif*, *zây*, and *lâm*, which belong to the Divine Presence. Even if the letters of the Divine Presence come from seven spheres and those of the Human Presence from eight, there is no contradiction in their correspondence; rather, the difference between divinity and worshiper is established.

On the letter *nûn*

In the very way the letter *nûn*[178] is written—it is a hemisphere—there are marvels that can be heard only by one who has firmly girded his loins with the loincloth of unreserved admission *(taslîm)* and has so realized within himself the spirit of death that he is incapable of conceiving of the slightest disputation or superfluous *(tatallu')* curiosity. The first sign of the spiritual and intelligible *nûn* can be seen in the *nûn*'s dot as it stands over the lower part of the letter, which is half of the circumference. The dot that goes with the written *nûn* placed at the beginning of the line is the place where the intelligible *alif* that forms the circle's diameter is set *(markaz).*[179] The final dot, in which the form of the *nûn* is interrupted and ends, constitutes the "head" (that is, the initial point) of this intelligible and imaginable *alif (al-ma'qûla al-mutawahamma)*. Let us suppose that the *alif* arises from its reclined position; it will stick itself above the *nûn*, and then the letter *lâm* will appear. Half of the *nûn* represents a *zây*; keeping the existence of the *alif* (and thus of the *lâm*) in mind, the *nûn* from this point of view signifies "human eternity" *(al-azal al-insânî)*, just as *alif, zây,* and *lâm* already expressed divine eternity, but with this difference: that eternity is apparent for the Divine Truth, because It is eternal in Its Essence, with clearly nothing preceding It or inaugurating Its existence. One individual who realized the truth spoke of "Universal Man" *(al-insân al-azalî)*, thus connecting man to eternity.[180] But eternity, which is hidden within him, remains unknown, since it is not apparent in his essence. One aspect of his existence by which it is possible to speak of eternity in his regard is that existence can be seen on four different planes *(marâtib)*; existence in what is mental *(dhihn)*; in being-entity *('ayn)*; in the spoken word *(lafz)*, and in writing *(raqm)*, which will be dealt with later in the book, God willing.[181] From the perspective of the existence of Man in the divine form, through which he exists as an essential entity *('ayn)* in the eternal beginningless knowledge that God has of him in his state of immutability *(fî hâl thubûtihi)*, man, also, exists in eternity without beginning *(azalan)*. By virtue of the concern that divine knowledge has for him, he finds himself in a situation comparable to that of the accident whose "localization" *(tahayyuz)* is due to the fact that it is inherent in substance. Man is thus "localized" (in divine knowledge) through dependence *(bi l-taba'iyya)*.[182] Because of this, eternity remains hidden in him, but it also remains hidden because of its own eternal realities, detached from this form that is specific, intelligible, and receptive to both eternity and contingency, as we explained in the *Book of the production of circles and tables*.[183] The work is worth consulting, for the question is developed in it, and we will refer to it again, as the occasion arises, in certain chapters of the present work. Manifestation of the secret of eternity, as in the case of *nûn*, is even better achieved and established in *sâd* and *dâd*, through the existence of a perfect circle in them.[184] Thus the essential realities of *alif, zây*, and *lâm*, which are specific to the divine, lead back to those of *nûn, sâd*, and *dâd*, which are specific to the servant. The Divine Truth is qualified by secrets that we have been forbidden to reveal in books. At the most, the individual who is in possession of them can share them with those who are worthy, whether their knowledge and their source of inspiration *(mashrab)* are identical to his, or whether they have reached the highest degrees of admission without reserve *(taslîm)*. His secrets are forbidden to anyone who does not fall into one of these two categories. Look into yourself regarding this subject, and note what evidence you can find; then you will possess marvels whose dazzling beauty stuns the intelligence.

Angelology and numerology:
The Intermediary Angel between God and man

The rest of the letters—of which there are eighteen [...][185] belong to the angels. We have already stated that human presence is comparable to the Divine Presence, or rather that the two are identical, since both entail three degrees: the Realm of the senses, the angelic, or spiritual Realm, and the world of the Almighty *(mulk, malakût, jabarût)*. Each of these degrees entails three others,[186] which gives a total of nine. Then, if the three from the world of the senses are multiplied by six, the sum of the letters in the divine and human presences, or the six specific days during which the three letters from the divine realm brought the three from the world of the creatures into existence, what we obtain is eighteen, or the existence of the Angel. The same process then takes place for the divine. Nine spheres for projection *(ilqâ')* go to God, and nine for reception *(talaqqî)*[187] go to man.

From each of the essential realities of the nine divine spheres, subtle bonds *(raqîqa,* pl. *raqâ'iq)* extend out toward the nine human spheres, and from these, subtle bonds reciprocally go back toward the divine spheres. Wherever these bonds meet, the angel itself is the meeting point, and it is there that the angel comes into existence *(hadatha).* This newly arrived fact of existence is thus the angel itself. If it bows with its whole being toward one of the sets of nine spheres, the other side attracts it. It thus comes and goes *(yataraddadu)* from one to the other [...].[188] Let us return to what we were saying then. The nine spheres[189] are at the same time seven spheres. Actually, the world of the senses is in itself an intermediate world *(barzakh)*; that makes one. It has an outer face, which makes two, and an inner face, which thus makes three. The world of Power *(jabarût)*[190] is an intermediate world, and thus the fourth. It has an outer face that is the inner side of the world of the senses, and an inner face, which is the fifth world. And finally, the world of the Inner Realm *(malakût)* is, in itself, an intermediate world: the sixth. Its outer face is the inside of the *jabarût*; its inner face is the seventh world, and there is no other. Such is the form of the heptad and the ennead *(is-sab'iyya, al-tis'iyya).* If we now take the three, and multiply them by seven, we get twenty-one. When we take away the three that belong to Man, we are left with eighteen, the station of the Angel, that is, the set of spheres from which man receives inspiration *(mawârid).* Let us proceed likewise with the three divine worlds; their multiplication by seven gives the spheres from which God projects toward His servant the knowledge that it pleases Him to inspire *(wâridât).* If we look at them from the divine side, we speak about the spheres of "Projection" *(aflâk al-ilqâ')*; and from Man's side, the spheres of reception *(aflâk al-talaqqî).* If we take the divine and human enneads together, the angel comes into existence from their being joined. This is why God brought nine spheres into existence: the seven heavens, the "Footstool" and the Throne, or, said another way, the sphere of the heavenly bodies and the dark sphere *(al-falak al-atlas).*[191] [...]

The Principles and Production of the Physical World

Know that there are marvels in the mixing of these principles. Heat and cold, being opposites, do not mix, and thus cannot produce anything of themselves; such is also the case for wetness and dryness. The opposite of an opposite cannot mix with anything other than the opposite of its opposite, so these principles can never engender anything but four elements. This is why they are opposed, two by two, since, if such were not the case, their composition would surpass what their specific realities entail. Composition would not be able to take place from more than four principles *(usûl)*, since the number four includes the fundamental numbers: three plus four make seven, and two more make nine, plus one makes ten. Choose any number to compose. No other numeral offers this peculiarity, just as there is no perfect number other than six, since it can divide itself into half, into thirds, and into sixths.[192] Thus heat and dryness mixed with one another, producing fire; heat and humidity produced air; cold and wetness resulted in water; and cold and dryness became earth. See how air is formed from heat and humidity; it is the vital breath *(nafas)*[193] that animates sensate life; through its blowing it moves all things, water, the earth, and fire; things move through its movement, since it is life and movement, the effect of life. Such are the four elements *(arkân)* engendered by the mother principles *(al-ummahât al-uwal)*.

Know next that these principles have no effect in composite beings other than that of their own reality, without mixing. Heating comes from heat alone, just as drying and contraction come from dryness. When you see fire dry a spot where there is water, do not think that it is heat that has dried it, since fire is composed of both heat and dryness: heat made the water get warmer; the drying took place through desiccation [...]. These principles are thus incompatible among themselves, and come together only in form,[194] in accord with the reality specific to each of them. One of these principles is never found alone in a form; they are always together, like heat and dryness, for example. Heat could not be there alone, since nothing other than it can come from it.[195]

The Common Origin of Letters and the First Principles

"God—glory be to Him—brought these forms into existence: water, fire, air, and earth. And He caused them to transmute into one another: fire becomes air and air again becomes fire, just as *tâ'* is changed into *tâ'* and *sîn* is changed into *sâd*.[196] Actually, the letters were brought into existence from the spheres that the mother principles[197] came from. The earth and letters come out of the same sphere: *thâ', tâ', tâ', jîm* (with the exception of its "head," half of the curve in *lâm*, the "head" of *khâ',* two thirds of the *hâ'*, the "dry" *dâl*, *mîm*, and *nûn*.[198] Water and the letters *sîn*, *ghayn*, *tâ'*, *hâ'*, *dâd*, the "head" of *bâ'* and its dot, the extension of the "body" of *fâ'*, the "head" of *qâf* and part of its curve, as well as the lower half of *zâ'*'s circle all come from the same sphere. The sphere that air comes from also gives rise to the last part of *hâ'* (the part that forms its circle), the "head" of *fâ'*, the curve in *khâ'* that forms a semi-circle, the upper half of the circle in *zâ'* with its vertical stroke, and the letters *dhâl*, *'ayn*, *zây*, *sâd*, and *wâw*. From the sphere that gives rise to fire come the letters *hamza*, *kâf*, *bâ'*, *sîn*, *râ'*, the "head" of *jîm*, the body of *yâ'* with the exception of its "head," the middle of *lâm*, and the body of *qâf*, without the "head."

All the letters come from the essential reality of *alif*, however. It is their sphere, for both spirit and sense perception.[199] Likewise, there is a fifth existent, which is the basis for the elements. This is a point of disagreement among speculative thinkers who are partisans of the science of natures *(ashâb 'ilm al-tabâ'i' 'an al-nazar)*[200]; the "Sage" mentions it in the *Ustuqusât*[201] without adding any information useful to one interested in studying the question. I have no knowledge about that, since I studied physics with the philosophers. It just happened that one of my companions came to see me with the book in his hand, because he was studying medicine. He asked me to clarify these questions as they are understood via the knowledge we acquire through intuitive revelation *(kashf)*, as opposed to study. He then read me the book, and I noted the point of divergence I just mentioned. Were it not for that, I would not have known that there were differences of opinion on the matter. Actually, for us, there is nothing other than something true *(al-shay' al-haqq)* here, such as it is in itself. For us, there is no point of divergence, since God, from Whom all knowledge comes—through both emptying the heart of all reflective thought and a predisposition toward receiving inspired knowledge *(wâridât)*—is the One who instructs us on something, such as it is at its most basic level, without this knowledge either remaining general or becoming perplexing *(min ghayri ijmâl wa lâ hayra)*. We thus know things according to their essential realities, whether they are isolated (in the intellect), whether they come into existence via the composition of elements, or whether they are divine realities; we express no doubt about any of this. This is where our knowledge comes from, and God—glory be to Him—is our teacher *(mu'allîm)* by virtue of a prophetic heritage that has been preserved and protected against any insufficiency, generality, or exteriority in knowledge[202] [...]

He who knows that the elements *(tabâ'i')* and the universe composed from them are in extreme indigence and need in relation to God, from Whom they get both their entities and the harmony of their composition *(ta'lîf)*, knows that the cause of the universe is the essential realities of the Divine Presence: the most beautiful Names and the sublime attributes, each according to its own specific reality. We made a sufficiently strong case for this in the *Book of the Production of Schemas and Circles*[203] and we will address this issue further in the remainder of the book.[204] Such is the eternal cause of causes that unceasingly brings the "mothers" into harmonious composition, and engenders the "daughters."[205] Glory be to Him, glory be to Him, the Creator of the Earth and the Heavens![206]

From Division into Four to Division into Six Degrees

So the elementary spheres *(basâ'il)* that those who rely primarily on their intellects *(al-'uqalâ')* restrict themselves to considering realities are divided into four degrees. We thus have the letters of the divine coming forth from the seven spheres; those of Man, coming from the eight; those of the Angel, from the nine, and those of the Jinn of fire, from the ten. They do not envision any extra divisions, incapable as they are of perceiving what is really at issue, since they are subjugated by their intellects, while those who have experienced the reality of things *(al-muhaqqiqûn)* are subjugated by their Lord, the King, the Truth—glory be to Him, and exalted may He be. They also are the recipients of unveiling that the others do not enjoy.

The elementary spheres considered by those who have experienced the reality of things entail six hierarchical degrees *(martaba* pl. *marâtib)*: the first degree, the degree of Him who imposes the Law, the Divine Truth, is that of *nûn*. It is binary *(thunâ'iyya)*, for we know God only through ourselves. He is our Adored one, and it is through us that He is known in His perfection. This is why *nûn* belongs to him, being binary, since it has two simple elements: *wâw* and *alif.*[207] *Alif* relates back to Him, and *wâw*, to "the idea of you" *(al-alif lahu wa l'wâw li-ma, nâka)*, and in existence there is none other than Allâh and you, for you are the *khalîfa*[208] [...].

The second degree is the degree of Man, the most perfect and the most universal of all the beings that submit to the Law from an existential point of view; he is the most accomplished and the most balanced from the creational point of view. A single letter corresponds to this degree, the *mîm*, which is ternary because its simple elements are three in number: *yâ', alif,* and *hamza.*

The third is that of the different kinds of jinn, be they of light or of fire.[209] This degree is quaternary, its letters being *jîm, wâw, kâf,* and *qâf.*

The fourth is that of the animals *(bahâ'im),* and is quinquenary; its letters are the "dry" *dâl, zây,* the "dry" *sâd,* the "dry" *'ayn, dâd,* and the "dry" *sîn, dhâl, ghayn,* and *shîn.*[210]

The fifth is that of the vegetable world *(nabât);* it is sextenary, and has *alif, hâ',* and *lâm*[211] as letters.

The sixth is that of the mineral world *(jamâd);* being septenary, its letters are *bâ', hâ', tâ', yâ', fâ', râ', tâ', thâ', khâ',* and *zâ'.*[212]

We will deal with all these letters later, God willing. The aim of this book is to reveal—like lights of understanding and dazzling references—a few of the secrets of existence. If we overtly addressed the mysteries of these letters and what their essential realities imply, our hand would quickly fatigue, the nib of our pen would grow dull, and our ink would go dry. Sheets and tablets could not contain them, even if they were "*unrolled parchment.*"[213] This knowledge belongs to the words God spoke: "*If the sea were made of ink...*" or "*Were every tree that is in the earth (made into) pens and the sea [to supply it with ink], with seven more seas to increase it, the words of Allah would not come to an end*" (Q. 18: 109 and 31:27). There is a secret here, and a marvellous hint for whoever gives his attention to it and discovers the meaning of these words. If this knowledge were the product of reflection or speculation, man might be confined to a quite imminent period of time *(la 'nhasara l-insân fî aqrab mudda).* But the inspirations *(mawârid)* that have come from the Divine Truth—exalted may He be—flow unceasingly into the servant's heart. His angelic spirits full of goodness and justice descend upon such beings, bringing mercy from the world of Mystery, from His abode, and knowledge[214] from Him. God distributes His gifts unceasingly, and the flowing of his grace does not stop; the receptacle is always available, sometimes through ignorance, sometimes through knowledge. If the servant prepares himself, makes himself available, and purifies and polishes the mirror of his heart, he will receive both the perpetual divine gift and, in a single instant, what the ages would not be able to entrust, so vast is this intelligible sphere, and so narrow is this sphere of the senses. How then might that whose end and whose borders cannot be conceived be interrupted? This is what the order given by God to His Messenger—may peace be upon him—clearly expresses: "*And say, Lord, let me grow in knowledge!*" (Q. 20:114).[215]

THE ISOLATED LETTERS
Chapter 2, Section I, Part II

The letters:
worlds and hierarchy

Know—may God give us Help—that letters are a community whose members receive the word of God and are bound by the Law *(mukhâtabûn wa mukallifûn)*. They have messengers just as we have. As such, they have names that only those on our path who have received the gift of unveiling know. The world of Letters is endowed with the purest of languages and the clearest of eloquence. The letters are distributed in accord with the way the world is commonly considered to be divided. Among them, we thus find:

• The world of the Almighty *(jabarût)*, for Abû Tâlib al-Makkî.[216] We tend to call this world the world of Immensity *('azama)*; this is *hâ'* and *hamza*;

• The upper world, or that of the Celestial Realm *(malakût)*: the letters *hâ'*, *khâ'*, *'ayn*, and *ghayn*;

• The intermediate world *(al-'âlam al-wasat)* or, for us and most of our companions, the world of *jabarût*: the letters *tâ'*, *thâ'*, *jîm*, *dâl*, *dhâl*, *râ'*, *zây*, *zâ'*, *kâf*, *lâm*, *nûn*, *sâd*, *dâd*, *qâf*, *sîn*, *shîn*, and *yâ'* as a consonant[217];

• The lower world, or the Realm of the Senses *('âlam al-mulk wa l-shahâda)*: the letters *bâ'*, *mîm*, and *wâw* as a consonant;

• The world where the sense realm mixes with the intermediate realm: the letter *fâ*[218];

• The world from the mixture of the intermediate world of *jabarût* with that of *malakût*: the letters *kâf* and *qâf*; mixture takes place at the level of the hierarchical degree *(imtizâj al-martaba)*. The letters *tâ'*, *zâ'*, *sâd* and *dâd*[219] mix in with them on the level of spiritual quality *(al-sifa al-rûhâniyya)*;

• The world of the mixture between *jabarût* as a place of Immensity and *malakût*: the letter *hâ*[220];

• The world that is like the worlds we know, where we cannot tell whether they come out of our world or enter into it: *alif*, as well as *wâw* and *yâ'*, which are weak letters.[221]

All these letters are worlds. Each of the worlds receives a messenger of its own kind, and a divine law by which its beings are bound to worship. The letters have modalities that are subtle and coarse. From divine discourse they receive only order and non-interdiction. Among them we find the common and the elite, the elite of the elite, and the pure quintessence of the elite of the elite.

• The common are *jîm, dâd, khâ', dâl, ghayn,* and *shîn*;

• The elite of the elite are: *alif, yâ', bâ', sîn, kâf, tâ', qâf, tâ', wâw, sâd, hâ', nûn, lâm,* and *ghayn*;

• The quintessence of the elite of the elite: *bâ'*;

• The elite that surpasses the common by one degree, the letters that begin the suras, like *Alif-Lâm-Mîm* and *Alif-Lâm-Mîm-Sâd*, of which there are fourteen: *alif, lâm, mîm, sâd, râ', kâf, hâ', yâ', 'ayn, tâ', sîn, hâ', qâf,* and *nûn*[222];

•The pure quintessence of the elite of the elite...[223];

• The world of messengers *(al-'alam al-mursal)*: *jîm, hâ', khâ',* and *kâf*[224];

• The world of those attached to God, and to whom the creatures are attached: *alif, dâl, dhâl, râ', zây,* and *wâw;* they represent the world of sanctification among the cherubic letters[225];

• The world of those for whom acquiring divine qualities is of utmost importance (...)[226] for men of light;

• The world of those for whom the realization of essential truths is of the utmost importance: *bâ'* and *fâ',* for men of secrets, and *jîm*[227];

• The world of those who have reached the station of reunion *(maqâm al-ittihâd)* [...][228]; and

• The world whose elementary natures are mixed *(al-'âlam al-muntazij al-tabâ'i')*. [...][229]

We have thus told you[230] what you, yourself, should put into practice in the matter of the world of letters; it will help you reach the stage where the world is unveiled, where you can discover its realities, and comprehend the meaning of the divine word: *"And there is not a single thing that does not glorify Him with praise, but you do not understand their song of glory"* (Q. 17:44). If the song of glory that beings sing were the very fact of their state *(tasbîh hâl)* alone, as some speculative thinkers maintain, what then would be the importance of *"but you do not understand...?* [...]

Alif-Lâm-Mîm in sura *al-Baqara*

I looked at the beings of this world, wondering upon which of them, more than others, I might expand my remarks, and I found that it was the world of the elite *(al-'âlam al-mukhtâss)*, the world of the beginnings of the suras, in the unknown sense,[231] like *Alif-Lâm-Mîm* in *al-Baqara, Alif-Lâm-Mîm-Sâd* in sura *al-A'râf, Alif-Lâm-Râ'* in sura *Yûnus* (among others) and those like them.

I shall then make a few short remarks about *Alif-Lâm-Mîm* in *al-Baqara,* the first sura in the Qur'ân that begins with these letters in the non-explicit *(mubham)* sense, in the manner appropriate for divine secrets.

I may add a few observations on the following verses, even though they are not part of this chapter. I did so after receiving, as usual, a command from my Lord. I do not speak until I have been authorized to do so, and, similarly, I will stop when a stopping point is given to me.

Both this work, and others, are unlike the books of other authors, and the procedure we are following cannot be compared to the procedures others follow. Authors are free to make choices, even if their choices are forced or determined by the knowledge they are imparting. In his work, an author expresses what part of his thought he chooses to express, or what his subject matter entails, or what the question with which he is dealing requires, until such point as he has done what he has set out to do. That is not the way it is in our works: these are devoted, diligent hearts, both poor and devoid of knowledge, on the threshold of the Divine Presence studying what the opening in the door allows to be seen. If questions were asked of them while in that station, they would not hear, as they lose all sense perception. Should an injunction from the other side of the veil be made manifest to them, they immediately hurry to conform to it and to compose text in accord with the details they are told. It may be that something is projected to them that is unlike what they have been in the habit of writing: speculative thought, data from exterior knowledge, or the exterior relationships among things such as these relationships is known by scholars; this is due to some hidden correspondence that only the people of unveiling are conscious of. But even stranger things happen to us; some things are projected into this heart that it is ordered to transmit, without it knowing them at that specific moment, for some reason known only to divine wisdom, which escapes created beings. No author who writes a book dictated by divine projection is limited by his knowledge of the subject matter at hand. He might include in it something that to the normal listener seems to belong to another order, depending on what is projected to him; but for us, it deals precisely with this subject, for reasons that only we know, like the dove and the crow who lived together because both limped. After receiving the order to write down what I am now about to "project," I have no choice but to do so.[232] [...][233]

On the isolated letters

Know that only those who can grasp intelligible forms *(ahl al-suwar al-ma'qûla)* know the reality of the beginnings of the suras, in the unknown sense. The suras in the Qur'ân begin with a *sîn*, which signifies submission to legal worship *(al-ta'abbud al-shar'î)*, or the outside of the wall *(sûr)* where both punishment and ignorance of the meanings of the suras reside. The inside of the wall is written with a *sâd (sûra)*; this is the station of divine mercy, or the knowledge of the essential realities encompassed by these suras, and this knowledge is the knowledge of Divine Unity.[234]

God—blessed and exalted may He be—had twenty-nine suras begin with these isolated letters, a number that represents the perfection of form: *"And We have ordained stages for the moon"* (Q. 36:39).[235] The twenty-ninth is the pole *(qutb)*, the sphere's axis, and the cause of its existence, as in sura *Al-Imrân*, which begins with *Alif-Lâm-Mîm-Allâh* [there is no god but Him, the Living, the Immutable] (Q. 3:1-2) without which the twenty-eight letters would have no stability.[236] Given their repetition in the Qur'ân, there are seventy-eight of these letters.[237] The "eight" are the true meaning of "and some" in the words of the Prophet—may peace be upon him: "faith entails seventy-some ramifications."[238] A servant has thus not penetrated all the secrets of the faith until he knows the essential realities of each of these letters in their respective suras.

To the objection that the specific meaning of "some" *(bid')* is unknown in the language—since it refers to a number from one to nine, why decide on the number eight?—my response is that I reached this number through personal unveiling, which is the path that I follow and the cornerstone that supports my knowledge in all fields. But I can also offer some insight in regard to the number. Ibn Barrajân—may God have mercy on him—did not deal with the issue in the same way in his book, but he did touch on the subject from an astrological *('ilm al-falak)* point of view. He hid his direct personal unveiling under this veil, when he predicted the conquest of Jerusalem in 583 (1187).[239] Similarly, we will veil such knowledge, or rather we will place a veil of numerical calculation over it.

We will say, then, that the "some" in sura *al-Rûm* means "eight."[240] Let us take the numerical value of the letters *A.L.M.* according to the "small estimation," which results in eight.[241] Let us add the eight from "some," which makes sixteen. We then take away one, because it comes from the *alif* that marks the beginning *(uss,* of letters and numbers), and fifteen remain, which we shall set aside. Let us begin the same operation again, by means of the "great sum," or "estimation."[242] Let us then multiply eight by seventy one, with the thought that we are dealing with years, and the product is 568. Let us add the fifteen that were set aside, which adds up to 583 years, that date of the conquest of Jerusalem, according to the reading *ghalabat-i-l-rûm...*, "the *Rum*s conquered..." In 583, the Muslims conquered and took control of the pilgrimage from the Infidels. [...][243]

God—glory be to Him—made the *alif* the first letter in writing; He made the *hamza* the first letter in pronunciation,[244] and He made the *nûn* the last. *Alif* represents the existence of Essence in its perfection, since there is no need to be moved by a vowel. *Nûn* represents half of the universe, the world of composition and the half of the sphere that appears to us from the sphere as a whole. The other half is the intelligible *nûn* located above the *nûn*. If the intelligible *nûn* were to show itself to the senses by transporting itself from the world of the Spirit, the circle would be completed. But God hid this spiritual *nûn* to which Existence owes its perfection. The *nûn*'s dot that is perceived by the senses was put there as an indication of this other *nûn*. The *alif* is perfect in all regards, but *nûn* is imperfect, just as the sun is perfect and the moon is imperfect, since it is effacement *(mahw)*, and its light is borrowed. *Nûn* is also all the trust *(amâna)* that Man has taken upon himself. His growth and apparition will be equal to his effacement and its total occultation *(sirâr)*.[245] It is a triad for a triad: the first, the setting of the moon of the divine heart in the One Presence *(ghurûb al-qamar al-qalbî al-ilâhî fî l-hadrat al-ahadiyya)*; the second is the rising of the moon of the divine heart in the Lordly Presence *(tulû' qamar al-qalb al-ilâhî fî l-hadrat al-rabbâniyya)*. Between these two, there is never-ending coming out and going back, step by step.[246]

> *[Ibn 'Arabî further explains this double triad, which expresses the Universal man's mediation between the manifested and the unmanifested via a threefold division of the isolated letters in the Qur'ân: the "singles" the "duals," and the "plurals."*[247] *These letters represent, respectively:*
> *1. The disappearance of any signs of the servant for all eternity* (fanâ' rasm al-'abd azalan) *or the sea of eternity-without-anteriority;*
> *2. The existence of signs of servitude in the present state* (wujûd rasm al-'ubûdiyya hâlan), *or the Muhammadan Isthmus* (al-barzakh al-muhammadî)[248]*;*
> *3. Eternity without posteriority in the unending arrival of divine inspiration* (al-abad bi-l-mawârid allatî lâtanâhâ).[249]*]*

Alif-Lâm-Mîm in Sura *al-Baqara*

In the *Alif-Lâm-Mîm* of *al-Baqara*, the *alif* is an allusive *(ishâra)*[250] reference to the knowledge of unity, and the *mîm*, to the imperishable kingdom; the *lâm* between them is a mediator, to ensure connection between the two.

Consider the line that the downward stroke of the *lâm* falls upon; the "trunk" of the *alif* stops at that point, and the *mîm* begins its growth there, then to descend from "the most excellent constitution" to "the lowest of low beings," the final point of the *mîm*'s root.[251] God—exalted may He be—said: "*We created man of the most excellent constitution, then we sent him back among the lowest of the low*"[252] (Q. 95:4-5).

The *alif*'s descending stroke toward the line is of the same order as the Prophet's words: "*Our Lord comes down toward the lowest heaven...*"[253] This heaven is the beginning of the world of composition, since it is Adam's heaven—may peace be upon him—and on this side of it is the sphere of fire.

The *alif* thus descended to the point where the line begins, from the station of Unity to that of the the origination of creatures; it was a descent of sanctification and transcendence, not of similarity and resemblance. *Lâm* was the mediator *(wâsita)*, playing both the role of Him who gives being and that of the beings in the universe *(al-mukawwin wa l-kawn)*, simultaneously. It is thus the Power[254] through which the world was brought into existence. In its descent to where the line begins, it looks just like *alif*. But, as a mixture of Him who gives being and of beings, it is not endowed with power over itself, but only over the creatures. Since this aspect of power is turned toward the creatures, without them it could not be attributed to the Creator; it is thus necessary that this attribute be related to the higher and lower creatures.

The *lâm* is not yet a reality when it reaches the line, since at that point it is on the same level as *alif*. By its very reality, it tends to go down over or under the line, as does the *mîm*.[255] It descended in order to bring the *mîm* into existence. But it was not able to descend in the form of the *mîm*, because in this case no letter other than *mîm* could have been brought into existence from it.[256] The *lâm* descended, forming a semicircle, the final point of which rejoined the line beside its point of departure. It thus became a noticeable hemisphere requiring an intelligible hemisphere, the two of which form a complete sphere.[257] This is how the entire universe, from the first being to the last, was produced in six days, species after species, from the first hour on Sunday to the last hour on Friday.[258] Saturday remained, dedicated to transfers from state to state, from station to station, and to transmutations from being to being, in an unchangeable, unchanged, and uninterruptable order.[259] Saturday is governed by cold and dryness, and among the heavenly bodies it corresponds to Saturn.[260]

Alif-Lâm-Mîm thus became an enveloping *(muhît)* sphere unto itself; the individual who completes the cycle knows the Essence, the Attributes, the Acts, and their objects. He who recites[261] *Alif-Lâm-Mîm* in accord with this essential reality and this personal unveiling is present through the All, for the All, and with the All. There is nothing left that he does not contemplate at this specific instant, except that he has knowledge of certain things, and of others he does not.

The *alif*'s transcendence, which keeps it from receiving vowels, is an indication that the Divine Attributes can only be grasped by Acts. As the Prophet—may peace be upon him—said: "*God was without anything, and He is as He was,*"[262] we turn toward what can be grasped by the intellect, and not toward its transcendent Essence. The idea of relationship *(idâfa)* cannot be grasped without two beings playing a part in it. Paternity cannot be conceived of without a father and a son, be they real or imagined; the same is true for the Divine Names, like the Possessor, the Creator, or the Producer of Beings, which, through their essential realities, call upon the world. This is pointed out in the letters *Alif-Lâm-Mîm* by the *lâm*, the attribute, being joined to the *mîm*, its effect and its act. The *alif*, which is a single essence, cannot be attached to any other letter when it is in an initial position. It is then the Straight Path, the path that the soul is asking for when it says "*Guide us on the straight path*" (Q. 1:6), the path of the realization of transcendence and unity. When the Lord of this soul—that is, the Word *(al-kalima)*—toward Whom it was ordered to go back in the sura of the Dawn,[263] had confirmed its request with *âmîn*, God approved of this confirmation and had the *alif* of *Alif-Lâm-Mîm* appear after "*nor of those who have gone astray.*"[264] He hid *âmîn*, which is an unmanifested reality from the Celestial Realm. "*He who says* âmîn *at the same time as the angels...*"[265] realizes it in what is unmanifested *(ghayb)*, which the doctors of the Law call "sincerity" *(ikhlâs)*; the Sufis call it "presence" *(hudûr)*; those who have realized the truth refer to it as spiritual energy *(himma)*, while we and others like us call it "divine solicitude" *('inâya).*[266] The *alif*, connected to itself in the Celestial Realm and in sensory manifestation, manifested itself and thus the difference between the eternal and the contingent came into being. Meditate on these lines we have just drawn, for in them you will find wonders!

The existence of the attribute about which we were just speaking is confirmed by the lengthening of the vowel in *lâm* and *mîm* when they are recited, as opposed to the *alif*.[267] When a Sufi says that the *alif* is written, but it is the *hamza* that is pronounced rather than the *alif*, why is that? Our response is that this confirms what we are saying. The *alif* cannot receive a vowel, since a letter is unknown as long as it is not moved by a vowel. When it is moved, the letter can be distinguished from others because of the vowel attached to it in a state of elevation, establishment, or lowering.[268] Essence is never known such as it is in reality, as is its indicator, the *alif*. It is God's representative in the world of letters, just as the human being is in the Universe, which is, itself, just as unknown as Essence; it cannot take a vowel, and cannot be known except via the negation of attributes *(salb al-awsâf)*. Just as it is impossible to utter a letter without a vowel, one cannot utter the *alif* itself, but only the *alif*'s name, and in so doing one pronounces the *hamza* moved by the vowel *a*.[269] The *hamza* is thus taking the place of the first production of being *(al-mubda' al-awwal)* here. The vowel *a* represents the attribute of knowledge (from which it comes) and the place of its coming into existence resides in the junction between *kâf* and *nûn*.[270]

[At this point, Ibn 'Arabî points out that in the name of the letter lâm, *the* alif *is pronounced, since it indicates that the vowel* a *is a long vowel. In this case, moreover, the* alif *is connected to the preceding letter. He explains these two facts as follows:]*

Its elongation is the secret of the request for substantial support *(sirr al-istimdâd)*[271] that entailed the attributes coming into existence in the receptacle of the letters. So there is no elongation without liaison. The letter is connected to the *alif* through its name "the Last," just as the *alif*'s extension takes place via the existence of the letter it is connected to. In order to come into existence, this letter needed the quality of Universal Mercy[272] and, therefore received "the movement of opening" *(harakat al-fath)*, meaning the vowel *a (al-fatha)*. When the *a* had received it, it was asked to express its gratitude. When the *a* asked how, the reply was: by letting the hearers know that your existence and the existence of your attribute are not for you, but they come from the essence of the Eternal—exalted may He be. Mention Him when you mention yourself, by the attribute specific to mercy. He made you the sign of Himself. This is why [the Prophet] said: "*God created Adam in the image of the All Merciful.*"²⁷³

The vowel in *lâm* is a sign of the Attribute (of Mercy), and thus of Essence. What about the other two vowels, *u* and *i*? The two corresponding semi-vowels, *wâw* and *yâ'*, are incapable of indicating Essence the way *alif* is. In marking the elongation *(madd)* of *u* and *i*, the letters *wâw* and *yâ'* are called "letters of deficiency," or "letters of causality" *(harf 'illa).* This terminology has a dual meaning, grammatical and ontological," which makes of the two semi-vowels, or semi-consonants, the symbol of doubling between the principle and its consequence, since the "cause" *('illa)* supposes a being "caused" or affected by it *(ma'lûl).* Elongation is the perceptible mark of their reciprocal relationship. On the level of Revelation *(wahy),* the *wâw* represents the bearer of the message and the *yâ'* represents the entity for whom the message is intended. It is for this reason that the Isolated Letters of the Qur'ân that have a *yâ'* of elongation within them *(mîm, sîn)* denote the Prophet and those that include a *waw* denote the Angel (cf. Qur'ân 68:1): "*Nûn, by the Pen...*"). The connection that stretches between them is the support *(madad)* that the higher world brings to the lower world in Revelation.

There must be a secret between the two via which the request for support takes place, and the bringing of this support *(al-istimdâd wa l'imdâd)* is the reason why causality is marked by elongation. When Revelation was given to the angelic messenger, if there had not been any relationship between him and the individual toward whom it was to be projected, the latter would not have been able to receive it. This nevertheless remained hidden from the Angel, who received Revelation. Because he is a higher spiritual being, his station is *wâw*. As a "deficient" *(mu'talla)* letter, it marks "elevation"²⁷⁴ and thus exaltation *('uluww).* We refer to him as the "angelic spiritual Messenger" whether we are referring to Gabriel or to another angel. Both some of the secrets of Divine Unity, and the Laws, were entrusted to the human messenger, and the request for support and the bringing of this support were given to the world of composition.²⁷⁵ The secret of the request for support remained hidden from him, and it is because of this that God commanded the Prophet to say: "*...And I do not know what will be done with either me or you*" (Q. 46:9); the Prophet also said: "*I am nothing other than a man, like you.*"²⁷⁶ Since he is in the lower world, the world of the body and of composition, we reserve for him the "deficient" *yâ'*, preceded by the vowel *i* as a sign of "lowering."²⁷⁷ The *wâw* and the *yâ'*, as causes of the existence of divine secrets in the doctrine of

Unity and the Law, received the gift of the secret of the request for support, and for this reason were prolonged. The difference between these two letters and the *alif* is actually due to the fact that they can lose this station by being vocalized by one of the three vowels or quiescents, while *alif* is never vocalized and, as a semi-vowel of elongation, is never preceded except by the vowel *a*. There is thus no relationship between *alif*, on the one hand, and *wâw* and *yâ'*, on the other. Being vocalized is both the station and the attribute of the latter two letters, while if *alif* were attached (as a semi-vowel) to the deficiency of causality *('illiyya)*, it would not belong to it by essence. From the perspective of the Eternal One—glory be to Him—the *alif* neither supports nor receives vowels. It does so only in order to take on the quality attached to a station, and it is as a *wâw* or a *yâ'* that it descends. What the *alif* stands for is eternal, while *wâw* and *yâ'*, whether they are vocalized or not, enter into existence *(hâdith)*. If such is the case, any written or uttered *alif*, *wâw*, or *yâ'* is nothing more than a sign *(dalîl)*. Any sign that is adventitious *(muhdath)* summons a being that causes it to come into existence *(muhdith)*; neither writing nor pronunciation can define what is happening here; it is, in reality, something manifestly unmanifest. Just as is the case for the isolated letters *Yâ'*, *Sîn*, and *Nûn*, the semi-consonants *(alif, yâ',* and *wâw)* are pronounced (representing His manifestation) but not written (which represents His non-manifestation). It is for this reason that we can actualize knowledge of the existence of the Creator, but not knowledge of His essence; likewise, we can actualize knowledge of the existence of *"There is nothing like His likeness"* (Q. 42:11) but not knowledge of its essence.[278]

Know, o you who receive *(al-mutallaqî)*, that everything that can be encompassed is a being that is either produced or created, and this is true of your receptacle *(mahall)*. Do not seek the Truth either inside or outside, for these are attributes of adventitious existence *(hudûth)*. But see the all in the all, and you shall see everything. The Throne is a united *(majmû')* being, and the "Footstool" is a separate *(mafrûq)* being:

> Oh you who seek to attain the being of Truth
> Return toward your essence. The Truth is in you; hold to it![279]

"*A.L.M.* That is the Book..."
(*dhâlika l-kitâb*)[280]

The demonstrative *(ishâra)*[281] refers to an existing being, even though it is marked with elongation; this happens because it denotes the Book, the separate being, the place of distinction. The letter *lâm* announces elongation in this station. "*The allusive indication* (ishâra) *is a call from afar*," according to the People of God.[282]

The *lâm*, moreover, belongs to the intermediate world *(al-'âlam al-wasat)*, and is thus the place of the attribute, since it is through the attribute that the contingent differentiates itself from the eternal.

Through the *kâf*, which is the pronoun for the singular form of "you," speech is addressed to an individual, to avoid confusion among the beings that are produced. We addressed this situation at length in our remarks about the divine words: "*take off your sandals!*" *(ikhla' na'lay-ka)* (Q. 20:12) in the *Book of Unitive and Distinctive Knowledge*.[283] What the command means is this: take away *lâm* and *mîm*, and what is left is *alif*, which transcends the attributes.

Distance was then put between the *dhâl*—which refers to the Book, the place of the second separation *(farq)*—and the *lâm* (from *li*) of the attribute—the place of the first separation—which allowed the Book to be read. This was done by the *alif*, which is the place of union *(jam')*. This took place so that the being that finds itself in separation does not imagine speech as coming from some other separation, since in that case it could never attain any other essential reality. It thus made the distinction via the *alif*, which became a veil between the *dhâl* and the *lâm*.[284] The *dhâl* wanted to connect to the *lâm*, but the *alif* stood in the way, saying "if you join him, it will be through me!" The *lâm*, also, wanted to connect with the *dhâl*, in order to give back what had been entrusted *(amâna)* to it. But here, again, the *alif* stood in the way, saying "you can meet him only through me!"

If we thus look at existence in a unitive or distinctive way *(jam'an wa tafsîlan)*, it is always found accompanied by the proclamation of unity *(tawhîd)*, indefectibly, just like One accompanies numbers. Two can never exist without one being added to its like; three could not be without one being added to two, and so on indefinitely. One is not the number, and yet, in itself, it is the number, in the sense that through it the number was made manifest. The number in its totality is one. If we subtracted one from a thousand, then one thousand's number, and its reality, would disappear. What would be left would be another reality: nine hundred ninety-nine. The moment that one is no longer in something, the thing no longer is, and conversely. Such is *tawhîd*, if you truly realize what its meaning is. "*And It is with you wherever you are*" (Q. 57:4).[285]

"That" is a nonspecific word *(harf mubham)* that is made more specific by "the Book," which is its reality. "The Book" *(al-kitâb)* is preceded by the two letters of determination and specificity *(al-ta'rîf wa l-'ahd)*, the *alif* and the *lâm* of *Alif-Lâm-Mîm*, even though they appear in a different form here. There, they were in the place of union *(jam')*; here, they are at the first door of distinction *(tafsîl)*, meaning: the distinction of the intimate secrets of this sura in particular, and not of the other. This is how the hierarchy of realities in existence is arranged.

"That is the Book." What this refers to is the "inscribed book, since there are three archetypes of books: the "drawn" *(mastûr)* book, the "inscribed" *(marqûm)* book, and the "unknown" *(majhûl)* book. We explained the meaning of the written and the writer *(al-kitâb wa l-kâtib)* in *The Book of divine dispositions for the reform of the human realm*, in chapter 9; it might be worth consulting at the present time.[286]

Since they are undimensional, essences *(dhawât)* should be able to be distinguished from one another in some other dimension: quality *(wasf)*. The "inscribed" book is thus qualified by the fact of its being inscribed, and the "drawn" book by the fact of its being drawn. The "unknown" book, from which all qualification has been removed, is in itself either a quality—which is why it cannot be qualified—or an unqualified essence. Unveiling teaches us that this "unknown" book is a quality called "Knowledge," and the hearts of the divine words are its receptacle. Do you not see that God said "*Alif-Lâm-Mîm. The descent of the Book...*" (Q. 32:12) and "*Say: "He had it descend through His knowledge..."* (Q. 4:166)? This speech was addressed to the *kâf* in *dhâlika* (that is, to you) through the attribute of knowledge: the *lâm* in *li*, which was lowered by the descent,[287] since His transcendent essence cannot be perceived. So God said to *kâf*—which is also Divine Speech[288]: "*That book,*[289] *which descended toward you, is My knowledge, not yours.*" "*There is no doubt about it*" for those who understand essential realities. I send it down as a guide for those who take Me for protection. It is you who came down, and You are the receptacle."[290]

Every book comes from an archetype *(umm)*. You will never know the archetype of this unknown book, because it is an attribute neither of you nor of anyone else; nor is it an essence. If you wish to realize that, consider the way in which knowledge becomes real in its knower, or the way that the thing seen is actualized in the person who sees. It is not the thing, and it is not something other than its essence.[291] Consider the degrees *(darajât)* of *là rayba fîhi hudan li-l-muttaqîn*: "There is no doubt about him, a guide for those who take refuge in God," and in His "mansions" *(manâzil)*, as will be said later, and meditate on what I have just told you.

Untie the knot of the *lâm-alif* in the word *lâ (rayba)*, and what is left is two *alifs*, since the form of the "root" *(ta'rîqa)* of the *lâm* reappears in the *nûn* of *al-muttaqîn*.[292] The *alif* actually comes after the *lâm* through the Divine Name "the Last" *(al-Akhîr)*, and thus represents the knowledge the servant gains by himself, according to the words of the Prophet: "He who knows himself knows his Lord." This is why knowledge of *lâm* precedes that of *alif*, and is a sign *(dalîl)* that it is coming. The two letters do not get confused to the point of becoming a single essence, but each is differentiated from the other by its essence. The sign and the thing indicated *(al-dalîl wa l-madlûl)* do not come together, but are rather joined by a bond *(râbit)*: the place where the *lâm* is connected to the *alif*.

Multiply the two *alifs* by one another and the result is a single *alif* represented as such.[293] This is the reality of the connection *(ittisâl)*. Similarly, multiply the adventitious by the eternal in the domain of the senses and the result will legitimately be adventitious; when this operation is performed, the eternal remains hidden, and this is the reality of connection and union. "*And when your Lord said to the angels: I am going to establish a representative on earth*" (Q. 2:30).[294] This point of view is diametrically opposed to what Junayd told the man who sneezed: "*When the adventitious is confronted by the eternal, no trace of it remains*," because Junayd was speaking from a different spiritual station.[295]

Do you not see how the *lâm-alif* in *lâ rayba fîhi* remained connected to the level of the "Pedestal" *(kursî)*, thus making two essences appear: لا and leaving the secret of their connection unknown. Then, when the two letters went back toward the Throne, the Throne separated them, and they took the form ل ا. The *lâm* appeared in its reality, since no being in the station of liaison and reunion *(maqâm al-ittisâl wa l-ittihâd)* was able to bring it back to its own form. We had already sent the *lâm*'s semicircle,[296] which was hidden in the *lâm-alif*, toward the world of composition and sensory manifestation. What was then left were two *alifs* separated from one another. We multiplied one by one, just like one multiplies something by itself; the result was an ا. One covered the other. One was the cloak *(ridâ')*; it was the one that appeared, the *khalîfa*, the being produced *(mubda')*. The other was the one that put on the cloak *(murtadî)*, the One that remained hidden, the Eternal, the producer of beings *(mubdi')*. The One wearing the cloak only knows its inside—the state of union—while the cloak molds itself to the shape wearing it.[297] If you say "one," you are speaking truthfully; if you say "two essences," you are also speaking truthfully, whether you see it with your eyes or through unveiling. He who composed the following lines, by God, was quite correct in saying:

> Subtle is the glass, subtle the wine;
> Similar is their form, and ambiguous.
> As if it were wine, but not a wine glass;
> A wine glass, but not wine.[298]

The outside of the cloak will never know the person wearing it; it will only know the inner facet of its own essence, which is its veil. Thus, only knowledge knows the True God, and only praise is truly capable of praising Him. You know Him only with knowledge—your veil—as an intermediary. You contemplate only the knowledge that remains within you *(al-'ilm al-qâ'im bi-ka)*,[299] even if that knowledge should be in perfect correspondence with its object. Your knowledge remains in you and is your object of contemplation and worship. If you follow the way of expression that is proper for essential realities, be careful of saying that you know the object of knowledge. You actually know only knowledge, and it is knowledge that has knowledge of its object. Knowledge and the Known are separated by unfathomable seas. The secret of the relationship between them, given the distance that separates the essential realities between them, is a sea upon which it is difficult to embark. In no case does the obvious expression of the doctrine *('ibâra)*, or even an allusive *(ishâra)* indication of it, allow it to be passed beyond. Only personal unveiling can perceive it, through veils that are so numerous, so subtle, so imperceptible, and so fine that they cannot even be felt when they cover the eyes of inner vision. If they are so difficult to perceive, what can be said about their Creator? So notice where the individual is who says "I know this thing through such-and-such thing, whether it is something adventitious or something eternal! That may be true for the contingent, but the eternal is infinitely less accessible, because there is nothing like it. Where does one reach knowledge about Him? How does one even get some of that knowledge?[300]

THE PROPERTIES OF LETTERS
CHAPTER 2, SECTION I, PART III

The letter sâd

[...] Know that even though I was of the opinion that the secret of this "dry"[301] *sâd* could be perceived only during sleep, this is only because I, myself, received it in a dream, as a gift from God. It is for this reason that I judged that God nevertheless does give such gifts to us during our sleep, but also when we are awake. When the time came for me to compose this passage, one of my companions read a passage about the secrets of letters back to me so that I could correct errors made by copying too quickly. When he reached *sâd*, I told the companions about its importance to me, that sleep was not necessary to receive the secret, but that is how I had received it. I described my state to them, and the group then dispersed. The next day, a Saturday, we had our usual meeting in the Sacred Mosque, facing the Yemenite corner of the Most-Venerated Ka'ba. One participant in our meetings was the Meccan resident *(mujâwir)*, the shaykh and *faqîh* Abû Yahyâ Abû Bakr b. Abî 'Abdallâh al-Hâshimî al-Tuwaytmî al-Tarâbulusî—may God have mercy on him. When we finished our reading, he said: "Yesterday while I was sleeping I saw myself in a seated position, and you were lying on your back. You were talking about *sâd*, and I spontaneously began to recited this verse:

Sâd *is a noble letter and the* sâd *in* sâd *is even more veracious.*

You asked me—I was still asleep—what proof I had, to which I replied:

Its form is a cycle and no form preceded it in time."

Still enwrapt in his vision, he added that I was delighted with his reply.

When he was finished with his story, I felt a moment of joy about this vision *(mubashshira)* in which I had played a part, and for the supine position I was in, because that is the sleeping position of the prophets—may peace be upon them. It was the state of the person at rest, free of both occupations and preoccupations, ready to receive, face to face, whatever news might come from heaven. I was surprised at his revelations, and he, for his part, was fully assured regarding the state I had described to my companions during our meeting the night before. *"And We forgave him for that, and he enjoyed a closeness to us, and an excellent return"* (Q. 38:25).[302] It is indeed a noble, magnificent letter. In pronouncing it, God was giving His promise through the station of "totalizing Words," the place of Muhammadan contemplation in its nobility, in the language of worship. This sura contains marvellous signs regarding both the attributes of the prophets—may peace be upon them— and the imperceptible secrets of the entire universe. In the vision itself, there are as many secrets as there are in the sura. This vision is a sign of immense wealth, a wealth that is as substantial for the person who had the vision as for the person for whom it was seen and who was contemplated by God in it. Both individuals benefit from the blessings of the prophets mentioned in the sura. Their enemies among the unbelievers, but not the believers, will be struck by the misfortune the sura announces. We beg God, for both them and us, to preserve us in this world and in the next.[303]

Knowledge of the *lâm-alif* in *lâ*

When the *alif* and the *lâm* kept one another company, each experienced a penchant for the other.[304] This penchant is amorous passion and interest, simultaneously. There is no penchant without the movement of love *(haraka 'ishqiyya)*. The *lâm*'s movement is thus essential, and the movement of the *alif* is contingent. The *lâm*'s power was exerted on the *alif* in order to get the *alif* to move. In this case, the *lâm* is stronger than the *alif*, since it is more smitten; its spiritual energy *(himma)* has a more perfect existence and better efficiency. The *alif* is less in love, and its spiritual energy is less attached to the *lâm*, which we see in its inability to stand up straight. The one with the greater spiritual energy necessarily takes the initiative for the act in the eyes of "those who have experienced the reality of things" *(muhaqqiqûn)*. This is the lot of the Sufi and the station he does not know how to get beyond. If he nevertheless does manage to move himself into the station of the *muhaqqiqûn*, he will certainly reach a level of higher knowledge. According to this knowledge, the *alif*'s penchant is not due to the effect of the *lâm*'s spiritual energy on it, but rather to the full descent of subtle graces upon the *lâm*, so that amorous desire takes possession of it. Do you not see the *lâm* bend its downstroke so that it can envelop the trunk of the *alif*, for fear that it might escape? The *alif*'s penchant toward the *lâm* is thus a descent comparable to God's descent to the lowest heaven, and the *lâm*'s fear is like the fear of "men of the night" during the last third of the night.[305]

The *lâm*'s penchant is something that is known by both the Sufi and the *muhaqqiq*. It is due to a necessary cause, and the only difference of opinion on this issue concerns the reason for its leaning. For the Sufi, this penchant is the leaning that is experienced by those caught up in the ecstasy of love, and who are looking for this ecstasy. For them, the penchant fully actualizes the station and the state of desire and loving attachment *(al-'ishq wa l-ta'ashshuq)*, while the *alif*'s penchant is that of a reciprocal relationship, and of reunion *(al-tawâsul wa l-ittihâd)*, which is why the forms of the two letters are similar [...].[306] This provokes the state of amorous desire. The sincerity of this desire engenders orientation toward the Desired One *(ma'shûq)*. The sincerity of such an orientation leads the Desired One to a connection with the One In Love. For the *muhaqqiq*, the reason for the penchant is knowledge that is common to both, but each according to his own reality. We, and those who, with us, have been raised to the highest degree of realizations—to that level beyond which there is no other—do not make the same remarks, since a difference arises in this question. We must first observe which existential presence *(hadra)* the two letters are coming together in, since amorous desire is itself a partial presence that participates in all the others. What the Sufi says is true; knowledge is also a presence, and thus the words of the *muhaqqiq* are also true. Nevertheless, the Sufi and the *muhaqqiq* have reached only a limited realization, as if they were seeing through only one eye.

It is our contention that the first existential presence where these two letters come together is the presence of the origination of existence *(hadrat al-îjâd)*, which is:

lâ	i-lâ-ha	il-la	al-lâ-hu
1	2	3	4
No	God	except	the God[307]

This presence is the presence of both creation and the Creator. The *lâm-alif (lâ)* appears twice negatively here (1 and 3), and twice affirmatively (2 and 4). The penchant of the Absolute Being, which is the *alif* in this presence, leans toward the origination of existence; the penchant of conditioned existence, which is the *lâm*, leans toward the origination of existence at the time when things are brought into existence. This is why the *lâm* came out in the Divine Form. Each of the realities specific to these two letters is absolute in its hierarchical abode *(manzila)*. So understand, if you can, and if not, make a retreat *(khalwa)*, and attach your inspiration *(himma)* to God the All-Merciful until such time as you do know. When He conditions Himself after His Being is determined and his own being has appeared to itself, it is then *(verses)*:

> *For the Divine Truth, it is God, and for man, it is man,*
> *at the time when existence arrives,*
> *and for the Qur'ân, it is the Qur'ân.*
> *For sight, it is vision at the time of contemplation,*
> *at the time of discourse with God it is hearing for the ear.*
> *Look at us with the eye of union* (jam'),
> *you shall find us in difference* (farq),
> *and hold fast to this,*
> *since the Qur'ân, in what it joins together,*
> *is the recognition of difference* (furqân).

Every being should have an attribute attached to it by which it faces a similar or opposite attribute in the Divine Presence. If I say "opposite" without limiting myself to "similar," which certainly is the case, I do so out of a desire to reform both the Sufi's heart and that of the person who has climbed through the earliest degrees of true realization, for such is their source of inspiration. They do not know what is higher than they and what we are referring to until God takes them by the hand and allows them to contemplate what He has had us, also, contemplate.[308] [...]

Dive into the sea of the incomparable Qur'ân if you have tremendous ability to hold your breath. Otherwise, limit yourself to studying the books of those who write commentaries on its outer meaning; do not dive, for you shall perish, for the sea of the Qur'ân is deep. If the diver had never aimed at places that are close to the shore, he would never have found his way back out for you. The prophets and their heirs, the guardians of prophetic knowledge *(al-waratha al-hafaza)*, are those who come to these places out of mercy for the universe. "Those who stand still" *(al-wâqifun)*[309] after they arrive have been detained without ever returning from the depths. No one has gotten any profit from them, nor have they profited from anyone. They dove, or rather they were led, down to the bottom of the ocean. They dove for eternity. They shall never return. May God show His kindness to al-'Abâdâni, Sahl b. 'Abdallah al-Tustarî's teacher! When Sahl asked him if the heart prostrates itself, his reply was "Forever!"[310] Better yet, may God share His grace with His Messenger! When he was asked whether the pious visit *('umra)* was part of the pilgrimage: "Is it for this year, or forever *(li-l-abad)*?" he replied, "forever and forever (or for eternity's eternity, *li-abad al-abad*)."[311] *'Umra*'s entry into the pilgrimage is a permanent spiritual reality in the abode of perpetuity, and is felt by the chosen ones in Paradise every year at the corresponding time (in eternity). They say "What is that?" and the answer they receive is "*'Umra*, on the pilgrimage": the breath of the Spirit, delights, the flowing of pure, noble grace drowning the faces of the chosen ones with light and making them more beautiful still.

When you dive into the sea of the Qur'ân—may God help you—do so in search of the two shells that hold the two jewels, *alif* and *lâm*. Their shells are the word and the verse that contains them. If the word refers to a divine act, attach the letters to this station; if it refers to a divine name, do likewise, and do so also if it regards the Essence. Even if it was not in specific reference to the letter, the Prophet suggested this in his invocation: "*I take refuge in Your pleasantness against Your anger*": "in Your approval," the leaning of the *alif*; in your anger, the leaning of the *lâm* (words concerning the Divine Names—*kalima asmâ'iyya*); in Your absolution, the leaning of the *alif*, against Your punishment, the leaning of the *lâm* (words concerning Acts—*kalima fi'liyya*); "in You," the leaning of the *alif*; "against You," the leaning of the *lâm* (words concerning the Essence—*kalima dhâtiyya*).[312] See how marvellous and sublime the secret of prophecy is, and how it aims both near and far! He who speaks of these two letters, *lâm-alif*, without maintaining awareness of the presence he is in, is not an accomplished knower. [...][313]

Come to an inner realization of all we have been speaking about. Pick your *alif* up out of its sleep[314] and untie the knot of your *lâm*. In the knot that ties the *lâm* to the *alif* there is a secret that cannot be told. I could only expand upon my explanation of the stations of *lâm-alif* if I were speaking with someone willing to listen the same way he would listen if the man upon whom the Qur'ân came down were speaking, if he, himself, were explaining its meaning.[315] But this book aims at conciseness; this chapter is already growing long, and my discourse, although it is synthetic, is growing lengthy, so numerous are the hierarchical degrees and the letters. [...][316]

Knowledge of the alif *and the* lâm *in* al

Know that after it is untied, after the abrogation of its form, after the showing of its secrets, and even after the disappearance of its name and the way it is drawn out, the *lâm-alif* reappears on the level *(hadra)* of genus, of specification, of determination, and of magnification.[317] The *alif* being that which is specifically divine, and the *lâm* that which is human, these two letters signify genus, since mentioning *alif* and *lâm* is tantamount to mentioning the universe as a whole, and Him Who gives it its being. If your being is extinguished by separating from God and taking on the condition of creation,[318] mention of *alif* and *lâm* certainly signifies the Divine Truth *(al-haqq)* and the creature *(khalq)*. This is what genus means for us. In the *lâm* itself the downstroke belongs to God—exalted may He be—and the semicircle in the *lâm*'s curve that can be seen, which remains after the *alif* has turned its downstroke back upwards, is nothing other than the *nûn* of creation. The spiritual, unmanifested semicircle is the circle of the Celestial Realm *(malakût)*.[319] The *alif,* which shows the circle's diameter, is that of the divine command, the *kun*.

All this is really just so many species and classes of the most universal genus that there is: the Reality of realities *(haqîqat al-haqâ'iq)*. It wanders endlessly, eternal in the eternal, but not in itself; adventitious in adventitiousness, but not in itself. It cannot be considered to be either existing or not existing. Not being existent, it cannot be qualified by either eternity or adventitiousness, as will be shown in the sixth chapter of the present book.[320] [...][321]

On the vowels
Chapter 2, section II

On the knowledge of vowels or the minor letters through which we distinguish words

There are six vowels among the consonant-letters. It was through them that God brought words—which are like them—into existence. They are "elevation" *(raf')*, "establishment" *(nasb)*, and "lowering" *(khafd)*: vowels for the declined letters. They are "opening" (fath), "contraction" *(damm)*, and "retirement" *(kasr)*: vowels for the stable letters. The foundations of language are "suppression" *(hadhf)* and thus death or "rest" *(sukûn)*, following the movement of vowels. Such is the state of the worlds: so take note of this strange life on a dead earth.

Know—and may God assist us through a spirit emanating from Him—that we had first begun to speak about the vowels in the section on letters by explaining why they are called the minor letters. Then we were of the opinion that it was useless to mix the world of vowels in with the world of consonant letters before putting the letters into order and adding them to one another to form one of the elements of language *(kalima min al-kalim)*. Their order *(intizâm)* corresponds to God's words regarding our creation: "*When I have shaped him and blown a breath of My spirit into him*" (Q. 15:29 and 38:72). This concerns the vowels coming upon the letters after the "shaping" of the letters. They then reappear in "another constitution,"[322] which we call "word" *(kalima)*, just as an individual in our species is called "man." In this way, the world of words *(kalimât)* and individual terms *(alfâz)* came into being starting from the world of consonant-letters. Letters are the material elements *(mawâdd)* of words, like water, earth, fire, and air for the constitution of our bodies. The spirit emanating from the divine command *(al-rûh al-amrî)* was blown into him, and he became a man, just as the winds that were predisposed to do so received the breath of this spirit, and became a fire genie *(jânn)*, and likewise for the lights, and they became angels.[323] Most words *(kalim)* resemble man, and the smaller number of them angels and the jinn—both are actually jinn[324]—like the particles *bi, li, la*; the particles of the oath: *wa, bi,* and *ta*; the *wa* and *fa* of coordination and imperatives, like *qi* (protect!), *shi* (denounce!), and *'i* (be attentive!).[325] This category aside, all the other words could not be more similar to man. But this category is itself similar to man's inner being, since in reality, man is *jânn*.[326] [...]

On words and speech

God's Messenger—may God give him grace and peace—said: "I received the totalizing words *(jawâmi' al-kalim)*"[327]; God said: "*And He sent His words* (kalimatu-hu) *down upon Mary* (Q. 4:171) and, also in reference to her: "*She believed in the truth of the Words* (kalimât) *of her Lord*" (Q. 66:12). Elsewhere it is said that the emir cut off the thief's hand. Actually, the individual upon whose order an act is committed is the one who performs the act. It was on behalf of God that Muhammad projected—pronounced—the words of the entire universe, with no exception whatsoever. From the universe, by himself, he projected the spirits of the angels and most of the higher world; other beings were projected upon his order, and came into existence through intermediaries *(wasâ'it)*. Thus, like a spirit praising and magnifying God, until the time that the seed sown begins to form in your limbs, it must have undergone a number of transfers and cycles in a single world, and then changed itself, in each new world, into the form of a specific species. The totality of beings thus comes back to him who received the "totalizing Words" *(jawâmi' al-kalim)*. At the time of the Raphaelian Reality *(haqîqa isrâfiliyya)*, emanating from the Muhammadan Reality, which itself is attached to God's, a breath was emitted, just as God—exalted may He be—said: "*The Day We blow into the trumpet*" (Q. 27:87), or, according to another version: "*wherever we blow...*"[328] Raphael is the one who blows, but God brings the breath back to Himself. The breath emanates from Raphael, the trumpet takes it in, and the divine secret that resides between the two is the meaning *(ma'nâ)* that is established between him who emits the breath and him who receives it, just as happens with the particles that establish a bond between two words.[329] Such is the secret of the sacrosanct, transcendent, divine act about which neither the person who emits the breath nor the person who receives it has any knowledge. The breath giver needs do nothing more than exhale, the fire nothing more than light, and the lamp nothing more than go out; lighting and going out will take place via the divine secret *(al-sirr al-ilâhî)*. The breath was blown, "*and, with God's permission, there will be birds*" (Q. 3:49).[330] God said: "*The trumpet shall be blown*,[331] *and all those who are in the heavens and all those upon the earth shall swoon, except those whom God wishes, and then there shall be a second blast, and they shall be standing up, beholding*" (Q. 39:68). The breath is unique, as is the individual who exhales it; the difference comes from what is being blown into *(al-manfûkh fîhi)*, according to the predisposition of beings. The divine secret between one and the other is hidden in all cases. O brothers, be attentive to this divine command, and know that God is inaccessible, and all wise *('azîz hakîm)*. No one can reach the knowledge of the deep reality of absolute divinity *(kunh al-ulûha)* and it is in no way appropriate that it be perceived. May it be exalted and glorified in its inaccessibility and its sublimity! The entire universe, from the first of the beings to the last is conditioned; one conditions the other, one adores the other; their knowledge goes from them to them; their very realities, springing forth from themselves by virtue of the imperceptible divine secret, return to them. Glory be to Him whose power has no rival and whose goodness is without equal. There is no God but Him, the Inaccessible, the All-Wise.

Now that you have understood the meaning of "totalizing Words" and the knowledge that encompasses all things *(al-'ilm al-ihâtî)* and the meaning of the divine light—which are privileges of the Secret of existence, of the Pillar under the celestial cupola, of the Foot of the throne and the Cause of the immutability of all things in its immutable being *(sabab thubût kulli thâbit)*,[332] that is, of Muhammad (upon him be God's grace and peace)—know that, from the perspective of the world of letters, there are three of these Words: an independent *(ghaniyya)* essence that subsists by itself; an essence indigent *(faqîra)* in respect to the first, which does not subsist by itself, and whose quality *(wasf)*—which, by essence, it is to seek independent essence—returns to this independent essence (which takes it on as a quality, this quality not belonging to indigent essence except by concomitance—*musâhaba*—and belonging just as much to independent essence from the perspective of indigent necessity—*faqr*); and a third essence that connects two essences to one another, whether they are independent, indigent, or independent and indigent. The essence that establishes this bond *(al-dhat al-râbita)* is indigent with respect to the existence of the two others. Indigence and necessity are thus the fact of all essences, in the sense that they all need one another, albeit in different ways. Independence *(ghinâ)* in the absolute belongs to God alone, the Most Rich *(al-ghanî)*, the Most Praised, by His essence.

Let us then refer to independent essence as "essence" *(dhât)*, indigent essence as "adventitious fact" *(hadath)*, and the third essence as "bond" *(rabîta)*. The words of language *(kalim)* are limited to these three realities, essence, adventitious fact, and bond, which are the Totalizing Words. A great number of species enters into each of these genera, although there is no need to deal with them individually in the present work. We did refer to them at some length in our commentary on the Qur'ân. The reader interested in seeing an analogy with what we just mentioned is referred to the writings of the grammarians and their division of the words used in language into nouns, verbs, and particles, or to the identical system used by logicians.³³³ [...]³³⁴

There are two sorts of movements, those that are bodily and those that are spiritual. There is a great variety of species in both of these, and they will be dealt with in the book. At present, we shall speak only about the "movements-vowels" *(harakât)* in language, both spoken and written. The written vowels are like bodies, and the spoken vowels are like their spirits. The letters that are changed by vowels *(mutaharrikât)* are either "firmly established" or "stable" *(mutamakkin)*, or they are "of changing color" *(mutalawwin)*. [...]³³⁵

Know that the spheres of the vowels are the same as the spheres of the consonants that support them in pronunciation and writing; one needs only to look in order to verify this. The same simple elements, states, and stations correspond to them as to the letters; God willing, we shall return to this topic in the "Book of Principles" devoted to the science of letters.³³⁶

"Coloration" *(talwîn)* and "stability" *(tamkîn)* concern essence as much as they do adventitious fact and the bond...³³⁷ even though the original *(asl)* state of the letters is stability or invariability *(binâ')*, a state that for us is comparable to the primordial nature *(fitra)*.³³⁸ There are secrets here for the one who knows how to find them. Just as, through parents, the child emerges from the relative primordial state *(al-fitra al-muqayyada)*, but not from the absolute primordial state, so are the letters fundamentally stable in the degree of their being *(maqâm)*, and they are unmovable, unchangeable, invariable, and completely quiescent in their state *(hâl)*. When the speaker wishes to communicate to his listener what is in his soul, he needs to produce a coloration. So he puts the sphere from which the vowels emanate into motion, according to Abû Tâlib (al-Makki).³³⁹ Some others say that the sphere's motion comes first; that pronunciation and writing come from the same sphere. Here is a subject of study for those who aspire to the direct vision *(mu'âyana)* of realities. We are in complete agreement neither with Abû Tâlib nor with the other, since both were speaking the truth from their point of view, but neither went far enough. So we say that the first divine realities *(al-haqâ'iq al-uwal al-ilâhiyya)* turn toward the upper spheres in the same way as they do toward the receptacles wherein their effects are produced *(mahâll âthârihâ)* in the opinion of others than Abû Tâlib. The spheres receive each of these realities, depending on their hierarchical ranking. For others than Abû

Tâlib, the closer these spheres are in subtle nature *(latâfa)*[340] to the divine realities, the quicker they get their effects, because nothing else is occupying them, and their receptacles are unadulterated by attachments to others. The purity of their receptacle allowed him to think of spheres as the efficient cause. He should have known that these first realities turn toward the exhalations *(anfâs)* of man that correspond to them by their subtle nature, and then they move the upper sphere that the world of breaths corresponds to, which is Abû Tâlib's teaching. The upper sphere then causes movement in the appropriate limb, depending on the goal sought, through the effect of this correspondence. The upper sphere, despite its subtle nature, is the first degree of "thickness" *(kathâfa)* and the last of subtlety, in contrast to the world of our breaths. Thus the teachings agree, since, for us, there is no room for divergence on our path; there is but one being destined for revelation, or destined for even more *(kâshif wa akshaf)*. Now you can understand what we were referring to, and you can realize it: it is a marvellous secret, one of the greatest of God's secrets, which Abû Tâlib made reference to in his *Qût*.[341] [...]

NOTES
TO 'THE SCIENCE OF LETTERS'

¹ Cf. *Futûhât* I, 51 (end of ch. 1).

² *Harf* (pl. *hurûf*) refers generally to the consonant, in contrast to the vowel, but as may be observed, the use of this word is much broader. It will almost always be translated as "letter," but occasionally "consonant-letter," in contrast to the vowel.

³ The author later explains (p. 84) that he preferred not to mix the world of vowels in with that of the *hurûf.*

⁴ The idea of edge is found in the etymology of *harf,* which refers to the side of something, its edge, or its cutting edge. *Harf* thus intersects with the meaning of *hadd* (pl. *hudûd*): "border," cutting edge," and "definition." Ibn 'Arabî himself brings the two words together in the expression taken from the "Monday prayer" *(wird yawm al-ahad)*: "One, single, such as He was before the Letters of the Limits *(hurûf al-hudûd),*" *Majmû'at al-ahzab,* collated by Ahmad Diyâ' al-Din Kamûshkhânî, Istanbul, 1298 A.H., reprod. n.d., p. 41. *Hurûf* and *hudûd* were also closely correlated in Isma'îlî esotericism; see especially H. Halm, *Kosmologie und Heilslehre der frühen Ismâ'ilîya,* Wiesbaden, 1978, pp. 38-48. To explain the meaning of *harf,* lexicographers cite expressions like *harf al-jabal,* "the slope of the mountain," or its "peak" *(a'lâ-hu al-muhaddad)*; in the latter case, the sense of limit is connected to that of elevation, which is not unrelated to the role letters play in bringing things into existence and the expression "higher letters" *(hurûf 'âliyât)* used by Ibn 'Arabî in a famous poem. In the Qur'ân, *harf* means "side," and thus "aspect," or "point of view" in the verse: *"And among men there are those who adore God from one side* ('alâharf)*; if good happens to such a man, he feels satisfied with it, but if trials occur to him, he turns*

his face (inqalaba 'alâwajhihi). *He has lost this world and the next.*" (Q. 22:11). From this meaning we also get that of "version" in Qur'ânic readings *(harf* pl. *hurûf)*. The *tahrîf* or alteration of the meaning of the Scripture by the People of the Book means not only the displacement of meaning, but also its inversion: "*They alter the words from their places* (yajarrifûna l-kalim 'an mawâdi'ihi)", Q. 4:46 and 5:13. On *harf,* see also: Qurtubî, *al-Jâmi' li-ahkâm al-qur'ân,* Cairo, 1952, I, 65-68, *Lisân al-'arab,* X, 385-386 and Fîrûzâbâdî, *Basâ'ir dhawî l-tamyîz fî latâ'if al-kitâb al-'azîz,* Cairo, 1385, A.H., II 452.

[5] *Futûhât* I, 292-297; O.Y. IV 341-345, paragr. 469-506.

[6] Cf. *Futûhât* I, 92-98, ch. 3; O.Y. II 90-118, paragr. 77-130.

[7] Cf. *Futûhât* I, 101-117; O.Y. II 132-218.

[8] Cf. section on vowels, and ch. 20.

[9] See the section devoted to eschatology (p. 94-124) in volume I.

[10] *Futûhât* I, 98-101; O.Y. II 119-131, paragr. 131-135.

[11] *Ibid.,* I, 57-58.

[12] On the *afrâd,* see M. Chodkiewicz, *Seal of the Saints,* index, s.v.

[13] See note 7.

[14] It is probably because of this that the isolated letters are just the first degree of the Elite.

[15] To use René Guénon's expression.

[16] *Futûhat* I, 65.

[16] *Futûhat* I, 65.

[16] *Futûhât,* I, 65.

[16] *Futûhât,* I, 65.

[17] On the initiatory hierarchy, see especially *Futûhât,* II, 6-16, ch. 73, and M. Chodkiewicz, *op. cit.,* ch. 6.

[18] Literally, "It is not there that you should build your nest" *(laysa 'ushshaka an...).*

[19] *Futûhat* I, 82 (l. 10-12).

[20] On this expression, see *Futûhat* I, 59. The letters whose meanings are unknown remind us that the sura is like an enclosure *(sûr)* whose inner part will remain unknown until the meaning of its spiritual from *(sûra)* is perceived.

[21] The look *(nazar)* is not a reference to speculation here, but rather to direct perception of the divine realities, since it is identified with *'ilm al-ladunî,* the knowledge received directly from God by al-Khadir (see Q. 18:65).

[22] *Futûhat* I, 82 (l. 18-24).

[23] Depending on the position of the lips, whence the name given to the vowels: *a = fatha* "opening"; *u = damma* "joining, uniting"; *o = kasra* "retirement" (according to André Roman's translation, *Étude de la phonologie et de la morphologie de la koiné arabe,* Aix-en-Provence, 1983, see the index of technical terms).

[24] *Futûhat* II, 390-478, ch. 198 on the Breath, or Exhalation *(nafas).*

[25] *Futûhat* I, 167-169, ch. 20; O.Y. III, 88-99. On the translation of this

chapter, see below, note 36.

26 Cf. the hadith: "Every newborn child comes into the world with the primordial nature; it is his parents who make him a Jew, a Christian, or a Zoroastrian..." (Bukhârî, *Sahîh*, *tafsîr*, sura 30 VI 143). There are several versions of this hadith.

27 At issue here are the "different" *(alfâz mutabâyina)* words for a single kind of being; the "univocal " *(mutawâti'a)* words, meaning a specific genus for several kinds of beings, like "animal"; "ambiguous" *(mushtaraka)* words, or words that share a variety of meanings, like *'ayn*, which means eye, source, essence, among other things; and synonyms *(mutarâdifa)*. All of these categories, in turn, have a number of subcategories.

28 *Futûhat* I, 89 (l. 26-28).

29 *Ibid.*, 92 (l. 24-28).

30 In the introduction to *Kitab al-Mîm wa l-Wâw wa l-Nûn*, Ibn 'Arabî reminds us that he had already dealt with the letters at length in the *Futûhât al-Makkiyya*, and that he had devoted a chapter of moderate importance to the subject in *al-Fath al-Fâsî* "the Fez Revelation," in which he says that it (he does not specify whether "it" refers to the work, or the chapter) is titled *al-Mabâdi' wa l-Ghâyât bimâ tatadammanuhu hurûf al-mu'jam mim al-'ajâ'ib wa l-âyât*. It is likely that this is the same work as the previously mentioned work with the same title. What is important is the mention of Fez, the city where the Shaykh al-Akbar received one of the announcements of his designation as Seal of Muhammadan Sainthood, cf. *Futûhat* III, 514, and Chodkiewicz, *Seal of the Saints*, p. 92, and ch. IX). The importance of the science of letters for Ibn 'Arabî is thus closely connected with this role.

31 *Futûhat* I, 191, ch. 26; O.Y., III, p. 196-208, paragraph 161-175. See also *ibid.*, I, 274, ch. 51 on the inspiration of *sîmîyâ* among the jinn.

32 *Ibid.* I, 190.

33 *K. al-Mîm wa...*, p. 4 f; *K. al-Tajalliyât*, p. 1 (regarding the etymology of *tilasm*); see also *'Uqlat al-mustawfiz*, p. 67 (regarding *falak al-hurûf*).

34 On Ibn Masarra, see below, p. 427f.

35 Cf. *Futûhât* II, 134, in response to Tirdidhî's question 154.

36 See note 25. This chapter was translated, preceded by a considerable introduction by Michel Vâlsan: "The Islamic references to the 'Symbolism of the Cross'" in *Études traditionnelles*, 171, pp. 49-61 and 275-283, and 1972, pp. 62-72.

37 On the relationship between *kun* and *huwiyya* from the point of view of the science of letters, see especially *Futûhât* I, 168; I, 190; II, 331-332; *K. al-Mîm...*, p. 9; *K. al-Yâ' wa huwa K. al-huwa*, pp. 1 and 8. See also these names for the Universal Man, taken from the "Prayer over the Prophet": "...*On the point of the* basmala *that encompasses what will be and what was, and on the time limit of the Decree that turns on the circumferences of the worlds; on the secret of Ipseity that is infused into everything, and is detached and isolated from*

everything..." (trans. M. Vâlsan, in *Études traditionnelles*, 1974, p. 243).

[38] See note 24.

[39] *Futûhât* II, 122, reply to Tirmidhî's question 140; IV, 291-292, and *Kitâb al-alif wa huwa K, al-Ahadiyya*, p. 12, where *alif* is called *qayyûm al-hurûf*, since "all things are attached to it, and it is attached to nothing." *Alif* shares this graphic particularity with five other letters *(dâl, dhâl, râ', zây,* and *wâw)*, or six, if *lâm-alif* is included. In a "special composition" *(tarkîb khâss)*, these seven letters are the letters of the Supreme Name. Cf. *Futûhât* II, 122, question 138.

[40] *Futûhât* II, 144-145, ch. 76, on spiritual combat *(mujâhada)*.

[41] *Ibid.*, II, 352, ch. 178.

[42] *Ibid.*, II, 122.

[43] At another degree, they may be seen as names for Angels, and are in this case a key for astrology. Cf. *Futûhât* II, 120-122.

[44] Many of the Divine Names begin with the letter *mîm*, for example.

[45] On the Supreme Name, see especially the replies to Tirmidhî's questions 131 to 138, *Futûhât* II, 120-122.

[46] "Apudity" is the fact of being near to *('inda)*. For this whole passage, see *ibid.* II, 122, question 139. According to a hadith, one of the Prophet's most frequent oaths was "By Him who upsets hearts *(wa muqallibi l-qulûb)*, cf. Bukhârî, *Sahîh, k. al-tawhîd*, IX, 145. A different hadith explains the meaning of the words: "the heart of each of Adam's sons is between two of the All Merciful's fingers, like a single heart that he turns wherever he wants." Cf. Muslim, *Sahîh, k. al-qadar*, Istanbul, 1332 A,H,, VIII, 51. For the other versions, see *Concordances et indices*, V, 554-560, and Tabarî, *Jâmi' al-bayân* Dâr al-ma'ârif, VI, 213-220 regarding Q. 3:8. Turning, or upsetting, hearts also has a basis in the Qur'ân; cf. 24:37, and 6:110.

[47] On the symbolism of *hamza*, cf. above, p. 395.

[48] *Futûhât* II, 421, ch. 198.

[49] *Ibid.*, IV, 424.

[50] *Ibid.*, II, 591, ch. 275.

[51] The first lines of one of the poems introducing the chapter on love, *Futûhât* II, 320, ch. 178—translated by M. Gloton with the title *Traité de l'amour*, Paris, 1986. This expression of the relationship between the letter and the meaning is based on the passage on the meaning of *harf* =letter, and that of *harf* = particle. Ibn 'Arabî actually takes the definition from the third part of Sîbawayh's words: "a particle bringing a meaning" or "that came to express a meaning" *(harf jâ'a li-ma'nan)*; cf. *Kitâb*, Beirut, 1967, p. 9 (whence the name of the particles: *hurûf al-ma'ânî*). Another passage from Ibn 'Arabî comments on this line: "*The entire world is a letter (or a particle) that came to express a meaning. This meaning is* Allâh, *so that His decisions* (ahkâm) *may be made manifest in the world, for God Himself cannot be a place for the manifestation of His decisions. The meaning never stops being attached to the letter, and, likewise, God is with the world. 'And He is with you wherever you are.'*" (*Futûhât* III, 148).

⁵² On phonetics, cf. *EI2* III, 617-620: *hurûf al-hijâ'* and VI, 127-128: *makhârij al-hurûf.* See also the study on the system of consonants and vowels in the Arabic grammatical tradition by A. Roman, *Étude de la phonologie et de la morphologie de la Koiné arabe*, Aix-en-Provence, 1983. See also the expanded study of the work of a great grammarian by 'Abd al-Kader Méhiri: *Les théories grammaticales d'Ibn Jinnî*, Tunis, 1973, 3rd part: Ibn Jinnî's theory of phonetics.

⁵³ The terminology Ibn 'Arabî used in calligraphy was perhaps Andalusian. Among his references on how letters are to be written, he mentions the formation of certain letters based on others. An illustration of this can be seen in a 9th century A.H. manual; cf. 'Abd al-Rahmân Ibn Sâ'igh (770 A.H. - 845 A.H.), *Tuhfa*, Tunis, 1967, plate pp. 104-105.

⁵⁴ On the question of whether the *hamza* is fully a letter, Ibn 'Arabî points out that Jâbir held that *alif* supported by *hamza* is a half letter, and the *hamza* the other half. Cf. *Sharh Khal' al-na'layn* ms from Suleymanye, Shehit Ali, no. 1174 f. 135b.

⁵⁵ On Jâbir's identity and on the dates of his works, see *EI2*, II, 367-369; Paul Kraus, *Jâbir Ibn Hayyân, contribution à l'histoire des idées scientifiques dans l'islam*, vol. I: *Le corps des écrits jabiriens*, Cairo, M.I.E., no. 44, 1943; H. Corbin, "Le Livre du Glorieux de Jâbir Ibn Hayyân," in *Eranos Jahrbuch*, no. 18, 1950, pp. 52-56 and P. Lory, *Jâbir Ibn Hayyân. Dix traités d'Alchimie*, Paris, 1983, Sindbad ed. pp. 34-51.

⁵⁶ P. Kraus, *Jâbir Ibn Hayyân*, vol. 2: *Jâbir et la science grecque*, Cairo, M.I.E. no. 45, 1942, pp. 155-156.

⁵⁷ *Ibid.*, p. 159.

⁵⁸ Corbin, "Le Livre du Glorieux," p. 83.

⁵⁹ P. Kraus, *Jâbir Ibn Hayyân*, vol. 2, p. 187.

⁶⁰ Corbin, *op. cit.*, p. 77.

⁶¹ P. Kraus, *op. cit.*, p. 187, from the *Kitâb al-khamsîn*.

⁶² P. Kraus, *Jâbir Ibn Hayyân, Essai sur l'histoire des idées scientifiques dans l'islam*. Vol. I: *Textes choisis*. Paris/Cairo, 1935, p. 100.

⁶³ Cf. *ibid.*, pp. 392-399 and P. Kraus, *Jâbir et la science grecque*, pp. 224, 241 and schemas p. 139. Cf. also Corbin, *op. cit.*, pp. 75-77. Corbin also studied how Jâbir's work was expanded upon by Haydar Amolî, a spiritual Shi'ite (8th/14th century): "La science de la balance et les correspondances entre les mondes en gnose islamique," article from *Eranos Jahrbuch*, reprinted in *Temple et contemplation*, Paris, 1980. Amolî's primary reference is Ibn 'Arabî, and like him, the science of letters developed in Qur'ânic commentary; cf. pp. 105-108, the interpretation of the 19 letters in the *basmala*.

⁶⁴ Cf. the passages from Ibn 'Arabi in *Inshâ' al-jusûm al-insâniyya* cited by Kraus from the manuscript in the Escorial (*Jâbir et la science grecque*, p. 244, note 11) and from the *Kitâb al-mîm wa l-wâw wa l-nûn* (pp. 5-6) concerning, each in turn, the articulation and the writing of letters in connection with the voices and shapes of animals.

⁶⁵ There is also a close correlation between letters and the initiatory hierarchy in Jâbir, especially in the "Livre du Glorieux" *(Kitâb al-mâjid)*. The esoteric Shi'ism that Jâbir was connected to is nevertheless expressed in terms that are quite different from the *tasawwuf*. In H. Corbin's presentation, which followed Massignon's, there was an attempt to identify the three tendencies represented by the three letters *('ayn, mîm,* and *sîn)* with 'Ali, Muhammad, and Salmân (or the imam, the prophet, and the initiator, or the Silent One, the Pronouncer, and the intermediary). In relation to the function of letters, Corbin points out the intermediary function of the *sîn*, unifying—between the *samît* and the *nâtiq*— the letter in the sense of "on the border between what was Pronounced and Silence." The role of *Mâjid* then looks like the synthesis of all these aspects by the balance of the "balance of letters," or the Universal harmony. The interpretation of the *basmala* by Haydar Amolî, mentioned above, is somewhat similar, since it posits a correspondence between the imams and the metaphysical (the Divine Names) and cosmic (the Heavenly Bodies) principles.

⁶⁶ See *EI2*, III, 1098-1103; according to Y. Marquet, the *Rasâ'il* were written between 350/961 and 370/980; see *La philosophie des Ikhwân al-safâ*, Algiers, 1975, p. 8. But for A. Triki, *Néoplatonisme et aspect mystique de la création de l'univers dans la philosophie des Ikhwan al-safa*, Algiers n.d. (circa 1975), pp. 7-14, the could have been composed as early as the late 3rd/9th century.

⁶⁷ Jâbir made room for music in connection with the letters, see, e.g., the *Kitâb al-ikhrâj ma fî l-quwwa ilâ l-fi'l*, in Kraus, *Jabir Ibn Hayyan, Textes choisis*, pp. 11 and 14.

⁶⁸ *Rasâ'il Ikhwân al-safâ*, Beirut, 1957, I, 219-221.

⁶⁹ We might also note that the 6th letter leads the earliest theoretical chapters back in the direction of microcosmic inner applications by setting up a correspondence between arithmetic and geometry on the one hand, and amending the soul and improving the character on the other, using the kind of philosophical language adopted by the Ikhwân.

⁷⁰ *Rasâ'il*, III, 84-87.

⁷¹ *Ibid.*, III, 85.

⁷² *Ibid.*, III, 122.

⁷³ *Ibid.*, III, 86.

⁷⁴ On the fifth element in Jâbir, cf. P. Kraus, *Jâbir et la science grecque*, pp. 152-153.

⁷⁵ Cf., III, 95 and 115: Pythagoras is believed to have established the rules of music and made the "lute" after hearing in his heart the movement of the spheres and the sounds produced by the rotation of the heavenly bodies. Music thus aims at restoring such hearing.

⁷⁶ *Rasâ'il*, III, 144-145.

⁷⁷ On *suryâniyya* language, see R. Guénon's article on the science of letters cited below. In this part of the letter, the reference to Adam shows that it was a primordial language, but this does not keep the Ikhwân from using the same

word to refer to the Syrian language (p. 144).

78 On the relationship between the Hindu and Islamic sciences of letters, see below, note 155, in reference to M. Valsân's article, "Le Triangle de l'Androgyne et le monosyllabe *ôm*."

79 For the Arabic text, see the Cairo edition (1978), and the analysis and translation in A. Roman, *Étude de la phonologie et de la morphologie de la Koïné arabe*, pp. 233-274.

80 Ibn Sînâ, *Tis' rasâ'il fi l-hikma wa l-tabî'iyyât*, Cairo, 1908, pp. 134-142.

81 *Abjad* refers to the alphabet listed in numerical order as in Hebrew or Greek.

82 L. Massignon: "La philosophie orientale d'Ibn Sînâ et son alphabet philosophique," in *Mémorial d'Avicenne IV*, IFAO, Cairo, 1954, pp. 1-18. See also Corbin's remarks on the article in *Avicenna et le récit visionnaire*, Tehran, 1954, pp. 320-324.

83 The case of Al-Mughîra b. Sa'îd is usually cited; in 119/737, he revolted against the Abbâsid al-Mansûr in Kufa. Bits of his teachings we can see in heresiographical literature suggest incompletely understood hermetic or gnostic precedents regarding the teaching of the Universal Man seen as the "Man of Light." Cf. al-Baghdâdî, *al-Farq bayna l-firaq*, Beirut, 1973, pp. 229 and Shahrastânî, *al-Milal wa l-hihal*, Cairo, 1969, I, 69-72. On the man of light, see H. Corbin, *The Man of Light in Iranian Sufism*, Boulder & London, 1978, ch. 2, and on Mughîra: Corbin, *Histoire de la philosophie islamique*, Paris, 1964, p. 112.

84 See an analysis of it by H. Halm, *Kosmologie und Heilslehre der frühen Ismâ'îliya*, Wiesbaden, 1978, p. 38f. On his work attributed to Ja'far's son of Mansûr al-Yamân, written in the second half of the 4th/10th century, see p. 168.

85 From this perspective, *'arsh* and *kursî* are seen as divine attributes representing, respectively, the inner and the outer sides of reality.

86 "Pronouncers" of the Law or of Revelation, meaning the prophets. These letters are *alif, bâ', tâ', thâ, jîm, hâ',* and *khâ',* or the first letters of the alphabet.

87 *Kûnî qadar* represents the primordial couple. The use of the first word, *kûnî* (the feminine form of *kun*) in the feminine probably refers both to the reflection, in the Universal Soul, of the divine aspect of all possibilities, and the exterior, which appears first. *Kûnî* is thus the "follower" of the imam *(tâlî)* and *qadar* ("determination") the Intellect or First One *(sâbiq)*. The *kitâb Khazâ'in al-adilla* identifies the seven letters of *kûnî qadar* with Adam, Abraham, Moses, Jesus, Muhammad, and the *qâ'im*; or with pairs of ideas that seem to preside over the destiny of human beings, cf. H. Halm, *Kosmologie...*, p. 55, note 4.

88 The *Kitâb al-zîna*, by the Ismâ'îli *dâ'î* Abû Hâtim al-Râzî (d. 322/934) entails a passage on letters that is much more reminiscent of the teachings of Jâbir, and those of the *Ikhwân al-safâ*, as well as connecting the science of letters

to that of the Names taught to Adam. See the excellent presentation of this passage by G. Vajda, "Les lettres et les sons de la langue arabe d'après Abû Hâtim al-Râzî," *Arabica*, no. 8, 1961, pp. 113-130.

[89] Cf. Tabarî, *Jâmi' al-bayân*, Cairo, 1969, I, 206; the letters are interpreted by Ibn 'Abbâs as the Supreme Name of God. See also P. Nwiya, *Exégèse coranique et langue mystique*, Beirut, 1970, pp. 64-166, in regard to Ja'far al-Sâdiq, especially P. Nwyia, like Massignon in regard to Hallâj, does not appear to distinguish the *jafr* in this spiritual interpretation clearly; what is at issue is certainly two different traditions, even though they do end up converging to a certain extent, as is seen later. The essential part of the early Sufi interpretations of the Isolated letters was collected by Sulamî in his *tafsîr*, the *Haqâ'iq al-qur'ân*; although this work is still in manuscript form, part of it was used by Rûzebehân Baqlî in his *'Arâ'is al-bayân*, edited a number of times in India. See also M. Valsân's introduction to Qâshânî's commentary on the Isolated letters, *Études traditionnelles*, no. 380, Nov.-Dec. 1963, pp. 256-262.

[90] *Luma'*, Cairo, 1960, pp. 124-125 *(bâb mâ qîla fî l-hurûf wa l-asmâ')*.

[91] A friend of Hallaj who died, also, in 309/922. He was also one of the early representatives of *tasawwuf* exegesis. His commentaries were gathered from the *Haqâ'iq al-qur'ân* by P. Nwyia in *Trois oeuvres inédites de mystiques musulmans*, Beirut, 1973, see intro. pp. 25-32.

[92] Qushayrî, *Risâla*, Cairo, 1972, I 53.

[93] P. Nwyia, *Exégèse coranique*, p. 365, according to the ms. of *K. nazâ'ir al-qur'ân*. This passage was also cited by 'Abd al-Fattâh Baraka, *al-Hakîm al-Tirmidhî*, Cairo, 190, p. 321. See also a text from the *'Ilm al-awliyâ'* on the relationship between the letters and the Names, cited by Ibrâhîm al-Juyûshî, *al-Hakîm al-Tirmidhî*, Cairo, 1980, p. 288.

[94] Questions 130-142. *Khatm al-awliyâ'*, ed. O. Yahyâ, Beirut, 1965, pp. 305-313 and *Futûhât* II, 120-123.

[95] Sahl al-Tustarî, *Risâlat al-hurûf*, which includes a *fasl fî-l-qur'ân*, edited by M. Kamâl Ja'far in his study *Sahl b. 'Abdallah al-Tustarî*, Cairo, 1974, pp. 366-375, based on a single manuscript from Chester Beatty in Dublin.

[96] See below, trans. from ch. 2, p. 478.

[97] Compare with the relationship among letters with the *hayûlâ* in the *Ikhwân al-safâ*. Ibn 'Arabî attributes use of the term *al-haba'* to Imam 'Ali, and later to Sahl, cf. *Futûhât* I, 121.

[98] *Al-quwwa al-rûhâniyya al-mufarrida*.

[99] *Al-kun al-a'zam allâdhî qâla-hû li-l-kull*.

[100] This is an early wording of a teaching later developed by Ibn 'Arabî. Since beings are manifestations *(mazâhir)* of the Divine Names, the Names do not exist as such, except through the beings they manifest.

[101] This passage might be explained through the words of an anonymous master, but reported by Sarrâj: "The Supreme Name of God is *ALLâH*. If the

alif is taken away, what remains is *LiLâH* (= "to Allah"). If the first *lâm* is removed, what remains is *La-Hû* (= "to Him") and thus pointing *(ishâra)*. If the second *lâm* is removed, what remains is *Hâ'*. All the secrets are contained in *Hâ'*, since its meaning is *Huwa* (= "Him," the "Self")." *Luma'*, p. 125.

102 "Spirit" *(rûh)*, feminine in gender here, probably corresponds to the way Jâbir uses it, in the sense of the Stoic *pneuma*, or to ether, the element of the celestial sphere, or the fifth element.

103 *Risâlat al-hurûf*, pp. 367-369.

104 *Ibid.*, p. 370.

105 *Alif, lâm, qâf, hâ', nûn, mîm, kâf, tâ'*, and *sad*.

106 Cf. *Futûhât* I, 121 (ch. 20).

107 L. Massignon included a certain amount of information about the letters in *La Passion d'al-Hallâj* (Paris, 1975), but the information was scattered throughout the work in such a way that it was not always possible to know how much of it came specifically from Hallâj's teaching.

108 L. Massignon and P. Kraus, *Akhbâr al-Hallâj*, Paris, 1936, trans. p. 100, Arabic text p. 95 (the translation was slightly modified).

109 *Ibid.*, trans. p. 80, text p. 53. The reference is to *alif*, the symbol of *tawhîd* like the "good word" is similar to a tree *"whose trunk..."* (Cf. Q. 14:24).

110 *Ibid.*, p. 79, text. p. 51.

111 Al-Hallâj, *Kitâb al-Tawâsîn*, ed. L. Massignon, Paris, 1913, p. 14 in the *Tâsîn al-Sirâj* on the Principial Light of the Prophet.

112 *Ibid.*, p. 35. in *Tâsîn al-nuqta*. The *mîm* is juxtaposed with the Divine Name "the Last" *(al-Akhir)*, which is reminiscent of the relationship between the *mîm* and the *nûn* in *al-Rahmân* and the *mîm* in *al-Rahîm* in Ibn 'Arabî's commentary on the *basmala*, cf. *Futûhât* I, 108-109.

113 *Ibid.*, p. 66, *Tâsîn al-tanzîh*; see also Ruzbehân Baqlî, *Sharh-l-shathiyyât*, ed. H. Corbin, Paris/Tehran, 1960, p. 540.

114 Cf. p. 476.

115 Edited by M. Kamal Ja'far in *Min qadâyâ al-fikr al-islâmî*, Cairo, 1978, pp. 311-344, followed by the edition of the *Kitâb al-i'tibâr*, pp. 346-360, where the idea already explained in the *khawâss al-hurûf* is further developed; that is, that what we discover in this world by going up toward the world above coincides exactly with what the Prophet brought down from above. The intellect actually comes from divine light, even though one cannot get out of the enclosure *(hawza)* of prophecy without severing one's direct connection to God *(al-inqitâ' 'an walâyat Allâh)*. This manner of expressing relationships in philosophical wisdom *(hikma)* and prophecy is discussed by Ibn 'Arabî.

116 Ibn 'Arabî states that the procedure he uses for the science of letters is analogous to that followed by Ibn Masarra al-Jabalî, who aimed not at the physical properties of the letters but rather at their spiritual secrets. Cf. *Kitâb al-mîm wa l-wâw wa l-nûn*, p. 7.

117 Ibn Masarra can be explained without recourse to a pseudo-Empedocles,

as Asîn Palacios did in his *Abenmasarra y su escuela*, Madrid, 1914. According to Ibn 'Arabî especially, what was known about Ibn Masarra before his texts were edited by M. K. Ja'far has been reported by R. Arnaldez, in *EI2* III, pp. 892-896.

118 As in Sahl, we see this vision—unitive and distinctive, at the same time—to be the foundation of Ibn 'Arabî's interpretation. Moreover, this perspective allows the uncreated nature of the Divine Word and the created nature of the letters to be defended, both at the same time. This is, at least, what Qushayrî (granted, he is an Ash'ari) sees in relation to Sahl al-Tustarî (*Risâla Qushayriyya*, Cairo, 1972, I, 54).

119 The hundredth, the Supreme Name, is the realization of this "list."

120 M. K. Ja'far, *Min qadâyâ al-fikr al-islâmî*, p. 348.

121 Unfortunately, we have been unable to examine the *tafsîr* manuscript of Ibn Qasî's companion Ibn Barrajân (d. 536/1141).

122 On Ibn Qasî, who was a complex individual, see *EI2* III, pp. 839-840.

123 Shehit Ali's manuscript of the *Khal' al-na'layn*, no. 1175 (115f), includes Ibn 'Arabî's commentary. The Shaykh al-Akbar sees a somewhat mitigated stance in Ibn Qasî: sometimes respectful, sometimes quite critical, particularly in regard to the number of letters, cf. f. 135b.

124 On *nûn*, cf. *Khal'*, folios 45b, 46, and 48.

125 On him, see A. J. Arberry, *The mawâqif and mukhâtabât* of M. Ibn 'Abd al-Jabbâr al-Niffarî, London, 1935, pp. 1-3, and P. Nwyia, *Exégèse coranique*, pp. 351-353.

126 See P. Nwyia, *op. cit.*, pp. 363-379.

127 Cf. *Mawâqif*, p. 58: *al-harf wa l-mahrûf* (the letter and what it limits).

128 P. Nwyia, *Trois oeuvres inédites*, pp. 212-213.

129 *Ibid.*, p. 305.

130 It is undoubtedly of significance that Ibn 'Arabî cites Niffarî for the first time in the *Futûhât* at the end of chapter 5, at the end of a commentary on the *Fâtiha*. Cf. *Futûhât* I, 115; ed. O.Y. II, 204, paragraph 290.

131 Presented and edited by Dr. A. 'Alam al-dîn al-Jundî, Tunis, 1977. There are plans for an expanded edition of this text, the *Nahw al-qulûb al-kabîr*.

132 Ibn 'Ajiba (d. 1229/1809-1810) wrote a Sufi commentary on the *Ajurrûmiyya*; cf. J. L. Michon, *Le soufi marocain Ahmad Ibn 'Ajîba et son mi'râj*, Paris, 1973, pp. 281-282.

133 In his article on Bûnî (*EI2*, suppl. 156-157), A. Dietrich remarks that only Hâjjî Khalîfa places his death in 622/1225. Ibn al-Zayyât (d. 814 A.H.) indicates that his tomb is in a Qarâfa *turba* in Cairo, although he does not specify the date of his death (*Kawâkib sayyâra*, re-ed. Baghdad, n.d., p. 268).

134 Al-Bûnî, *Shams al-ma'ârif al-Kubrâ*, Cairo, n.d., popular ed., 4 vols under one cover. The author and his work are similarly problematic. Toufic Fahd, who mentions ancient manuscripts of the *Shams*, believes that an early, abbreviated version might be attributed to al-Bûnî; cf. *La divination arabe*, re-ed. Paris,

1987, Sindbad ed., pp. 230-232; see also p. 237. In the printed version, the work ends with a mention of "*the chain of transmission* (sanad) *of our teachers.*"

135 On the *awfâq*, cf. *EI2*, suppl. article "*Budûh.*"

136 On the *zâ'irja*, see T. Fahd, *op. cit.*, pp. 219-224 and below, n. 142.

137 Cf. note 134.

138 Cf. the advice that follows chains of transmission: "*It is incumbent upon you to sweep away the veils that cloud your inner vision and to turn toward the tablet, which is the manifest Book of Allah, his immutable secret and his eternal treasure. God said: 'And you do not see within your very selves' (Q. 51:21)."* He who does not know his book, which is his very self *(huwa huwa)* is not, himself, his very self *(fa-laysa huwa huwa)*, *Shams al-ma'ârif* (IV 123).

139 *Ibid.*, II, 85 and III, 85.

140 Often, in Ibn 'Arabî's lineage, like the Yemenite 'Abd al-Karîm al-Jîlî (d. between 805 and 829 A.H., cf. Najâh al-Ghunaymî, *'Abd al-Karîm al-Jîlî wa makânatu-hu fi l-Fikr al-islâmî*, typewritten thesis, Cairo, Al-Azhar, 1976, p. 140) in his commentary on the *basmala*: *al-Kahf wa l-raqîm fi sharh bismillâhi l'rahmâni l'rahîm*, Hyerabad, 1336 A.H., or in the remarkable little work that ties the most metaphysical of meanings of the symbolism of letters to thoughts on the *awfâq*: *Haqîqat al-haqâ'iq allatî li-l-haqqi min wajh wa min wajh li-l-khalâ'iq*, Cairo, 1982. Closer to us, we might cite the letter by the Damascus Shaykh 'Umar al-Attâr (1242-1308/1826-1890): *hâdhihi risâla... a'rabat 'an maknûn asrâr al-hurûf wa l-asmâ'*, Damascus, 1301 A.H., which shows deep impregnation by the Shaykh al-Akbar's work. Even closer is the commentary on the *basmala* by Shaykh Ahmad al-'Alawî of Mostaganem (d. 1936): *al-Unmudhaj al-farîd fi ma'nâ intiwâ' al-kutub al-samâwiyya fi nuqtati bismillâhi-l-rahmâni l-rahîm*, Algiers, 1345 A.H. It might be added that manuscript libraries hold a great number of treatises on the "letters and names" that have yet to be studied.

141 Ibn Khaldun, *Al-Muqaddima*, first eastern version, ed. Mbarek Redjala, Aix-en-Provence, 1983, 2nd vol.

142 Ibn Khaldûn, *Muqaddima*, reprod. Ed. Quatremère, Paris, 1858, pp. 137-146, followed by a long poem by Abû l'Abbâs al-Sabtî on the *zâ'irjat al-'âlam*, "*the circular tablet of the universe that is shaped like a large circle encompassing other concentric circles, some of which are related to the celestial spheres and the others to elements, to sublunar things, to spiritual beings, and to events of all kinds and to different kinds of knowledge. It can be used to predict the future*" (Dozy, *Suppl.* I 577). The letters play a preponderant role in the *zâ'irja*. For further information, see also T. Fahd, *op. cit.*, p. 243-245.

143 See also Ibn Khaldûn, *Shîfâ' al-sâ'il li-tahdhîb al-masâ'il*, Beirut, 1959, pp. 53-56. The passage, which is nearly identical to the one in the *Muqaddima*, maintains that this knowledge is a later deviation from the *tasawwuf*, although it still attempts to describe it meticulously.

144 The chapter on *jafr* is the last chapter in the third part, which is devoted

to the *dawla* (State, dynasty). In it, Ibn Khaldûn offers his widely-shared opinion that the traditions regarding the *Mahdî* that are common in the *tasawwuf* come through Shi'ism. On *jarf*, see T. Fahd, *op. cit.*, pp. 219-224 and *EI2* II, 386-388.

145 *Shams al-ma'ârif*, I, 65-76.

146 According to the tradition of *tafsîr*, interpretation of the isolated letters by the *hisâb al-jummal* or numerical value of letters was practiced by the Medinan Jews in predicting how long the Muslim community would last. It was interpretation of these letters alone that Muqâtil (d. 150 A.H., the author of the oldest of the *tafsîr*) dealt with. Cf. Ed. 'Abd-allah Shahâta, vol. I, Cairo, 1969, pp. 17-21. With considerable circumspection and no mention of Muqâtil, Tabarî used the tradition later in his *Jâmî' al-bayân*, I, 216-218.

147 Trans. M. Vâlsan, *Études traditionnelles*, no. 380, Nov.-Dec., 1983, p. 266. See also the unfortunately too brief remark by M. Vâlsan, pp. 259-260.

148 Such was the case for C. Huart, who published *Textes persans relatifs à la secte des Houroufis*, Leiden, 1909. The *Hurûfiyya* are a quite peculiar branch of Shi'ite esoterism whose teachings are partially based on the symbolism of letters; cf. *EI2*, "Hurufiyya," III, 620-622.

149 R. Guénon, "La science des lettres" published in the *Voile d'Isis*, February 1931 and reprinted in *Les symboles fondamentaux de la science sacrée*, Paris, 1962, pp. 68-74.

150 Among whom was al-Bûnî. The title of his work "Le soleil suprême des connaissances" can be related to the "solar" meaning of the word *suryânî*. On the *suryâniyya* language, see also Ahmad b. al-Mubarak, *Kitâb al-Ibrîz*, Cairo, 1961, pp. 213-216.

151 Guénon does not appear to have known about Jâbir's work related to these remarks.

152 R. Guénon, "Les mystères de la lettre *Nûn*," in *Les symboles fondamentaux de la science sacrée*. On the other hand, information concerning the cosmic and eschatological significance of the letter *nûn* is more closely correlated with other details scattered throughout the Islamic tradition as seen in Ibn Masarra, Ibn Qasî, or al-Bûnî.

153 Cf. "Al-Rûh," "Note sur l'angélologie de l'alphabet arabe" and "La chirologie dans l'ésoterisme islamique," articles reprinted in *Aperçus sur l'ésotérisme islamique et le taoiste*, Paris, 1973. Mention should also be made of "Tétraktys et le carré de quatre," in *Symboles fondamentaux*, pp. 125-130; there is no mention of letters, but reference is made to the *Ikhwân al-safâ*, and these are remarks about the numbers 4 and 6, which are not unlike those in the second chapter of the *Futûhât*. See also "Un hiéroglyphe de Pôle" (*ibid.* pp. 131-136), which deals with the symbolism of the letter *qâf* and the relationship between the letters and the initiatic hierarchy; see also *Le Symbolisme de la croix*, 1931, p. 137, n. 2.

154 See M. Vâlsan, *Symboles fondamentaux*, annex III, pp. 462-468, and *Études trad.*, March-April 1961, pp. 99-107.

155 M. Vâlsan, "Le Triangle de l'Androgyne et le monosyllabe ôm," *Études traditionnelles*, from 1964 to 1966.

156 M. Vâlsan, *Études trad.*, March-April 1961, pp. 99-107.

157 Vâlsan's other contributions in this area are the introduction to Qâshânî's commentary on the isolated letters, *Études trad.*, Nov. - Dec. 1963, pp. 256-262, where passages from chapter 2 in the *Futûhât* are cited, as well as the article titled "Références islamiques du symbolisme de la Croix," in *Études trad.*, March-June 1971, p. 49-57, followed by the translation of chapter 20 from the *Futûhât* on "La science propre à Jésus," *Études trad.*, 1971, pp. 62-72. Ibn 'Arabî's treatise "Le Livre du Nom de Majesté" *(Kitâb al-jalâla)* translated y M. Vâlsan in *Études trad.*, June-July-August and December 1948 contains considerable information about the symbolism of the letters in the Name *Allâh*. After Vâlsan's death, Charles-André Gilis published a note on the symbolism of the letters *alif, wâw*, and *mîm*: "Remarques complémentaires sur OM et le symbolisme polaire," in *Études trad.*, July, August, September, 1975. This note follows the information made available in "Triangle de l'Andrygyne" and is based on a number of Ibn 'Arabî's texts, the *Kitâb al-mîm wa l-wâw wa l-nûn*, and chapters 2, 5, and 198 in the *Futûhât*. See also Ch.-A. Gilis, *Le Coran et la fonction d'Hermès*, Paris, 1984, p. 36-39 regarding the *alif-lâm-mîm* in sura Al 'Imrân. Jean Cantein's research on letters also bears mentioning: *Phomèmes et archétypes, contextes autour d'une structure trinitaire*, AIU, Paris, 1972, a comparative study on the symbolism of the three vowels, and a collection of articles: *La Voie des lettres: tradition cachée en Israël et en Islam*, Paris, 1981. Among other matters, the isolated letters and their role in the Qur'ân is dealt with, although the author refers to Ibn 'Arabî only indirectly.

158 Cf. above, p. 396 and below, note 283.

159 In *Rasâ'il*, Hyderabad, 1948.

160 *Kitâb al-azal*, p. 12.

161 Knowledge and Mercy are the divine attributes described as "enveloping," or "embracing." This is why Knowledge and Mercy, *sharî'a* and *haqiqa* always go together in relation to the servant's state of perfection in the Shaykh's work.

162 The title of chapter 2 (*Fut.*, I, 51, l. 32-33) is "On the knowledge of the hierarchical degrees of the letter-consonants and the vowels in the universe and their counterparts among the Divine Names; and on the knowledge of words, of sciences, of the scholar, and what is known."

163 The letters of the alphabet are called *hurûf al-mu'jam*. *Mu'jam* has the same root as *'ajamî* (non-Arab) and *'ajama*, which means "to speak Arabic poorly, and thus incomprehensibly." According to the Ibn 'Arabî's terminology, *'arabî* denotes that which is clearly expressed, while *'ajamî* refers to that which is unsayable, and can be expressed only via symbolic allusion. (Cf. J. Cantreins, "arabe et 'barbare,'" in *La Voie des Lettres*, Paris, 1981, p. 81ff.) A letter is said to be *mu'jam* when it has diacritical marks to distinguish it from another letter with an identical shape. Whence the use of *mu'jam* in reference to a lexicon or a

dictionary, which brings us back to the object of this chapter, since the words, and thus the lexicon, are produced through the combination of elements whose meanings remain unclear until they are in some way put together.

[164] That is: (3 x 7 = 21) + (3 x 8 = 24) + (4 x 9 = 36) + (18 x 10 = 180) = 261.

[165] *Alif*, which is not a letter in itself, accompanies all the other letters in the same way that the transcendent One or the transcendent Self accompanies beings. Receptivity to the contradictory qualities also makes the equivalent of the "Universal Reality" *(al-haqîqa al-kulliya)*, "*which belongs neither to God, nor to the world, which is described neither by existence nor by nonexistence, nor by contingence or eternity; it is in the eternal, described by it, eternal and in the contingent, described by it, contingent, etc.*" *(Futûhât* I, 119, ch. 6).

[166] Here we see an early indication of the role played by the phonetic classification of letters according to the places in the mouth where they are pronounced *(makhârij)*. The letters that have a cold nature in common are the pharyngeal letters *(hurûf al-halq)*.

[167] These numbers are obtained via a counting system that is analogous to that explained in note 164.

[168] That is, all the letters except *alif* and the six pharyngeal letters, which are listed here in the numerical order of the *abjad*.

[169] *Lâm-alif* is considered to be a letter by itself because it combines either with the *alif* (of prolongation) that is not phonetically a letter-consonant, or with the *hamza* (vocal stress), which is a consonant, but which has no graphically stable existence (it is written like a small *'ayn* with no tail, and stands upon the *alif*, the *wâw*, or the *yâ'*, or else it is written above the line.)

[170] This question comes up later as a "complement" *(tatmîm)*: "*Know that heat and humidity constitute physical life. If humidity had a specific sphere like the other principles that play a part in the mixture of elements* (mazja), *the cycle of this sphere would know an end, its power would cease, as it is manifest in accidental life* (al-hayât al-'aradiyya), *life would then be annihilated or transferred. Now the specific reality of life requires that it not be annihilated; it thus has no sphere of its own. This is why the Creator—exalted may He be—told us that the final abode is the true life...*" *(Futûhât*, I, 55, l. 2-6).

[171] Cf. *Futûhâ,t*, I, 292-297.

[172] *Kitâb al-mabâdi' wa l-ghâyât fî mâ tahwî 'alayhi hurûf al-mu'jam min al-ajâ'ib wa l-âyât*. See the introduction to the translation of this chapter, p. 399 and note 30. O. Yahya mentions three manuscripts with this same title in the libraries of Istanbul; *Histoire et Classification*, p. 347, *R.G.* No. 380. It is not known whether their text is identical to the poem on the letters, three manuscripts of which are in Damascus (cf. R. al-Malih, *Firhist Makhtûtat... al-Zâhiriyya, al-tasawwuf* II, 598-600). Edited after *Rûh al-Quds*, Damascus, 1970, it includes all the introductory poems in the list of qualities of letters (*Futûhât*, I, 65-77 and 84) in the same chapter 2.

[173] This verse was uttered by Iblîs who, after refusing to prostrate himself

before Adam, replied: "*I am better than he: You created me from fire, and him from clay*" (verse 12). On the igneous nature of the jinn, see also Q. 15:27, and especially 55:15. In his commentary on the latter verse, Ibn 'Arabî shows that Iblîs's words "*I am better than he*" are the result of his perspective being limited to the four elements, where fire is superior to earth. Cf. all of chapter 9: "On the knowledge of existence of spirits created from the flames of fire *(al-a wâh al-mârijiyya al-nâriyya)*," *Futûhât*, I, 131-134.

174 The name for each of these three letters is likewise composed of three letters.

175 Ibn 'Arabî also devoted a letter to the idea of *azal*: the *Kitâb al-azal*, in *Rasâ'il*, Heyderabad, 1948,. Cf. p. 436.

176 The scriptural origin of this expression is found in a hadith on the creation of Adam: God created Adam in His (his) form (or: in his image: *'alâ sûratihi*). He was sixty cubits tall. After creating him, he said: Go greet that group, meaning a group of seated angels, and listen to the words they use to greet you, for they will become your salutation, and that of your progeny. Adam said to them: "Peace be upon you," and they replied: "Peace be upon you," to which they added "and God's mercy, too." Thus, each man who enters Paradise does so in the form of Adam; he is sixty cubits tall. "*Since that time, men have continually gotten shorter up to the present day.*" Cf. Ibn Hanbal, *Musnad*, II, 315 and 323; Bukhârî, *Sahîh, Kitâb al-isti'dân*, I; VIII, 62, and Muslim, *Sahîh, Kitâb al-janna*, 28, commentary by Nawawî, XVIII, 178. In this version, the form can be interpreted as relating to God or to Adam; both possibilities are looked at by Ibn 'Arabî, although he most commonly refers to the meaning of divine form, using as a basis a version that is not found in the recognized collections of traditions: "According to the form of the All-Merciful *('alâ sûrat al-Rahmân)*." Nawawî rejects the authenticity of the version, although Ibn Hajar al-'Asqalânî appears to accept it (cf. *Fath al-Bârî*, XI, 2; see also VI, 281), although he does so without offering any information about it. One further mention of the form relating to either God or Adam is seen, with occasional variations, in the hadith: "*When one of you strikes (or fights), let him avoid the face, because God created Adam in His form.*" Cf. Ibn Hanbal, *Musnad*, II, 244, 251, 434, 463, 519, and Muslim, *Kitâb al-birr*, 115, commentary by Nawawî, XVI, 165. In this particular commentary, Nawawî clearly interprets the expression as meaning the divine form. There are other hadiths that mention the form of God, as in: "*In a dream, I saw my Lord in the most beautiful of forms...*" although Ibn 'Arabî was not referring to these.

177 The letters specific to each level of existence represent the realities that are constitutive or essential *(haqâ'iq)* to it. The attributes, however—which are one of the realities specific to the Divine Presence—simultaneously express relationship *(nisba*, pl. *nisab)*. An attribute can thus be attached, or attributed *(nusibat)*, to the level of the divine as well as to the human, by virtue of their correspondence.

178 See introduction, figure I.

¹⁷⁹ *Markaz* refers to the center, in geometry, but etymologically it refers to the place where a point is stuck, like a lance: a comparison suggested by the trunk of the *alif*.

¹⁸⁰ *Azalî* is an adjective of relationship *(nisba)* marked by the suffix *î*. Man is thus attached to eternity, like he is ordinarily attached to his tribe, his ethnic group, his city or country of origin, etc. One wonders about the *muhaqqiq* that Ibn 'Arabî fails to mention.

¹⁸¹ Cf. *Futûhât*, II, 309, ch. 117.

¹⁸² The purpose of this detail is as much to help a public familiar with Aristotelian logic, if not through philosophy then at least through theology, to understand the idea of immutability *(thubût)* (cf. Introduction, p. 110) or man's "place" in divine knowledge as it is to justify metaphysically the use of such terminology.

¹⁸³ *Kitâb inshâ al-dawâ'ir wa l-jadâwîl*, ed. Nyberg, in *Kleine Schriften des Ibn al-'Arabî*, Leiden, 1919.

¹⁸⁴ See figure 5 at the end of the introduction.

¹⁸⁵ They are listed in the order of their numerical value, as on page 2.

¹⁸⁶ Corresponding to the three letters of each presence.

¹⁸⁷ Of knowledge.

¹⁸⁸ Ibn 'Arabî specifies here (p. 54, l. 21-27) that, properly speaking, there is no bowing *(mayl)* in the angel's movement, but that, like Gabriel, the angel moves vertically upward, or downward *(haraka mustaqîma wa mankûsa)*. The angel is thus the opposite of the *jinn narî*, whose movement is limited to the four directions on the horizontal plane. Man, however, moves in three, or six, directions, which clearly is to be related to the three or six short and long vowels. On the list of the qualities of the letters, p. 65-78, the movement of the line that forms each letter, ascending, descending, curving, or a mixture of these, is mentioned and later related to the different directions of spiritual energy *(himma)*; upward movement, toward God; downward, toward creation; curving or horizontal movement, the relationship between him who gives being and him who receives it; a mixture, leading to the knowledge of two realities. See p. 83 (l. 25-28).

¹⁸⁹ On the cosmic importance of the number nine and its relationship to the science of letters, see also *Futûhât* I, 169 (ch. 20), and M. Vâlsan's translation, p. 68.

¹⁹⁰ In Ibn 'Arabî, *jabarût* is an intermediary between *mulk*, the realm of the senses, and *malakût*, the inner realm. On the order and name of these three worlds, see above, p. 454.

¹⁹¹ *Atlas* means black, or grayish. Dozy translates *al-falak al-atlas* as *coelum ambiens*, the heaven that encompasses all heavens; Titus Burckhardt does so as *ciel non étoilé*, or *sans étoiles*, meaning "starless sky." Cf. *Clé spirituelle de l'astrologie Musulmane d'après Mohyiddîn Ibn 'Arabî*, in *Études traditionnelles*, 1950; reprod. Archè, Milan, 1974. *Futûhât* I, 52 (l. 4) and 54 (l. 35).

¹⁹² The perfect numbers are those that are equal to the sums of their divisors

or aliquot parts. On perfect numbers in Islam, see the references noted by P. Kraus, *Jâbir Ibn Hâyyan*, vol. 2, p. 199, note 2.

[193] On the divine breath of exhalation that produces the substantial aspect of beings, see the introduction to this chapter, pp. 408-409.

[194] As is noted later, p. 56 (l. 1), form *(sûra)* means the combination of two of the realities that give existence *(ta'lîf haqîqatayn)* to the physical world; in other words, one of the four elements.

[195] There are two sorts of realities *(haqâ'iq)*: those which the intellect conceives by itself *(murfadât)*, like life, science, the spoken word, sensation, and of course those just dealt with; and those which exist only through the existence of composition *(bi-wujûd al-tarkîb)*; heaven, earth, the universe, man stone, etc., due to the mixing of elements which are themselves the first products of composition (p. 55, l. 30-32); I, 55 (l. 15) and 55 (l. 30).

[196] For example, in the word *mustafâ*, the *tâ'* of which is changed into an emphatic *tâ'*, because it is preceded by another emphatic letter: *sâd*.

[197] *Al-ummahât al-uwal*; this appears to refer to elements.

[198] The division of letters appears to relate to graphic criteria here. The "head" of a letter is its first part. The "dry" letters are those letters that have no dots. The author does not explain the reason for the name. Cf. p. 83 (l. 30-35).

[199] According to sensual perception, because it represents, phonetically, prolonging the voice *(imtidâd al-sawt)*, and graphically, the extension of the dot.

[200] The "Partisans of natures" or naturalists *(ashâb al-tabâ'i, or al-tabâ'iyyûn)* are, for the Muslim heresiographers, those *"who explain the generation of the universe by the interaction of the four fundamental 'natures.'"* cf. Gimaret, "Bibliographie d'Ash'arî: un réexamen," *Journal Asiatique*, 1985, p. 228, note 14. The doctrine of the fifth element is also specific to them, cf. Kraus, *Jâbir Ibn Hayyân*, vol. II, p. 152, note 2. See also p. 154, note 2, on the Pythagorean origin of its being called ether *(atir)* and the Stoic origins of its description as *al-rûh* (= *pneuma*) in Jâbir, see also all of page 155.

[201] *Al-Hakim*, who was a philosopher and medical doctor, is probably referring to Hippocrates or his commentator, Galen, whose *Kitâb fî l-ustuqusât 'alâ ra'y Buqrât* was translated by Hunayn b. Ishâq , cf. F. Sezgin, *Geschichte des Arabischen Schrifttums* III, p. 86 and 146. The word *ustuqus* is a translation of the Greek *stokheîa*, which referred to Aristotle's elementary bodies. M. A. Goichon notes that "*as opposed to* rukn *(pl.* arkân*) and* 'unsur *(pl.* 'anâsir*), it refers to the element that enters composite bodies as a part.*" Cf. *Lexique de la langue philosophique d'Ibn Sînâ*, Paris, 1938, p. 5. Once again, the issue of the fifth element comes up toward the end of this chapter (pp. 92, l. 3 f), in the third section on knowledge, to illustrate how possible it is to use analogies to learn about manifestation. See also *Futûhât*, I, 138-139, ch. 2; O.Y. II, p. 310.

[202] What follows here (p. 56, l. 21-26) is a commentary on Q. 36:69: "*We have not taught him poetry, nor is it fitting for him; this is but a reminder for people, and a plain Qur'ân.*" Through its images, poetry is a general, allusive form

of expression. The knowledge of the heirs to prophecy is actually beyond "global" *(ijmâl)* and distinctive *(tafsîl)* knowledge, since it includes both aspects at the same time, like divine knowledge itself, and—also like divine knowledge—it entails both outwardness and inwardness at the same time, since all opposites are resolved in God, Who is both the Outside and the Inside.

203 See above, note 183.

204 See ch. 4: "On the cause of the beginning of the world and the hierarchical degrees of the Most Beautiful Names relative to the entire universe" (I, 98-101).

205 That is, the principles of the physical world and the elements.

206 *Futûhât* I, 56 (l. 3-30).

207 As is explained below (*Fut.* I, p. 81, l. 30-33), the simple elements (*basâ'it*, as the elementary spheres) of a letter are the letters that its name are composed of . In the case of *nûn*, its name is composed of two *nûn*s and a *wâw*, thus of two letters; *wâw*, in turn, is composed of two *wâw*s and an *alif*, and thus also of two letters. It is noteworthy that the sum is still three letters, which brings us back to the triadic nature of the Divine and human Presences in the preceding model. It might also be noted that, from the point of view of the graphic symbolism of the *nûn*, whose name entails two *nûn*s, or two half-circumferences, allows us to draw a complete circle representing the whole sphere on the metaphysical level or, on the cosmic plane, the farthest sphere *(al-falak al-aqsâ)*, which encompasses all the others. (On the relationship between the production of the spheres and of phonemes, see also *Futûhât*, I, 82, l. 2-3.) Thus Ibn 'Arabî here considers only the *alif* and the *wâw*, respective signs of the divine and the human *(as ma'nâ)* in the total sphere of existence represented by *nûn*.

208 Regarding the distribution of letters into six degrees, we must bear in mind that the numeric value of *wâw* is six, the perfect *(tâmm)* number, as was stated earlier. On *wâw* and the symbol for the Universal Man, see especially the translation of Ibn 'Arabî's *Livre du Nom de Majesté* by Michel Vâlsan, *Études trad.*, 1948, pp. 146, 147, note 1.

209 Cf. above, p. 442, note 173.

210 These nine letters are actually only five, in the way they are formed; they are different only in their lack of dots (the "dry" letters), or by one or more dots.

211 That is, six letters: *alif, lâm, fâ', hâ', hamza,* and *nûn.*

212 These ten letters are reduced to seven by their form.

213 Cf. Q. 52:3, the Qur'ânic symbol for the unfurling of manifestation in the form of writing.

214 Cf. Q. 18:65, regarding al-Khadir.

215 *Futûhât*, I, 56 (l. 33) - 57 (l. 23).

216 Al-Makkî, the author of a famous manual of *tasawwuf,* spent his childhood in Mecca, later lived in Basra, and died in Baghdad in 386/996; cf. *EI2*, I, 157, and, for his biographical references, Kahhâla, *Mu'jam al-Mu'allifîn,* XI, 27,

and Sezgin, *Geschichte des Arabischen Shrifttums*. We have found no mention of the hierarchy of worlds in the *Qût*, let alone the quite specific question regarding the relationship between the movements of vowels, man's breathing, and the movement of the spheres which Ibn 'Arabî nevertheless explicitly mentions as being in the *Qût* (*Futûhât*, I, 87, l. 8-18; see p. 486). It may be that editions of the *Qût* are incomplete. There is nothing really surprising about Abû Tâlib's interest in this science, since he is in Sahl al-Tustarî's spiritual lineage.

217 The intermediary world is also that of the Angel, as these eighteen letters suggest. *Jabarût* is not unlike the angel Gabriel (*Jabrâ'îl*, in Arabic), or like *jabara*—in the sense of regluing, resoldering, or reuniting—or like Jâbir, if we are dealing with a symbolic name.

218 *Fâ'* is pronounced with the lower lip (outside the cavity of the mouth itself) comes in contact with the upper teeth (inside the mouth).

219 *Kâf* and *qâf* are pronounced in the same place: the uvula *(lahât)* or the back part of the tongue *aqsâ l-lîsân*; the only real difference is that the *kâf* is pronounced slightly more forward than the *qâf*. Their relationship to the other four letters is undoubtedly a question of quality of *isti'lâ'* (at least for the *qâf*), that is, the tendency of the tongue to rise up toward the palate, which produces the emphasis.

220 *Hâ'* is midway between the farthest place back in the throat and the midpoint (where it is pronounced in front of the *'ayn*). We should note here that the difficulty in identifying worlds is due in part to the terminology Ibn 'Arabî uses, and to the fact that he has four worlds in mind: *'azama*, *malakût*, *jabarût*, and *mulk*, in contrast to the habitual division into *jabarût*, *malakût*, and *mulk*. In his consideration of the in-between areas, or areas where they mix together, he reaches seven worlds, as in part I. See p. 156.

221 This eighth world, which both is, and is not, part of the universe, seems to refer to the Spirit *(al-Rûh)* as the originator of existence, which is the breath *(nafas)*. In his commentary on the *Fâtiha*, the number eight is related to the letter, which has that numeric value, the *hâ'* in *al-Rahmân* (cf. *Fut.*, I, 106, l. 31-33), the *alif*, the *wâw*, and the *yâ'* under consideration here are the prolongation of the three vowels by stretching out either their sound *(imtidâd al-sawt)* or the air *(imtidâd al-hawâ')*. See *Futûhât*, II, 391, the chapter on *nafas*, regarding the *alif* as an "air letter" *(al-harf al-hâwî)*.

222 Cited in the order of their appearance in the Qur'ân.

223 Sixteen letters, only five of which do not belong to the preceding degrees. The reason for this distribution of letters is unclear.

224 The first three letters have the same shape, and are distinguished from one another only by the absence or presence of a dot; the *kâf* has a nearly identical form, although it is a mirror image.

225 When written, these six letters are connected to the letters that precede them, but not to the letters that follow them. They are thus like the Cherubim *(karûbiyyûn)*, "spirits enthralled by the Divine Majesty"; "they know only Him,

and see only that which they know of Him." They correspond to the *afrâd* (the forlorn) in the human world (cf. *Futûhât* II, 19). In the angelic and human world, these beings thus play a role that has to do with sanctification or affirmation of divine sainthood *(taqdîs)*, and lead those who are like them toward transcendence, whence the necessity for men to become attached to them, but not vice-versa.

226 This is a reference to twelve letters, all of which have at least one diacritical mark, with the exception of *hâ'* (without a dot), which replaces the *jîm* (with a dot), occupied by the next category.

227 First of all, three types of spiritual realization appear here: *ta'alluq*, which is connection to essence; *takhalluq*, which is the acquisition of a divine quality; and *tahaqquq*, which is the realization of essential truth. The difference between men of light *(ahl al-anwâr)* and men of secrets *(ahl al-asrâr)* corresponds to the differences between the numerical values of letters in the "eastern" and "western" *abjad*. We will encounter this difference again in the list of the properties of letters. It goes without saying that from Ibn 'Arabî's perspective, the latter are superior to the former.

228 What follows are thirteen letters that have no diacritical marks. These letters are called "dry" *(yâbisa)* when they are differentiated from the letters of the same shape that do have diacritical marks *(mu'jama)*. The three first letters on this list form the name *ahad* ("one"). Ibn 'Arabî specifies that there are two stations in the "meeting." One is elevated, and the other is even more so.

229 The worlds of Letters are then divided into four or five species *(ajnâs)* corresponding to the numbers of letters that have the same graphic shape in common (p. 59, l. 3-7).

230 *Qad qasasnâ 'alayka*. Ibn 'Arabi is here using a Qur'ânic expression that concerns prophetic stories, since each of these stories *(qissa)* contains a teaching to be meditated upon, as it has a meaning deeper than the apparent meaning of the story (*'ibra*, cf. Q. 12:3 and 79:26). *Qassa* also means following someone's tracks, or coming back on one's own tracks (cf. Q. 18:64). He is thus inviting his reader to follow the "tracks" made by letters, in order to delve, through them, into the mystery of the Book of Existence, to understand the world's song of glory or praise, and for this reason he comes back to what, to his readers, constitutes the least strange world, that of the isolated letters of the Qur'ân.

231 *Awâ'il al-suwar al-majhûla*, which might mean either "the unknown beginnings of the suras," or "the beginnings of the unknown suras." The next part of the text shows that we should favor the first meaning, but that the second could come from the relationship between the *sûra-sûra* relationship, an enclosure, or outer form and inner form.

232 On the "projection" and the "reception" of knowledge, see the introduction to this chapter, pp. 392 and 447.

233 What follows is a series of questions relating to the isolated letters (p. 5a, l. 24-28), already dealt with in the commentary titled *al-Jam' wa l-tafsîl*.

234 A reference to Q. 57:13: "*The day when hypocrites, both men and women, say to those who believed: wait for us, so that we might use a little of your light! They will be told: go back whence you came and search for light. Then a wall* (sûr) *will be raised up among them, with a door in it; inside it, there shall be mercy, and outside, punishment.*" The particular walls or enclosures that the *sûras* constitute thus pertain to the protective veil of the rigors of the Law, which is placed over intelligible realities, pure mercy. The isolated letters at the beginnings of the suras may be considered to be this door. Their unknown meaning is an appeal to delve into the mystery, through fulfillment of the Law, as is shown by the hadith about the "ramifications" of faith that are alluded to later. Regarding the relationship between *sîn* and *sâd*, it must be noted that the numerical value of *sîn* according to the eastern alphabet is identical to that of *sâd* in the western alphabet (60).

235 Elsewhere, Ibn 'Arabî identifies Man, in the plenitude of his primordial being and his singularity *(al-insân al-mufrad)*, with the moon, in relation to this verse and the 28 letters of the alphabet (cf. *Futûhât*, I, 302, ch. 62; see also II, 440-441, ch. 198, paragraph 20, where the astrological dimension of the 28 mansions is carefully studied relative to the perfection of the human form).

236 From the point of view of pronunciation, the *alif* of liaison in *Allâh* cannot in this case connect the name to what precedes (since the *m* of *Mîm* is not vocalized, at least in one of the possible readings), and should thus be seen as a *hamza*, that is, the 29th letter. As will be seen later, this change from the non-manifest to the manifest relates to the institution of the divine *Khilâfa*. As Guénon has pointed out, moreover, the *alif* is seen as being "polar" *(qutbâniyya)*, and the sum of the values of its letters is equal to that of the *qutb*. Cf. "Un hiéroglyphe du Pôle," in *Symboles fondamentaux de la Science sacrée*, p. 133. C.A. Gilis has pointed out the importance of this reference to the pole in his translation of the passage in chapter 198, devoted to the phrases in the *shahâda*, cf. *Le Coran et la fonction d'Hermès*, p. 37. Let us bear in mind that *Allâh* is the specific *dhikr* of the *qutb*, cf. *Futûhât*, III, 248, ch. 355. At the graphic level, the 29th letter is not the *hamza* that has no specific written form, but the *lâm-alif*. It is remarkable that it does not appear either in writing *A.L.M.* or in *Allâh*, in the first case because only the letter *lâm* is written, and not its name; in the second, because the *alif* is superscribed, and thus hidden as the pole.

237 This passage is comparable to the one in the *Kitâb al-isrâ ilâ l-maqâm al-asrâ* titled *munâjât asrâr mabâdi' al-suwar* (intimate conversation regarding the secrets of the beginnings of the suras), pp. 76-80, in *Rasâ'il*.

238 This hadith frequently cited by Ibn 'Arabî, is reported with a number of variations, according to Abû Hurayra: "*The faith entails 78 ramifications* (shu'ab) *(or 68). The most excellent is saying* lâ ilâha illâ'llâh*; the least, removing a hazard from one's path; and modesty is a ramification of the faith*" (Muslim, *Sahîh Imân* 58; Istambul, 1329 A.H., I, 46 and Nasâ'î, *Sunan Imân* 16, Cairo, n.d., with glosses by Suyûtî, VIII, 110).

239 Abû l-Hakam 'Abd al-Salâm Ibn Barrajân, who taught in Seville and was accused during Almoravid times of pretension to the *imâma*, was taken into captivity in Morocco, where he died in 536/1141 (*EI2*, III, 754-755). Other than this passage, Ibn 'Arabî cites him especially for the doctrine of "the Truth through which things are created" *(al-haqq al-makhlûq bihi)*, one of the aspects of the *haqîqa muhammadiyya* (cf. *Futûhât*, I, 297; II, 60, 104, 577; III, 77). In the *Mawâqi' al-nujûm*, Cairo, 1965, p. 142, this prediction is cited from the work of Ibn Barrajân, *Idâh al-Hikma*. There is a copy of this *tafsîr* in Istanbul: Sulaymanié Mahmud Pasha 3 and 4, copied in 596 A.H. However, the text appears to be different from the other manuscripts of Ibn Barrajân's *tafsîr*, like Suleymanié, Reïsulkutab 30 and 31 (copied from 667 A.H. and 1168 A.H.). See also Cârullah 51M and Dâmâd Ibrâhîm Pasha 25-26-27. (In a note, O. Yahya points out the reference to the commentary on this verse in the latter manuscript, cf. *Futûhât*, I, 267.) Ibn Barrajân was also the author of a treatise on the Divine Names, composed before the *tafsîr*: *Tarjumân al-haqq al-mabthuth fî l-amr wa l-khalq*, Paris, B.N. Arabic collection 2642, and also of a *Kitâb al-irshâd* that is compared to his *tafsîr*.

240 Cf. Q. 30:1-4: "1. A.L.M.; 2. The Rûm were victorious; 3. on the closest earth, but they, after their victory, will be vanquished; 4. in a few years; commanding belongs to God, both beforehand and after, and that day the believers will rejoice; 5. God's rescue; He rescues whom He wishes, and He is the All-Powerful, the All-Merciful; 6: the Promises of God! God does not break His promises, but most men do not know; 7. Thoughtless about their being from the beyond, they experience an outer side of life in this world." Ibn Barrajân, and later Ibn 'Arabî, refer to reading Ibn 'Umar's verses 2 and 3: *ghalabati l-rûm... sa-yughlabûn*, while all other readers, keeping in mind the historical circumstances of Revelation, read: *ghulibat-i-l-rûm... sa-yaghlibûn*: "The Byzantines have been vanquished... they will be victorious." Cf. Tabarî, *Jâmi' al-bayân*, XXI, 11f. Regarding the meaning of *bid'*, "some," Tabarî reports a number of traditions about a wager Abû Bakr made with the Quraysh in Mecca for a period of five years, after which the Prophet reminded him that *bid'* means from 3 to 9. On the orientalist literature regarding these verses, Rudi Paret, *Der Koran*, Kommentar und Konkordanz, 1977, p. 388. "The closest land" means Syria *(al-Shâm)*. The two possible readings of this prophecy refer to past and future situations being overturned in this central eschatological land that Syria, in the broad sense, is.

241 *al-jazm al-sahhîr*, the method of calculating that entails reducing tens to ones: A.L.M. = 1 + 30 + 40 = 1 + 3 + 4 = 8.

242 *Al-jummal al-kabîr* or *jazm*, which keeps track of tens (and hundreds): A.L.M. = 1 + 30 + 40 = 71.

243 *Futûhât*, I, 58, l. 13; 60, l. 9. Here, as later (in I, 81, o. 29-30), Ibn 'Arabî is expressing his desire to write a work about "the marvellous secrets" of numbers. He then reminds us that knowledge of the fourteen isolated letters confers "*Knowledge of the reality of how things come into existence and the solitude of the*

Eternal in the Attributes that are His for all eternity" (*tafarrud al-qadîm bi-sifâtihi al-azaliyya*). This knowledge of transcendence ends up contrasting with that of Man. He sees a sign of this in the fact that the first of the letters is *alif*, and the last is *nûn*.

244 An *alif* at the beginning of a work cannot be pronounced without the vocal stress marked by the *hamza*.

245 Ibn 'Arabî thus chose to consider *nûn* as the last of the letters, which it is neither in the numeric nor in the written alphabet, because of its lunar symbolism. The last night of the lunar month *(sirâr or sarâr)* entails total effacement of the light reflected from the sun. The night can be the 29th or the 30th, which allows for the inclusion of *lâm-alif* (the symbolism of which will be discussed at length later) in the counting of letters. The reference to the "trust" is an indication of the relationship between the *nûn* and the Universal Man, and especially with the *Khalîfa* that is alluded to in the verse: "*We offered the trust to the heavens and the earth, but they refused to take it, and were afraid of it. But man took it, and in truth, he showed himself to be unfaithful to it, and unjust, and full of ignorance*" (Q. 33:72). This *amâna* is to be compared to the necessarily hidden role of the *umanâ'*, the repositories of the divine secret God has entrusted to men. See *Futûhât*, II, 20.

246 *Futûhât*, I, 60, l. 17-23. This latter passage, which is deliberately obscure, illustrates the complex relationships between the first and the last of the isolated letters, *alif* and *nûn*, as well as their meaning for the highest level of spiritual realization, that of the Universal Man. The three elements of the first triad are: 1. the movement of descent, the setting; 2. a half circle, with the arc pointing upwards (design), since the adjective *qalbî*, "relating to the heart," suggests this shape, that of an inverted heart, as *qalb* also means "turning over"; 3. the One Presence, that is, with no relationship to the manifested. This thus entails a leaving, or an exit. The return toward creatures is marked by the rising of the moon, by the appearance of a crescent that is also shaped like the *nûn* or the heart (design); the third element is the lordly presence, that is, turned toward the creatures. We thus see the symbol of the two *nûn*s, united by the diameter or the *alif* lying on its side, as was seen above. This diameter is one of the names for the Universal Man, in Ibn 'Arabî's prayer over the Prophet: "*The diameter of the One, drawn between the "Two Arches" of Unity and Oneness*" (*khatt al-wahdat bayna qawsay l-ahadiya wa l-wâhidiyya*), see the translation by Michel Vâlsan in *Études traditionnelles*, Nov. - Dec. 1974, p. 245. On the other hand, the word "three" or "triad" is reminiscent of the triangle; the union of two semicircles, one turned upwards, and the other turned downwards can thus be compared to the union of the two triangles on Solomon's seal. Their common center, though not seen, is precisely the *nûn*'s dot [design] = [design star of David] "The exit and the return step by step" *(qadam bi-qadam)* indicates the strong correlation between the degrees of universal manifestation and the steps of realization.

247 Depending on whether it is a single letter, like the *nûn* in sura 68 or the

qâf in sura 50; two letters, like the *tâ'-hâ'* of sura 20 or the *yâ-sîn* of sura 36; three letters, like the *alif-lâm-mîm* of sura 2, among others; of four letters: *alif-lâm-mîm-sâd*, as in sura 7; or five, as in *kâf'-hâ'-yâ'-'ayn-sâd* in sura 19, etc.

[248] On this idea, see the introduction, p. 58. The idea of *barzakh* is developed here through a commentary on Q. 55:19-20 "*He separated the two seas so that they flow freely; between them is an isthmus beyond which they do not pass.*" (p. 60, l. 27-33).

[249] We might recall the two ways the Prophet is referred to in Ibn 'Arabî's prayer: "*The Mediator of 'descents' from the Heaven of pre-eternity toward the Earth of Perpetuity*" (wâsita l-tanazzul min samâ' al-azaliyya ilâard al-abadiyya)... "*The Intermediary located between the Manifested and the Unmanifested: 'He separated the Two Seas that touch' and regarding the place where the ephemeral touches the Eternal: 'Between them there is a barrier over which they do not spill'*" (Prayer, cf. n. 246, pp. 245, 247). The *lâm* in the following passage symbolized this role as intermediary and Mediator *(wâsita)*.

[250] The meaning of *ishâra*, an allusive or demonstrative indicator, is developed later, in regard to *dhâlika l-kitâb*, "That is the Book."

[251] Cf. intro., fig. 2. Here, the translation emphasizes the vegetable symbolism connected to these calligraphic terms: *asl* (trunk) also means beginning, or foundation; *ta'rîq*, which is the name for the "tail" on the *mîm*, literally means "the fact of having taken root." The relationship between the *alif* and the *mîm* is reminiscent of the two trees, one straight and the other leaning.

[252] *Asfala sâfilîn*. We have attempted to translate the last part of the verse as closely as possible [French: "*Nous avons créé l'Homme dans la plus excellente constitution, puis nous l'avons renvoyé au plus bas des êtres bas*"]; its syntactically somewhat unusual nature was noted by the earliest commentators on the Qur'ân, like al-Farrâ', *Ma'ânî al-Qur'ân*, Cairo, 1972, III, 277.

[253] Here is the text of the hadith: "*Our Lord comes down to the lowest heaven nightly, during the last third of the night, and says: 'Who is that calling Me, that I may answer him? Who is asking My forgiveness, that I may forgive him?'*" (Bukhârî's version, *Sahîh*, VIII, 88, *K. al-da...awât*, 13). On the many versions of this hadith, cf. *Al-Ahâdîth al-qudsiyya*, Cairo, n.d., I, 72-74.

[254] *Qudra*, with the double meaning of ability and possibility.

[255] Written alone, both *lâm* and *mîm* finish below the line: [arabic letters]. Initially or in the medial position, they connect to the letters that follow on the line [arabic letters].

[256] The author is thus thinking of the *lâm* written either as the last letter in a word or as an isolated letter here, independent of the way it is written in *alif-lâm-mîm*, where the *lâm* is connected to the *mîm* on the line.

[257] Cf. intro., fig. 3.

[258] Sunday *(al-ahad)* is the first day of the week.

[259] On Saturday's being a day of passage, cf. Ibn 'Arabî, *Tanazzul al-amlâk*, Cairo, 1961, p. 193-195.

²⁶⁰ Saturn corresponds to the 7th heaven and the mixture of cold and dry produces the earth, the last of the elements.

²⁶¹ *Qara'a*, as Ibn 'Arabî frequently reminds us, also means "to bring together."

²⁶² According to 'Ajlûnî, this version of the hadith is Ibn Hibbân's and Al-Hâkim al-Nisâbûrî's version, from Burayda; cf. *Kashf al-Khafâ'*, II, 130, no. 2011. Ibn 'Arabî mentions more than once that the phrase "*and He is now...*" is a later addition; see for example, *Futûhât* I, 41, and O.Y., I, 189, paragraph 240, and II, 56, question 23, etc. Bukhârî offers two versions according to Imrân b. Husayn, IV, 128-129, *Bad' al-khalq* I: "*... God was and nothing else was...*" and IX, 152, *tawhîd* 5: "*God was and nothing else was before Him...,*" which goes back to the idea of *azal*, as Ibn 'Arabi underscores (e.g., in *Fut.* I, 152; O.Y., II, 384, paragraph 597). It is interesting to put this hadith into context (according to Bukhârî, *tawhîd*): "*'Imrân b. Husayn reports: 'I was at the Prophet's house—may grace and peace be upon him—when a group from the Banû Tamîm came. The Prophet said "Receive the good news, o Banû Tamîm!" They replied, "you announced good news, so give us some gift." Then some men from Yemen came in. The Prophet said "Receive the good news, o People of Yemen, for the Banû Tamîm did not accept it!" They replied, "We do accept it. We came to learn about the religion and to ask you about the Beginning; what was it?" He replied: "God was, and nothing else was before Him. His Throne was upon the water, and then he created the Heavens and the earth, and wrote all things in the Remembrance (dhikr)."' 'Imrân added: "A man then came to find me, and said: 'O 'Imrân, go catch your camel, which is running away!' I went out to look for it, and at one point the mirage that was keeping me from seeing it broke. By God, I would have preferred that it run away, and that I had not had to get up.*"

²⁶³ Q. 89: 27-28: "*O peaceful soul, return well pleased and well pleasing toward your Lord.*"

²⁶⁴ The mention of *amîn* is all the more remarkable here since, like *A.L.M.*, it precedes the commentary on the *Fâtiha*, and it will no longer be mentioned in chapter 5. *Amîn* is not actually part of the written or recited Qur'ân, although it "seals" recitation of the *Fâtiha* in canonical prayer. In common prayer, the imam says *amîn* in a low voice, and those with him say it louder, like the audible echo of an unmanifested sound, to reinforce the invocation of the last part of the *Fâtiha*: "*Guide us on the straight path... nor of those who have gone astray.*" When written, this invocation begins with an *alif (ihdi-nâ)*, as do *Amîn* and *A.L.M.*; at the end, *alif* is the graphic symbol of verticality and the phonetic symbol for the occultation, and thus of transcendence, since it is never pronounced as such. The *alif* "United to itself" that is mentioned below appears to be a reference to the writing of *âmîn*, where the *alif* is actually double (one pronounced as *hamza*) and the other elongated). Ibn 'Arabî alludes to the importance of the order of the letters in *âmîn* in recitation (*Futûhât* II, 101, question 100). The relationship between the writing of *A.L.M.* and *A.M.N.* is in any case evident, since, as we have seen, the *lâm* is composed of *alif* and *nûn*. Finally, *Amîn*

appears to be identified with the Word "Lord of the Soul" in this case, and thus with the transcendent, unmanifested face of the Spirit, which explains the relationship to *A.L.M.* where the mediating *lâm* is an *alif* in its first part. On *Amîn* as the name of the Word, but also of God, and on its not only conforming, but also affirming, role, see Michel Vâlsan's in depth study of all the Islamic traditions, in "Le triangle de l'androgyne et le monosyllabe '*Om*,'" in *Études traditionneles*, 1970, pp. 82-89 and 132-134.

265 Cf. the hadith "*When one of you says* âmîn*' and the Angels in heaven do likewise, if his speech coincides with that of the Angels, his prior sins will be forgiven*," Bukhârî, *Sahîh*, I, 188; IV, 138. An identical tradition is reported in regard to the response to the imam's words when standing back up after bowing. As is also the case for the *khalîfa*, the imam speaks for God: "*God listens to him who praises Him*" and those in attendance reply, following the example of the angels: "Allâhumma, *our Lord! to You be praise!*" cf. *Sahîh* I, 191 and IV, 139.

266 A hermeneutic hierarchy that corresponds to the four degrees of understanding the Qur'ân; cf. *Futûhât*, I, 188, ch. 25. The tradition the division is founded on: "*There is no verse that does not have an outer* (zâhir) *and an inner* (bâtin) *meaning, an edge* (hadd) *and a higher* (muttala') *point of view*" is not usually admitted by the traditionists, even though it was reported by Ibn Hibbân (cf. O.Y., *Futûhât* III, 187, paragraph 153). Ibn 'Arabî claims that it is authentic for the "people of unveiling." Nevertheless, Tabarî , citing his source as Ibn Mas'ûd, reports it in this form: "*The Qur'ân was revealed according to the seven modalities* (harf, *pl.* ahruf). *Each* harf *has an outer and an inner face* (zahr-batn); *each* harf *has its edge and each edge, a higher point of view*," *Jâmi' al-bayân*, ed. Dâr al-Ma'ârif, I, 22-23.

267 The name of the letter *alif* contains no long vowels, in contrast to *lâm* and *mîm*, whose long vowels are elongated six times the value of a short vowel *(madd lâzim)* in *tajwîd*, or Qur'ânic orthoepy.

268 That is, the three case endings, marked by the vowels *u, a,* and *i*, respectively. See the passage on vowels below.

269 In Arabic, a word cannot begin with either a nonvocalized consonant or a vowel, whence the necessity for the vocal emphasis of the *hamza*. *Alif* receives the vowel *a*, since its name *fatha* means "opening," and will be interpreted below (p. 62, l. 8) as "*the attribute of the opening of existence*" (sifat iftitâh al-wujûd). Use of the word *mubda'* in reference to the *hamza* is related to the divine name *badî' al-samâwâti wa l-ard*: "the Inventor"—i.e., the Creator "working without a prior model" of the heavens and the earth," since the *hamza* is the first manifestation of the unmanifested. See also *Futûhât* II, 421, ch. 198 on the name *al-Mubdi'*.

270 The first manifestation of being is the word *KuN*, meaning "Be!" (*fiat*, in Latin). The *wâw* in the root *KWN*, "to be," is hidden, although it reappears when the being produces, as in the verse "*And when He decreed something He had only to say 'be!* (kun) *and it was* (fayakûn)" (Q. 2:118). See also

Futûhât I, 61, l. 2-61, l. 33.

271 The root *MDD* is an expression of two meanings at the same time: (primarily vocal) extension or prolongation *(madd)*, and (primarily spiritual) succor or support *(madad)*. The word *mâdda* (that which extends itself, meaning "matter,") comes from the extension meaning.

272 *Al-sifat al-Rahmâniyya*, connected to the "Exhalation of the All Merciful" *(nafas al-Rahmân)*.

273 *Futûhât* I, 62, l. 2-7. On this last hadith, see note 176.

274 The case marked by the ending *u* or *û* (i.e., the vowel *u* followed by a *wâw* of prolongation) is called *raf'*, or "elevation" in the transitive sense.

275 Revelation thus clearly appears as the "cause" of manifestation, via the substantial and "material" *(mâdda)* extension of the *Nafas al-Rahmân*. But the way this extension takes place must remain hidden from both the Angel and the Prophet. The hierarchy of states of Being relies on the difference between *wâw* and *yâ'*, just as the existence of manifestation relies on the difference between *wâw* and *yâ'*, on the one hand, and *alif* on the other.

276 Part of a hadith in which the Prophet, realizing that he had erred in his opinion regarding the pollination of palm trees, clarified by saying, "*That was merely an opinion I was stating. If it seems like it might be useful to you, do it. I am nothing more than a man like you, and my opinion can be true or false. But as soon as I say 'God said...' I am incapable of uttering falsehood in regard to 'God*" (Ibn Hanbâl, *Musnad* I, 163).

277 *Khafd*. The case marked by the vowel *i* or *î* (followed by a *yâ'*) is that of the complement of a noun or a noun governed by a preposition, thus a noun in a state of dependence, while "elevation" *(raf')* is the case of the subject or the attribute.

278 On the "Likeness" *(mithl)*, see the commentary on the *Fâtiha*, *Futûhât*, ch. 5.

279 *Futûhât* I, 62, l. 12-29.

280 The first part of the verse can be considered a nominal phrase, and thus translated in this way. But it is generally understood as "That book (subject), no doubt upon it (predicate)."

281 The demonstrative *dhâlika* actually entails three words: *dha*, the demonstrative pronoun, properly speaking; *li*, the sign of elongation *(al-lâm li-l-bu'd)* and *ka* (or *Kâf al-mukhâtab*) the sign that a specific person is being addressed, since this is a question of a second person personal pronoun. (In ancient usage, little of which survived in the Qur'ân, the word *dhâlikum* was used to address several individuals). *Dhâlika* can be translated as "that, o you!" The grammatical term for the demonstrative, *ishâra*, means "sign" (made by the finger or another part of the body), or "indication." In *tasawwuf*, it refers to the transmission and the reception of a truth in direct relation to the spiritual state of the person for whom it is intended. In Qur'ânic reading, *ishâra* is the particular understanding of the divine words by the reader as he is personally and directly addressed at that very instant. It is thus the very letter *Kâf* (you!) that is the

basis of the principle of the allusive, interior interpretation of the Qur'ân. On the Qur'ânic and prophetic bases of *ishâra* in Ibn 'Arabî, see the translation of *K. al-i'lâm bi-ishârât* by M. Vâlsan, "Le livre d'enseignement par formules indicatives des gens inspirés," in *Études traditionnelles*, 1967-68 (1967, pp. 56-57). See also P. Nwyia's article "*ishâra*" in *EI2*, IV, 119.

282 As O. Yahya points out, this phrase is found in the introduction to Ibn al-'Arîf's *Mahâsin al-majâlis* (d. 536/1141), ed. M. Asin Palacios, Paris, 1933, p. 76, but it is not certain that it is by Ibn al-'Arîf himself.

283 The *K. al-maj' wa l-tafsîl fi asrâr (ma'ânî) al-tanzîl* is mentioned by Ibn 'Arabî in his *Fihrîs* (number 5, ed. K. 'Awwâd, *Revue de l'Académie Arabe de Damas*, no. 29-30, 1954-55, pp. 356-357. See also O. Yahya, *Histoire et classification*, p. 266, no. 172). In it, he specifies that this commentary does not stop at verse 59 of sura *al-Kahf* (sura 18), that is, just before the episode of the meeting between Moses and al-Khadir, and that each verse in it is interpreted from three points of view: Majesty *(jalâl)*, Beauty *(jamâl)*, and Perfection *(kamâl)*, a station of balance between the two preceding aspects of Divine Mercy and Divine Harshness. This station, he adds, has no relationship to the first two, and it is from this point of view, specific to the perfect Muhammadan Heir *(al-wârith al-kâmil al-muhammadî)* that he deals with "*the secrets of letters, of words, and of the minor letters that the vowels are, and of living or dead quiescence* (sukûn)." This lack of relationship is also seen between the first two aspects and the third in the interpretation of *ikhla' na'layka*, in relation to the *alif*s transcendence.

284 Phonetically, this *alif* is a mark of the *a* in *dhâ* being drawn out, but the argument here relies on the way it is written: the letters that follow cannot be attached to either the *dhâl* or the *alif*; graphically, the *alif* is thus isolated between the *dhâl* and the *lâm*.

285 Cf. for example, *Futûhât* III, 494, ch. 379, where this same idea is developed in relation to this verse.

286 See the edition of the *Tadbîrât al-ilâhiyya fi islâh al-mamlaka al-insâniyya*, in *Kleinere Schriften*, p. 180: after mentioning the elements necessary for writing (the Pen, the Inkwell *(Nûn)*, the Tablet and the Right Hand), Ibn 'Arabî adds: "*The Tablet is thus the receptacle for writing. Let us call it "the Written" (or "the Book": al-kitâb). The latter is divided into "inscribed book" and "drawn book." God said: "By the Mountain* (Tûr) *and by a drawn book" (Q. 52:1-2) and "An inscribed book" (Q. 83: 9-20). God thus gave His word via that which is "drawn out" and informed us that that which is "inscribed" is found in two places:* Sijjîn *(the abode of the damned) and* 'Illiyûn *(the abode of the chosen ones). The "drawn book" is found in the world of spirits, and the "inscribed book" is found in both the world of mystery and that of sensory manifestation. From the point of view of essential realities, the "inscribed" and the "drawn" are identical, as authentic unveiling shows. However, since the beings of the Supreme Pleroma see only the side of the Book that is facing them, that of the world of Divine Order* ('âlam al-amr), *for them, the Book*

is *"drawn"*; on the other hand the Man who can bring the upper and the lower together in himself is able to see both sides. For him, the Book is *"inscribed"*... In regard to the third book, the Qur'ân does not mention an *"unknown"* book, but rather *"a hidden book,"* according to a hierarchy that is reminiscent of the one mentioned in: *"No, certainly I give my word by the setting of the stars (fragmented and distinctive Revelation) and it is a word—if you only knew—that is impressive. It is a noble Qur'ân, in a hidden* (maknûn) *book."* (Q. 56:75-78).

287 The *lâm* is "lowered" or "abased" *(makhfûd)*, because it contains the vowel *i*, the sign of the case ending called "lowering" *(khafd)*. Since the *i* is not the mark of a case here, it might have been better to say *maksûr*, "broken," or "withdrawn," in line with the characteristic of the articulated vowel. But using logical analytical terminology *(i'râb)*, Ibn 'Arabî is undoubtedly emphasizing the fact that the three dimensions of being signified by these vowels are not limited to the letters playing a specific role in grammar.

288 Or the Divine Word whose name *(al-kalimatal-ilâhiyya)* begins like *kun* (*fiat*, "let it be") with a *kâf*.

289 The second translation of *dhâlika al-kitâb*, "that book," is not mentioned here.

290 Because the Attribute is not distinct from the Essence. A hadith cited later implicitly leads to the interpretation of *hudan li-l-muttaqîn* as "a guidance for those who fear." The verb *ittaqâ*, of which *muttaqîn* is the plural agent participle, literally means not "to fear," but rather "to protect oneself." Pious fear *(taqwâ)* consists in seeking protection in God against God Himself, an example of which is the Prophet's invocation "I take refuge in You against You"; cf. p. 478.

291 *Fa-laysat wa laysat ghayrahâ*. To explain this phrase, O. Yahya goes to the Ash'arite doctrine of Attributes (cf. *Futûhât* I, 286, note 8), but, as the rest of the passage shows, what was most at issue was the mystery of knowledge.

292 *Lâm-alif* is written as two *alifs* tied together at the base. Cf. fig. 4. Since the *lâm* is tied to the *alif*, it is no longer written ( ) but rather ( ) [characters do not appear in original text -ed.]. As was seen above, *lâm* is broken down into an *alif* and a *nûn*, which reappears in the last letter of the verse: the *n* in *muttaqîn*, whence the reference to the Divine Name "The Last" (the first letter of which is an *alif*, like the name "the First" *(al-Awwâl)*.

293 Just as is the case with 1 x 1 = 1, when one *alif* follows another, they are written as a single *alif*, albeit topped by a sign of elongation, the *madda*. Moreover, the way the *alif* is drawn coincides with that of *one* in numbers of Indian origin. See fig. 4.

294 The indirect, but necessary, relationship between divine occultation and the appearance of injustice *(zulm-zulma)* in the institution of the *khalîfa* might be noted; it stands out clearly in this verse, and in the rest of the story of Adam.

295 See the commentary on *al-hamd* in the *Fâtiha*: *Futûhât* I, 103, ch. 5.

296 The *nûn* belonging to the world of the senses.

297 The word *ridâ'*, for Ibn 'Arabî, refers to *"the perfect servant, created in the*

divine form, bringing together the realities of the possible and of the divine, the most perfect manifestation that there is..." (*Futûhât* II, 103). It gets its origin from a *hadith qudsî* ("Grandeur is My mantle, and immensity is My loincloth" (*al-kibriyâ' ridâ'î wa l-'azama isârî*), Ibn Hanbal, *Musnâd* II, 248; see also Ibn 'Arabî, *Mishkât al-Anwâr*, trans. Michel Vâlsan: *La Niche des Lumières*, Paris, 1983, pp. 38-39. From this tradition, Ibn 'Arabî concludes as follows: "*Since we are the grandeur of God before His Face and the veil contemplates the Veiled, God confirms that we will see Him. Al-Ash'arî (or the Ash'arite) is correct to cite these words of the Prophet, 'You shall see your Lord' at the same time as the words (spoken by God to Moses), 'You will not see Me' (Q. 7:143). The cloak has an outer side and an inner side. It sees God with its inner side... and supports him who claims that it will be possible to see God, while with its outer face, it does not see Him, and supports the Mu'tazilite (who denies the possibility of such vision). The cloak is, of course, one and the same entity..."* (*Futûhât* IV, 246). See the other references noted by S. al-Hakîm, *al-Mu'jam al-sûfî*, pp. 529-531. A quick reference in the text that follows (p. 64, l. 16) to rogations for rain *(istisqâ')*, a prayer during which the imam turns his cloak over, is suggestive both of the exceptional nature of such contemplation in the world, and of the state of absolute indigence that it supposes.

[298] Attribution of these two verses has yet to be established. Emir 'Abd al-Qâdir al-Jazâ'iri cites them for the first time attributing them to Sâhîb Ibn 'Abbâd, and a second time declaring that Shaykh al-Akbar attributes them to al-Hasan b. Hâni' and Ibn Khallikân to Ibn 'Abbâd; cf. *Mawâqif* I, 205, no. 103 and 221, no. 109 (communication from Michel Chodkiewicz).

[299] This might also be translated, transitively, as "the knowledge that maintains your existence."

[300] *Futûhât* I, 63, l. 1-64, l. 14. This fundamental question, as the Shaykh reminds us, comes up again in the third part of this chapter.

[301] Keeping the *hamza* in mind.

[302] This verse regarding David is found in sura *Sâd*, which gets its name from the name of the isolated letter it begins with. The sura lists some of the trials the prophets were subjected to. Addressed primarily to the Prophet Muhammad, more specifically, it tells the stories of David, Solomon, and Job, and quickly thereafter, stories about other prophets; it ends with Iblîs's refusal to prostrate himself before Adam, and with the mission God gave him to tempt men "until the end of known time" (v. 81). This cyclical backtracking clearly relates to the form and the meaning of the letter *sâd*.

[303] *Futûhât* I, 71, l. 14-34.

[304] "Penchant" is to be understood both as is, and figuratively. In one style of writing the *lâm-alif*, only the *alif* is leaning; in the other, the *lâm* and the *alif* are leaning symmetrically. See intro., fig. 4.

[305] See note 253, above. The translation expands slightly on the meaning, in order to bring out the parallel between the *lâm*'s fear of losing the *alif*, and the fear of the "men of the night" of letting its spiritual benefit escape them. The lit-

eral meaning is as follows, however: "like God's descent toward the lower heaven, and it is *(wa hum)* the men of the night in the last third." This initiatory category may thus be identified as the upper covering of the world, between heaven and earth, a mediating role that is fundamentally that of the *lâm*.

306 Ibn 'Arabî brings up a spelling issue here (p. 76, l. 6-8): which letter is to be vocalized first and with which should one begin? Both possibilities result from the fusion and the similarity of the two letters.

307 In the Arabic text the letters of the *shahâda* are detached in such a way that they highlight the four *lâm-alif*s it contains.

308 This relates back to the third section on knowledge.

309 A *wâqif* is the saint who, once he reaches his goal, stands waiting, turned only toward God. Cf. *Futûhât* I, 251, ch. 45: "*He who is not sent back (toward the creatures) no longer has in him any face turned toward the universe. He remains there, standing* (wâqifan). *He is also called a* wâqif..." Most of this chapter can be considered to be the development of this passage. See Michel Vâlsan's translation: "*Sur celui qui 'reveint' (vers les créatures) après être 'parvenu' (à la Vérité suprême) et sur Celui qui le fait revenir,*" in *Études traditionnelles*, 1953, p. 125f.

310 On Abû Habîb Hamza b. 'Abdallah al-'Abâdânî, one of Sahl's teachers but otherwise very little known, cf. *Risâla Qushayriyya*, Cairo, 1972, I, 106, and Ghazâlî, *Ihyâ' 'ulûm al-dîn*, Beirut, n.d., III, 74. Prostration of the heart is mentioned more than once by Ibn 'Arabî in reference to this reply; cf. *Futûhât*, II, 20, 32, 34, 102; III, 86, 250, etc.

311 The *tamattu'* in question here consists in completing an *'umra* upon his arrival in Mecca, removing the sacredness around oneself, and then retaking *ihrâm* at the moment of the pilgrimage *(hajj)*. This version of the hadith is from Ibn Mâja, *Sunan manâsik*, I, Cairo, 1972, p. 992. Bukhârî, *Sahîh...umra*, 6, III, 4, offers the Prophet's only reply as: *li-l-a-bad*; the same is true for Nasâ'î, *Sunan hajj*, 71, Cairo, 1930, V, 179 and Dârîmî, *Sunan manâsik*, 34, II, 47: *li-abadin abadan*.

312 Most of the collections of hadith report this invocation with a few variations. See, e.g., Ibn Hanbal, *Musnad*, I, 96: "...*according to 'Alî, the Prophet—upon him be peace—said at the end of the* witr:...[same text] *"I cannot list all the praise that belongs to You. You are as You have praised Yourself."* See other commentaries on this invocation, *Futûhât* II, 155 and 157; III, 183.

313 Reference (p. 77, l. 2-6) to a few examples of *lâm-alif* in the Qur'ân.

314 Cf. the beginning of this chapter, p. 444.

315 The Shaykh is making a strong claim for his role as Muhammadan heir.

316 *Futûhât*, I, 75, l. 32-77, l. 9. Ibn 'Arabî adds that the liaison and the correspondence or the affinity *(munâsaba)* of the letters among themselves is a vast subject all by itself, and one of which this passage is but an example. Once again, he refers his reader to his commentary and to the work he was in the process of composing, the *Mabâdi'*.

317 *Jins, 'ahd, ta'rîf,* and *ta'zim*, the different grammatical roles the article *al* plays.

318 *Fa-in-fanîta 'an al-haqq bi-l-khalîqa*. This form of extinction *(fanâ')* is the highest, because it is a return toward the creatures and total occultation of the attributes of divinity. It thus inaugurates the first genus, that of humans, in this case, and the principle of separation and division. In contrast to *lâm-alif*, *alif* and *lâm* are separated in writing, since no letter can attach itself to the *alif*.

319 Cf. pp. 444 and 459-460.

320 On *haqîqat al-haqâ'iq*, or *al-haqîqat al-kulliyya*, see *Futûhât* I, pp. 118-119.

321 *Futûhât* I, 77, l. 20-27.

322 Cf. Qur'ân 53: 44-47: "*...and it is He who causes death and life, and He creates the couple, male and female, out of a drop of sperm at the moment it is ejaculated, and it is He who brings forth a second constitution* (al-nash'at al-ukhrâ)."

323 This passage deals with the same material as the beginning of the chapter, but from a different point of view.

324 The Qur'ân does not draw a clear line between the Angels and the Jinn, since it refers to Iblîs disobeying the angels: "*They prostrated themselves, except for Iblîs; he was one of the jinn, and he transgressed his Lord's order.*" (Q. 18:50).

325 Words formed from a single consonant are rare in Arabic. Other than a few particles *(hurûf)*, the three imperatives cited come from roots whose first and last letters are a *wâw* and a *yâ'* that disappear in the imperative form.

326 The word *jânn* in the sense of a subtle being of igneous nature appears in two suras, where its creation is linked to that of man: "*We have created man from a putrid clay in a dry and sonorous* (salsâl) *land. Earlier, We created the* jânn *from the fire of a torrid wind*" (Q. 15: 26-27; verse 29 on the insufflation of the Spirit was cited earlier, in the beginning of this section); "*He created man from a dry and sonorous land, like baked earth* (fakhkhât) *and He created the* jânn *from a bright flame of fire*" (Q. 55:14-15). Although we are unable to address all the symbolism in these verses, it is to be noted that earth has been transformed by breath and flame, and thus made receptive to sound. *Salsâl* might be compared to *salsalat al-jaras*, "the ringing of a bell," one of the modalities of the primordial sound and of Revelation. The creation of the *jânn* before or after the man of clay, explains why he may be considered as the inner "double" of man. On this point, see note 173.

327 The word *jawâmi' al-kalim* appears in a hadith listing a certain number of the Prophet's privileges, all the versions of which are transmitted by Abû Hurayra. The following version underscores the bond between the "Totalizing Words" and the role of Seal of the Prophets, and integrates into this meaning a parable that is more often cited as an independent hadith: "*I received six things more than other prophets: I was granted Totalizing Words; I was rescued by fright (placed in the hearts of enemies); booty was made legal for me; the earth was instituted for me as a praying spot and a way of purification; I was sent to all creatures, and through me the prophets were sealed. The prophets and I are like this parable: a man built a palace. He finished every last detail except the placing of one brick.*

When men saw the palace, they said 'how beautiful this construction is! If only the last brick had been laid!' 'Am I not that brick?'" (Ibn Hanbâl, *Musnad,* II, 411-412. Id. Muslim, *Sahîh masâjid* 6, Istanbul, II, 64: without the parable.) In other, shorter versions, the "Words" are mentioned with rescue through fright, and receiving "keys of the treasures of the earth" in a dream, cf. Bukhârî, *Sahîh ta'bîr,* 11 (IX 47); Muslim, *ibid.*; *Musnad,* II, 268.

328 Muhammadan Reality encompasses all the realities of manifestation, including the angels, and especially Isrâfîl, whose trumpet blast closes the cycle and announces the following one, as is seen in the verse cited below. On the trumpet *(sûr)* which, according to one hadith, is actually a horn containing the forms *(suwar)* of the beings in the intermediate world *(barzakh),* cf. *Futûhât,* I, 305-306, ch. 63.

329 Particles *(hurûf),* contrary to the other parts of speech, denote neither a being nor its modalities. They express only meanings or ideas *(ma'nâ,* pl. *ma'ânî)* which establish the bonds among other words (e.g., attribution, localization, coordination, oaths, etc.).

330 The following part of this verse, which reproduces Jesus' words, underscores the relationship between breath and the resurrection: "... *I heal the blind and the leper, and I return life to the dead, with God's permission...*"

331 Verbs are here in the passive accomplished: the act is impersonal and the events are already completed.

332 On the idea of *thubût,* cf. p. 36f.

333 Here Ibn 'Arabî is referring to the question of *masdar* (the word for an adventitious fact) and the fact of its preceding the verb.

334 *Futûhât,* I, 85, l. 23-86, l. 17.

335 The *mutalawwin* letters are letters that carry the vowels of the declination, both complete (Zayd-u-n, Zayd-a-n, Zayd-i-n) and incomplete (Ahmad-u, Ahmad-a). The *mutamakkin* are the final consonants whose vowel is invariable *(hâ'ulâ'i,* etc.), or all the other consonants at the beginning of, or inside, a word. Cf. p. 86, l. 32-35.

336 This refers to properties that were listed in the third part of section I.

337 For example, like a verb whose unfinished mode is considered to be declined *(marfû', mansûb)* or a particle, like *qad*; when it precedes a *hamza,* the vowel of the latter is moved toward it in certain Qur'ânic readings (Warsh): *qad 'aflaha = qad-a-flaha.*

338 On the human and original *fitra,* see *Futûhât,* II, 70, question 73.

339 On Abû Tâlib, see note 216.

340 "Subtle" *(lâtif)* and "thick" *(kathîf)* should thus be understood as meaning informal and formal manifestation, per R. Guénon.

341 *Futûhât* I, 86, l. 29-87, l. 18.

THE END OF THE JOURNEY

Denis Gril

ON BEING LIBERATED FROM STATIONS
CHAPTER 420

This short chapter (Fut. IV, 28-29) *titled* "On knowledge of the 'mid-way stop' in which one is liberated from the stations (manâzalat al-takhallus mina l-maqâmât)" *is an important example of analysis and hermeneutical synthesis in Ibn 'Arabî's expository methodology. Its organization hinges around a sentence from the Qur'ân spoken by the Hypocrites* (al-munâfiqûn) *who were secretly supporting the coalition* (al-ahzâb) *of Bedouin tribes, Jews, and the Quraysh against the Muslim community in Yathrib (the pre-Islamic Medina):* "O people of Yathrib, you will no longer have a place to stand *(lâ muqâma lakum)*; come back!" *(Q. 33:13). The entire chapter is constructed on three words whose roots, through their correlation guide the line of thought:* Yathrib, *root* TH R B, *to which the idea of opprobrium is attached;* lâ muqâm *which, in another lesson, can be read* lâ maqâm: *"non-station"; and the verb* raja'a, *"to come back" or "to return," in one of its uses in the Qur'ân.*

Entering a spiritual station (maqâm) *is primarily the acquisition of knowledge. Thus, one who has passed through and gathered within himself the totality of the stations* (al-jâmi' li-l-maqâmât) *goes beyond the specific knowledge that each station procures, since the search for knowledge supposes an infinite liberation from one's own limits. The* maqâmât, *whose cognitive and existential role is to create a distinction* (tamyîz) *between different degrees of Being, should thus be gone beyond, and their authority or their limitative law* (hukm) *abolished in what looks like a non-station.*[1] *In this non-station, the contradiction is resolved between any conditioning* (taqyîd) *necessary for the signs and the stages of divine knowledge, on the one hand, and, on the other, the absolute character* (itlâq) *of Being that those signs and stages point to, as is expressed in the verse:* We shall make them see Our signs on the horizons and in themselves" Q. 41:53).[2] *The fact that something is conditioned supposes the existence of an Absolute, but calling God an absolute is conditioning Him by making a distinction between Him and manifestation, since "distinction is conditioning"* (al-tamyîz taqyîd). *The tradition "He who knows himself knows his Lord" likewise contains a dual indication of identity and difference*[3] *that is resolved in a higher kind of knowledge in which "He is the very being of all things"* ('ayn kulli shay'). *From this perspective, those beings that were conditioned and distinguished earlier are no more than the "different forms" of a First Ipseity* (huwiyya ahadiyya).[4] *In this chapter, this expression of the doctrine of Self is based on the idea of return* (rujû'). *The command ("Come back!") is juxtaposed with the numerous verses of the Qur'ân in which the passive voice indicates the both necessary and impersonal nature of the return:* "And to God belongs the non-manifested of the Heavens and of the earth, and toward Him everything is returned" (Q. 11:123).

Liberation from the stations is thus translated by an overturning of habitual perspectives. On the level of initiation, the relationship between stations and states maqâmat, ahwâl) *is reversed. It is no longer the stations that constitute the degrees of spiritual progression, but rather the states, since—as pure gifts from God—they come from Essence, while the stations represent fulfillment by the Divine Attributes of the Law governing the hierarchy of Being. Likewise, this same non-station, where all the elements of Being are perceived like so many multiple functions and, simultaneously, like one single reality, is translated by the reintegration of all these elements, even the most negative of them in appearance, since even when they appear to be negative, they are never anything other than mistaken claims* (da'âwâkâdhiba). *This is the meaning of this surprising reference to the Yathrib Hypocrites, who are doomed by the Qur'ân to the lowest degrees of Hell,[5] but kept integrated into the Community by the Prophet. The double reference to the name of Yahtrib and Joseph's words means that not only is opprobrium a part of the Whole, but that it is also the agent of Return. As we know from exegetical tradition, the Prophet himself used these words of reconciliation again at the time of the Conquest of Mecca:* "It is reported that while holding on to the two uprights of the door to the Ka'ba on the day of the Conquest (fath) *the Messenger of God—may grace and peace be upon him—asked the Quraysh:* "What do you think I am going to do with you?" *They replied:* "Something good, we think. Are you not a generous brother, the son of a generous brother? Now you have the power to act." *Then* the Prophet declared: *"I will tell you what my brother Joseph said: 'Let no disgrace fall upon you today.'"*6

Just as the historical community is reintegrated, the Prophet incorporates within himself all the different kinds of knowledge related to both all the different aspects of the Universal Man and all the degrees of Being. Thus, only Muhammad's heir is likely to be liberated from the stations. This non-station can just as well be defined as the supreme station, or the station of Proximity (maqâm al-qurba).7 The most universal dimension of the Prophet's mission is of course manifested by access to the *"Lauded Station"* (al-maqâm al-mahmûd), *or the final intercession for all beings.* The linguistic relationship between intercession (shafâ'a) *and the even numbered "pair"* (shaf') *allows the Shaykh al-Akbar to state, albeit allusively, that the final accomplishment of the Prophetic mission reveals its most important role, that of adding "something more"* (amr zâ'id) *to the divine loneliness of non-manifestation. The Prophet Muhammad is the specific individual through whom this "extra thing" comes into existence and returns to its beginning. Only his heir could say it in words like this:*

> (verses):
> There is, in existence, nothing but Him,
> look at Him as I have looked at Him, you will find Him in the Self.
> He who seeks to prove His existence is setting up dialectics;
> in his heart there is nothing of him but semblances and likenesses
> If He were not, no eye would look through the one that is looking,
> If He were not, no mouth would pronounce His name.
> Utter a judgment about Him, by Him, while you are in non-existence,
> Hold firmly to it, since there is nothing in the universe but Him.
> By Allah, were it not for the existence of the True,
> His words would not be received in the existence of the universe,
> were it not for Him!

God—exalted be He—said: "*O people of Yathrib, you have nowhere left to stand, return!*" (Q. 33:13). He who gathers together all the stations has no station left, as is required both by "He who knows his soul knows his Lord"8 and by the verse: "*We shall have them see Our signs on the horizons—meaning signs pointing toward these stations—as well as in their world*" (Q. 41:53). By their very conditioning, these signs, being conditioned, simultaneously condition what they stand for—their Meaning—even though they point toward His absolute nature: absoluteness is a conditioning, since conditioning is a distinction.[9] The knowledge that the gnostics have of Him—exalted may He be—thus does not come from the vision of exterior and interior signs, since such signs indicate either a being conditioned in an absolute, or an absolute in a conditioned being. The gnostics see Him as the essential identity of all things *('ayn kulli shay')*.

A created being (Joseph) said to those who had behaved badly toward him and had broken the bonds of relationship: *"Let no disgrace fall upon you today!"(Q. 12:92)*. It is even more common that God act in such a manner toward the individual who has behaved badly toward Him and broken the bonds of relationship.[10] Clearly, whoever breaks this bond is doing so without knowing what it entails, since the bond is not truly broken and, it might be added, still remains. It remains for the individual who knows of such matters; it is broken for the individual who does not know.

Everything comes back to God.[11] But the return to God of things that have been the objects of mistaken claims does not mean that God is different from what He was before, where they are concerned. He has in no way changed, regardless of whether these claims try to associate themselves with Him or whether everything returns to Him.

The only reason the station is there is to establish a distinction, but if there is only a single being, what should it distinguish itself from? Thus, there is no station, but only a single ipseity *(huwiyya ahadiyya)* with a diversity of forms. Zayd is one, in that he is a being *(ahadiyy al-'ayn)*. If there were nothing in existence but him, he would not be different from anything, and nothing would be different from him, since we have not supposed the existence of any entity other than Him. There would be no station by which he could distinguish himself from another, since there would be no Other. Nevertheless, his hand is different from his foot, his head is different from his breast, as is his ear from his eye; each of his limbs is different from the others, and each of his internal faculties has a function and a location that is different from the others. Forms in a single entity *('ayn wâhida)* with neither distinction nor station can thus be different from one another. We, ourselves, belong to Him just as the limbs and the faculties of each one of us does. From whom, then, would we differentiate ourselves, since He does not differentiate Himself from us? However, as we have established, we differentiate ourselves from one another. Functions and stations are not attributed to our limbs, but to us. We say: Someone seized hold of Someone; Someone walked toward Someone; Someone heard Someone's words; Someone saw Someone. None of this is attributed to an instrument, to a faculty, or to a limb. *"And toward Him everything is returned"* (Q. 11:123) and *"To Him belongs the decision and to Him you shall be returned"* (Q. 28:70 and 88).[12]

Know that the only one liberated from the stations is the heir to Muhammad —may peace be upon him— he to whom God has given the totalizing words *(jawâmi' al-kalim)*,[13] the knowledge of all the names, and the knowledge of the first and the last; "the entire hunt is in the belly of the onagre."[14] From whom would we be different if the entire universe is in Muhammad's—may peace be upon him—heir? He is thus liberated from the law *(hukm)* that the stations were exercising upon him, and it is now he who is exercising his law over them, according to what he has been entrusted with by spiritual states, since he is the most learned, the most wise.

It is the totality of the Divine Names that manifest the stations, and it is according to them that the judge administers the law *(yahkumu l-hâkim)*, and there is no judge but God; where He is concerned, the Word is not changed.[15] The Word is the law, and God judges according to the Word. So be attentive to judgment, and upon whom, by what, in regard to what, judgment is rendered; be attentive to who the judge is; you shall know who the individual liberated from stations is: it is he who has no station.

The "Lauded Station"—which God has praised and where He will establish Muhammad (may peace be upon him)—is the station of the intercession of God's Messenger. He will intercede on the Day of Resurrection so that angels, messengers, prophets, saints, and believers intercede in turn, and so that God will save from the Fire, or will bring into Paradise those who have never done anything good, until such time that there is no one left in the Fire but the People of the Fire, meaning those who are destined to remain there. God keeps them there in a condition and in a complexion such that if He let them out to enter into Paradise with that complexion, they would experience torment, and entry into Paradise would harm them, just as the fragrance of the rose causes harm to scarabs. God answers the Prophet's request in this station. If the answer requires the manifestation of more than one thing, there is intercession, whether this thing is even or odd; what matters is that it be something extra *(zâ'id)*.[16]

It is impossible to free oneself from states; they are a gift to us from God, and they belong to His very Essence (verses):

A state imposes its law; we are under the authority of states.

In the universe there is nothing but God and man.
Our condition is to be meditated upon, if only you fully understood it!
Other than the All-Merciful, everything is the object of meditation.
We are the stars that set in the west,
and only the sun and the moon appear.
Effacement is in us, for our greatest good,
but only the man endowed with vision knows this.
Fear nothing; other than the All-Merciful,
there is no real being, nor power to decide, nor efficiency.
To Him all beings in creation are returned,
as are the Decree, the judgment, and destiny.
He is Existence; He bears no prejudice.
Evil could have no effect on His creatures.
Evil does not return to Him; our Creator is too majestic.
Such is the news that was brought by the messengers.

He who knows wandering and guidance does not notice distance. He knows that God does not abandon His creatures senselessly, any more than He abandoned them at the time of the first creation. Even if He has not given them entrance into the abode of the blessed, God, in His all-encompassing mercy, will not doom them to an eternity of damnation. Why would He do this when He, Himself, is the Cloak?[17] In this station He ransoms Himself, and makes Himself the target for the enemy's arrow.[18] It is He Who has mercy, both final and perpetual, for ever and ever.[19] *"And God—praise be to Him—tells the truth and He guides us upon the straight path"* (Q. 33:4).

ON PROXIMITY
CHAPTERS 73 AND 161

The two texts presented together here because of their complementarity relative to one another concern the highest degree of sainthood, the "station of proximity" (maqâm al-qurba). *This* maqâm *is located before prophecy, but after the degree of "confirmer of truth"* (siddîqiyya) *incarnated in Abû Bakr, one of the closest, if not the closest, of the Prophet's Companions, and the first of his successors. Ibn 'Arabî is well aware of the difficulties affirmation of this* maqâm *arouses, since it appears, in a way, to run counter to the verse:* "They will be with those upon whom God has given His grace: the prophets, the 'confirmers of the truth' *(siddîqîn)*, the martyrs and the saints" *(Q. 4:69), where the* siddîq *are mentioned just after the prophets, in contrast to the excellence of Abû Bakr among the companions, and thus among the saints (which is accepted by Sunni Islam).*[20] *The response to these two possible objections is offered in the two texts translated here. The first, in reply to Tirmidhî's question:* "Where are the abodes of the People of Proximity?" *sums up the first difficulty, through both a precise hierarchization of prophetic duties and the definition of a* siddîq *as a "follower"* (tâbi') *of a prophet and an affirmer of his message. The conclusion to chapter 161, devoted to the "station of proximity," raises the second difficulty by affirming the union in Abû Bakr of both this station and* siddîqiyya, *which is tantamount to saying that no being is closer to the Prophet than he, but not that there is no intermediate station between* siddîqiya *and prophecy.*

Each of these two passages occupies a place in the Futûhât *that stresses its importance for the doctrine of sainthood. One follows the answer to the first question in Tirmidhî's "Seal of the Saints"* (Khatm al-awliyâ)*: "How many abodes do the saints have?"*[21] *The other, in the section devoted to stations* (maqâmât), *concludes a series of chapters in which the author* "reviews one after the other, first in general terms, and then relative to their relationship to the human condition on the one hand, and to the angelic condition on the other, the "stations" of sainthood, of prophecy, and of the missions of Messengers *(risâla)*, all the while reminding us that, in a way, we are here dealing with three concentric spheres, and that the first, that of *walâya*, encompasses both the others: every *rasûl* is a *nabî*, and every *nabî* is a *walî*. He concludes his study with a chapter rich in biographical information, in which he deals with the "station of proximity" that represents the plenitude of sainthood, in accord with what the word's etymology in Arabic implies."[22]

Walâya *and* qurba *actually both mean "proximity," which, Ibn 'Arabî reminds us, is a divine quality.*[23] *However, the form* qurba[24] *suggests a specific, elective quality of divine proximity in which all beings participate. In the all-encompassing sphere of* walâya, *the* maqâm al-qurba *refers to the supreme degree in each of the hierarchical levels* (tabaqât) *occupied by the messengers, the prophets, and the saints. But is it important to note that this division can be expressed just as easily in terms of prophecy: the prophecy that instigates the sacred laws* (nubuwwat al-sharâ'i), *"general" or universal* ('âmma) *prophecy, and "free" or absolute* (mitlaqa)—*meaning not conditioned by the form of a revelation—prophecy. This latter category, that of those saints who are the "People of Proximity," is defined in terms of prophecy, because they are its heirs.*[25]

The word used, both generally and in the Qur'ân (those who are close, muqarrabûn) *underscores the participation of all these degrees in the supreme election. The Qur'ân's use of this word refers to the higher angels (Q. 4:172) as much as it does to Jesus (Q. 3:45),*[26] *and "those who go beyond," and as much to the Companions of the Right Hand as to those of the Left (Q. 56:11 and 88). This affinity with the supreme Pleroma* (al-malâ' al-a'lâ) *gives us a sense of why the men of this* maqâm *are not in any way affected by the lightning and thunder of the Resurrection, since the return has already taken place for them.*

The preceding also explains the subtlety of the relations between lawgiving prophecy and "free" prophecy in the person of Moses and al-Khadir, whose story, in its Qur'ânic and prophetic version, is the scriptural basis for the maqâm al-qurba. *In the* Jawâb al-mustaqîm, *the first version of the reply to*

Tirmidhî's questions, Ibn 'Arabî calls al-Khadir "one of the leaders of this abode" (min ru'asâ hâdhâl-manzil).²⁷ *There are two points to bear in mind regarding the relationship between these two individuals. While for Moses the role of messenger emanates purely from divine election* (ikhtisâs), *the station of al-Khadir constitutes an acquisition* (iktisâb) *due to his having passed through all the stations. But when all is said and done, the "knowledge from within God"* (al-'ilm al-ladûnî) *with which he is gratified is a pure divine gift in the same sense that Moses' mission is. The fact that he possesses knowledge that Moses did not possess in no way invalidates the Superiority of the Messenger. The delicateness of their relationship comes from the fact that they both received "gustative"* (dhawq) *knowledge from God. A pure gift, like the spiritual state, it imposes its law and its effects. This is why Moses, motivated by divine jealousy in terms of keeping the Law, was unable to do anything but contest acts that, exteriorly, broke the law.*

We see Moses' denial again at another level, among the initiated, most of whom are not familiar with this maqâm. *Probably because of his exemplary character, Ibn 'Arabî emphasizes Ghazâli's error in denying its existence, pushed as he was by a jealous zeal to defend the superiority of Abû Bakr.*²⁸ *The Shaykh al-Akbar also tells us of the feeling of strangeness, of singularity, of solitude that took hold of him when he first went into this station, without even knowing its name, in a time and place that are noted specifically for a reason that must be important. The* afrâd, *the "forlorn" or the "loners" is actually another name for those who reach this station, escaping from both the ordinary conditions of humanity and even the eyes of the "Pole," who is nevertheless one of them.*²⁹ *Concealed by God and taking personal responsibility for hiding their state in order to keep the divine secrets entrusted to them, they show themselves to fellow humans only with ordinary exterior appearances, and express their spiritual states only through the transmission of hadiths or stories about the saints.*³⁰ *This was precisely the case for Abû 'Abd al-Rahmân al-Sulamî, who was the author of a treatise on the* malâmatiyya, *where the* afrâd, *or "faithful repositories"* (umanâ'), *constitute the elite. There is consequently nothing surprising about Sulamî, incarnated spirit that he was, coming along to teach the Shaykh the name of this station and comfort him in his solitude by reminding him of the example set by al-Khadir, moreover, he found a reference to this* maqâm *in one of al-Sulamî's works.*³¹ *Ibn 'Arabî likewise noted, based on one of Abû Madyan's teachings, that al-Khadir—while following his own law—respected the order given by Moses to leave him, out of consideration for the high rank of the Messenger. But he adds an extra dimension to the allusive information of his predecessors: that of the universality of*

*Muhammad's message and his heritage: after Muhammad's arrival, al-Khadir should have followed his law.*³² *This remark is in line with two others, one on the possible multiplicity of the sacred laws before the time of Muhammad, and the other on the fact that those who are defining legal statutes while engaged in juridical thought* (ijtihâd) *are supported, whether they are aware of it or not, by the influence of this supreme station. This is where the possibilities for differences of opinion that* ijtihâd *entails begin; but they can also be resolved here, if reflective thought is corroborated by intuitive unveiling* (kashf). *This is how the Muhammadan saint proceeds; following the example of the Prophet, he allies strict observance of the Law and of the order of things with the sole, universal, eschatological*³³ *authority of the Prophet's mission, which includes all the previous traditions, at the same time that it abrogates them as Laws. From this perspective, the double reference to Judaism in chapter 161 takes on a sense of universality. A series of bits of information found in chapter 420, like the proverb about the onager, the reverse of the* iktisâb-ikhtisâs *relationship in the spiritual stations and states, and the possibility of flaws in perfection are just some aspects, among others, of the station of proximity in which Muhammad's heir is freed from all the stations.*

Response to Tirmidhî's questions
(*Fut.* II, 41) *Chapter 73*

Question 2: Where are the abodes of the people of proximity?

Answer: Between the degree of confirmation of the truth *(saddîqiyya)* and that of lawgiving prophecy *(nubuwwat al-sharâ'i')*. Thus these abodes do not reach the rank held by the lawgiving prophet when universal prophecy as a whole is considered, and they do not belong to the abodes of the truth-tellers who come after the prophets and confirm what they say. These abodes are the station of those who are Close. God has brought them close to Him, either because He has chosen to do so *(ikhtisâs)*, independent of the deeds they perform, like Him who will rise up at the end of time *(al-qâ'im fî âkhir al-zamân)*³⁴ and those like him; or He has brought them close via the path of performing deeds *(ta'ammul)*, like al-Khadir and those like him. This station is the same one, but it can be reached either way, and this is how the messenger is distinguished from the prophet.³⁵ This station, which encompasses both prophets and messengers, is the station of those who are Close[36] and the "forlorn" *(afrâd)*. In this station, the human being joins the supreme Pleroma, and those who should be gratified by it are blessed by divine election.

The station is one that is acquired,[37] even though it can also be obtained through election; this is why the mission of the messenger *(risâla)* is said to be one of pure election. And that is correct, since the servant would be unable to acquire what comes from God—to Him be glory. He can work toward his goal, but not to obtain what emanates from God, once he has arrived. It is from there that "the knowledge emanating from God" *(al-'ilm al-ladunî)* springs, whence God has said regarding His servant Khadir: "*We have given him out of Our mercy a knowledge that is close to us, and we have taught him a knowledge that is close to Us* (min ladun-nâ) (Q. 18:65), which should be understood as follows: In Our mercy, We have given him a knowledge that is from Us and we have instructed him about Us. This knowledge is one of the four stations, which are knowledge of divine writing, knowledge of union and separation, knowledge of the light, and the "knowledge that emanates from God" (or: from within God).[38]

Know that the abode of the People of proximity connects their lives to the life hereafter. Therefore, they will not be struck by the lightning *(sa'q)* that will strike spirits (on the Day of Resurrection); they will even be among those whom God has excepted in His words: "*The trumpet will be blown, and those that are in the heavens and those that are on the earth will fall stricken, except those whom God has wanted.*" (Q. 39:68).

This abode is the highest, and the closest to God. Those who remain in it fit into three hierarchical levels *(tabaqât)*. One group has reached Him fully; these are the messengers—may the grace of God be upon them—each of which, to his degree, rises up in merit over the others (cf. Q. 2:251). Others are found in the second level; these are the prophets—may divine grace be upon them—who were not sent (to preach to men), but who worshiped God according to a law that is restricted to them alone. The same is true for those who follow them; those who do not follow them are not at fault, since God did not impose following them on anyone. They likewise rise up over one another in degrees and in merit. The third group represents the degree of "free" prophecy *(mutlaqa)*; no angel plays a part in the revelations they receive. On this side of these three hierarchical planes stand the confirmers of the truth who follow the messengers; even more on this side are the confirmers who follow the prophets without being forced to; and finally come the holders of the third rank, called also "those who have been brought close." There is a specific gustative knowledge *(dhawq)*, unknown to the others, that corresponds to each plane. This is why al-Khadir said to Moses—upon him be peace: *"and how could you bear that which you do not know by experience?"* (Q. 18:68). Now experience *(khubr)* means gustative knowledge, which is a "state knowledge" *('ilm hâl)*. Al-Khadir said to Moses: "I have knowledge that God taught me, and that you do not know; and you have knowledge that God taught you, which I do not know."[39]

On the station between
the confirmation of truth and prophecy:
the station of proximity *(maqâm al-qurba)*
(*Fut.* II, 260-262)
Chapter 161

Proximity is a divine quality and an unknown station whose effects even the elite among the messengers—upon them be peace—have managed to deny, despite the need they have of this station and the guarantee of integrity *('adâla)* and election God has made to those who have reached it. Such was the case for al-Khadir in his encounter with Moses; Moses was overcome by the effects of the jealousy God gave His messengers for the station of divine Law. For God's sake, Moses condemned and reiterated his disapproval, despite the warning that the holy servant gave him when each question was asked.[40] In his jealousy, he could do nothing other than make his opposition be known, since the Law was for him a "gustative" *(dhawq)* knowledge, and what he saw in others was foreign to him, even if it was a matter of authentic knowledge. However, gustative knowledge had the upper hand; his state *(hâl)* imposed its law. This is why it was revealed to God's Messenger—upon whom be grace and peace: *"Say: Lord, make me grow in knowledge!"* (Q. 20:114) and not: make me grow in spiritual state, since his disapproval would be found to have increased with it. By growing in knowledge, he increased in clarity, in unveiling, in breadth, in dilation, and in transcendent vision of the Faces that take off their veils and appear behind their curtains and canopies. Oppression and inconvenience disappeared; perfection was contemplated in the flaw.

Once I reached this sublime station, I somewhat allusively, suggestively, recited these verses:

I love the flaw in him whom I love,
without the flaw there would be no perfection, for those who know.
Perfection has not lessened the full moon that you see,
It is still a full moon for him whose thoughts are deep.
He sees it in its fullness, in all its clarity,
in the most perfect of states, both inside and out.
There was in the universe no confirmed flaw,
True Being would see its depleted value.
Through me, thus, True Being attains the perfection that includes flaws.
Look carefully at the contents of my verse.
A gazelle came from Paradise, her face under a veil; she was coming for me.
What was happening was in no way concealed from God.
I exclaimed: warm welcome to her to whom,
through the life of love, my breast has held so tightly.
I am overcome with love for her, regardless of my state,
in life, in death, at the resurrection and the final gathering.
One day the veil was removed from her face; the splendor of her graces
revealed that she was the Night of Value (laylat al-qadr).
I prostrated myself before her, out of love.
Seeing Him, I knew that I had attached myself to no one else.
I glorified God, glorified Him for having loved me,
since my innermost secret (sirr) *is what my appearance had smitten with love.*
Realizing that I am the very being of him whom I love,
I no longer fear either distance or the separation of lovers.
Baghdad is my abode, I have no other land,
but if Baghdad becomes ostentatious, I shall leave for my Egypt.[41]

I entered this station in the month of Ramadân, in the year 597. I was travelling, but had stopped at Igîsil, in the Maghreb. I went through the station, overwhelmed with joy. Finding no one there, I felt a sense of loneliness, and this reminded me of how Abû Yazîd (al-Bistâmî), who had reached it through humiliation and indigence, also found no one there. But this stop[42] is my homeland, and soon I no longer felt loneliness, for all beings, in essence, feel nostalgic for the land of their birth, and loneliness is a companion to foreignness.

When I entered this station and no longer felt isolated in it, I knew that if someone found me there, he would disavow me. I remained there, to explore all its nooks and crannies, one by one.[43] Without even knowing the name of this station, I realized it fully, and I knew what God has reserved for whomever He deigns to grant it to. I saw the divine commandments pass by in my honor, one after the other, and God's emissaries (*sufarâ*) descend toward me, eager to share their familiar company with me.

I resumed my travels in this state of solitude and isolation, for familiarity comes only with one's peers. I encountered a man of God at the stop called Angâl[44] and prayed the *'asr* in his mosque. Emir Abû Yahyâ b. Wâgiten, one of my friends, happened by. He was elated to see me, and invited me to stay with him. But I declined, and went down to stay with his secretary, with whom I had some familiarity. I complained to him of the isolation in which I found myself, in a station where I was nevertheless happy. We were engaged in a friendly discourse when someone's shadow appeared. I arose from by bed and went toward it, hoping to find some relief in it. It embraced me. I stared into it, recognizing Abû 'Abd al-Rahmân al-Sulamî[45], whose spirit had taken on flesh; God had sent him to me out of mercy.

"I find you in this station?" I asked with a note of surprise.

"I was seized while in it, and with it I died," he replied. "And I have not left it since."

I informed him of my loneliness, and the absence of a familiar companion in this station.

He replied: "The foreigner does feel loneliness. Now that you are here in this station, through the prescience of divine solicitude, give praise to God. O my brother, are you not satisfied that al-Khadir is your companion in this station? The prophet Moses, upon him be peace, disapproved of his state, even though God assured him of its integrity. Al-Khadir only let Moses see his outer form. It was his own state that Moses saw, and it was himself that he disapproved of. He was pushed to it under the influence of divine jealousy that God gave solely to His messengers; if he had waited, he would have seen. He was actually preparing to ask al-Khadir a thousand questions. All of them concerned things that had happened to him that he condemned, emanating from al-Khadir.[46]

On this subject, our friend Abul-Najâ, known by the name Abû Madyan, once said: al-Khadir understood the rank and the high degree of Moses among the messengers, so he obeyed his order, after his second remark, when he said: "*If I ask you about anything from now on, keep me no longer in your company!*" (Q. 18:76), for God has said: "*What the messenger gives you, take; what he forbids you to have, leave!*" (Q. 59:7). The third time, Moses forgot the state he was in when he said: "*Lord, in regard to the good which you have sent down upon me, I am poor and stand in need"* (Q. 28:24) and, despite his need, he had not asked for a salary for watering (the flock of Jethro's daughters). Al-Khadir then showed him the knowledge of the acts he disapproved of, and left. He added: *"I did not do it of my own accord"* (Q. 18:82), for he was following a law according to his Lord, and a path. This law was valid for al-Khadir during his time, but for us it was no longer so after the mission of Muhammad—upon him be peace and grace—because Muhammad is like the onager, "the entire hunt is in his entrails."[47]

"O Abû 'Abd al-Rahmân," I said, "I do not know any name by which to distinguish this station."

His reply was, "It is called the Station of Proximity; experience it fully!"

I experienced it, and saw that I was dealing with an immense station. Those who are learned in the Letter of the Law who engage in juridical reflection *('ulamâ' al-rusûm min ahl al-ijtihâd)* are taking a sure step into this station, but are doing so without knowing that they are in it. I have seen divine influence *(al-imdâd al-ilâhî)* originate from this station and spread out over them. This is why they disapprove of one another and accuse one another of error, for they do not have gustative knowledge of it, and they do not know via contemplation or unveiling from whom it flows. Each of them has a piece of the truth, just as each of the prophets before the Muhammadan era follows his revealed law and path. Believing in them is incumbent upon all the faithful, even if we need to observe their laws only to the extent that their legal definitions *(ahkâm)* coincide with those of our law. The doctors of the law who engage in juridical thinking are heirs to the prophets in the matter of legislation. Scriptural signs *(adilla)* are for them what revelation is for the prophets; differences of opinion among them are like differences in legal definitions. In any case, they are different from the messengers in their lack of intuitive revelations. The messengers confirm one another, as is also the case for the learned, who ally revelation with juridical thought, while those who are not endowed with it accuse one another of error.

If al-Khadir had said the moment that the messenger Moses joined him: "nothing you see me do will be done of my own initiative," Moses would not have disapproved of him, nor would he have opposed him. On the contrary, God had him speak the following words: *"God willing, you shall find me patient, and I shall not disobey you in anything"* (Q. 18:69).

Now there is no patience except for that which is unpleasant. If Moses had mentioned patience prior to the divine will, as the Muhammadan would have done, he would have had perfect patience and would not have contradicted al-Khadir. God mentioned it first, in order to teach Muhammad—upon whom be grace and peace. So he who wishes to acquire knowledge of God through His creatures, let him keep the orders of things set by His Wisdom, and put forward what God has put forward, and put last what God has put last. "He who places forward" *(al-Muqaddim)* and "He who places last" *(al-Mu'akhkhir)* are Divine Names. Thus, putting off what He has brought to the forefront, and bringing to the forefront what He has put off is a form of latent conflict that provokes privation. God—exalted be He—said: "*And do not say of something: certainly, I will do that tomorrow (without adding): unless God wills it*" (Q. 18:23-24). God put the exceptive condition in the last place, while Moses mentioned it first. Thus he was not able to have patience with al-Khadir; if he had mentioned it last, he would have been able to have perfect patience. This same verse is found in Hebrew, in the Torah.[48]

By Allah, by Allah, brothers in this Muhammadan tradition, hold strictly to these places where the presence of God *(mashâ'ir Allâh)* which God has shown us can be felt; do not stray beyond what He has drawn out for you! Do you not see that when he went up on the rocks of al-Safâ during the Farewell Pilgrimage, the Prophet—upon him be grace and peace—recited: *"Al-Safâ and al-Marwa are among the signs appointed by God"* (sha'â'ir Allâh) (Q. 2:158). Then he added: "I begin where God began."[49] He spoke those words in order to teach us, and to respect spiritual propriety *(adab)* toward God. If it had not been licit for him to begin the sacred run *(sa'y)* with al-Marwa, he would not have added these words. He preferred that with which God had begun, to the choice left by the conjunction "and."[50] God actually began with al-Safâ because of a secret known only to Him; whoever does not follow this order is deprived of the benefits of the secret. (...)

I will relate a startling anecdote regarding this subject. It was told to me by Mûsâ b. Muhammad al-Qurtubî al-Qabbâb, the muezzin from the minaret that is located between Bâb al-Hazûra and Bâb Ajyâd in the holy mosque of Mecca, in the year 599:

A man from Kairouan wanted to make the pilgrimage. He was vacillating between making the journey by the overland route, or by sea. Sometimes the land route seemed preferable, and at others, he preferred the sea. He said: the day after tomorrow, in the morning, I will ask the opinion of the first man I meet. Whatever he thinks is the best thing to do, I will decide. The first man he met was a Jew. It was hard for him, but he overcame his discomfort and said: "By God, I certainly shall ask his opinion."

"O Jew," he said, "I would like to ask your advice regarding this voyage; should I go by land or by sea?"

"Glory be to God," exclaimed the Jew, why are you asking me a question like that? Do you not know that in your own Book God is telling you: *"It is He who makes you go by land and by sea"* (Q. 10:22). He mentioned the land before the sea. If there was not a secret meaning intended by God, and one to which it would be best to conform, He would not have mentioned it first. The sea comes second, in case one does not have the means of traveling by land."

I was amazed by his words, and took the overland route. Never have I experienced a trip of the sort, by God! The Lord provided me with more goodness than I ever could have wished.

Abû Hâmid al-Ghazâlî denied this station [of proximity], declaring: "There is no station between the confirmation of the Truth *(al-Siddîqiyya)* and prophecy; he who tries to go over the neck of the confirmers of truth falls into prophecy; prophecy is a closed door." He also said: "do not go over the necks of the confirmers of the truth!"[51]

The lawgiving prophets are undoubtedly the highest of God's servants among men. It is nevertheless not inconceivable that God might grant the individual of lesser *(mafdûl)* merit knowledge that someone whose merit is greater *(fâdil)* does not have. The fact that the former distinguishes himself from the latter by this knowledge does not mean he is superior. On the contrary, al-Khadir said to Moses: "I possess knowledge that God has taught me that you do not have, and you have knowledge taught to you by God that I do not have."[52] He would not have said to him: I am more excellent than you. What's more, knowing the dignity of Moses and what was his due, he complied with the prohibition against keeping him as a traveling companion, out of respect for the station and the high rank that Moses held, as well as for his silence when al-Khadir left him. Moses did not retract his prohibition, knowing that al-Khadir could no longer hear him, especially when he said: "And I did not do it of my own initiative." Moses thus knew that he was only leaving him alone by divine command, and he raised no objection. Moses' goal was reached, as well as God's, which was to impart teaching *(ta'dîb)* to him. He learned that God has servants who possess knowledge different from his. The knowledge in question is just one of the kinds of knowledge that come through unveiling; it is held by a creature and conferred through the spiritual states of disciples progressing along the Way. What more could be said if it were a question of knowledge relative to transcendence, or to similarity[53] to the Divine Dignity!

The secret of Abû Bakr, the Confirmer of the Truth, comes from this station: the secret that was placed in him, and whose strength was manifested when the time came.[54] 'A'isha told God's Messenger when, during his final illness he ordered Abû Bakr to lead prayer: "he is a man in distress."[55] The Messenger knew the secret that had been placed in him, but it was not known by the Community. But the day that God's Messenger—upon him be grace and peace—died, all were upset, filled with consternation, and uttering words that were inappropriate for the situation, except Abû Bakr, the Confirmer of the Truth, who was untouched by anything that was happening. He climbed up the *minbar*, encouraged the assistants, and, in reference to the death of the Prophet—upon him be grace and peace—declared: "For him among you who adored Muhammad, Muhammad is dead, and for him among you who adored God, God is living and immortal!" Then he recited: "*You are doomed to death and they are doomed to death*" (Q. 39:30), and "*Muhammad is nothing but a messenger; messengers have passed before him. If he died or was killed, would you turn your heels?*" (Q. 3:144). The pain of the Muslims was soothed, to such point that 'Umar exclaimed: "It is as if I had never heard that verse before today!"[56]

Abû Bakr's attitude is very much in line with the words of the Prophet—upon him be grace and peace: "when it—that is, death—is stricken down, may none of the weepers further lament."[57] But before death has reached its term, weeping is praiseworthy. That is what Abû Bakr did when the Prophet stood up (one day) and declared: "What do you say of a man to whom God has left the choice and who has chosen to meet God?" Abû Bakr was the only one in the crowd to weep. He had understood that God's Messenger—upon him be grace and peace—was announcing his death to his companions. They disapproved of Abû Bakr's tears, although he knew better.[58] When the Prophet did pass away, the people moaned and wept, except for Abû Bakr, according to the words of the Prophet "when he is stricken down..." Abû Bakr's attitude was due to the secret that this station had conferred upon him.

What should thus be said is that there is no one between Muhammad and Abu Bakr, and not that there is no station between confirmation of the Truth and prophecy. The confirmer's duty is that of being a follower *(tâbi')* in faith. What the individual he follows denies, he denies; what he admits, he admits. He is such as he is, but he can also hold another station that does not govern this state. Know this!

NOTES
TO 'THE END OF THE JOURNEY'

¹ Cf. *Futûhât* I, 223; III, 105; *Mawâqi' al-nujûm*, p. 141: *"He who is blessed with this is the accomplished Muhammadan saint who has no* maqâm, *and who cannot be caught up with. The Book points out in this verse: 'O people of Yathrib...' that, on the one hand, there is no end, and, on the other, the issue at hand is the* maqâm *about which we just dealt*; *'Abâdila*, p. 55 and *Qurba*, p. 2, where this verse is said to refer to the *maqâm al-qurba*.

² Cf. *Futûhât* II, 116: *"The signs here are indications that they are places of divine manifestation"* and II, 151: *"The signs are indications that it is the Truth that is manifested in the places of manifestation of beings in the universe."*

³ Cf. *Futûhât* II, 298, chapter 17: "On knowledge": *God's Messenger said that there is no path to the knowledge of God other than that of oneself. He said: 'He who knows himself knows his Lord; and : 'He among you who knows himself the best is the one who knows his Lord the best.' He thus made you into a sign (or a guide:* dalîl*), meaning that He made your knowledge of yourself an indication of your knowledge of Him, either by describing you in the same way He has described Himself as Essence and attributes, and in yourself making him* Khalîfa *representing His place on His earth; or by considering the indigent necessity you have of him in your existence. These two aspects should be realized together. We see what God says about the science that regards Him, which is called 'knowledge': 'We will have them see Our signs on the horizons and in themselves until it appears to them that He is the Truth.' (...) If divine assistance allows us to fulfill both aspects at the same time, then we will know Him and it will be apparent to us that He is the Truth..."*

⁴ A passage from the *Kitâb al-Yâ'* or *Kitâb al-huwa*, pp. 12-13 in *Rasâ'il* quite

clearly establishes the connection between realization of the Self, the final goal of knowledge, and the return of the People of Yathrib:

"*Intimate conversation with the Self (munâjât al-huwa): O Self, You have made us absent to ourselves, and we found ourselves again by starting with ourselves, in absence (ghayb). Because of our absence, we wanted that which is absent to us of You when the Self reminded us what of You is absent in us. This is what it shouted to us: hold to that part of you that is absent to you, and you will see what of Us is absent to you. We sought assistance, and I received it. We requested support and I was supported; we sought to know how to delve into that, and I learned. We embarked on a sea without a shore in the Muhammadan vessel (or the sphere:* fulk-falak*) of Yathrib. The fish and the animals of the sea were stunned to see us unfurl all the sails and go off in search of that which has neither end nor limit. We received this call: 'O People of Yathrib, you will have no place to go; come back!' We went back in the direction of the shore whence we had set sail. But it became the sea again, such that our return was just like our departure: the quest for that which has neither limit nor eternity, neither beginning nor end. We pursued our crossing (or we were distraught:* juznâ *or* hirnâ*), asking for mercy. Then the Self addressed us as follows: 'O my servants, you have sought in Me a station where none other than I sees Me. I was in the thickest of clouds (*'amâ*) with nothing with Me, and I am just as I was, with nothing with Me, with your existence. This sea where you are is the "cloud" where you are. If you pierce through your own "cloud," you reach Mine, but never will you be able to pierce through it or to reach Me. You are in your own cloud with nothing with you, and this cloud is the Self that it is your task to fulfill. The Divine Form requires that you be where you are.' I asked: 'O self of the Self* (yâ huwa 'l-huwa), *what shall I do without the Self?' 'Immerse yourself in it,' He replied. I threw myself from the vessel, naked, stripping myself of its darkness. I drowned myself and found repose. I am there for ever and ever, and am in existence nothing other than myself, freed from the pain of the quest. I then heard the call of the Self: 'O he who is in all things! What can a thing do with a thing, when it is a thing?'"*

[5] Cf. Qur'ân 4:145. This should be looked at in light of the end of the chapter where those who are definitively doomed to the Fire are mentioned.

[6] Zamakhshari, *Tafsîr*, reprod. Tehran, II, 342, where a similar tradition is cited, with the appearance of Abû Sufyân. We have already noted that this individual was also involved in the Prophet's quotation of the proverb "the entire hunt is in the belly of the onager." (Cf. below, note 47).

[7] See below.

[8] On this hadith and its interpretation in Ibn 'Arabî's work, see M. Chodkiewicz, presentation and translation of Malyânî, *Épitre sur l'Unité Absolue*, Paris, 1982, p. 27-30.

[9] Cf. *Futûhât* I, 470: "God is conditioned by nothing other than absoluteness *(wa'llâhu lâ yataqayyadu illâ bi-l-itlâq)* and *ibid.*, III, 219: "Conditioning is a quality that intelligences and unveiling attribute and limit to possible beings.

They attribute absoluteness to God without knowing that it is a conditioning. Indeed, conditioning's foundation and the reason for being is distinction, so that essential realities are not confused. Absoluteness is thus a conditioning, since God, through it, differentiates Himself from that which is conditioned, and He conditions himself through absoluteness."

10 An implicit reference to the hadith: "The bond of kinship is a branch that has grown out of the All-Merciful. God said: he who approaches it, I approach him; he who breaks it, I break him." (Bukhârî, *Sahîh, adab* 13, VIII, 7.)

11 Cf. Qur'ân 11: 123: *"To God belongs the unmanifested of the heavens and the earth, and toward him all things are returned (passive voice)."* Cited later.

12 Qur'ân 28:88: *"Every thing is perishable except his (or His) face, and toward Him..."* The face or the essence of each thing is its ipseity.

13 On the *jawâmi' al-kalim*, cf. below, p. 482f and n. 327.

14 On the meaning of this proverb, cf. n. 47. These three sciences could possibly be interpreted as the triple heritage of the Prophet as Universal Man, Representative *(khalîfa)*, and Seal of the Prophets.

15 Cf. Qur'ân 59:29: *"The Word is not changed in Me, and I am not unjust toward servants."*

16 Intercession *(sharâ'a)* has the same root as *shaf'*, pair. This function, which falls first upon the Prophet, and then upon beings by hierarchical order, instigates duality, since it calls for the intervention of an extra being.

17 Ibn 'Arabî plays on the assonance between *radâ* (dam) and *ridâ* (mantle), which is one of the names for the Universal Man, since the "mantle" has two sides, one facing the individual wearing it, and the other the person looking at it, and for whom it is a "dam." But this face is not essentially different from the one that is turned toward God. The dam can thus not be eternal. On *ridâ*, see below, pp. 470-471, n. 297.

18 Bringing back to Him all the aspects of manifestation, both positive and negative.

19 This final paragraph is in rhymed prose.

20 On the attacks against Ibn 'Arabî in this regard, see M. Chodkiewicz, *Seal of the Saints*, p. 114, n. 27.

21 *Futûhât* II, 40.

22 M. Chodkiewicz, *op. cit.*, pp. 55-56.

23 Cf. in the Qur'ân the divine name *al-qarîb*, "near" (2:186, 11:61; 35:50), and *aqrab* "closer" (50:16, 56:85).

24 "Proximity" in the more general sense is *qurb*; the addition of the *a (tâ' marbûta)* is the sign of a particular modality.

25 Cf. M. Chodkiewicz, *op. cit.*, pp. 137-138. Especially the *K. al-qurba*, p. 8, in *Rasâ'il* that emphasizes the idea of heritage.

26 Due to his angelic forebears and his role as "Seal of Universal Sainthood." As M. Chodkiewicz has pointed out, *"the arrival of the second Seal will definitively close the* maqâm al-qurba," *op. cit.*, p. 173.

²⁷ Cited in a note by O. Yahya in his edition of the *Khatm al-awliyâ'*, Beirut, 1965, p. 144.

²⁸ See also *K. al-qurba*, p. 6 and *Dhakhâ'ir al-a'lâq*, p. 181. We have not been able to find Ibn 'Arabî's two citations (ch. 161) in Ghazâlî's work. Other than this chapter, other passages confirm that Abû Bakr's excellence is in no way questioned by the Shaykh al-Akbar. Cf. for example: *"...I asked ('Alî): 'Where is Abû Bakr?' 'Up in front,' he replied. I stepped into the white light behind the dais of the unmanifest, and there I found Abû Bakr—may God's blessing be upon him—at the summit of the degree."* (*Tajalliyyât*, pp. 36-37, in *Rasâ'il*, and ed. O. Yahya, with commentaries, in *al-Machreq*, 1967, pp. 291, 293-294.)

²⁹ Cf. *K. al-qurba*, p. 4. On the *afrâd*, see M. Chodkiewicz, *op. cit.* index and especially pp. 106-107 and 137.

³⁰ Cf. *Futûhât* I, 252, chapte 45; I, 181, ch. 23 (the corresponding Qur'ânic verse is "Houris confined to the pavillions" (55:74).

³¹ Abû 'Abd al-Rahmân al-Sulamî, the master of Nishapur, died in 412/1021. A number of passages from his work on the initiatory categories presage ideas later developed by Ibn 'Arabî. The latter, in his conclusion to the *K. al-qurba* (p. 9) claimed to have found the name of the *maqâm* in one of Sulamî's books. The *Jawâb al-mustaqîm* specifies that what is at issue is the *Aghâlît al-sûfiyya* (cf. ed. of the *Khatm al-awliyâ'*, p. 144) probably identical to the *Ghalatât al-sûfiyya* (cf. Sezgin, *Geschichte des arabischen Schrifttums*, Arabic trans, Cairo, 1978, II, 501). There are, however, other mentions of the *qurba* in his work, like this passage announcing, among others, chapter 420 in the *Futûhât*: *"Each station bathes him in a light and a brilliance far greater than the preceding one, until he has passed through all the stations and reaches the very end. He then remains with the Truth, with no station, no place, no name, no trace, no quality, no pretension, no vision, no contemplation, and no petition. It is, as has been said, as if he did not exist and the Truth is as if It had never ceased to be... Then he becomes aware of inner knowledge, meaning the divine secrets that God unveils to his "faithful repositories"* (umanâ') *among the saints. It is in regard to "the knowledge of what is from God"* (al-'ilm al-ladunî) *that God said: 'And they found one of Our servants to whom We had given a mercy from Us and whom We had taught Knowledge from Ourselves'* (Q. 18:65)... *It is the time that he is allowed to hear the Word, to discover its meanings, and to be gratified with the understanding of what he hears. This hearing, this contemplation of meanings of the Word, and this understanding get him nearness* (taqrîb) *and proximity* (qurba)." (*Darajât al-sâdiqîn*, pp. 147-149, in *Tis'rasâ'il*, Turkish ed. and trans by Sûleyman Ates, Ankara, 1981). The word *qurba* also appears in the introduction to Sulamî's letter on the *Malâmatiyya wa l-sûfiyya wa ahl al-futuwwa*, Cairo, 1945, p. 87.

³² Cf. the hadiths concerning Moses and Jesus on this subject.

³³ Cf. ch. 420 on the *maqâm al-mahmûd*. It is probably with this intention that the *Mahdî* is mentioned among those who receive the *maqâm al-qurba* by divine election.

34 On the *Mahdî*, see below, ch. II.

35 That is, by election.

36 The sentence means that this station encompasses all those who reach it in one way or another. The messengers and the prophets are not mentioned only by analogy, but because—as we see from the remainder of the text—they participate *a fortiori* in this station. In the Qur'ân, only one prophet is mentioned specifically as being one of "those who are Close": "the Messiah Jesus, son of Mary, in a verse about the Annuncuation (3:45); this is considered to relate to his role as "Seal of the Saints."

37 A reference to the classical distinction in the *tasawwuf* between the *maqâm* acquired through spiritual effort and the state *(hâl)*, which is a gift from God; cf. *al-Risâla al-Qushayriyya*, Cairo, 1972, I, 236 and *Futûhât*, II, 385, ch. 193.

38 On these four sciences, see the reply to Tirmidhî's first question, *Futûhât*, II, 40.

39 This sentence is taken from a long hadith transmitted by Ibn 'Abbâs, which contains a commentary on the story of Moses and al-Khadir; cf. Bukhârî, *Sahîh*, *bad, al-khalq*, IV, 187-190 and *tafsîr, sura 18*, VI, 110-117.

40 Cf. Qur'ân 18:71, 74, 77.

41 The opposition between Baghdad and Misr (Egypt, or the capital of Egypt) is in all probability a literary reference. In Ibn 'Arabî's poetry, Baghdad, the seat of the caliphate, refers to the station of the *qutb*, cf. *Tarjumân al-ashwâq*, ed. Nicholson, re-ed. London, 1978, no. 30, verse 12, p. 32, and notes on the translation, p. 113, no. 54, v. 6-7, trans. and notes, pp. 140-141, no. 56, verse 1, p. 43 and 142 notes (information from M. Chodkiewicz). In the context of this chapter, *Misr* relates to the station of those who those who escape the gaze of the *qutb*, the *afrâd*.

42 The station in this case is called *manzil*, meaning spiritual abode, or stopping place. With it, Ibn 'Arabî is noting the correlation between the geographical location of the event and its spiritual location.

43 Its "nooks" *(zawâyâ-hu*, pl. of *zâwiya)* and "crannies" *(makhâdi'uhu*, pl. of *makhdi')*. *Makhdi'* should perhaps be understood in its technical sense here of "closet," a concealed place where the *qutb* hides from the *afrâd*, and where—without them knowing it—he clothes them with the robes of investiture. Ibn 'Arabî attributed use of this word to 'Abd al-Qâdir al-Jîlânî. Cf. *Istilâhât*, p. 13, *Futûhât*, II, 80, 130, and S. Hakîm, *Mu'jam*, 384-385.

44 The spelling of these two stopping places is incorrect in all the editions. At issue are the names of two places along the road from Marrakesh to Salé. Cf. al-Isrisî, *Nuzhat al-mushtâq*, the consecrated part of the Maghreb, ed. and trans. Hadj Sadok, Algiers, 1983, ch. 37. On Igisil, see also al-Tâdili, *al-Tassawwuf*, no. 249; ed. Faure and ed. A. Tawfîq, p. 423 and note 327.

45 See the introduction to this passage.

46 The three acts that Moses criticizes in al-Khadir—putting a hole in the boat, killing the young man, and not asking for a salary in exchange for a service—correspond to three episodes in the life of Moses that did not, outwardly,

conform to the Norm: crossing the Red Sea, killing an Egyptian, and watering the flock of Shu'ayb's (Jethro's) daughters. Al-Khadir is thus just reflecting Moses' image back to him, but Moses is judging al-Khadir, and thus himself, according to his own state, which is the establishment of the Law.

47 Here is how this expression, which subsequently became a proverb, originated: three men were out hunting; one brought back a gazelle, the second a hare, and the third is said to have declared "the whole hunt is in the onager's belly," since the onager, all by itself, is worth as much as all other game. According to one tradition, Abû Sufyân had asked permission to speak with the Prophet. He was made to wait until everyone else had been seen. Then Abû Sufyân said: "if you had the chance, you would have received all the stones between the two sides of the wadi before you met with me!" To this, the Prophet replied: "*the entire hunt is in the onager's belly*" (cf. *Lisân*, I, 116, the article *Fara'* and 'Ajlûnî, *Kashf al-Khafâ'*, II, 121, who considers this hadith to be *mursal*). The Prophet was teaching Abû Sufyân a lesson in humility in acting the way he did; by citing the proverb in reference to him, he was flattering one of the great Quraysh lords, since what he was saying was: if I make you wait, it is because you are the most highly thought of among the Quraysh; now all the other Arabs will allow me to have them wait. It might be noted that the indirect appearance of Abû Sufyân here, who was one of early Islam's fiercest enemies, is perhaps not coincidental. It marks the reintegration of all human elements, even the most negative, into the Muhammadan community, which is nothing more than the reflection of universal manifestation. In reference to Ibn 'Arabî's text, when he applies the proverb-hadith to Muhammad's heir, we can see an example of knowledge and virtues coming together, symbolized by the different kinds of game. A reference to the noble origin of the Seal of Muhammadan Sainthood might also be seen in this old Arabian expression.

48 To which verse is Ibn 'Arabî referring, and from whom did this information come? The expression "God willing" does not appear to come from the Bible, with the possible exception of *Ecclesiastes* 39:6: If the Lord, the Great, wishes," It can also be seen in the New Testament, but this is not a case of a "Hebrew" text; cf. James 4:15: "Instead, you should say 'if the Lord wills, we shall live and we shall do this or that,'" and Peter 3:17: "For it is better to suffer doing good, if such is the will of God, than doing evil." Moreover, the saying "If the Name wishes" is current in Judaism, although it is neither Biblical nor Talmudic. (Information from M. Chodkiewicz.)

49 On this tradition, see Tirmidhî, *al-Jâmi' hajj*, no. 38, and *tafsîr hadith*, no. 15, and *Concordances et indices*, I, 148.

50 The *wâw* is an indicator of simple coordination, with no idea of temporal or logical succession (as opposed to *fâ*).

51 See the introduction to this chapter.

52 See note 39.

53 The expression should possibly be understood as: *min al-'ilm al-muhkam*

wa al-mutashâbih.

[54] Cf. the tradition: *"Abû Bakr is not superior to you in fasting or prayer, but in something that has been placed in his heart."* This tradition does not appear in the primary collections of the Sunna, or even in the vast corpus of al-Muttaqî's *Kanz al-'ummâl.* According to al-'Ajlûnî, it is reported by al-Hakîm al-Tirmidhî in the *Nawâdir al-usûl,* cf. *Kashf al-Khafâ',* II, 190.

[55] *Rajul asîf,* or in some versions: *raqîq* (with a sensitive heart). Bukharî, Muslim, Tirmidhî, etc., report several versions of this way of referring to Abû Bakr as imam; cf. Ibn al-Athîr, *Jâmi' al-usûl fî ahâdith al-Rasûl,* VIII, 595-600.

[56] These words of Abû Bakr's after the Prophet's death are reported by Ibn Hishâm, *al-Sîra al-nabawiyya,* Cairl, 1955, IV, 656. On Abû Bakr's firmness on this occasion, see also Ghazâlî, *Ihyâ' 'ulûm al-dîn,* IV, 473.

[57] See, e.g., Abû Dâwûd, *Sunan,* III, 188 (*Janâ'iz* II) and *Concordance et indices,* I, 211.

[58] See the different hadiths reporting this in Ibn al-Athîr, *Jâmi' al-usûl,* VIII, 586-588.

BIBLIOGRAPHY

Abû Tâlib al-Makkî: *Qût al-qulûb*, Cairo, 1961.
Abû Zayd, Nasr Hâmid: *Falsafat al-ta'wîl*, Beirut, 1983.
Addas, Claude: *Ibn 'Arabî ou la quête du Soufre rouge*, Paris, 1989.
Addas, Claude: *Ibn 'Arabî: The Voyage of No Return*, Cambridge, 2000.
Addas, Claude: *Quest for the Red Sulphur: The Life of Ibn 'Arabî*, Cambridge, 1993.
Alchimie, see Ibn 'Arabî: *Futûhât*, translated extracts.
Asin Palacios, M.: *El islam cristianizado*, Madrid, 1931; French tr.: *L'islam christianisé*, Paris, 1982.
Asin Palacios, M.: *El mistico murciano Abenarabi*, Madrid, 1928.
Austin, R. W. J.: *Ibn al 'Arabî: The Bezels of Wisdom*, New York, 1980.
Austin, R. W. J.: *Sufis of Andalusia*, London, 1971.
Balyânî, Awhad al-Dîn: *Epître sur l'Unicité absolue*, tr. M. Chodkiewicz, Paris, 1982.
Bezels, see Ibn 'Arabî: *Fusûs al-hikam*.
Böwering, G.: *The Mystical Vision of Existence in Classical Islam: The Qur'ânic Hermeneutics of the Sufi Sahl al-Tustarî* (d. 283/896), Berlin, 1979.
Al-Bûnî: *Shams al-ma'ârif al-kubrâ*, Cairo, s.d., popular edition in 4 volumes.
Burckhardt, T.: *Clé spirituelle de l'astrologie musulmane*, Milan, 1974; English translation as *Mystical Astrology According to Ibn 'Arabi*, Louisville, 2002.
Chittick, W.: "Death and the World of Imagination: Ibn al-'Arabî's Eschatology," *Muslim World* LXVII (1987).
Chittick, W.: article "Eschatology" in *Islamic Spirituality I*, S. H. Nasr, ed., New York, 1987 (Vol. XIX of "World Spirituality: An Encyclopedic History of the Religious Quest").
Chittick, W.: article "Ibn al-'Arabî and His School" in *Islamic Spirituality II*, S. H. Nasr, ed., New York, 1991 (Vol. XX of "World Spirituality: An Encyclopedic History of the Religious Quest").

Chittick, W.: *Imaginal Worlds: Ibn al-'Arabi and the Problem of Religious Diversity*, Albany, 1994.
Chittick, W.: *Ibn al-'Arabî's Metaphysics of Imagination*, New York, 1989.
Chittick, W.: *The Self-Disclosure of God: Principles of Ibn al-'Arabî's Cosmology* Albany, 1998.
Chittick, W.: *The Sufi Path of Knowledge: Ibn al-'Arabî's Metaphysics of the Imagination*, Albany, 1989.
Chodkiewicz, M.: "Ibn 'Arabî: la lettre et la loi," parts in the collection, *Mystique, culture et société*, ed. M. Meslin, Paris, 1983.
Chodkiewicz, M.: *Le Sceau des saints: Prophétie et sainteté dans la doctrine d'Ibn 'Arabî*, Paris, 1986; English translation as *Seal of the Saints*, Cambridge, 1993.
Chodkiewicz, M.: *An Ocean Without Shore: Ibn 'Arabî, the Book and the Law*, Albany, 1993.
Chodkiewicz, M.: *The Seal of the Saints: Prophethood and Sainthood in the doctrine of Ibn 'Arabî*, Cambridge, 1993.
Corbin, H.: *L'imagination créatrice dans le soufisme d'Ibn 'Arabî*, Paris, 1958; 2nd ed., 1977; New English translation as *Alone with the Alone: Creative Imagination in the Sufism of Ibn 'Arabî*, Princeton, 1998.
Elmore, G.: *Islamic Sainthood in the Fulness of Time: Ibn al-'Arabî's "Book of the Fabulous Gryphon"* Leiden, Brill, 2000.
El-Saleh, S.: *La vie future selon le Coran*, Paris, 1971.
Encyclopaedia Iranica, ed. E. Yarshater, London, 1982.
Encyclopedia of Islam, 1st and 2nd editions (EI^1 and EI^2).
Ernst, C. W.: *Words of Ecstasy in Sufism*, Albany, N.Y., 1985.
Fahd, T.: *La divination arabe*, Strasbourg, 1966; 2nd ed. Paris, 1987.
Al-Farghânî, Sa'îd' al-Dîn: *Mashâriq al-darârî*, S. J. Âshtiyânî, ed., Tehran, 1357/1978.
Furûzânfar, B.: *Abâdîth-i Mathnawî*, Tehran, 1334/1955.
Fusûs, see Ibn 'Arabî: *Fusûs al-hikam*.
Fut. or *Futûhât*, see Ibn 'Arabî: *al-Futûhât al-Makkiyya*.
Al-Ghazâlî: *Ihyâ 'ulûm al-dîn*, Cairo, 1326.
Al-Ghazâlî: *al-Maqsad al-asnâ*, ed. F. A. Shehadi, Beirut, 1971.
Al-Ghazâlî: *La perle precieuse (K. al-durrat al-fâkhira)* tr. L. Gautier, Leipzig, 1977; *The Precious Pearl*, tr. J. I. Smith, Missoula Montana, 1979.
Graham, W. A.: *Divine Word and Prophetic Word in Early Islam*, The Hague, 1977.
Ghurâb, M: *Al-Fiqh 'inda' l-Shaykh al-Akbar*, Damascus, 1981.
Guénon, R.: *Les symboles fondamentaux de la science sacrée*, Paris, 1962.
Al-Habashî, Badr: *Kitâb al-inbâh*, ed. and tr. D. Gril, *Annales Islamologiques* XV (1979).
Al-Hakîm, S.: *al-Mu'jam al-sûfî: al-hikma fî hudûd al-kalima*, Beirut, 1401/1981.
Halm, H.: *Kosmologie und Heilslehre der frühen Ismâ'îlîya*, Wiesbaden, 1978.
Hirtenstein and P. Beneito, The Seven Days of the Heart, Oxford, 2001.
Hirtenstein, S.: *The Unlimited Mercifier: The Spiritual Life and Thought of Ibn 'Arabî*, Oxford, 1999.
Ibn 'Arabî: *Dîwân*, Cairo, Bûlâq, 1271 h.
Ibn 'Arabî: *K. al-fanâ' fî'l-mushâhada*, tr. M. Vâlsan, *Le livre de l'extinction dans la contemplation*, Paris, 1984.

Ibn 'Arabî: *Fusûs al-hikam*, ed. A. Affifi, Cairo, 1346/1946; *The Bezels of Wisdom*, tr. R. W. J. Austin, New York, 1980; A translation and commentary by Bursevi, I. H., Oxford, 1986; *La sagesse des prophètes*, partial tr. Titus Burckhardt, Paris, 1955.

Ibn 'Arabî: *al-Futûhât al-Makkiyya*, Cairo, 1329, 4 vol.

Ibn 'Arabî: *al-Futûhât al-Makkiyya*, ed. Osman Yahya, Cairo 1392-1413/1972-92 (14 volumes to date, corresponding to one third of volume 1 of *Futûhât* above). Translated extracts of the *Futûhat:*
—Chapter 167: *L'alchimie du bonheur parfait*, tr. S. Ruspoli, Paris, 1981; partial tr. from the same chapter by G. Anawati, *Revue de l'Institut Dominicain d'Études Orientales du Caire*, Mélanges 6 (1959-61).
 Chapter 178, II 320: *Le traité de l'amour,* tr. M. Gloton, Paris, 1986.
—Chapter 198, *fasl* 9, II 405-420: *Le Coran et la fonction de'Hermès*, tr. C. A. Gilis, Paris, 1984.
—Chapter 262 and 263: tr. M. Vâlsan, *Études Traditionnelles,* July-October 1966.

Ibn 'Arabî: *Kitâb al-Isrâ' ilâ al-maqâm al-asrâ'* (*Rasâ'il* I, no. 13, pp. 1-92), Hyderabad, 1948.

Ibn 'Arabî: *Kitâb al-i'lâm bi-ishârât ahl al-ilhâm;* tr. M. Vâlsan, "Le Livre d'enseignement par formules indicatives des gens inspirés," *Études traditionnelles*, 1967-68.

Ibn 'Arabî: *Kitâb al-istilâhât al-sûfîya;* tr. R. T. Harris, *Journal of the Muhyiddîn Ibn 'Arabî Society*, III (1984); (*Rasâ'il II*, No. 29).

Ibn 'Arabî: *Kitâb al-jalâla;* tr. M. Vâlsan, *Études Traditionnelles*, June, July, August and December, 1948.

Ibn 'Arabî: *Al-kawkab al-durrî fî manâqib Dhî al-Nûn al-Misrî;* tr. R. Deladrière, *La vie merveilleuse de Dhû-l-Nûn l'Égyptien*, Paris, 1988.

Ibn 'Arabî: *Khutbat al-Kitâb* (prologue des *Futûhât Makkiyya);* tr. M. Vâlsan, *Etudes Traditionnelles*, 1953.

Ibn 'Arabî: *Kitâb al-Bâ'*, Cairo, 1954.

Ibn 'Arabî: *Kitâb mawâqi' al-nujûm*, Cairo, 1965.

Ibn 'Arabî: *Kitâb Mishkât al-anwâr fî mâ ruwiya 'an Allâh min al-akhbâr,* Aleppo, 1349/1927; tr. M. Vâlsan, *La niche des lumières*, Paris, 1963.

Ibn 'Arabî: *Majmû'at al-ahzâb,* assembled by Ahmad Diyâ' al-Dîn Kamûshkhânî, Istanbul, 1298 h.

Ibn 'Arabî: *Muhâdarat al-abrâr,* Cairo, 1906, 2 vol.

Ibn 'Arabî: *Rasâ'il Ibn 'Arabî*, Hyderabad, 1948.

Ibn 'Arabî: *Risâlat al-anwâr fî mâ yumnah sâhib al-khalwa min al-asrâr* (*Rasâ'il* I, no. 12, pp. 1-19), Hyderabad, 1948; tr. R. T. Harris, *Journey to the Lord of Power,* New York, 1981.

Ibn 'Arabî: *R. al-ittihâd al-kawnî;* tr. D. Gril, *Le livre de l'Arbre et des Quatre Oiseaux*, Paris, 1984.

Ibn 'Arabî: *Rûh al-quds*, Damascus, 1964.

Ibn 'Arabî: (attributed) *Shajarat al-Kawn*, tr. A. Jeffery, "Ibn 'Arabî's *Shajarat al-Kawn*," *Studia Islamica*, vol. X and XI; tr. M. Gloton, *L'arbre du monde*, Paris, 1962.

Ibn 'Arabî: *Tanazzul al-amlâk min 'âlam al-arwâh ilâ 'âlam al-aflâk,* ed. Ahmad Zakî Atiya & Tâhâ 'Abd al-Bâqî Surûr, 1961.
Izutsu, T.: *A Comparative Study of the Key Philosophical Concepts in Sufism and Taoism: Ibn 'Arabî and Lao-Tz⁻u, Chuang-Tz⁻u,* Tokyo, 1966.
Izutsu, T.: *Sufism and Taoism,* Tokyo, 1983.
Jâmî: *Naqd al-nusûs fî sharh naqsh al-fusûs,* ed. W. Chittick, Tehran, 1977.
Journey, see Ibn 'Arabî: *Risâlat al-anwâr* tr. Harris.
Kraus, P.: *Jâbir Ibn Hayyân, contribution à l'histoire des idées scientifiques dans l'Islam,* Cairo, 1943 (M.I.E. no. 44).
Lings, M: *Muhammad,* New York, 1983.
Massignon, L: *Essai sur les origines du lexique téchnique de la mystique musulmane,* nouvelle édition, Paris, 1968; translated as *Essay on the Origins of the Technical Language of Islamic Mysticism,* Notre Dame, 1997.
Meyer, F: "Ein kurzer Traktat Ibn 'Arabîs über die A'yân al-Thâbita," *Oriens* 27/28 (1981).
Michot, J: *La destinée de l'homme selon Avicenne: le retour à Dieu* (ma'âd) et *l'imagination,* Louvain-la-Neuve, 1987.
Mishkât, see Ibn 'Arabî: *Kitâb Mishkât al-anwâr.*
Morris, J. W.: "Ibn 'Arabî's Esotericism: The Problem of Spiritual Authority," *Studia Islamica* LXIX (1989).
Morris, J. W.: "Ibn 'Arabî and His Interpreters," *Journal of the American Oriental Society* 106, 3 and 4 (1986) and 107, 1 (1987).
Morris, J. W.: "The Spiritual Ascension: Ibn 'Arabî and the Mi'râj", *Journal of the American Oriental Society* 108 (1988).
Morris, J. W.: *The Wisdom of the Throne: An Introduction to the Philosophy of Mulla Sadra (K. al-Hikmat al-'arshîya),* Princeton, 1981.
Mu'jam, see al-Hakîm: *al-Mu'jam al-sûfî.*
Murata, *Chinese Gleams of Sufi Light,* Albany, 2000.
Murata, *The Tao of Islam: A Sourcebook on Gender Relationships in Islamic Thought,* Albany, 1992.
Nyberg: *Kleinere Schriften des Ibn al-'Arabî,* Leiden, 1919.
Ormsby, E. L.: *Theodicy in Islamic Thought: The Dispute over al-Ghazâlî's "Best of All Possible Worlds,"* Princeton, 1984.
O.Y., see Ibn 'Arabî: *Futûhât,* ed. Osman Yahya.
al-Qaysarî, Dâwûd: *al-Tawhîd wa'l-nubuwwa wa'l-walâya,* ed. S. J. Âshtiyânî, Mashhad, 1357/1978.
Qushayrî: *al-Risâla,* ed. 'Abd al-Halîm Mahmûd & Mahmûd ibn al-Sharîf, Cairo, 1972–74, 2 vol.
R. al-anwâr, see Ibn 'Arabî: *Risâlat al-anwâr.*
R.G., see Yahya, O.: *Histoire et classification.*
Radtke, B.: *al-Hakîm al-Tirmidhî: Ein islamischer Theosoph des 3/9 Jahrhunderts,* Freiburg, 1980.
Rasâ'il, see Ibn 'Arabî: *Rasâ'il Ibn 'Arabî.*
Râzî, Fakhr al-Dîn: *Sharh asmâ' al-husnâ, wa huwa al-kitâb al-musammâ Lawâmi' al-bayyinât,* ed. Tâhâ 'Abd al-Ra'ûf Sa'd, Cairo, 1976.
Roman, A.: *Etude de la phonologie et de la morphologie de la koiné arabe,* Aix-en-Provence, 1983.

Sakhâwî: *al-Qawl al-munbî*, Ms. Berlin 2849, Spr. 790.
Sarrâj, Abû Nasr: *al-Luma' fî'l-tasawwuf,* ed. R.A. Nicholson, Leiden, 1914.
Sceau, see Chodkiewicz, M.: *Le Sceau des saints.*
SEI: The Shorter Encyclopaedia of Islam, Leiden, 1965.
Sells: *Stations of Desire: Love Elegies From Ibn 'Arabî,* Jerusalem, 2000.
Sha'rânî 'Abd al-Wahhâb: *Al-yawâqît wa'l-jawâhir* & *Al-kibrît al-ahmar,* Cairo, 1369h.
Smith, J. I. & Haddad, Y.Y.: *The Islamic Understanding of Death and Resurrection,* New York, 1981.
Al-Suyûtî: *al-Jâmi' al-saghîr,* in al-Munâwî, *Fayd al-qadîr,* Beirut, 1972.
Vâlsan, M.: "Les références islamiques du 'symbolisme de la croix,'" *Études Traditionnelles,* 1971 et 1972.
Vâlsan, M.: "Le Triangle de l'Androgyne et le monosyllabe Ôm," *Études Traditionnelles,* 1964 to 1966.
Wensinck, A. J. et al: *Concordance et indices de la tradition musulmane,* Leiden, 1936–69.
Word, see Graham, W.: *Divine Word and Prophetic Word...*
Wolfson, H.A.: *The Philosophy of the Kalam,* Cambridge Mass., 1976.
Wronecka, Joanna: "Le *Kitâb al-isrâ' ilâ maqâm al-asrâ'* d'Ibn 'Arabî," *Annales Islamologiques,* XX (1984), containing translated extracts.
Yahya, O.: *Histoire et classification de l'oeuvre d' Ibn 'Arabî,* Damascus, 1964.

INDEX OF QUR'ANIC REFERENCES

Sura : Aya — Pages

1 : 1 — 88.
     6 — 168.

2 : 2 — 115.
     4 — 74.
     30 — 174.
     31 — 145.
     106 — 99.
     115 — 22.
     118 — 212.
     152 — 94.
     158 — 238.
     169 — 84.
     185 — 69.
     196 — 88.
     233 — 75.
     236 to 241 — 6.
     238 — 69, 100.
     251 — 233.
     268 — 84, 85.
     276 — 95.
     282 — 66, 122.

3 : 8 — 190.
     11 — 88.
     12 — 165.
     18 — 88.
     45 — 230.
     47 — 14.
     49 — 38, 183.
     59 — 14.
     84 — 74.
     144 — 240.

4:   46 — 188.
     69 — 229.
     97 — 31.
     105 — 78.
     126 — 74.
     145 — 243.
     166 — 173.
     171 — 183.
     172 — 230.

5 : 2 — 88.
     9 — 84.

         13 — 188.
         95 — 88.

 6 :   73 — 14.
         92 — 23.
         110 — 190.
         152 — 75.
         153 — 79.

 7 :   17 — 152.
         42 — 75.
         54 — 31.
         143 — 216.
         156 — 39.
         184 — 67.
         185 — 67.

 8 :   13 — 88.
         29 — 66.

 9 :   37 — 54.

 10 :   1 to 2 — 117.
         2 — 16.
         22 — 239.
         63 to 64 — 97.

 11 :   13 — 102.
         61 — 244.
         114 — 100.
         123 — 224, 227, 244.

 12 :   3 — 206.
         64 — 88.
         92 — 226.

 14 :   10 — 11.
         10 to 11 — 67.
         24 — 195.
         48 — 88.

 15 :   9 — 75.
         26 to 27 — 218.
         27 — 201.
         29 — 28, 120, 182, 218.
         37 — 18.

 16 :   40 — 14.
         101 — 99.

 17 :   44 — 27, 163.
         78 — 100.

 18 :   23 to 24 — 238.
         50 — 218.
         64 — 206.
         65 — 66, 188, 204, 233, 245.
         68 — 234.
         69 — 237.
         71 — 246.
         76 — 236.
         82 — 237.
         109 — 160.
         110 — 67.

 19 :   8 — 14.
         35 — 14.

 20 :   12 — 20, 30, 172.
         15 — 91.
         96 — 34.
         129 — 102.
         114 — 160, 234.

 21 :   3 — 67.
         69 — 103.
         83 — 88.

 22 :   5 — 102.
         11 — 188.
         29 — 23.
         30 — 96.
         32 — 96.
         78 — 69.

 23 :   24 — 67.
         62 — 75.

 24 :   21 — 84.
         26 — 84.
         37 —190.

 25 :   23 — 95.

26 : 145 — 67.

27 : 87 — 183.

28 : 24 — 237.
70 — 227.
88 — 227, 244.

29 : 53 — 102.
56 — 31.

30 : 8 — 102.
1 to 7 — 208.

31 : 27 — 160.
29 — 102.

32 : 12 — 173.

33 : 4 — 68, 85, 97, 228.
13 — 11, 223, 225.
72 — 209.

35 : 4 — 102.
13 — 102.
50 — 244.

36 : 15 — 15.
39 — 165.
69 — 203.
82 — 14.

37 : 96 — 18.

38 : 25 — 177.
72 — 120, 182.

39 : 5 — 102.
6 — 247.
10 — 31.
30 — 240.
37 — 88.
42 — 102.
68 — 183, 233.

40 : 7 — 92.
9 — 92.

51 — 96.
67 — 102.
68 — 14.

41 : 6 — 67.
53 — 23, 224, 225.

42 : 11 — 53, 90, 171.

43 : 77 — 102.

46 : 3 — 102.
9 — 170.

48 : 29 — 84.

51 : 21 — 197.

52 : 1 to 3 — 214.
3 — 204.

53 : 9 — 9.
42 — 90.
44 to 47 — 218.

55 : 14 to 15 — 218.
15 — 201.
19 to 20 — 210.
72 — 37, 245.

56 : 11 — 230.
75 to 78 — 215.
85 — 244.
88 — 230.

57 : 3 — 33.
4 — 22, 92, 115, 173.
13 — 207.
28 — 66.

59 : 7 — 236.
29 — 244.

64 : title — 96.
9 — 96.

65 : 7 — 75.

66 : 1 — 78.
       12 — 183.

68 : 1 — 170.

71 : 4 — 102.

74 : 30 — 103.

76 : 1 — 15.

79 : 26 — 206.

83 : 9 to 20 — 214.

89 : 27 to 28 — 211.

95 : 4 to 5 — 30, 167.

96 : 18 — 103

112 : 3 to 4 — 137.

INDEX / GLOSSARY

Aaron : 41.
'abd : servant : 18, 29, 55.
Abd al-'Azîz al-Mahdawî : 4, 19.
Abd al-Qâdir al-Jazâ'irî (Emir Abdel Kader) : 5, 13.
abdâl : see badal.
Abraham : 4, 20, 103, 192.
Abû Bakr al-Siddîq : 208, 229, 231, 240, 245, 248.
Abû Hanîfa : 81 .
Abû Hurayra : 207, 218 .
Abû Ishâq b. Qarqûl : see Ibn Qarqûl.
Abû Tâlib al-Makkî : 161, 204.
'âda : accustomed order : .
adab : courtesy : 122, 141, 238.
Adam : 28, 31, 32, 48, 54, 84, 102, 117, 132, 133, 136, 145, 167, 170, 192, 194, 201, 215, 216.
'adam : nonexistence : 14-15, 48.
aflâk : see also falak : 108, 110, 156.
afrâd : solitary saints : 37, 113, 188, 206, 231, 233, 246.
ahad : the One the Unique : 93, 145, 206.
ahadiyya : Unity : 15, 224, 226.
ahkâm (see also sing. hukm) : statutes : 91, 190.
— al-mumkinât : statutes of possibilities : 12.
— al-shar' : legal statutes : 6.
ahl : people
— al-anfâs : of the breath : 38.
— al-anwâr : of light : 206.
— al-asrâr : of secrets : 206.

— al-dhikr : of memory, of Qur'an : 75.
— al-ilqâ wa-l-talaqqî : of projection and reception : 112.
— al kitâb : of light : 206
— al-nar : of the fire : 87.
— al-suwar al-ma'qûla : who can grasp intelligible forms : 165.
— al-tadânî wa l-taraqq : of reciprocal closeness and progressive elevation : 112.
ahwâl : see hâl.
'A'isha : 240.
akhbâr al-nabawiyya : traditions of prophetic origin : 81.
âkhira : next other world : 87.
akhlât : humors : 66.
'âlam *al-saghîr*: microcosme : 27.
'Alî b. Abî Tâlib : 24.
'âlim : knower, see plural 'ulamâ'.
amâna : responsibility : 115, 166, 172, 209.
Amîn : 122, 145, 211, 212.
'âmma : ordinary people : 87.
amr : affair commandment entity thing : 30, 134, 214, 225.
anbiyâ' : see sing. nabî.
Andalusia : 3, 25, 61.
Ansârî : 9.
'aqîda : credo : 21, 50.
'âqil : judicious person : see plural, 'uqalâ'.
'aql : reason : 21, 28, 134;
— al-awwal : First Intellect : 18.
al-Aqsâ (Mosque of) : 4.
a'râd : honor : 260.
ard : earth : 31, 53.
'ârif bi-Llâh (pl. 'ârifûn bi-Llâh) : knower of Allah : 21, 23, 25, 30, 37, 63, 94, 96.
'arsh : throne : 110, 116, 135, 193.
arwâh : spirits : see singular, rûh.
asl (see also pl. usûl) : principle, root : 138, 185, 210.
asmâ' (see also sing. ism) : divine names : 29, 75, 88, 108, 124, 180.
astrology : 25, 36, 165, 190, 207.
athar : effect : 124.
Avicenna : see Ibn Sînâ.
Awhad al-Dîn al-Kirmânî : 32.
awhâm : see wahm.
awliyâ' (see also sing. walî) : friends, saints : 10, 11, 13, 30, 34, 38, 40, 42, 49, 62, 99, 123, 136.
awtâd (sing. watad) : pillars : .
a'yân (see also sing. 'ayn) : entities : 75.
— al-thâbita : immutable entities : 15, 16, 28, 33, 48, 52, 110, 120.
'ayn (see also pl. a'yân) : entity essence self eye : 46, 75, 109, 154, 189, 224, 226;
— al-Haqq : God Himself : 41.
— al-wâhid : Reality of the One : 226.
— thabita : immutable entity : 17.
azal : eternity without beginning : 109, 139, 147, 148, 154, 201, 211.
'azama : tremendousness : 161, 205, 216.

INDEX / GLOSSARY • 261

al-Azdî al-Iskandarî, 'Abd al-Wahhâb (qadi) : 79.
bâb al-asrâr : the chapter of secrets : 12, 13.
bâb al-raqm : the door of writing : 135.
bâb al-wasâya : 40.
badal (pl. abdâl) substitution : 119.
badî' : Originator : 126, 212.
Badr al-Habashî : see al-Habashî.
Baghdad : 61, 235, 246.
balgham : phlegm : 66.
Baqara (second surah of Qur'an) : 30, 114, 115, 118, 163, 167.
barzakh : isthmus, intermediate imaginal world : 32, 92, 110, 156, 166, 210.
basmala : 29, 110, 134, 136, 140, 189, 191, 192, 196.
Basra : 142, 204.
Bastâmî : see Bistâmî.
bâtin : nonmanifest or inner : 34, 212.
birr al-wâlidayn : filial piety : 33.
Bougie : 4.
Bûnî, Abû'l-'Abbâs : 25.

Cairo : 4, 5, 6, 44, 50, 144, 196.

dahr : time, eternity ; divine name : 15, 61.
Damascus : 5, 45, 200.
darakât : degrees of hell : 92.
darajât : spiritual degrees : 91, 92, 174.

Dâwûd b. Khalaf : 60, 98, 100.
dhât : essence : 112, 121, 180, 184.
dhawq : direct personal experience : 21, 50, 231, 234.
dhikr : invocation : 8, 75, 122, 136, 207, 211.
Dhû'l Nûn al-Misrî : 9, 32.
dîn : religion : 33.
djinn : see jinn.
dunyâ : lower world : 87.

Ecija : 95, 104.
Egypt : 144, 235, 246.
Eve : 117, 132, 145.

falak (see also plural, aflâk) : sphere :
— al-aqsâ : ultimate sphere : 108, 151.
— al-atlas : dark sphere : 156, 202.
— 'ilm al-f. : see astrology : 165
falsafa : Greek philosophy which was translated into Arabic : 36, 135.
fanâ' : extinction annihilation : 166, 218.
faqr : poverty : 85, 184.
al-Fârâbî : 91.
al-Farghânî, Sa'îd al-Dîn : 49.
fard : legally obligatory act : 75, 97.

faqîh (pl. fuqahâ') : jurist : 80, .
fatâ : young hero : 20, 22-24, 36, 42, 51, 54, 107.
Fâtiha : the opening sura of Qur'an : 14, 19, 29, 30, 110, 115, 126, 140, 141, 144, 146.
fath : opening, conquest : 168, 182, 224.
fayd al-aqdas : holy effusion : 15, 48.
Fez : 4, 101, 189.
fi'l (pl. af'âl) : act, operative virtue : 123, 138.
fiqh : jurisprudence: 39, 61, 62.
fitra : primordial nature : 121, 185, 219.
furqân : discrimination division: 66, 179.
futuwwa : heroic generosity : 8, 20.

Gabriel : 170, 202, 205.
ghafla : inattention forgetfulness: 8.
ghafûr : forgiving : 84.
ghanî : rich : 184.
ghayb (pl. ghuyûb) : unseen : 53, 55, 90, 137, 168, 242.
ghayra : jealousy : 95.
al-Ghazâlî : 239.
ghinâ' : independence: 184.

habâ' : principal substance : 31, 33, 53, 137.
Habashî, Badr al : 49, 55.
hadd (pl. hudûd) : prescription penalty : 135, 187, 212.
hadîth : 70, 102.
— qudsî : 10, 22, 46, 55, 61, 92, 102, 104.
hadra : presence : 178, 181.
Hafsa : 78.
hajj : pilgrimage : 72, 100, 217.
hajjîr : see hijjîr.
hâl : spiritual state : 9, 10, 11, 46, 82, 185, 234, 246.
Hallâj : 55, 194, 195.
haqîqa (pl. haqâ'iq) : reality : 19, 28, 29, 42, 59, 85, 86, 99, 118, 137, 152, 201, 203.
— al-haqâ'iq : reality of realities : 181.
— al-kulliya : universal reality: 200.
— al-muhammadiyya : muhammadan reality : 18, 30, 31, 32, 41, 52, 208.
haqq : Real, God, Truth : 17, 41, 48, 68, 82, 85, 90, 150, 180.
haraka (pl. harakât) : movement, vowel-movements : 28, 29, 63, 120, 131, 185.
harf (pl. hurûf) : letter : 24, 25, 26, 38, 107, 113, 116, 128, 141, 142, 150, 170, 173, 187, 188, 190, 199, 200, 212, 218.
hayra : perplexity : 10, 11, 13, 158.
hayûlâ : prime matter : 53, 131, 134, 194.
hijâb (pl. hujub) : veil : 14.
hijjîr : motto, verse used in invocation : 47.
hikma : wisdom : 69, 195.
himma : spiritual energy : 118, 168, 177, 179, 202.
hudûd : see hadd.
hudûth : temporal origination, adventitious : 109, 153, 171.

hujub : see hijâb.
hukm (see also pl. ahkâm) : judgment, authority, command : 223, 227.
huwa : He, Him, the Self : 115, 125, 138, 139, 195, 197, 243.
huwiyya : divine ipseity : 125, 139, 189, 224, 226.

'ibâda (pl. 'ibâdât) : worship : 60, 68.
ibâha : antinomianism, licit, permissive : 17, 59, 72, 75, 83, 100.
ibn al-waqt : child of the moment : 65.
ibdâ' : origination : 134, 135.
Ibn 'Abbâs : 23, 78, 194, 246.
Ibn 'Atâ', Ahmad : 136.
Ibn Barrajân : 165, 196, 208.
Ibn Hazm : 61, 63, 64, 98, 99, 100, 102.
Ibn Khaldûn : 143, 144, 198.
Ibn Masarra al-Jabalî : 124, 140, 146, 195, 196, 198.
Ibn Qarqûl, Abû Ishâq Ibrahîm : 79.
Ibn Qasî : 50, 141, 196, 198.
Ibn Sînâ : 134, 135.
Ibn Taymiyya : 17, 48, 49, 59, 100, 103.
Ibn Tufayl : 90.
Igisil : 4, 246.
ihsân : perfection : 29.
ijmâ' : consensus: 61, 63, 64, 65, 66, 67, 68, 73, 74.
ijtihâd : judicial, interpretation : 62, 64, 65. 67. 76, 78, 99, 100, 232, 237.
ikhlâs : sincerity : 168.
Ikhwân al-Safâ' : 53, 130, 133, 139, 145, 146, 193, 194, 198.
iktisâb : acquisition: 120, 231, 232.
ilâh : God, divinity : 153.
ilhâm : inspiration : 77, 90, 101, 120.
'ilm : knowledge, science : 24, 25, 26, 38, 107, 128.
— al-'aql : knowledge acquired through the intellect : 21.
— al-ahwâl : knowledge the states : 21.
— al-'âlam : knowledge of the laws of cosmology : 36.
— al-asrâr : science of secrets : 21.
— al-awliyâ : science of the saints : 123.
— al-hurûf : science of letters : 24, 25, 26, 38, 107, 128.
— al-ihâtî : knowledge that encompasses all things: 184.
— 'isawî : Christic knowledge : 124.
— al-ladunî : knowledge from God, knowledge of what is from God : 62, 120, 188, 230, 233, 245.
— al-nazarî : science of metaphysical speculation : 120.
— al-salb : via negativa : 28.
ilqâ' : projection: 6, 110, 112, 155, 156.
imân : inner faith : 29, 87.
India : 133, 145, 194, 215.
insân : human being : 32, 206;
— al-azalî : universal or eternal man : 109, 154.
— al-kâmil : perfect human being : 20, 23, 27, 30, 32, 33, 35, 45, 52.

— al-kullî : universal man : 20.
irâda (pl. irâdât) : will : 66.
'Isâ : see Jesus.
ishâra (pl. ishârât) : allusion : 115, 167, 172, 175, 195, 210, 213, 214.
ism : (see pl. asmâ').
'isma : immunity from error : 50, 92, 103.
isrâ' : nocturnal ascent : 7, 20, 23.
Istanbul : 5, 208.
isti'dâd : preparedness : 17, 62.
istihâla : transmutation : 111.
ittihâd : reunion : 117, 163, 174, 178.
ittisâl : conjunction : 117, 174.

jabarût : mightiness : 110, 155, 156, 161, 162, 202, 205.
Jâbir b. Hayyân : 124, 128, 130, 131, 143, 146, 191, 192, 195, 198, 202, 203, 204.
Ja'far al-Sâdiq : 124, 128, 194.
jam' : union : 115, 117, 172, 173, 178.
jamâd : inanimate : 160.
jamâl : beauty : 214.
al-Jarrâh, Abû Muhammad : 19, 49.
jawâmi' al-kalim : totalizing words : 121, 183, 218, 227.
Jerusalem : 4, 25, 165, 166.
Jesus : 4, 12, 26, 38, 52, 53, 121, 124, 192, 219, 230, 245, 246.
al-Jîlî, Abd al-Karîm : 12, 48, 197.
jinn : 3, 53, 54, 67, 88, 109, 112, 141, 142, 152, 159, 160, 182, 189, 201, 202, 218.
jism (pl. jusûm) : body : 33, 87.
Joseph : 224, 225, 226.
Junayd : 66, 174.

Ka'ba : 3, 4, 7, 22, 23, 36, 53, 63, 176, 224.
Kairouan : 238.
kalâm : speech : 21, 22, 28, 36, 50, 132, 138.
kalima (pl. kalim) : word : 127, 168, 180, 182.
kamâl : perfection : 214.
kashf : unveiling : 22, 25, 89, 111, 120, 135, 158, 232.
kawn (pl. akwân) : engendered existence : 114, 129, 167.
khabar (pl. akhbâr) : tradition : 66, 67, 70, 71, 75, 81, 82, 139.
Khadir : 38, 62, 66, 188, 214, 230, 231, 232, 233, 234, 236, 237, 238, 239, 246. 247.
khal' al-na'layn : the 'taking off of the sandals' of Moses : 30, 50, 141, 196.
khalîfa : vicegerent : 112, 114, 117, 159, 174, 196, 209, 212, 215, 242, 244.
khalq : creation: 41, 134, 135, 137, 181.
khalwa : spiritual retreat : 41, 90, 179.
al-Kharrâz, Abû Sa'îd : 136.
khatâ' : error : 75, 76.
khatm al-awliyâ' : seal of saints: 39, 136, 230, 245.
khâssa : elect : 22, 87, 113.
khawâss : elite : 123, 130;
— al-asmâ' : properties of the Names : 124.

khayâl : imagination : 31, 41, 53, 123.
Khiḍr (see Khaḍir).
khilâfa : representation : 40, 207.
khitâb : address : 115.
kibrît al-ahmar : Red Sulphur: 50, 144.
Konya : 5, 45.
kufr : infidelity : 84.
kursî : footstool : 30, 110, 116, 135, 139, 174, 193.
kun : "be", the fiat of existence : 16, 125, 134, 137, 138, 139, 146, 181, 189, 193, 212, 215.

latâfa : subtlety : 122, 186.
lawh al-mahfûz : guarded tablet : 90.
lawh al-qadar : table of assigned destiny : 144.
laylat al-qadr : the night of value : 235.

madad : support : 170, 213.
madhhab (pl. madhâhib) : doctrinal position school : 61, 81, 82, 112.
— zâhirî : 61, 63, 81, 98.
Maghreb : 3, 79, 143, 235, 246.
mahall : locus receptacle : 116, 171.
al-Mahdawî : see 'Abd al-'Azîz.
Mahdî : 10, 143, 144, 198, 245.
mahmûd : praiseworthy : 14, 225, 245.
mahw : effacement: 166.
malak (pl. malâ'ika) : angel : 82, 88.
malakût : inner realm: 110, 155, 156, 161, 162, 181, 202, 205.
malâmatiyya : 231.
malâmiyya : blameworthy : 35, 37, 39, 42, 55, 94.
Mâlik b. Anas : 65, 76.
ma'lûh : vassal of God : 153.
ma'nâ (pl. ma'ânî) : meaning : 126, 183, 204, 219.
manzil (pl. manâzil) : spiritual stage mansion : 9, 10, 14, 47, 76, 86, 92, 108, 112, 116, 152, 174, 246.
maqâm (pl. maqâmât) : spiritual station : 9, 10, 11, 12, 46, 90, 91, 185, 223, 224, 229, 230, 231, 242, 245, 246;
— al-ittihâd : station of reunion : 163.
— al-qurba : station of proximity : 4, 37, 225, 229, 230, 234, 244, 245.
ma'rifa (pl. ma'ârif) knowledge : 108, 139.
martaba (pl. marâtib) : level : 27, 108, 109, 112, 150, 154, 159, 162.
Marwa : 238.
mawârid : inspiration [divine] : 156, 160, 166.
Masrûq b. al-Ajdâ' : 65, 101.
mazhar (pl. mazâhir) : locus of manifestation : 16, 35, 194.
Mecca : 3, 4, 5, 18, 22, 51, 79, 204, 208, 217, 224, 238.
Medina (see also Yathrib) : 4, 36, 54, 223.
mi'râj (pl. ma'ârij) : spiritual ascent : 10, 29, 37, 45, 89.
mithl : likeness symbolic image : 53, 213.

Moses : 4, 20, 25, 30, 34, 38, 84, 102, 193, 214, 216, 230, 231, 234, 236, 237, 238, 239, 246, 247.
mubâh : licit : 97.
mubashshira : dream vision/glad tidings : 177.
mubdaʻ : originated thing : 114, 169, 175.
mubdiʼ al-mubdaʼât : producer of beings : .134, 212.
Mudawwir : 95.
muhaqqiq (pl. muhaqqiqûn) : verifier, realizer of reality : 112, 118, 159, 178, 202.
muhdath : temporally originated : 171.
muhyî : Lifegiver : 26.
mukallaf : subject to legal obligations : 17, 108, 150.
mukallif : He who imposes the law : 108, 112, 150.
mulk : kingdom, possession: 96, 110, 155, 202, 205.
munâjât : intimate conversation: 243.
munâzala : midpoint encounter : 94.
muntaqim : avenger : 88.
al-Murâbit, Abû ʻAbdallâh : 19, 49.
murîd : willing 52, 65: .
Mûsâ b. Muhammad al-Qurtubî al-Qabbâb : 238.
mushâhada : contemplation : 112.
mustanad ilâhî : divine basis : 16, 39, 42.
mutakallim (pl. mutakallimûn) : theologan : 21, 50.
mutashâbihât : *equivocal* verses : 109, 122.
mutawâtir : authoritative [tradition] : 70, 71.

al-Nâbulusî, Abd al-Ghanî : 5, 33.
nabî (pl. anbiyâʼ) : prophet : 230.
nafas al-Rahmân : the All-Merciful breath : 53, 121, 213.
nafs (pl. anfâs) : soul self : 38, 71, 122, 126, 134, 186.
nahy (pl. nawâhî) : interdiction : 30, 72.
nâʼib (pl. nuwwâb) : substitute : 35, 114.
naql : narration : 71.
nâr : fire : 32, 66, 87, 152, 198.
naskh : abrogation : 71.
nass (pl. nusûs) : formal text : 64, 72.
nazar : speculation : 22, 67, 68, 158, 188.
nisba (pl. nisab) : relationship : 201, 202.
nisyân : forgetting God : 8, 75.
niyâba : deputyship : 35.
nubuwwa : prophecy : 18, 135, 230, 232.
nûr : light : 32, 97.

Qabbâb : see Qurtubî.
qadâʼ : predestination : 84.
qadar : divine decree, determination : 84, 135, 144, 193.
qâdî : judge : 80.
qadîm : eternal : 17.
qâʼim : subsistent, that which raises or is raised up : 135, 193, 232.
qalb : heart : 166, 209;

— al-wujûd : of the universe : 3, 22.
— murâqabat al-q. : guarding the h. : 92.
Qâshânî : 49, 143, 194, 199.
qidam : eternity : 16, 153.
qiyâs : reasoning by analogy : 63-68, 73-75.
Qûnawî Sadr al-Dîn : 5, 48.
Qur'ân (as a subject in itself; see also Quranic Index) : 19-20, 25, 29, 30, 61, 62, 63, 64, 71-72, 77, 119, 127, 139, 140, 147, 179-180, 212.
— al-kabir : the great Quran (the universe as,) : 16, 27.
— brother of : 27.
— "I am the Q." : 19.
qurb : proximity : 230, 244, 245.
Qurtubî, Mûsâ b. Md al-Qabbâb : 238.
Qushayrî : 20, 142, 196.
qutb (pl. aqtâb) : pole : 11, 12, 28, 36, 52, 118, 164, 207, 246.
quwwa : faculty force : 137.

rabb : Lord : 18, 29.
rahîm : All-Compassionate : 30, 84.
rahma : mercy : 42, 87.
rahmân : AllMerciful : 38, 42, 201, 205.
rasûl (pl. rusul) : messenger : 27, 113, 230.
ra'y : personal opinion : 73, 74, 75, 78, 79, 80, 81.
ridâ' : mantle : 89, 117, 174, 215, 244.
risâla : divine message : 230, 233.
rizq : subsistence : 34.
rubûbiyya : lordship: 109, 131.
rûh (pl. arwâh) : spirit : 195, 203, 205.
rujû' : return : 224.
rukn (pl. arkân) : the four elements : 66, 157, 203.
rusul : see rasûl.
Ruzbehân Baqlî Shîrâzî : 9, 140, 194.

sa'âda : felicity: 79.
sabab (pl. asbâb) : cause : 184.
Safâ : 238.
safrâ' : yellow bile: 66.
sâhib al-asrâr : the repository of divine secrets : 21, 50.
Sahl al-Tustarî : 137, 140, 142, 146, 205.
Salâh al-Dîn Yûsuf b. Ayyûb, Nâsir (Saladin) : 80.
salâm : peace : 18.
salât : prayer : 38, 69, 72, 75, 100.
salb : negation : 28, 169.
Salé : 3, 4, 246.
sâlik : traveler : 11, 20, 40, 91.
Sarrâj, Abû Nasr al- : 194.
sawdâ' : black bile : 66.
shafâ'a : intercession : 88, 225.
Shâfi'î, Imâm : .

shahâda : formula of profession of faith : 140, 217; visible as opposed to ghayb : 55, 162.
shahwa : desire, passion : 129.
shar' : religious law or way : 6, 96, 165.
Sha'rânî : 13.
shâri' : lawgiver : 60.
shirk : idolatry, polytheism : 83.
shu'ab al-îmân : branches of the faith : 46, 113.
shuhûd : contemplation or witnessing : 96.
siddîqiyya : confirmer or confirmation of the truth : 229, 239.
sidq : sincerity truthfulness : 8, 16, 67, 71.
sifa : quality, attribute : 139, 162, 212, 213.
sirr (see also plural, asrâr) : secret, inmost consciousness : 131, 169, 183, 235.
sitr : veil : 84, 85.
sukr : intoxication : 71.
Sulamî : 231, 236, 245.
Spain : 225.
sunna : 62, 63, 66, 67, 68, 70, 71, 72, 74, 75, 81, 100.
sûra (pl. suwar) : form : 82, 113, 137, 165, 188, 203, 206, 207, 219.

tabaqât : hierarchical levels, categories : 39, 230, 233.
tafsîr : commentary, explication : 30, 194, 196, 198, 208.
tahaqquq : realization of the essential truth : 206.
tahlîl : licit : 83.
tajaddud al-khalq : see tajdîd al-khalq, khalq al-jadîd.
tajallî : theophany : 41.
tajdîd al-khalq : perpetual creation : 30, 41.
taklîf : legal obligation : 16, 74, 96.
takhalluq : to assume the character traits of God : 113, 206.
takwîn : formation; engendered existence : 89, 125, 134, 135.
talaqqî : reception : 112, 155, 156.
ta'lîf : harmonious composition : 111, 114, 126, 159.
talwîn : coloration : 185.
tanzîh : incomparability of God : 28, 37, 42.
taqlîd : imitating: 74.
taqrîb : nearness : 245.
taqwâ : reverence for God : 215.
tarjumân : interpreter : 27, 29, 52.
tarkîb : composition: 89, 91, 190, 202.
tasarruf : free disposal : 96, 143.
tasawwuf : mystic way : 8, 9, 20, 103, 124, 130, 131, 136, 137, 140, 141, 143, 146, 192, 194, 196, 197, 204, 213, 246.
tashbîh : similarity, immanence : 28, 37, 41, 42, 109.
tawba : repentance : 8, 96.
tawhîd : divine unity : 87, 112, 115, 122, 172, 173, 195.
ta'wîl : spiritual interpretation : 30, 73, 101, 136.
tawakkul : absolute trust and reliance on God : 12.
thubût : immutability affirmation : 15, 16, 48, 121, 184, 202.
Tirmidhî : 39, 123, 136, 137, 190, 229, 230, 231, 232, 246, 248.

Tunis : 4, 32, 98, 99.
turâb : earth : 66.

'ubûda : servitude : 122.
'ubûdiyya : servanthood : 29, 101, 109, 166.
Uhud, Ohod : 27, 95.
'ulamâ' (sing. 'âlim) : knowers : 39, 64;
— al-rusûm : exoteric authorities : 237.
— biLlâh : true knowers of God : 123.
'ulûm : see 'ilm.
'uluw : exaltation, elevation : 170.
umanâ' : faithful repositories (of the divine secrets) : 209, 231, 245.
'Umar (caliph) : 23, 240.
umm : archetype mother : 173;
— al-Kitâb : Mother of the Book : 116.
umma : community : 27, 33.
ummahât : kingdoms: ;
— al-asmâ' : matrical Names : 28, 52.
— al-uwal : mother principles : 110, 157, 203.
'uqalâ' : judicious persons : 112, 159.
usûl (see also sing. asl) : sources : 60, 62, 63, 64, 76, 100, 157.

wahdat al-wujûd : Oneness of Being : 18, 41, 48, 65.
wahm (pl. awhâm) : illusion, mental representation : 123.
wahy : [direct] divine revelation : 170.
wajh al-khâss : specific aspect : 90.
wakîl : guarantor : 85.
walâya : sainthood; authority : 18, 35, 37, 38, 40, 101, 195, 230.
walî (see also pl. awliyâ') : saint : 9, 50, 230.
waqf (pl. awqâf) : religious foundation : 5.
wâqif : one who stands still : 141, 180, 217.
wâridat : inspired : 156, 158.
wârith : inheritor : 10, 214.
wâsita : intermediary : 167, 210.
watad (see plural, awtâd).
wujûb : obligation : 72, 74, 83.
wujûd : Being existence : 48, 127, 203, 212.

Yahyâ (John the Baptist) : 102.
yaqîn : certitude : 8.
Yathrib (see also Medina) : 223, 224, 225, 242, 243.

zâhir : manifest, apparent : 34, 91, 212.
zakât : legal alms : 72, 100.
zamân : time : 232.
zulm : injustice : 215.
zulma : darkness : 215.